Agile Manufacturing

Forging New Frontiers

Agile Manufacturing

Forging New Frontiers

Paul T. Kidd

 ADDISON-WESLEY PUBLISHING COMPANY

Wokingham, England • Reading, Massachusetts • Menlo Park, California
New York • Don Mills, Ontario • Amsterdam • Bonn • Sydney • Singapore
Tokyo • Madrid • San Juan • Milan • Paris • Mexico City • Seoul • Taipei

© 1994 Addison-Wesley Publishers Ltd.
© 1994 Addison-Wesley Publishing Company Inc.

Cover designed by Viva Design Ltd, Henley-on-Thames and printed by The Riverside Printing Co. (Reading) Ltd.
Typeset by Meridian Phototypesetting Ltd, Pangbourne.
Printed in Great Britain by T.J. Press (Padstow) Ltd, Cornwall.

First printed 1994.

ISBN 0-201-63163-6

British Library Cataloguing in Publication Data
A catalogue record for this book is available from the British Library.

Library of Congress Cataloging in Publication Data
Kidd, Paul T.
    Agile manufacturing : forging new frontiers / Paul
T. Kidd.
        p.   cm.
    Includes bibliographical references and index.
    ISBN 0-201-63163-6
    1. Production planning.   2. System design.   I. Title.   II. Title:
Agile manufacturing.
    TS176.K517   1994
    658.5--dc20   94-19144
                                                            CIP

To Judith, Lucy, Tara and Dale

Preface

We stand today at the beginning of a new era in manufacturing. We are about to forge a new frontier. A new concept, **agile manufacturing**, promises to completely transform our manufacturing industries.

However, although agile manufacturing is a relatively new term, and we have yet to fully define the concepts, it seems from the many articles that are now appearing in our journals and trade magazines that our manufacturing enterprises are already practicing agile manufacturing. But are they? It seems to me that agile manufacturing is being interpreted as lean production, or flexible manufacturing, or computer integrated manufacturing (CIM). This is wrong.

My primary aim in writing this book was to contribute to the process of defining agile manufacturing, and to dispel any beliefs that it is just another way of describing lean production, flexible manufacturing or CIM. To me, it represents a quantum leap forward in manufacturing. Instead of just chasing after the Japanese by copying their techniques, we are trying to achieve a competitive lead by doing something they are not doing (yet).

Because agile manufacturing is new, and as yet, untried, I have not presented case studies of implementations. Many of our corporations today are undergoing massive transformations – re-engineering business processes, flattening hierarchies, empowering people, implementing lean production concepts and so on. The list is almost endless. But none of these massive transformations, on their own or taken collectively, constitutes the implementation of agile manufacturing.

Agile manufacturing is something that our corporations have yet to fully comprehend, never mind implement. It is the way business will be conducted in the next century. It is not yet a reality. Of course, this situation will change very rapidly. Over the next few years we can expect to see agile manufacturing more fully defined, and a few pioneering corporations moving into the frontier of implementation.

It seems to me, however, that we are being held back from this quantum leap and exploring this new frontier by the baggage of our traditions and conventions, and our accepted values and beliefs. I believe that if we are to achieve agility in our manufacturing enterprises, we should fully understand the nature of our existing cultures, values, and traditions. We should achieve this understanding as a prelude to their consignment to the garbage can of historically redundant ideas.

However, in writing this book, I also had in mind the need to begin to map out the way forward. I firmly believe that agile manufacturing implies a revolution in the way we go about designing and implementing manufacturing systems, technologies, and organizations, and in the way we conduct our business. I also believe that it has radical implications for our technologies. In the future we will be devoting much of our efforts to developing systems that will lever the skills and knowledge of our people.

Readership

This book is aimed at a diverse group of people: chief executive officers, managers, manufacturing strategists and integrators, and engineers in manufacturing industry. It is primarily of use to those engaged in the broad areas of manufacturing strategy and systems design, integration and implementation.

The book covers a wide range of subject material, including management accounting, technology, psychology, organizational science, systems theory, design methods, software engineering and manufacturing strategy. I can guarantee that a specialist in any of these fields will be able to find fault with some aspects of the text. But to do so would be to miss the point completely. The book is not aimed at specialists, but at those who have to transcend the narrow specialisms of monoprofessionals, to gain a broad picture of the whole enterprise in all relevant dimensions, taking into account all the interrelationships between them.

The contents will also be useful to those engaged in determining research policy, and those involved in manufacturing research. Such people need to begin to question whether what they are doing is right for agile manufacturing.

Much of the material in the book is based on the results of investigations that have been undertaken over a period of ten years. Some of the material is, of course, not new. The way that it has all has been combined, related and applied is new.

Structure

Reflecting the diverse readership, the book is structured in self contained units. A short introduction sets the scene for the remaining chapters.

Part I focuses on providing an overview of agile manufacturing. Chapter 1 provides a definition of agile manufacturing, and considers the nature of the emerging competitive environment and the business case for agile manufacturing. A conceptual framework is also proposed along with some primary generic features. Chapter 2 deals with what I have called the four core concepts of agile manufacturing.

Part II of the book is concerned with understanding the revolutionary changes implied by agile manufacturing. Chapter 3 provides an overview of the types of changes that we must face up to. In Chapter 4, the nature of our existing management accounting paradigm is described. Changing this paradigm is a key leverage point for any long term change strategy. The nature of our existing organizational, control, technological and design paradigms are considered in Chapter 5.

The third part of the book deals with the process of designing agile manufacturing enterprises. This covers several issues: the concept of agile manufacturing enterprise design (Chapter 6), the process by which we need to design our enterprises (Chapter 7), interdisciplinary design (Chapter 8) and the question of management accounting and investment appraisal for agile manufacturing (Chapter 9).

Part IV focuses on the question of skill and knowledge enhancing technologies. Chapter 10 examines our traditional technology oriented approaches, and introduces what I have called a skill oriented approach. A conceptual framework for skill and knowledge enhancing technologies is also presented. Chapter 11 presents a detailed case study based on computer based technologies for machine tool systems.

Finally Part V provides an overview of issues, problems, research needs and likely future developments (Chapter 12).

I hope that readers will find the book interesting and stimulating, and that it will encourage people to learn more about agile manufacturing, and actively participate in the forging of this new frontier.

Acknowledgements

The copyright of Figures 1.1, 1.8 and 6.3 belongs to Manufacturing Knowledge Inc. They are reproduced with permission. These figures may be reproduced provided that attribution is made to Manufacturing Knowledge Inc. and their appearance in this book.

The copyright of Figure 3.9 belongs to Digital Equipment Corporation and I am grateful to Dr Charles Savage for his permission to reproduce this diagram.

The copyright of Figures 2.3, 3.6, 6.1, 6.2, 8.10, 10.1, 10.2, 10.3 and 12.1 belongs to Cheshire Henbury. They are reproduced with permission.

The copyright of Figures 9.1 and 9.2 belongs to CAM-I. These figures are taken from *The CAM-I Glossary of Activity-Based Management* (1991) (Raffish N. and Turney P.B.B., eds.), Arlington: CAM-I. They are reproduced in this book under the copyright permission granted in the above publication.

In Chapter 6, I refer to a tool called HITOP. HITOP is a trademark of the Industrial Technology Institute, Ann Arbor, MI.

Early work on the development of skill and knowledge enhancing technologies was undertaken in collaboration with Professor Howard H. Rosenbrock at the Control Systems Centre, UMIST, Manchester, England. Professor Rosenbrock was also one of the first engineers to challenge our traditional manufacturing paradigms. His vision of a different type of manufacturing, based on the enhancement of human skills and knowledge, inspired the writing of this book.

I should like to acknowledge the help of various people with the writing of this book. Thanks are due to Dr Charles Savage and Professor Jim Browne who both reviewed the first draft and made constructive and detailed criticisms. Thanks are also due to Tim Pitts of Addison-Wesley for his help and suggestions for transforming the reviewers' comments into a revised and much improved manuscript.

Finally, I would like to express my thanks to my wife Judith, and my three children Lucy, Tara and Dale, for putting up with my obsession to complete this book on time.

Paul T. Kidd
June 1994
Manufacturing Knowledge Inc.
Louisville, KY

Contents

Introduction

Manufacturing industry is on the verge of a major paradigm shift. This shift will take us away from mass production, way beyond **lean manufacturing**, into a world of **agile manufacturing**.

We spent most of our time during the 1980s and early 1990s copying the Japanese. Now we may be about to teach the Japanese something. For a change, US manufacturing industry is realizing that it has very little to gain, in the long term, by copying what other people are doing. There is now a growing realization that global preeminence in manufacturing can only be achieved through innovation. We can learn from others, but in a highly competitive world, we can only become world leaders if we develop new ideas that take us beyond the state-of-the-art.

Since the 1950s our manufacturing industries have been dominated by the paradigm of mass production, which has led to enormous wealth creation and supported an ever increasing standard of living. But there has been a price to pay for this prosperity. As our factories became geared up to producing large volumes of low variety and low cost products, they became inflexible and lost the capability to respond to rapid shifts in market conditions. This was not a problem, as long as everyone was playing the same mass production game, but it is now clear that our Japanese competitors were not playing this game. Over an extended period the Japanese, in effect, developed their own manufacturing paradigm, what today we call lean manufacturing. This is so called, because it is concerned with manufacturing products with less of everything – less time to design, less inventory, less defects, and so forth.

Lean manufacturing was not developed overnight. The Japanese gradually worked away at the development of their manufacturing paradigm, with companies like Toyota acting as pioneers, in much the same way that Ford pioneered mass production. By the late 1970s many Japanese enterprises were starting to outperform our own. Today, in the

1

1990s, there are some industrial sectors where several of our enterprises have become wholly or partly owned by the Japanese. The fact of the matter is that, both in the US and Europe, there has been a gradual loss of competitiveness. As the lean manufacturing paradigm became established in Japan, generating competitive edge for those Japanese companies who were using it, the mass production paradigm, dominant in US and European industry, was contributing to this loss of competitiveness, which has now become a major economic problem.

How are we going to restore our competitiveness? Should we adopt lean manufacturing in our own enterprises? Should we mimic the Japanese? Or should we do something different and better?

Without doubt there are now a significant number of people who believe that we have to adopt lean manufacturing. But in adopting this approach we run the risk of forever chasing after a moving target, for the Japanese are not going to stand still and wait to be outperformed by US and European enterprises. The Japanese will keep innovating and perfecting their methods. Thus, adopting lean manufacturing can only be a short term measure aimed at doing something to close the competitive gap. In the longer term, if we want to catch up with and overtake the Japanese, lean manufacturing is not the answer. What we need to do is something that the Japanese cannot do.

Enter agile manufacturing. This is not another *program of the month*. Nor is it another term for **computer integrated manufacturing** (CIM), or any number of other fashionable buzzwords. Agile manufacturing is primarily a business concept. Its aim is quite simple – to put our enterprises way out in front of our primary competitors. In agile manufacturing, the aim is to combine the organization, people and technology into an integrated and coordinated whole. The agility that arises from this can be used for competitive advantage, by being able to respond rapidly to changes occurring in the market environment and through the ability to use and exploit a fundamental resource – knowledge.

Fundamental to the exploitation of this resource is the idea of using technologies to lever people's skills and knowledge. People must be brought together, in dynamic teams formed around clearly identified market opportunities, so that it becomes possible to lever one another's knowledge. Through these processes is sought the transformation of knowledge and ideas into new products and services, as well as improvements to existing products and services.

The concept of agile manufacturing is built around the synthesis of a number of enterprises that each have some core skills or competencies brought to a joint venturing operation, based on using each partner's facilities and resources. For this reason, these joint venture enterprises are called virtual corporations, because they do not own significant capital resources. This helps to make them agile, as they can be formed and changed very rapidly.

Central to the ability to form these joint ventures is the deployment of advanced information technologies and the development of highly nimble organizational structures to support highly skilled, knowledgeable and empowered people. Agile manufacturing builds on what is good in lean manufacturing and uses what can be adapted to Western cultures, but it also adds the power of the individual and the opportunities afforded by new technologies.

Agile manufacturing enterprises will be capable of responding rapidly to changes in customer demand. They will be able to take advantage of the windows of opportunity that, from time to time, appear in the market place. With agile manufacturing will come new ways to interact with customers and suppliers. Customers will be able to gain access to manufacturers' products and services, and easily assess and exploit their competencies, enabling achievement.

The key to agility however, lies in several places. An agile enterprise needs highly skilled and knowledgeable people who are flexible, motivated and responsive to change. It also needs new forms of organizational structures that engender non-hierarchical management styles and stimulate and support individuals, as well as cooperation and team working. Agile manufacturing enterprises also need advanced computer based technologies.

To achieve agile manufacturing, enterprises will have to bring together a wide range of knowledge in the design of a manufacturing system that encompasses suppliers and customers, and which addresses all dimensions of the system, including organization, people, technology, management accounting practices, and so on. Most importantly, the interrelated nature of all these areas needs to be recognized, and an interdisciplinary manufacturing systems design method adopted as standard practice. This means going beyond the multidisciplinary approaches that are currently being adopted, and looking at areas between professions.

There is, however, a fundamental problem, a barrier which hinders progress in this area of interdisciplinary design. For the past 200 years or more, the industrialized world has organized knowledge into well defined boxes, represented by professional groups often working in separate departments. Anything that did not fit into those well defined areas of knowledge was ignored or allowed to fall through the cracks created between professions. This resulted in such countermeasures as design for manufacture, where attempts are being made to overcome the problems that have arisen from fundamental operating philosophies.

Manufacturing has tended to treat organization, people and technology issues independently, and for the most part this division of knowledge worked well in the past. However, this approach does not work very well today, because over the last 10 years or so the world has changed enormously and has become much more complex. Technologies have become more sophisticated, markets more global and dynamic, and people more demanding, both as customers and as employees. The traditional paradigms which fostered the growth of manufacturing industry have started to shown signs of breaking down. We are now entering a new era, and as manufacturing begins to move from the old industrial era to the new knowledge intensive age, new paradigms are being forged. Agile manufacturing is a new paradigm. It is highly likely that it will form the basis of 21st century manufacturing strategy.

Interdisciplinary design will form the basis of designing agile manufacturing systems in the new knowledge intensive era. Interdisciplinary design, however, means more than just applying knowledge from other domains, such as psychology and organizational science, to the design of agile manufacturing systems. It also implies looking into the unexplored areas between these disciplines and the areas where they overlap, to find new insights, new knowledge and new and original solutions. This is one of the most important challenges that managers, system designers and integrators will face in the years ahead, for interdisciplinary design leads us to new approaches and new ways of working and of thinking. However, to successfully adopt an interdisciplinary design method, we also need to:

- Challenge accepted design strategies and develop new and better approaches.
- Question established and cherished beliefs and theories, and develop new ones to replace those that no longer have validity.
- Consider how we address organization, people and technology, and other issues in the design of manufacturing systems, so that we can achieve systems that are better for performance, for the environment and for the people who form a part of these systems.
- Go beyond the automation paradigm of the industrial era, to use technology in a way that makes human skill, knowledge, and intelligence more effective and productive, and that allows us to tap into the creativity and talent of all the people involved.

The challenges faced with respect to all these issues are enormous. The world of manufacturing is very complex. There is a massive number of interconnections between the various components and elements. A manufacturing enterprise is so complex that, in the past, it has been impossible to cope with it as a whole, and it has been necessary to reduce it into manageable areas which have tended to be examined separately.

In this respect we have copied the scientific method, but the end result has been that our knowledge of manufacturing is divided into well defined boxes such as industrial engineering, mechanical engineering, software engineering, industrial psychology, and so on. There is, however, no natural law stating that knowledge of manufacturing should be divided in this way. These subjects are man-made, and the divisions between them are more a matter of convenience than anything else.

More correctly, it should be said that the division of knowledge into these boxes was a matter of convenience. This is no longer the case. In fact it is now a handicap, a barrier to progress in the field of agile manufacturing.

In the past we managed reasonably well with this way of organizing knowledge. It resulted in some problems, but on the whole the benefits seemed to outweigh the costs. In the past however, we did not have to deal with some of the complex technological systems that have been designed and built over the past few decades, or with the complexities of rapidly changing market conditions, and with the several other factors which make the world of manufacturing very complex.

Increasing technical sophistication, of course, has been vitally important to the development of all aspects of civilization, including manufacturing industry. It could be said that technology is the axis, pivot and springboard of development, for without technology there would be no progress. No books to stir the imagination. No cars, no planes, no houses, no radios, no televisions, nothing. That is the power of technology. Without knowledge and access to technology, civilization cannot develop. If a society has no access to technology it becomes trapped in a time warp, that of primitive existence.

Without technology there would be no manufacturing, but manufacturing is more than technology. It is also about people and how they and technical resources are organized. Manufacturing is about organization, people, technology, management accounting, business strategy, and so on. It is also about the connections between all these dimensions. In the past we have tended to ignore not only the connections, but also some of the dimensions. We have placed too much faith in technology, using technology to compensate for inadequacies elsewhere, and trying to solve all problems as though they were technical problems.

All the relevant dimensions of agile manufacturing are written in different books and taught by different people. The education system teaches limited and discrete lumps of knowledge. Even when a broad range of disciplines is taught, which sadly is still uncommon, there is rarely any indication of how these different areas of knowledge interrelate. These relationships, however, lead to a new vision of manufacturing.

If agile manufacturing is to be successful, it must break with bad practices. We aim to show how better and more effective manufacturing systems and technologies can be designed based on the insights derived from the relationships between different areas of knowledge. However, to make the transition we need to:

- Examine and define the underlying conceptual framework on which agile manufacturing enterprises will be built.
- Explore and understand the nature of the mass production paradigm and the nature of the cultural and methodological difficulties involved in the transition to agile manufacturing.

- Define a methodology for designing a 21st century manufacturing enterprise.

Our new vision of manufacturing will be based on a systems perspective of technology, organization and people, tied to clear business vision and goals. This will help us to understand the full complexity of designing a 21st century manufacturing enterprise, and the way that the past mass production paradigm still limits our thinking today. Most of all, this systems perspective will help us to see how to approach the task of designing an agile manufacturing enterprise. The issues that are addressed in the chapters that follow are: defining what we are about, understanding the present and how it limits our progress, and the means by which we will bring about agile manufacturing.

PART ONE

Agile manufacturing

1

A 21st century paradigm

Introduction

The term **agile manufacturing** came into common usage with the publication of the report *21st Century Manufacturing Enterprise Strategy* (Iacocca Institute, 1991). Agile manufacturing has been used to refer to other concepts such as **flexible manufacturing** and **lean production**, as though synonymous. This chapter presents a definition of agile manufacturing and its conceptual framework.

What is agile manufacturing?

Agility is defined in dictionaries as quick moving, nimble and active. This is not the same as flexibility, which implies in the manufacturing sense, adaptability and versatility. It is now an accepted assumption that flexibility is a requirement for the competitive markets of today, but on its own, will not deliver agility. Flexibility should be regarded as a necessary condition, which does not include agility.

Lean manufacturing (Womack, Jones and Roos, 1990) is so called because it is concerned with doing everything with less (Jones, 1992). In other words, the excess of wasteful activities, unnecessary inventory, long lead times, and so on have been cut away through the application of, for example, just-in-time manufacturing, concurrent engineering, overhead cost reduction, improved supplier and customer relationships, and total quality management. However, lean manufacturing is not the same as agile manufacturing, because leanness and agility are two different concepts. Sometimes the terms are used interchangeably, but this is not appropriate. Again, lean manufacturing is necessary for agile manufacturing, but it is not sufficient. Computer integrated manufacturing and the computer integrated enterprise can be considered in the same light. When computers are linked across applications, functions and enterprises, agile manufacturing is not achieved. What is achieved however, is a necessary condition for agile manufacturing, that is, rapid communications and the exchange and reuse of data.

So, if agile manufacturing is not flexible manufacturing, or lean manufacturing, or computer integrated manufacturing, then what is it? The answer is that it is something that is partly concerned with combining these concepts, introducing some additional ones, then using them to make a quantum leap forward in our thinking about manufacturing, recognizing the capabilities that emerge from our new vision.

To understand agile manufacturing, we should consider the Iacocca Institute report (1991). This makes three key points:

(1) A new competitive environment is emerging, which is acting as a driving force for change in manufacturing.
(2) Competitive advantage will accrue to those enterprises that develop the capability to rapidly respond to the demand for high quality, highly customized products.
(3) To achieve the agility that is required to respond to these driving forces and to develop the required capability, it is necessary to integrate flexible technologies with a highly skilled, knowledgeable, motivated and empowered workforce. This must be done within organizational and management structures that stimulate cooperation both within and between firms.

Agile manufacturing can be considered as a structure within which every company can develop its own business strategies and products. The structure is supported by three primary resources: innovative management structures and organization, a skill base of knowledgeable and empowered people and flexible and intelligent technologies. Underpinning these three primary resources is a methodology of integration. Agility is achieved through the integration of these three resources into a coordinated, interdependent system. In simple terms therefore, agile manufacturing can be considered as the integration of organization, highly skilled and knowledgeable people, and advanced technologies, to achieve cooperation and innovation in response to the need to supply our customers with high quality customized products. This concept is illustrated in Figure 1.1.

The Iacocca Institute report also describes the concept of agile manufacturing in terms of several company scenarios. The teams of industrialists responsible for producing the report produced a set of competitive foundations and common characteristics, systems elements, and enabling

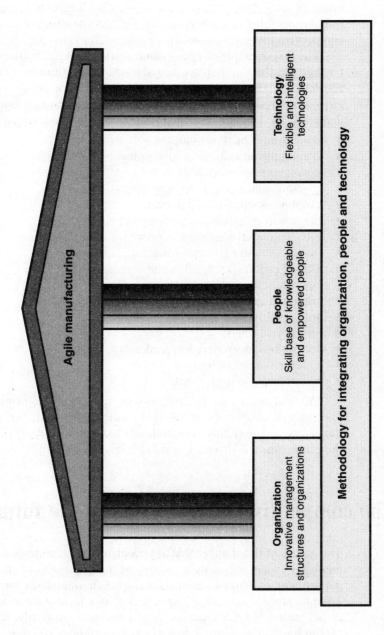

Figure 1.1   The structure of agile manufacturing enterprises. *Source:* Manufacturing Knowledge Inc. © 1993. Published with permission.

The figure, displayed rotated, shows "Agile manufacturing" supported by three pillars:

Organization — Innovative management structures and organizations

People — Skill base of knowledgeable and empowered people

Technology — Flexible and intelligent technologies

all resting on a base: **Methodology for integrating organization, people and technology** subsystems for agile manufacturing. These were collectively referred to as a new infrastructure for manufacturing.

We will refrain at this point from listing the system elements and enabling subsystems. These are addressed in Chapter 6. The competitive foundations and characteristics of the infrastructure consists of four competitive foundations and 18 enterprise characteristics.

The first principle of agile manufacturing is that an enterprise should be built on the competitive foundations of continuous change, rapid response, quality improvement and social responsibility in terms of environment and employees. The agile manufacturing enterprise, as defined in the Iacocca Institute report, possesses the characteristics of:

- concurrency in all activities;
- continuing education for all employees;
- customer responsiveness;
- dynamic multi-venturing capabilities;
- employees valued as vital assets;
- empowered individuals working in teams;
- environmental concern and proactive approach;
- accessible and usable information;
- skilled and knowledgeable employees;
- open systems architectures;
- right first time designs;
- total quality philosophy;
- short cycle times;
- technology awareness and leadership;
- enterprise integration;
- vision based management.

We will return to the concept of agile manufacturing when we present our conceptual framework, but before that, we will review the emerging competitive environment to establish clearly the nature of the prime business drivers behind agile manufacturing.

The competitive environment of the future

The nature of the changes that are occurring in the competitive environment is well described by members of the organization and efficiency department of Philips International in their important book, *Flexible Manufacturing. Integrating Technological and Social Innovation* (Bolwijn *et al.*, 1986). These changes are concerned primarily with a shift of emphasis away from a primary concern about price, to addressing simultaneously, and without trade-off, issues of price, quality and customer choice.

When we look back over several decades it is quite apparent that some notable changes have occurred in the market place for manufactured goods. Price has always been the most important competitive factor for most of our manufacturing companies. In this type of economic regime the emphasis that we have placed traditionally on reducing costs can easily be understood. In order to remain competitive and profitable in a price driven market environment, we continually had to reduce our costs, and traditionally we tried to achieve this objective through mass production (economies of scale), product rationalization, division of labor, and the application of technology to achieve increased capacity, improved machine utilization, automated production and the de-skilling and elimination of direct labor.

During the 1970s and 1980s price competitiveness became less important, and quality and other issues such as delivery performance, customer choice and so on became equally important competitive factors. This need to provide customers with better quality products and greater choice, and the increased demand for more customizing of products, coupled with rapid technological developments, resulted in the pursuit of manufacturing and product innovation, and the continuous revision and updating of products. These customer demands, coupled with the need to reduce costs, led towards a drive to reduce inventory levels, improve quality and increase flexibility. Consequently, in addition to achieving reduced costs, improved quality and greater flexibility were required.

World markets are becoming more international, dynamic and customer driven, and competition on price alone is no longer a viable business strategy for most manufacturing companies. Other non-price competitive factors have become equally important. These market changes do not mean that the need to reduce costs has become unimportant. Product price is still a relevant competitive factor, but a competitive price alone is not enough, because customers are also demanding a wide range of high quality products. This has instigated change in business and manufacturing strategies.

As we move towards the next century we are likely to see an acceleration of the existing trend towards tailoring of products to meet customer needs. Although this trend has been described as a move from mass production to one of a kind production (Browne, 1992), the actual change in market conditions is more complex than this because there will still be a whole range of company specific conditions that will govern our strategic choice (Atkinson, 1990). A more realistic and simplified representation of the changes that are now occurring is illustrated in Table 1.1. Basically the emphasis will be on moving away from competition on price alone, to competition on price, quality and choice. This can be based on large volumes of mass produced items with many variants, or on low volumes of diversified quality products.

Table 1.1 A simplified classification of business strategies.

	Price competition	*Price, quality and choice competition*
High volume manufacturing	Low variety and mass production	High variety and customized mass production
Low volume manufacturing	Small batch and make to order production	High variety and high quality production

As Table 1.1 illustrates, it would be a mistake to believe that changes in business strategies imply that price competition is dead. In fact there is the opportunity for the most innovative companies to offer a diverse range of low price high quality products. The important point about these changes in markets is that we are now faced with the trends shown in Figure 1.2, that is, reductions in production volumes, increasing product variety, shorter product life cycles (as companies strive to keep their products up to date and respond to customer demand) and a reducing number of repeat orders. These trends show no signs of abating in the foreseeable future. The questions to be asked therefore, are what implications do these trends have for the source of economic growth and what will the impact be of these trends on the economics of manufacturing?

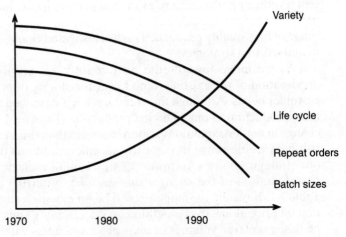

Figure 1.2 Market trends.

Economies of scale versus economies of scope

The prevailing economic paradigm is based largely on the concept of economies of scale and is referred to by economists as the cost-price driven model. This cost-price driven model is illustrated in Figure 1.3. It is based on a cycle in which product standardization and automation of production leads to unit cost reductions, which in turn leads to price reductions, which gives market growth, leading to larger scale production, which in turn leads to opportunities for more standardization and more automation, and so on.

This is the basis of our mass production enterprises, which have become the dominant mode of production in much of the Western industrialized world. It could be argued that the extent to which mass production has come to dominate these economies does vary. For example, it is commonly believed that mass production is more dominant in the US because of the large size of their internal market, than it is in Western European countries (UK, Germany, France and so on) where markets are much smaller, more diverse and fragmented. It could however, be argued that in some sectors, European manufacturing industry is more mass production focused than is the case in the US (Womack *et al.*, 1990). This apart, the paradigm of economies of scale based on mass production is one of the important aspects of our traditional approaches to manufacturing.

It is now believed in some circles that the cost-price driven mechanism of economic growth is becoming increasingly irrelevant (Ayres, 1990).

Figure 1.3   Economies of scale.

Over the past few decades a trend away from mass production has been observed. Economists are now discussing the emergence of a new paradigm of economic growth based on economies of scope (Goldhar and Jelinek, 1983). With this, competitive advantage is achieved from using the same equipment to produce products more cheaply in combination than separately. That is, equipment is not dedicated to only one product or product family. Rather, the same equipment is used to manufacture many products. Also, these products are manufactured in smaller batches, because of the organizational and technical capability to achieve rapid equipment set-ups when changing between products. Economies of scope is, therefore, an ability to convert fixed capital from one purpose to another. In simple terms, this means flexible manufacturing.

The concept of economies of scope is illustrated in Figure 1.4. There is one important point to note about this new paradigm. The proposed model of economic growth is not based on the simple chain reaction to events outlined for the cost-price driven model. It is clear that we are now faced with several mechanisms of interaction occurring between different stages. Also, as production cost is no longer the sole driving force for competitive performance, the role of technology is not so clear as it was previously.

We should now consider other factors that might play a key role in the generation of growth.

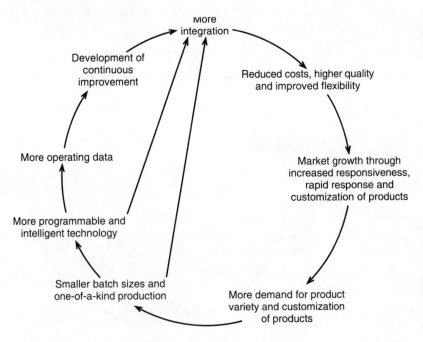

Figure 1.4　Economies of scope.

One of the characteristics of mass production is its reliance on a fairly lengthy product life cycle which allows recoupment of high development costs over a relatively long period. Product life cycles are, however, being reduced. The opportunity to recoup high development costs over a long period is therefore rapidly disappearing. Apart from the obvious need to reduce our time to market so that we can respond more quickly to changing market conditions, there are several other important economic implications of shorter product life cycles to be aware of.

The first is that product development costs will have to be reduced. This will imply a change of focus away from reducing manufacturing costs on a project-by-project basis, to overall cost reductions based on a holistic systems view that takes account of interactions between marketing and product development, design and manufacturing and so on. In other words there will be a major focus on right first time designs – right in the sense that products meet customers' needs, wishes and expectations, and right in the sense that they can be manufactured without difficulties and then easily maintained in the field. The second implication is that sales revenues will have to increase against a background of an increasingly competitive and dynamic market environment, which implies building and maintaining a world class performance. If we are to do more than just survive, performance must at least equal our best competitor's. But what we really have to do is to outperform them.

Most importantly however, the shift to short product life cycles will have profound implications on the cash flows in businesses and the impact of product failures on liquidity (von Braun, 1990). If we assume, for the sake of argument, that the sales revenue from a given product has a normal distribution, then over the life of the product, we would expect to see sales increase, reach a peak, and then fall off, as illustrated in Figure 1.5.

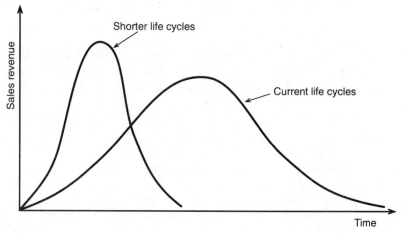

Figure 1.5 Effect of life cycle change on sales income distributions with total sales income remaining constant.

If the total sales revenue from a product over its life is maintained, that is, the area under the sales curve remains the same, then the effect of a shorter life cycle is simply to produce a faster generation of sales revenue and higher peak revenue.

This looks very attractive from the financial perspective! But beware, for there is a hidden trap here for the unwary. Life cycles cannot be continually reduced. There is some lower limit beyond which life cycles cannot go, otherwise there would never be any time to sell products. So what happens when this lower limit is approached?

In order to maintain sales income at a steady state, we need continually to introduce new products in such a way that the growth in the income from new products compensates for the loss of income from older products. Ideally, we want to see a real long term growth in sales, which implies generating more income from new products. When life cycles are reduced and total sales revenue derived from products remains unchanged, we will achieve an apparent increase in sales revenue as soon as we adopt shorter life cycles. This will happen for two reasons. First, we will generate our sales revenue at a faster rate, and second, the sales volume from older products will not decline as fast as those from newer products. The net effect of these two factors will be to produce an increase in sales revenue, which might be maintained for several years.

The increase will however, eventually flatten out and then reduce back to the previous steady state value. It will do this because we will not be able to keep reducing the life cycles and because older products will eventually be phased out. As we made the assumption that total sales revenue remained constant, then it must follow that after a period of transition to a shorter life cycle for our products, our total sales volume will be just as before.

So the effect of introducing short product life cycles will be that total sales grow, as long as life cycles continue to reduce. As soon as they stop reducing there is a return to previous levels.

Now, what happens if, as a result of shorter life cycles, the total sales for each product reduce rather than remain constant? Reduced total sales are a distinct possibility in a situation where there are shorter life cycles. When this situation arises it will be noticed, when product life cycles eventually stop decreasing, that the overall net effect will be a total steady state sales value, less than that achieved for longer life cycles.

Perhaps of more concern in the case of shorter life cycles, is the impact of product failure. This of course results in a loss of revenue. But with longer life cycles this loss is spread over many years. With shorter life cycles, the loss is more concentrated, even though the total sales loss might be the same. The net result of this concentrated loss of income could be a severe financial crisis. Shorter product life cycles therefore make companies more vulnerable to the financial effects of product failures.

The dynamics of competitiveness

Hayes *et al.* (1988) have pointed out that we do not always fully appreciate that our competitive position at any point in time is often less important than the rate of improvement of our competitive position as compared to our competitors. Manufacturing competitiveness is a dynamic process – it is not static.

Rate of change in competitive performance needs, therefore, to be related to the rate of change of competitors, as illustrated in Figure 1.6. The competitive performance of world class performers is continually improving (a moving target). To catch up and overtake them, others must achieve a rapid change in competitive performance, and to stay ahead must keep improving competitive performance at a faster rate than the competitors. If the rate of change is allowed to fall off to any degree, then it will only be a matter of time before the competitors take the lead again.

In order to understand how to maintain competitive advantage, it is important to appreciate the mechanisms of innovation. From time to time new discoveries lead to technological breakthroughs, which have a revolutionary impact. These innovations spawn whole new industries, new products and new ways of doing things. Examples of revolutionary developments include the steam engine, the Bessemer blast furnace, the dynamo, telephone communications, manned flight, transistors and many others. However, all these technologies, once introduced, have been subject to on going improvements over a long period. None of these improvements produce the same impact as the initial innovation. Small-scale innovations, nevertheless, are a vitally important part of the innovation process.

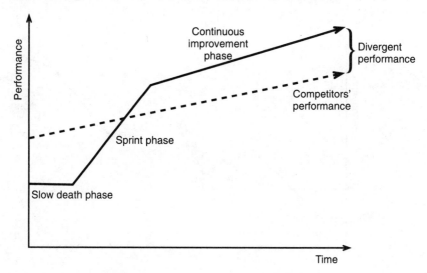

Figure 1.6 The dynamics of competitive position.

Rapid changes in competitive performance are only likely to come about through revolutionary changes. This means that we have to get involved in making *big-bang*, that is, major and highly innovative changes to the order of things (in terms of organization, people, technology, products and processes and so on). Once a competitive edge has been achieved through such innovative changes, it is more likely to be sustained by smaller and more incremental changes involving continuous improvements to products, processes, organization, people and technology. But we should also be looking to make revolutionary changes again at some point in the future, as our competitors will also be seeking to make rapid improvements in their competitive position.

Thus, in an innovation process, we experience revolutionary changes, but in between there is a process of incremental improvement. Although revolutionary breakthroughs happen from time to time, they are much rarer than is popularly believed, and breakthroughs that are hailed as revolutionary often turn out to be less revolutionary than prophesied. The majority of improvements most often come from small, regular, and continuous incremental improvements in all areas of the business. It is through the cumulative effect of all these smaller-scale innovations that an advantageous rate of change in competitive performance can be sustained.

The important point about the dynamics of competitiveness is that it is an interactive system. We must occasionally make revolutionary changes, because although the cumulative effects of incremental change can be significant, our competitors will want to make revolutionary changes in order to overtake us once again. Thus we have a situation of the type shown in Figure 1.7, where we must periodically seek to achieve

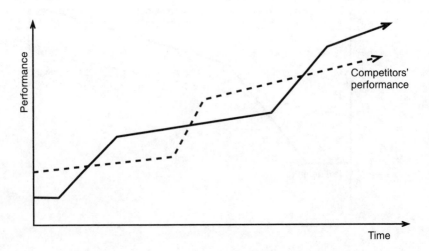

Figure 1.7   The interactive dynamics of competitive position.

a sprint (Tranfield and Smith, 1990) in our competitive performance. In between these sprints, these periods of rapid and revolutionary change, we must be implementing incremental changes.

Thus our businesses will be in a state of continuous change and innovation. It has been argued (Hayes *et al.,* 1988) that achieving a culture of continuous change involves establishing a learning organization, where lessons learnt in one project are applied in other projects, and where an environment is created that unleashes the creative potential of people, throughout the enterprise.

The business case for agile manufacturing

Analysis of the emerging competitive environment leads us to state the business case for the development of agile manufacturing. This is done with reference to the issues raised in the previous section, which are reiterated.

First, in the cost driven mass production paradigm, technology played a key role in the strategies for growth and improvement of competitiveness. With the economies of scope scenario, technology still plays an important and key role, but flexibility and continuing improvement are also required. Flexibility is partly a product of technology, but it is also partly a product of organizational and management structures and practices, and partly a product of people; their attitudes, abilities, motivation, skills, and so on. Continuous improvement and innovation is primarily derived from people, but technology, organizational and management structures and practices play an important role in fostering and supporting improvement and innovation. The first conclusion therefore is:

> In an economic system dominated by economies of scope we can no longer afford to concentrate on technology alone. We need to focus on organization, people and technology and the interrelationships between the three.

Second, when product life cycles become shorter and shorter we expose the weaknesses built into our manufacturing enterprises developed primarily to serve mass production. We no longer have the luxury of long development times and even longer periods in which to recoup our development costs. This trend to shorter product life cycles means that we must reduce significantly both the cost and time to develop and introduce new products. Moreover, as shorter product life cycles and increasing competition indicate a decrease in sales revenues, we must develop the capability of rapidly responding to and accurately assessing every commercial opening and window of opportunity. We must therefore not only focus our attention on the new product development and introduction process, but the whole enterprise. We must ensure that we get the right products to our customers at the right price and at the right time, but in a way that maximizes the benefits and returns to our businesses. To do this we must rethink fundamentally every aspect of our enterprises. Our second conclusion therefore is:

> In the emerging competitive markets we must be prepared to develop a new enterprise infrastructure, fundamentally different from what exists today, which delivers certain characteristics and capabilities, enabling customer focus and choice, innovation, rapid response and quality, at the lowest cost.

Third, in a short product life cycle environment the effect of product failure could have a devastating effect on liquidity. We must therefore ensure right first time products. This has enormous implications for the methods of designing and introducing products, and the procedures for ensuring that unfavorable or inappropriate developments are identified and terminated. Our third conclusion therefore is:

> The commercial risks inherent in the emerging competitive environment are much greater, which means that risk sharing, management and elimination, and the need to get things right, are crucial to success. This implies that we tap into every ounce of intelligence in businesses and back this intelligence up with suitable advanced technologies.

Finally, competitiveness is not static, it is dynamic. More than this, it is interactive. We are always engaged in a battle for supremacy. Our final conclusion therefore is:

> We must create an enterprise culture of continuous change. There must be continuous change, based on periods of rapid revolutionary change and longer periods of incremental change. But change must not just be a part of everyday life, it must be accepted and welcomed.

The argument for agile manufacturing is that market conditions are such that only companies which achieve a high level of market driven innovative capability are likely to be successful in the long term. Market driven innovative capability is likely to become the main source of competitive advantage, and this will have profound implications for everyone in enterprise infrastructures. Innovation and creativity will become key parts of day-to-day work, and all job descriptions throughout the company will include substantial elements of experimentation, learning and development work. Companies will have to organize around innovation networks linking all the people, not just those traditionally associated with innovation. We will not, in future, be grouped around neat organizational boxes determined by functions and bureaucracy, but around networks. This is the new vision of manufacturing. This is agile manufacturing.

A conceptual framework for agile manufacturing

The Iacocca Institute refers to a new infrastructure for manufacturing. What we need first, however, is not a detailed infrastructure, but a definition of a conceptual framework. There is also the danger, at this stage, that we might see an infrastructure as a prescription for success. A working definition of agile manufacturing has previously been provided, and the business reasons that lie behind the development of the concept outlined. We will now provide a framework of essential concepts. The details of the required infrastructure, and how we might build our agile manufacturing enterprise, are left until later chapters.

Agile manufacturing should primarily be seen as a business concept that brings together many ideas. We are facing significant changes in competitive markets. We should stop fearing these changes and looking at them from the current perspectives of mass production. We should start to encourage the developments currently occurring in the competitive environment, and start to build agile enterprises, taking advantage of these forces.

To achieve this goal a whole new set of manufacturing concepts are needed. We need these new concepts in order to develop an appropriate manufacturing response to the emerging market conditions, to take advantage of new market opportunities, and to exploit business concepts, such as the virtual enterprise, which are made more practicable by new technologies. New manufacturing strategies are therefore needed.

The important point is that agile manufacturing is brought about by the integration of organization, people and technology into a coordinated interdependent system. This is where agility comes from. Thus our new strategies will be based upon the use of organization, people and technology, involving people, working in advanced organizations, supported by advanced technologies.

Agile manufacturing is now defined in terms of a conceptual framework. This is shown in Figure 1.8. Central to this framework is the enterprise built on the competitive foundations of continuous change, rapid response, quality improvement, social responsibility

---

Generic features model

- Integrated enterprises
- Human networking organization
- Enterprises based on natural groups
- Increased competencies of all people
- Focus on core competencies
- Virtual corporations
- An environment supportive of experimentation, learning and innovation
- Multi-skilled and flexible people
- Team working
- Empowerment of all the people in the enterprise
- Knowledge management
- Skill and knowledge enhancing technologies
- Continuous improvement
- Change and risk management

Core concepts

- Strategy to achieve agility
- Strategy to exploit agility
- Integration of organization, people and technology
- Interdisciplinary design methodology

Competitive foundations

- Continuous change
- Rapid response
- Quality improvement
- Social responsibility
- Total customer focus

Figure 1.8 A conceptual framework for agile manufacturing. *Source:* Manufacturing Knowledge Inc. © 1993. Published with permission.

and total customer focus. The first four of these are proposed in the Iacocca Institute report, but we have added one more – total customer focus. No importance is attached to the order in which these competitive foundations are listed. They are equally important.

We will create our agile manufacturing enterprise on these competitive foundations. The core concepts are:

- A strategy to become an agile manufacturing enterprise.
- A strategy to exploit agility to achieve competitive advantage.
- Integration of organization, people and technology into a coordinated interdependent system which is our competitive weapon.
- An interdisciplinary design methodology to achieve the integration of organization, people and technology.

We believe strongly that the goal of becoming an agile manufacturing enterprise is a strategy in itself, which is additional, but complementary and related to, normal business strategies. Furthermore, the strategy for becoming an agile manufacturing enterprise will be focused on this infrastructure issue of achieving the integration of organization, people and technology. And to achieve this integration we need to design a complete manufacturing enterprise addressing all components. This points to the need for an interdisciplinary approach. All this amounts to a big change in the way we think about our manufacturing enterprises and how we design them.

We now define the generic features of our agile manufacturing enterprise conceptual framework. We wish to achieve a high level of motivation in our people and to make use of their skills, knowledge, judgment, experience and creativity. Our organizations, management practices and technologies need to be developed to allow highly trained people, throughout our companies, to adapt their work strategies to the variety of situations that they will have to face. We must not only be more effective and responsive, but must make better use of people, and take into account their physiological and psychological needs.

In response to these needs we should focus our attention not on solutions, but on generic features. We must be able to adapt to changing circumstances. This implies open systems. These open systems will allow people a large degree of freedom to define the mode of operation of the system at any point in time, and to redefine the system as and when necessary.

A framework of generic features comprises:

- integrated enterprises;
- human networking organization;
- enterprises based on natural groups;
- increased competencies of all people;
- focus on core enterprise competencies;
- virtual corporations;
- an environment supportive of experimentation, learning and innovation;

- multi-skilled and flexible people;
- team working;
- empowering of all the people in the enterprise;
- knowledge management;
- skill and knowledge enhancing technologies;
- continuing improvement involving all people;
- change and risk management.

It should be stressed that these generic features are not a prescriptive framework for agile manufacturing, nor are they intended to be a prescriptive solution to the various problems that beset manufacturing enterprises. The needs of manufacturing companies are not generally amenable to prescriptive solutions.

One of the problems with the emerging competitive environment is that there are so many different types of manufacturing business: high volume and low variety, low volume and high variety, process, batch and jobbing, and long and short life cycles, with most businesses trying, within this complex environment, to differentiate and compete in a wide range of markets. This means that each business has its own specific set of critical competencies. As a result, there is a wide variety of them, and no prescriptive approach is likely to provide adequate solutions for a wide range of businesses.

This implies that the generic features outlined above need to be highly tailored to specific needs of manufacturing companies, or plants, or even product families. The preceding list should therefore be considered as a generic features model that provides us with a guide to the sort of building blocks needed to develop an agile manufacturing enterprise.

Some primary generic features

Many of the generic features outlined above are familiar topics. Integrated enterprises, increasing the competencies of people, multi-skilled and flexible people, and team working have all been discussed widely in the manufacturing literature during the 1990s. However, several aspects of the generic features model have only recently become topical, or are still less well known, so we will therefore mention something about these features.

Human networking organization and empowerment of all the people in the enterprise

Traditional organizations are modelled on the principle of hierarchy, with information flowing upwards, and control exercised from the top downwards. Traditionally our hierarchies have been very steep, and in recent years there has been a tendency to view these very steep hierarchies as a source of inefficiency, unnecessary cost and unresponsiveness. Consequently, there has been a growing consensus of opinion that these steep hierarchies should be flattened by removing several layers of management.

We have also advocated using information technology to achieve this organizational flattening, but more recently we have begun to realize that these layers of management are a direct result of the way we organize our manufacturing enterprises, and our desire to control and direct, in detail, the work of our people. Thus by changing our basic assumptions and desires, it becomes possible for us to conceive organizational flattening through new factory layouts and more decentralization of decision-making, rather than using information technology to make these changes.

In recent years there has been discussion about the importance of employee empowerment. One of the main characteristics of hierarchy is the belief that we have to control other people. Employee empowerment rejects this concept. We now believe that people should not be controlled, but managed by giving them a framework in which to act, and providing them with authority and responsibility to solve problems and to investigate and develop new ideas. They should not have to ask for permission to do this. It should be part of their everyday activities.

Employee empowerment involves people forming informal networks, as and when needed. To be able to do this effectively, we should provide an infrastructure to support empowerment. This infrastructure should consist of agreed procedures for keeping others informed, technology to facilitate communications, meeting rooms, time to undertake investigative and development activities and a performance measurement system to help people understand what is important strategically.

The concept of employee empowerment renders our older concept of hierarchial organizations, whether they be steep or flat, inappropriate. Thinking in terms of hierarchy is simply the wrong model on which to base agile manufacturing. What we need to be doing is using a new model, and this should be based on the concept of human networking organizations (Naisbitt, 1984; Savage, 1990), as illustrated in Figure 1.9. In the human networking organization everybody is networked together, not via computer networks, although invariably these will be needed and can be used to support human networking, but by interactions that occur between all people in the organization, in response to problems and the need to develop new products and so on.

The links that exist between people can be separated into two groups; critical linkages and regular linkages. Critical linkages are those which have a high degree of leverage in the market place, or which have the potential of generating important innovations which might lead to

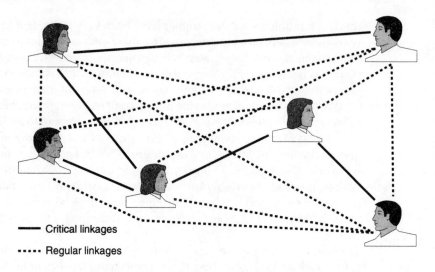

Critical linkages
Regular linkages

Figure 1.9   Human networking organization.

significant improvements. Regular linkages are those which have less immediate significance, or which deal with information sharing and so on, or which support the critical linkages. The important point about the classification of linkages, is that the description is not static. What is regular today, may become critical tomorrow, and vice versa. Part of our task is to identify critical linkages and the changes that occur in them and set the empowerment framework appropriately to respond to the changes.

Enterprises based on natural groups

In traditional organizations, people are often grouped around fragmented and specialized parts of the whole. This is largely a result of the desire to have simple organizational principles and rules, and to control people and to limit their range of actions. In these organizations, individuals only identify with a very small part of the overall system. Some of the consequences of this approach are problems with communications and flexibility of response, individuals frustrated because of the lack of control over their work, complexity and confusion and so on.

A natural grouping is one where people are centered around a part of the whole. This is meaningful to those concerned, makes organizational sense in terms of eliminating non-value added activities, improves communication, understanding, motivation and satisfaction, reduces complexity and confusion, and improves response times, throughput times, new product introduction times, system downtime, reliability and quality.

Natural grouping is applicable throughout the organization. It can be applied to office based work such as design and administration, to field operations such as sales and servicing, and to manufacturing. However, natural groups cannot be defined on a piecemeal basis. They should be developed for the whole manufacturing enterprise, or not at all. The reason is quite simple. Usually the whole of our manufacturing organization is inefficiently and badly designed. By tampering with bits, the inefficiencies are left in place, and the degrees of design freedom and the scope for organizational redesign are limited. At best, all that is achieved is limited incremental improvements, which may eventually be offset by continuing problems elsewhere. What is missed is the opportunity for major savings and improvements, on an enterprise wide basis, founded on clearly defined links with strategic objectives.

Focus on core enterprise competencies and virtual corporations

The concept of the core competencies of a corporation is defined (Prahalad and Hamel, 1990) to be a collective learning process focused on developing and coordinating a diverse range of skills and capabilities. These are like the hidden roots of a tree, giving corporations their strength. We should use them to form core products, for use in a diverse range of business operations. To external observers, some business operations might appear to be totally unrelated. However, the common thread that binds them together is the core competencies at the roots of the corporation, which are likely to be hidden from the external observer.

The idea behind developing core competencies is to focus on inherent strengths, or to direct corporations towards necessary competencies. This a strategic process. Corporations must then create competitive advantage by exploiting their core competencies. To do this it is necessary to develop core products which can then be used within an array of diverse end products. The aim is to rapidly enter emerging markets, invent new markets, and capture a competitive lead in established markets by dramatically changing customers' expectations, choice, and so on.

Prahalad and Hamel (1990) specify that core competencies should fulfill three criteria. First they should offer the potential to gain access to a wide variety of markets. Second, they should provide customers with a significant enhancement of the perceived benefits of the end product. Third, they should be difficult to copy.

It is unlikely that any corporation will possess all the core competencies that it needs. There are several ways that this situation can be corrected. Common wisdom would suggest developing supplier relationships or forming strategic alliances. Another way, advocated in the Iacocca Institute (1991) report, is the formation of virtual enterprises.

The definition of a virtual corporation within the concept of agile manufacturing is different from the common usage of the term. Davidow and Malone (1992) define a virtual corporation as one where traditional, well defined boundaries and edges have become blurred. An example of this blurring of edges is our relationship with component suppliers.

Traditional relationships are often adversarial and lacking in trust. There is little sharing of information and no working towards a common goal, although many of our enterprises are now working towards improved supplier relationships. Companies are sharing design and production data, and building long term relationships based on trust and collaboration. They are in effect building a seamless system, which gives the impression to the outsider that the supplier is part of the enterprise.

In agile manufacturing the term virtual corporation is used to mean something different. In this situation efforts are concentrated on building joint ventures with other corporations who have other distinctive and complementary core competencies allowing the creation of several companies, each with unique competencies. Thus, core competencies are selected from several companies and then synthesized into a single entity. For example, the design competency of one company might be combined with the manufacturing competency of another, with the distribution and logistics competency of another, to create a new company to design, manufacture and sell an innovative product. To the customer the enterprise looks like any other, but in fact it does not possess any design, manufacturing or distribution expertise or facilities in itself. The expertise and facilities of the partners in the venture are used by the virtual company. The collaborating partners are linked together electronically to share data and to facilitate the required team working and collaboration. The only physical resources actually deployed in the joint venture enterprise might be a small office to handle customer queries, orders, invoicing, collection of payments, distribution of payments to the partners, and so on.

The aim in agile manufacturing is to develop the agility to form these joint ventures rapidly so that changes in markets and windows of opportunity can be exploited. Part of the thinking is that this involves focusing attention on inherent strengths, core competencies, or development of new competencies. It is core competencies which will form the roots of activities in the commercial world.

An environment supportive of experimentation, learning and innovation

Most of us now believe that continuous improvement in products, processes and procedures is vital to competitive success. Likewise, we also see a high quality design process, in which we tap into all relevant sources of human expertise within our enterprises, as vital to gaining competitive advantage through market focused innovation.

The design process and continuous improvement activities rely on human skill, judgment, expertise and creativity. If these human qualities are not valued in all our people, then our human and financial resources are not only being wasted, but also the probability of making mistakes and taking the wrong decisions is increasing. Businesses now operate in an environment which is so hazardous, increasingly competitive and fraught with danger, that the continued existence of our companies depends on the day-to-day mobilization of every ounce of intelligence.

It is therefore extremely important that we recognize our people as vital assets, which involves developing a perspective that sees everyone as a source of innovation, knowledge and expertise rather than as a cost. When people throughout the enterprise are committed and motivated, and are used and treated appropriately, they can provide a high degree of leverage in the market place.

A key aspect of the process of continuous change and improvement and innovation is experimentation and the assessment of outcomes, that is, learning. We must therefore provide everyone with the opportunities for experimentation and learning. The knowledge acquired in this way must then be translated into a framework that leads to improved decision-making (Heim and Compton, 1992).

It is important, therefore, that the experimentation and learning processes be incorporated into the fundamentals of our operating philosophy. This not only requires the provision of opportunities for them, but institutionalization by making them a part of every person's job. An infrastructure is also required to support the processes. This infrastructure involves providing support personnel when required, tools to help define and monitor experiments, a mechanism for extracting and disseminating results, and procedures for incorporating these results into everyday practices.

Part of this infrastructure involves information sharing, which is about creating an open environment, where data, information and knowledge is shared by all. Such information sharing is not only an integral part of the process of gaining commitment, but necessary to support the participation of people in experimentation and learning. Without information, effective experimentation cannot be undertaken.

Information sharing is a two way process. It is about giving and sharing data, information, knowledge, ideas, visions, and so forth with others. It is also about others' response by sharing their own insights and knowledge. This helps team building and provides a fuller picture of the problems and difficulties faced by the companies.

Some data and information, however, may need to be protected for commercial reasons, but this should be kept to an absolute minimum. It may be better to share sensitive data rather than withhold it. Either way, it sends a powerful message. The former is positive (trust), the latter is negative (no trust). The benefits of sharing may well outweigh the risk of sensitive data falling into the wrong hands!

When information is being shared, and everyone is engaged in experimentation and learning activities aimed at innovation and continuous improvement, then companies are on the road to becoming *learning organizations*.

Knowledge management

Knowledge management is a process of managing and making better use of our enterprises' most expensive, most valuable and most under utilized asset – knowledge.

Knowledge is contained in people's heads, in company reports, policy manuals, case histories, in our company library, in our company's goals, objectives and plans, in its databases and knowledge-based systems and in many other repositories. Few companies, however, have any system for systematically coordinating, sharing, improving or exploiting this knowledge. Knowledge management is about recognizing that knowledge is as important as physical assets, and that it needs to be continually refined, developed, captured, shared, distributed, deployed and exploited for commercial advantage.

A knowledge management system should not be confused with knowledge-based computer systems. Knowledge management might well involve deploying knowledge-based systems, but more importantly, it involves defining our core competencies and seeking to develop knowledge in these areas, identifying areas where knowledge is weak or non-existent and doing something to remedy the situation, providing systems and procedures to ensure that all the people know what knowledge is available, providing access facilities and so on.

Skill and knowledge enhancing technologies

What is needed in the sphere of technological development is a new relationship between people as users of advanced computer based systems, and the computer technology itself: an intelligent relationship between computers and intelligent people.

We need to use technology to lever the skills of the people. Too often in the past we have taken the view that the user's role is to compensate for the inadequacies of the computer. The implication of this is that the people have to intervene in system operation; the people are still needed. We should now focus the design of these computer based systems on the principle that the user's role is not just to intervene but to be involved. This demands that we view people as desirable; our emphasis therefore needs to be on the view that people *should be needed*, rather than on our older ideas that people are *still needed*.

The differences between these two design perspectives are very important and we need to understand them clearly. In the former, people are viewed as complementary to the technology, while in the latter they are regarded as a necessity, perhaps even an unfortunate necessity. The first view encompasses the second, but not vice versa, and the one that we pursue has fundamental implications for the type of technology that we develop (Kidd, 1988, 1990).

The aim of adopting this design approach should not be to fossilize outdated techniques, but to:

- Ease the transition from old to new working methods.
- Create a flexible system which will allow our skilled users to develop working methods that are appropriate to each situation.
- Leave room for our users to develop and practice their skills and to contribute their skills, experience and judgment to the work process.

We should not therefore allow technical functionality to dominate. User acceptance, usability, user motivation, exploiting human resources, and other user needs should play an important part in the future development of manufacturing systems and computer based technologies.

Change and risk management

Two important characteristics of the emerging competitive environment in which agile manufacturing enterprises will operate are continuous change, which arises from our desire to respond rapidly to commercial opportunities, and increased risks, which arise from a more competitive environment and the consequence of product failure.

When we enter into a world where change is an everyday event, we need to be sure that we are making changes in the appropriate way and not causing problems. Thus, we have to ensure that changes are linked to corporate goals. When we are introducing new technologies, changing working practices, or developing new organizational relationships, structures, and so on, we must make sure that these changes are properly planned, their implications analyzed, the required goals clearly identified, and the resources needed made available. We must also consider and properly identify the human issues, so that potential conflict is avoided. We want our people committed, excess stress avoided, appropriate training available, and so on. In other words, we must manage the changes.

We must also manage risks. This means identification and analysis of potential risks and the use of measures to reduce, avoid and if possible to eliminate risks. In areas where risks are inherent, for example, in new product introduction, we must introduce methods to ensure a more systematic evaluation of ideas, so that bad or immature products and ideas are identified at an early stage, and not after vast resources have already been consumed in their development. This means that in addition to achieving a much improved market orientation in the product development process through techniques such as quality function deployment, we should also be deploying techniques such as stage-gate methods (Cooper, 1990) and rapid prototyping, which allow us to manage risks more effectively.

Concluding comments

This chapter has outlined the meaning of agile manufacturing. Of central importance is the idea that, after spending the past 200 years trying to get people out of manufacturing systems, it will now be necessary to start putting them back. We need to use people to transform their knowledge into ideas for new and improved products and processes, and discover better ways of doing things. This change of emphasis requires the development of a whole new approach to manufacturing. In the following chapters consideration is given to the important concepts needed to bring about agile manufacturing systems.

We will begin the process by looking in more detail at the key to agility, the fundamental concept of integrating organization, people and technology.

Key points

- It is important not to confuse agile manufacturing with flexible manufacturing, lean manufacturing or computer integrated manufacturing.
- Agile manufacturing should primarily be seen as a business concept.
- Agile manufacturing could be seen as another buzzword, a fad, a flavor of the month, a quick fix or a prescription. In fact it is none of these. It should be seen as a business opportunity which requires creativity and innovation to turn it into enhanced competitiveness and profitability.
- The business drivers for agile manufacturing are primarily concerned with achieving quantum leaps in competitiveness and performance, and making life difficult for our competitors.
- It is important and necessary to develop a good understanding of what agile manufacturing is about before embarking on the development of its capabilities.
- Agile manufacturing has several generic features which have to be designed into the agile manufacturing infrastructure.
- Agile manufacturing requires the integration of organization, people and technology into a coordinated whole. This is what delivers agility. Agility is not a function of one single dimension.

References **35**

References

Atkinson J. (1990). Flexibility and skill in manufacturing establishments. *IMS Report 180*, Institute of Manpower Studies, Brighton

Ayres R.U. (1990). CIM: driving forces and applications. In *CIM: Revolution in Progress. Proc. final IIASA Conf. CIM: Technologies, Organisations, and People in Transition* (Haywood W., ed.), pp. 9–26. Laxenburg: IIASA

Bolwijn P.T., Boorsma J., van Breukelen Q.H., Brinkman S. and Kumpe T. (1986). *Flexible Manufacturing. Integrating Technological and Social Innovation*. Amsterdam: Elsevier

Browne J. (1992). Future integrated manufacturing systems: a business driven approach. In *Organisation, People and Technology in European Manufacturing* (Kidd P.T., ed.), pp. 17–30. Luxembourg: Commission of the European Communities

Cooper R.G. (1990). Stage-gate systems: a new tool for managing new products. *Business Horizons*, **33**, 44–5

Davidow W.H. and Malone M.S. (1992). *The Virtual Corporation*. New York: HarperCollins

Goldhar J.D. and Jelinek M. (1983). Plan for economies of scope. *Harvard Business Review*, November–December, 141–8

Hayes R.H., Wheelwright S.C. and Clark K.B. (1988). *Dynamic Manufacturing. Creating the Learning Organisation*. New York: Free Press

Heim J.A. and Compton W.D., eds. (1992). *Manufacturing Systems. Foundations of World Class Practice*. Washington DC: National Academy

Iacocca Institute (1991). *21st Century Manufacturing Enterprise Strategy. An Industry-Led View. Volumes 1 & 2*, Bethlehem, PA: Iacocca Institute

Jones D.T. (1992). Beyond the Toyota production system: the era of lean production. In *Manufacturing Strategy. Process and Content* (Voss C.A., ed.), pp. 189–210. London: Chapman & Hall

Kidd P.T. (1988). The social shaping of technology: the case of a CNC lathe. *Behaviour and Information Technology*, **7**, 192–204

Kidd P.T. (1990). Information technology: design for human involvement or human intervention? In *Ergonomics of Hybrid Automated Systems II* (Karwowski W. and Rahimi M., eds.), pp. 417–24. Amsterdam: Elsevier

Naisbitt J. (1984). *Megatrends. Ten New Directions Transforming Our Lives*. New York: Warner

Prahalad C.K. and Hamel G. (1990). The core competence of the corporation. *Harvard Business Review*, May–June, 79–91

Savage C.M. (1990). *Fifth Generation Management. Integrating Enterprises Through Human Networking*. Bedford MA: Digital Press

Tranfield D. and Smith S. (1990). *Managing Change. Creating Competitive Edge*. Kempston, UK: IFS

von Braun C-F. (1990). The acceleration trap. *Sloan Management Review*, **32**(1), 49–58

Womack J.P., Jones D.T. and Roos D. (1990). *The Machine that Changed the World*. New York: Rawson Associates

2

Four core concepts

Introduction

In Chapter 1 we proposed a conceptual framework for agile manufacturing, at the heart of which were four core concepts, being:

- A strategy to become an agile manufacturing enterprise.
- A strategy to exploit agility to achieve competitive advantage.
- Integration of organization, people and technology into a coordinated, interdependent system which is the competitive weapon.
- An interdisciplinary design methodology to achieve the integration of organization, people and technology.

In this chapter we will take a much closer look at these core concepts and describe and discuss some of the important issues.

Conceptual aspects of agile manufacturing

To retain and increase our competitive position in world markets, and to be able to respond to windows of opportunity, we need to be able to take full advantage of the potential for increased productivity, better quality and greater flexibility provided by more responsive and new forms of organizational structures. We also need to make better use of human skills, knowledge and experience, and to exploit the power of modern computer based technologies. To achieve all these goals we need skilled, cooperative and motivated people. Our traditional management hierarchies and methods of control must be eliminated. More participation is needed by people throughout the enterprise, in planning, designing and implementing new technologies and systems. Technical systems also need to be designed, not just to meet economic and technical goals, but to satisfy organizational and human requirements.

Agile manufacturing is a modern manufacturing concept that embodies these ideas. The importance of the human role in agile manufacturing is stressed. However, agile manufacturing should not be seen as a collection of management and organizational techniques, in which technology has no major role. A wide range of human abilities and characteristics are required in an agile manufacturing environment, and we must focus more of our attention on people issues, both to make full use of all our people's abilities and to create a good working environment for everyone.

To bring agile manufacturing to fruition, we have to overcome our belief that technology can provide the answers to all our problems. We should not treat non-technical problems as technical problems. A much more sensible approach is needed if our manufacturing companies are to compete in world markets. Reduced costs, improved quality, greater flexibility and rapid response capability are needed, without trade-off. We cannot do this with technology alone. We need a balanced manufacturing response, not a technological one. This demands the development of a new and broader vision of the factory of the future: a vision with a future.

Our new vision should not be technology oriented. Technology oriented manufacturing leads to a competitive dead end. Agile manufacturing is a broad, strategic, market driven approach that involves taking a balanced consideration of organization, people and technology in an integrative way.

Agile manufacturing is not technology oriented, but technology does, nevertheless, play an important role. The aim should be to create an environment for the exercise of human skills, judgment, creativity, knowledge and ingenuity and to make full use of modern computer based technologies. These two goals are essential requirements for future success in manufacturing.

A strategy driven approach

We can only benefit from agile manufacturing if we have a strategy of agility which will allow us to formulate a change plan to implement agile manufacturing and be competitive.

We need to develop an appropriate manufacturing strategy to meet market needs and exploit our agility by shaping market opportunities. Agile manufacturing is therefore based upon the need to adopt a market driven strategic manufacturing response.

With markets becoming more and more dynamic and competition increasingly being based on improved quality and customer responsiveness, the development of an appropriate manufacturing strategy is likely to have a major impact on our survival, success and growth. We therefore suggest that, in general, a strategy for agile manufacturing should be focused on designing an enterprise that will lead to:

- Faster response to highly variable customer demand patterns.
- Improved productivity.
- Opportunities for system wide innovation, learning and improvement.
- Improved product quality.
- Better utilization of expensive capital and improved return on investment.
- Improved customer and market focus and a better understanding of customer needs and closer customer relationships.
- Flexibility to cope with a wide range of batch sizes including one-of-a-kind production, and a wide range of products.
- Integration of suppliers into product development and manufacturing processes.
- Short-order capability and the ability to rapidly respond to new windows of opportunity.
- Capability to undertake multi-venturing through virtual corporations.
- Reduced operating expenses via reduced stock holding, less scrap and rework and reduced system down-time.
- Shorter design and manufacturing lead times.
- Reduced indirect labor and other overhead costs.
- More time and opportunities for management to tackle problems.
- System integrity and robustness.

These goals provide the basis for the agile manufacturing enterprise strategy. In general, the goals will only be accomplished by investing in organization, people and technology, so the strategy should address those areas. Chapter 6 provides a change management framework for that purpose.

Integrating organization, people and technology

Competitive advantage

Agile manufacturing is achieved through the integration of three primary resources into a coordinated, interdependent system. These three primary resources are: innovative management structures and organization, a skill base of knowledgeable and empowered people, and flexible and intelligent technologies. For brevity we refer to these simply as organization, people and technology.

Thus an important feature of agile manufacturing is the philosophy that competitive advantage is not only derived from technology, but also from appropriate and responsive organizational structures, appropriate work practices, and from the skills, knowledge, intelligence, experience and creativity of all the people involved.

We have often stated in the past that people's skills, knowledge, intelligence, experience and creativity are our most important assets (people make it happen!). We can state clearly that without people, agile manufacturing will not work, but the way that we deal with people issues needs to be fundamentally different to that of the past.

In agile manufacturing we are suggesting that appropriate organizational structures and people, with their unique abilities, actually provide us with improved competitiveness. In essence, therefore, the organization and people issues in manufacturing are not just a question of *human factors*, but are more a question of developing strategies that specifically set out to use organization, people and technology to achieve improved competitiveness (Kidd, 1991).

The differences between these two approaches are fundamental. In manufacturing, we have traditionally associated human factors with improving working conditions, making equipment easier to use, and smoothing the introduction of new technologies. Often we have not asked our human factors practitioners to consider whether the proposed technology is appropriate, or whether we are following the right manufacturing strategy. We have assumed that our technologies would remain fixed and our strategies would be unquestioned. We have asked our human factors specialists to design the interfaces to our technologies and to design work practices and jobs around our technologies, but we have assumed that we would not have to change these technologies and strategies.

We have used this approach for several reasons. First, many of our human factors specialists have not fully understood the technologies. Second, none of us has fully appreciated the interdisciplinary issues. For example, if our organizational structures emphasize decentralized control, centered on natural groups, then we did not consider that the new technology would need to be quite different from the original. At best, we asked our human factors specialists to adopt a multidisciplinary approach, but normally we expected them to work in isolation from other professionals.

Finally, we largely ignored the impact that organizational change and new work practices could have on business performance. Human factors experts argued that achieving a joint optimization of human and technical design issues would help avoid the implementation problems commonly encountered with new technology. In addition, joint optimization would enable the development of more effective systems, accounting for human needs. However, no one seemed to understand that organizational choice, and the role of people, can be used, along with technology, to satisfy business objectives.

A more sensible method would be to adopt a balanced approach, which would use organization, people and technology as three basic components of a strategy designed to deliver agility, thus satisfying market needs and exploiting opportunities. Instead of just looking to technology to provide improved competitiveness, we should instead address how the three elements can be combined to produce business benefits. Instead of looking for prescriptive solutions, which is often what technology offers, we should design appropriate organizations and work practices, define appropriate roles for people that make better use of their skills, knowledge, intelligence, experience and creativity, and then use our technologies in a way that reflects the needs of the people and the new organization and work practices. Instead of installing new technologies, and then adapting our organization and people to them, we should consider adapting the technologies to the desired organization and the roles that we want our people to undertake.

Balanced manufacturing

In the past we have tended to approach the development of advanced manufacturing systems and the associated computer based technologies, as a technology oriented activity. The direction that we should now be taking is based on a concept of balance. By this we mean that we should develop a new approach which integrates organization and people issues into the manufacturing systems development process.

Manufacturing systems design needs to incorporate modern organizational concepts and work practices. Instead of using technology only to improve business performance, we should also implement organizational innovation, and change our traditional work practices. The role of our production associates on the shop floor needs to be expanded and technologies are required to support all these changes. This type of thinking represents a sensible and balanced use of organization, people and technology. It is also good manufacturing systems engineering design practice.

The situation often experienced in manufacturing is represented in Figure 2.1. Too much emphasis has often been placed on technology, and the organization and people issues have been commonly regarded as matters of secondary importance. The imbalance between technical issues and the coverage of organization and people factors needs to be redressed. The desired situation is depicted in Figure 2.2. This figure does not imply that each element be given equal financial resources, but that the over-emphasis on technology be addressed. However, the idea of achieving balance should be viewed dynamically, as sometimes it will be appropriate to focus attention on technology. However, when we focus on technology, we must be careful not to forget about the organizational and people aspects. Likewise when we focus on the organization, we should not forget about the technologies we can use to improve effectiveness.

Thus our aim is not to shift from technology oriented manufacturing to a purely human and organization driven approach. We are proposing a balanced approach: one that gives serious consideration to the organization, people and technology. Our argument is that we need to take a broader view of manufacturing, always seeking the right mix and the right balance for each problem encountered. The three dimensions are complementary.

Balance is an important conceptual basis for the new paradigm of agile manufacturing. It will help us to address the interconnected

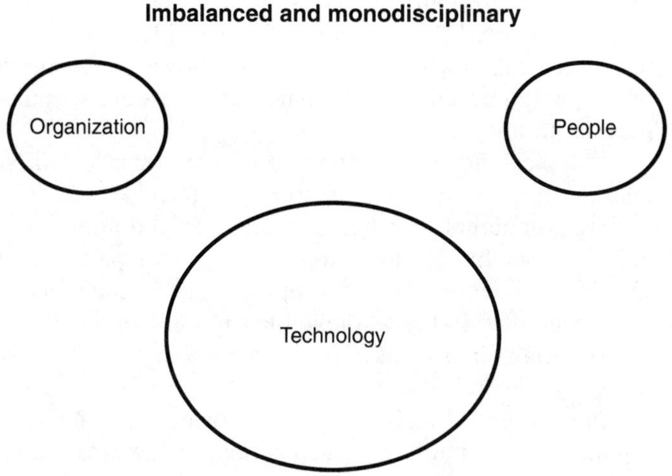

Imbalanced and monodisciplinary

Figure 2.1 Advanced manufacturing: the traditional imbalances.

Balanced and interdisciplinary

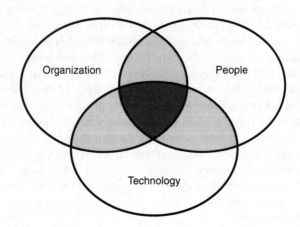

Figure 2.2   Advanced manufacturing: the desired balances.

elements of our overall manufacturing enterprise. A balancing capability avoids polarization from any perspective.

Human and computer integrated enterprises

The changes that we need to make to bring about agile manufacturing are illustrated in Figure 2.3. For many years CIM has been one of the major funded research areas. However, much of the work on CIM has been dominated by technological considerations. The concept of integrated manufacturing should not, however, be restricted to computers, data interchange, standards and software modules. This is only part of the story.

A typical dictionary definition of *integrate* is *to combine parts into a whole*. An integrated manufacturing enterprise cannot be achieved by linking computers together, sharing data and attempting to automate various tasks. Integration implies bringing the parts together, and organization and people are just as much a part of manufacturing systems as the technology. So the whole implies more than technology. Integration is more than simply linking computers and coordinating tasks such as design and manufacturing.

No amount of technology, on its own, can bring about integration. We also wish to integrate organizational structures, groups and people. To integrate people we have to motivate them to cooperate and work as teams, because only then will we achieve a truly integrated enterprise.

Do we work for the same company?

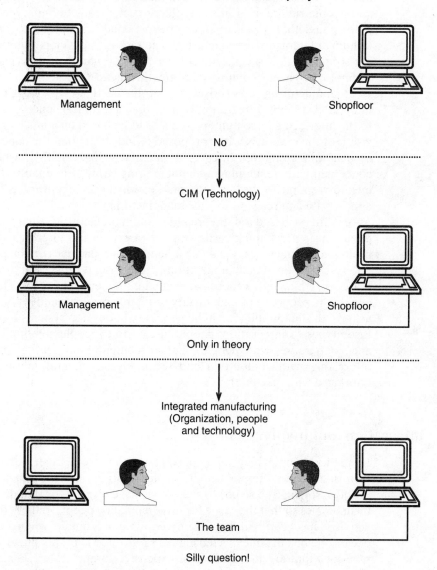

Figure 2.3 From traditional manufacturing and computer integrated manufac-turing to human and computer integrated manufacturing. *Source:* Cheshire Henbury. © 1989. Published with permission.

Integrated manufacturing therefore needs more than technology. It needs changes in attitudes, work practices, organization and people's skills. These changes are not only about adapting our existing organiza-tions, work practices and people to fit the requirements of computer interfaced technologies. We have argued that organizational structures and people can be used in a way that actually leads to improved competitiveness, that organization and people issues are not just a question of human factors in manufacturing. The task is to develop manufacturing strategies that specifically set out to use organization, people and technology to achieve improved competitiveness.

Manufacturing enterprises therefore need to be designed as integrated systems. Integration is more than a technical concept relating to the interfacing of computers. It needs to be based on a much broader vision of the enterprise. It is proposed (Kidd, 1991) that the concept of **human and computer integrated manufacturing** (HCIM), which is concerned with developing a manufacturing strategy to enable companies to respond to the dynamic markets of the 21st century, is highly appropriate and relevant to agile manufacturing.

HCIM is based on the realities of manufacturing, that is, it is people, using technology, who convert raw materials into high quality profitable products. People make it happen, not machines or computers.

To create an agile manufacturing enterprise, it is necessary to integrate everything into a coordinated and interdependent system. This will enable the provision of high quality profitable products and services. To achieve this integration it will be necessary to develop systems based on three types of integration: people integration (people communicating and cooperating with people), human–computer integration (people interacting with computers) and technological integration (machine interfaced with machine).

Integration and involvement

In reality, people play an important role in every aspect of manufacturing (for example condition monitoring, system diagnostics, problem solving and so on). However, we have often in the past designed technologies so that the scope for involvement by people in these diverse activities has been reduced to intervention, for example, when a failure occurs or when the unexpected happens. We often leave people to undertake jobs that are too difficult or expensive to automate (Bainbridge, 1983), or which require cognitive skills not easily replicated using computers.

Expert systems, neural networks, and so on now provide us with tools that automate some of these cognitive tasks. The more recent developments bring into sharper focus the problems that often arise when we gradually transform people's work from an active and participatory mode into a passive and interventionist mode.

People are often expected to respond to emergency situations and to unexpected events, with unknown results. To do this effectively they need knowledge of their systems. They also need an understanding of the effectiveness of this knowledge. Moreover, they must also develop appropriate skills. In addition, these skills need to be practiced with regularity if they are to be maintained (Bainbridge, 1983). The normal way in which this happens is by performing the various relevant tasks. However, over a period of time, many tasks have been automated. How then, are people to develop their knowledge base, understanding and the skills they require?

Similar problems have arisen in other decision-making situations. For example, expert systems could be used to generate switching plans to isolate part of a power distribution network. An expert system can also be used in the design of a mechanical component, or a compensator for a feedback control system. However, any design or plan produced by an expert system must be verified by someone to ensure that it is suitable for its purpose. People, therefore, have to exercise judgment over the results of the computer's work, but in order to do this, they must be knowledge-able and skilled practitioners.

How will people achieve the level of expertise required if the routes have been closed off? Well, one way of dealing with this type of problem is to arrange for systems to shut down automatically when anything goes wrong or when unexpected events occur. Another way is to provide train-ing, as in the case of airline pilots who use high fidelity flight simulators to learn how to deal with emergency situations and to practice their flying skills. A further method is to use the principle of vertical division of labor, and to create a hierarchical system where routine work is performed by relatively unskilled people, who are supervised by a smaller number of better trained, more highly skilled people.

There are many disadvantages associated with these approaches. For example, it may not be possible to automatically shut down a system when something goes wrong. Some conditions may not warrant such a drastic step. Furthermore, what effect would these shutdowns have on our throughput times, on our on-time delivery performance measures and so on? What additional costs would these shutdowns generate? High fidelity simulators, on the other hand, are expensive to build and to operate and hierarchies are inflexible and can be costly and bureaucratic.

None of these solutions are ideal and all have costs and associated problems, some of which are difficult to deal with. More importantly, all three approaches are reactive. We create problems by applying technologies, and then we seek responses by applying more technology. Would not a proactive approach be a better way forward? Such an approach would involve designing technologies that avoided the problems in the first place.

A dominant characteristic of much of our technology is that it is designed with the view that people will compensate for any technologi-cal inadequacies through a process of human intervention. Often however, we do not think through the implications of this, and consider whether people will be able to intervene adequately. This type of technology leads to very passive work and much activity is oriented towards intervention when something goes wrong or when unexpected and unknown events occur. This is an interventionist model (Kidd, 1990), which has become pervasive.

Many situations demand that people be knowledgeable and skilled. One way to achieve this is to design systems such that people are more active and are involved in decision-making activities even when it is possible to use automatic techniques. This is a participatory model (Kidd, 1990), which at the moment is far from normative.

In a participatory model, computer based technologies need to be used to support people. These technologies need to be skill and knowledge enhancing rather than skill and knowledge replacing. The technology should allow people to develop and practice their skills and knowledge.

Interdisciplinary design methodology

Manufacturing systems design is an interdisciplinary activity, and organization and people issues need to be addressed in parallel with technical issues, that is, using a concurrent engineering approach rather than a serial engineering one. This means making trade-offs between cost and performance and other factors such as, for example, job satisfaction and user motivation.

One of the primary concepts of agile manufacturing is concerned with the integration of organization, people and technology. To achieve this integration we need to adopt an interdisciplinary design methodology. The design paradigm that should underlie agile manufacturing is characterized by:

- A holistic systems based approach.
- Concurrent engineering concepts applied to the design of the manufacturing enterprise.
- Application of insights from the organizational and psychological sciences to the design of the technology and the overall manufacturing enterprise.
- Consideration of organization and people issues at all stages, from formulation of business strategy right through to the design and implementation of systems.

The design paradigm that should underlie agile manufacturing is closely related to the joint technical and organizational design method (see Chapter 6) and involves a different way of dealing with organization and people issues to that currently used in manufacturing industry. The vast majority of our manufacturing companies adopt a serial engineering approach to dealing with these aspects of design. We design and implement manufacturing systems, making trade-offs between cost and performance, and only then deal with organization and people issues. At this late stage however, these issues may have turned into problems that have to be dealt with retroactively. It is common to find that we cannot resolve these problems satisfactorily because by this stage many degrees of design freedom have been closed off.

The point here is this. At the beginning of any design, our knowledge about the design problem is quite limited. As the design proceeds our knowledge grows. However, as we move through the design process, the degrees of design freedom start to decrease. This situation is depicted in Figure 2.4. Thus, when we arrive at the stage of implementation and discover many problems relating to organization and people issues, we do not have much design freedom to deal with the problems.

For this reason, agile manufacturing needs a concurrent engineering approach to the design of manufacturing systems and computer based technologies. This implies that organization and people issues should be addressed right from the start of the design process and in parallel with technical issues. This also implies that we adopt an interdisciplinary method, where insights from psychology and organizational science are used to shape the system, and address the issues that lie between these various disciplines.

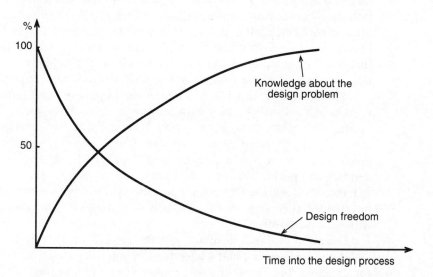

Figure 2.4   Changes in design freedom and knowledge about the design problem in relation to time into the design process.

This involves us in making, in addition to the usual cost-performance trade-offs, further trade-offs between technical options, costs, and performance, user acceptance, motivation, user skill requirements, implementation issues, job design and organizational structure. The benefits of this approach lie in the area of improved design and implementation processes, better system designs, more appropriate organizational structures and motivated and engaged people throughout the company.

However, using a concurrent engineering approach also implies that organization and people issues are considered as being relevant to the design process itself as well as issues that have to be addressed as part of the system design. Reported experiences of the design process (Klein, 1976; Perrow, 1983; Meister, 1987; Rosenbrock, 1989; Kidd, 1992) clearly show that problems are experienced when various professions and different departments have to collaborate. Concurrent engineering should seek to overcome these problems, which implies that we should be using insights from psychology and organizational science to shape the design process itself.

The design paradigm for agile manufacturing needs to be based on more iterative design models to enable the early realization of proposed systems using, for example, rapid prototyping and simulation. The spiral life cycle model developed for software engineering (Boehm, 1989), is one candidate for a new design model (see Chapter 7).

Design experience suggests that it is almost impossible to write a complete and detailed specification using formal and structured analysis methods alone. Some constraints, requirements and goals, implementation problems and so on are difficult to formulate and to predict, and often cannot be clearly expressed until a model or a mock-up system has been built. If we write a specification and present it to a client, it is likely that it will be accepted. When the system is built, it also likely to be said that some aspect of the system was not what was wanted or expected.

The reason for this is that some goals, constraints and difficulties remain tacit and only become explicit when the goals have not been met, or the constraints have been violated, or the difficulties have been exposed through use of the actual system. This is one of the reasons why much software is inadequate or inappropriate. In design, problem defining and problem solving are intertwined inherently. The writing of specifications, and the implementation and operation of systems are also intertwined. It is a major mistake to believe that the two can be separated without adverse effects.

During the design of manufacturing systems and computer aided technologies, there are many uncertainties and risks. Risk areas include, for example, organization and people issues, identification of system requirements and unforeseen problems that arise from new and relatively untried technologies. Our classical iterative linear models of design (for example the waterfall life cycle model) are not well suited to design projects that involve substantial risks (and many manufacturing systems projects fall into this category), because they are not sufficiently iterative, and because in the waterfall model, we only start one phase when we have completed the preceding phase. In projects where there is a significant level of risk, it is important to reduce the risk. This means identifying the risks and then focusing attention on the high risk areas, leaving other, less risk laden aspects, until later.

Thus systems elements with high risk need to be progressed rapidly, at relatively low cost, through various stages of design, to quickly identify and remedy any problems while the cost of change is still relatively low. This rapid progress can be achieved, not by writing detailed specifications, but by a whole range of risk reducing exercises such as the development of non-functioning models, simulation, user involvement in the design process, system mock-ups, development of short and precise system definitions and statement of essential requirements.

This process is based on several iterations following in rapid succession, involving elements of partial analysis, partial design and partial implementation, at the end of which we may well discard or change the design radically. As the process of iteration continues, the risk should reduce, and an acceptable design should begin to emerge, along with requirements, and eventually the design will stabilize, and attention can then be turned to the lower risk aspects.

Many of the risk reducing tools mentioned above also act as transitional systems, and can help to introduce users to systems still in the very early phases of design, thus giving people an opportunity to make an input to the design, to develop ownership of the design, and to learn something about the new systems long before they are ready for implementation and use.

Concluding comments

This chapter has focused on the four core aspects of the conceptual model of agile manufacturing proposed in Chapter 1. This completes the overview of agile manufacturing. These four core concepts form the starting point for a methodology for designing and implementing an agile manufacturing enterprise. This is addressed in Chapter 6.

Before addressing the creation of an agile manufacturing enterprise, it is important to understand fully the characteristics and culture of existing manufacturing. Some of the characteristics of our existing traditional manufacturing paradigms will now be examined in detail.

Key points

- There are four core concepts underlying agile manufacturing. All four are mutually interdependent.
- We need to develop a strategy to become agile, but we also need a strategy to exploit our agility.
- The strategy to develop agile manufacturing should focus on ways to achieve integration of organization, people and technology.
- To achieve integration of organization, people and technology we need to develop interdisciplinary design methodologies.
- It is the integration of organization, people and technology that delivers competitive advantage.
- There are many different forms of integration. Integration of technology is only one narrow view of integration.

References

Bainbridge L. (1983). Ironies of automation. *Automatica*, **19**, 775–9

Boehm B.W., ed. (1989). *Software Risk Management*. Washington DC: IEEE Computer Society Press

Kidd P.T. (1990). Information technology: design for human involvement or human intervention? In *Ergonomics of Hybrid Automated Systems II* (Karwowski W. and Rahimi M., eds.), pp. 417–24. Amsterdam: Elsevier

Kidd P.T. (1991). Human and computer integrated manufacturing: a manufacturing strategy based on organisation people and technology. *Int. J. Human Factors in Manufacturing*, **1**(1), 17–32

Kidd P.T. (1992). Design of human-centred robotic systems. In *Human–Robot Interaction* (Rahimi M. and Karwowski W., eds.), pp. 225–41. London: Taylor & Francis

Klein L. (1976). *A Social Scientist in Industry*. London: Gower

Meister D. (1987). Systems design, development and testing. In *Handbook of Human Factors* (Salvendy G., ed.), pp. 17–42. New York: John Wiley

Perrow C. (1983). The organisational context of human factors engineering. *Admin. Science Quarterly*, **28**, 521–41

Rosenbrock H.H., ed. (1989). *Designing Human-Centred Technology. A Cross-Disciplinary Project in Computer-Aided Manufacturing*. London: Springer–Verlag

PART TWO

Agile manufacturing and change management

3

The change implications

Introduction

The established practices that we use in manufacturing industry were developed when circumstances were very different to those existing today. In the past, the manufacturing environment was largely cost driven and was based on high volume, low variety markets, with low levels of competition. In this environment we found that management accounting techniques based on financial measures of performance, and management and manufacturing practices based on the application of division of labor, hierarchical control, centralization, de-skilling and so on worked reasonably well.

For example, when technology was applied to automate production and to de-skill people on the shop floor, generally it was found that this produced competitive advantage and made companies more profitable. Furthermore, failure to adequately address people issues during the design of production plant was not seen as a source of competitive disadvantage. Neither did product development processes based on a serial engineering model (the over-the-wall approach) constitute a major competitive disadvantage, because most companies used this method and there was little or no incentive to improve the product development process.

The profound changes that are now occurring in the market place have already initiated major changes in the way we do things in manufacturing industry. Our belief that the introduction of new technology to reduce costs will guarantee improved competitiveness and profitability has been challenged by concepts such as just-in-time manufacturing, concurrent engineering and so on. Furthermore, increased emphasis on quality and flexibility has meant that we have begun to realize that the skills of all the people involved are assets rather than costs to be minimized. Moreover, we have started to witness the emergence of organization and people issues as major design issues, and our traditional serial engineering approach to product development is now being displaced by the concurrent engineering model.

It is our assertion that the emergence of agile manufacturing as a new manufacturing paradigm has revolutionary implications for many of our traditional beliefs and practices. Agile manufacturing cannot be based on the traditional concepts of high levels of vertical and horizontal division of labor, de-skilling, standardization and so forth.

In this chapter we will begin to examine many of the major changes that will have to be brought about if this new paradigm is to become a reality. We will also consider some insights from the theory of change and change management, and these will be used to analyze the present situation, and to highlight some problem areas.

Agile manufacturing implies revolutionary changes

There is increasing awareness of the importance of issues such as organization, people, design process and so on. However, increased awareness has not always been accompanied by fundamental changes in values, beliefs and practices. The established paradigm has in many cases remained largely unaltered. On the whole, we have often chosen to modernize the traditional manufacturing paradigm, rather than replace it completely with new paradigms.

Organization and people issues illustrate very well the problem that we experience. While most of us now accept that these matters need to be considered in the design and implementation of manufacturing systems, we still adopt a fairly narrow orientation to how these issues should be considered. Our orientation is often restricted to forcing the organization to adapt to the technology, often at great cost, overcoming resistance to change. We commonly assume that resistance is derived from the reluctance of people to accept new technology. We rarely perceive that resistance might arise from a mismatch between the organizational, human and technological elements of manufacturing systems (Majchrzak and Gasser, 1992).

It is our belief that the fundamental changes that are now occurring in market conditions not only demand new techniques, but also a fundamental shift in paradigm. Paradigm shifts are however, difficult to achieve and may be opposed to preserve the existing paradigm. We all face tremendous problems when confronted with the need to make the transition from traditional manufacturing to a new manufacturing paradigm such as agile manufacturing. We *must* face up to the pain involved in making the required changes, and the first step must be to appreciate the limitations of our present approaches; to understand our past failures and the nature of the changes that we will have to implement.

Our past failures in advanced manufacturing

The implementation of CIM has not resolved the problems of quality and performance to schedule as anticipated. The failures associated with investment in advanced manufacturing technologies have tended not to be well documented. We do not advertise failure, even if it is recognized, which it sometimes is not, owing to its subjective nature. Also, as we shall see later, our traditional management accounting systems are not well adapted to identifying failure.

There is, however, increasing evidence that the design and implementation of advanced manufacturing technologies and systems has led to significant failures and disappointments. Failures include such actions as removing equipment once installed, and many disappointments include lower than expected quality and due date improvements and productivity gains (Browne *et al.*, 1988; Browne, 1992; Majchrzak and Gasser, 1992).

The results of the study undertaken by the MIT Commission on Industrial Productivity (Dertouzos *et al.*, 1989) points to several serious problems and weaknesses in the US manufacturing industry. Several key problem areas were identified by the Commission, being:

- Outdated business strategies.
- Short investment time horizons.
- Technological weaknesses in development and production.
- Neglect of human resources.
- Failures of cooperation.
- Government and industry at cross-purposes.

One study of a number of manufacturing enterprises (Voss, 1988) shows that all the firms examined achieved technical success. In other words, all the companies got their technical systems installed and fully operational, with all operating problems resolved. However, only 86% of these companies managed to achieve increases in productivity, and just over 57% realized other benefits such as improved flexibility, quality, throughput times and due date performance. Amazingly, only 14% of these companies managed to improve their competitiveness.

These figures are more interesting and alarming if we look at them from a different (and more sobering) angle. The fact that 86% of companies increased their productivity means that 14% failed to achieve any increases in productivity. Likewise, as only 57% realized other benefits, then 43% failed to realize other benefits such as improved flexibility, quality, throughput times and due date performance. And since only a mere handful, 14%, improved their competitiveness, the vast majority, 86%, did not achieve any improvement in their competitive performance.

Several major reasons have been identified for our failures. They include:

- Technology oriented rather than business and market focused investment plans.
- Inappropriate or non-existent business or manufacturing strategies, or both.
- Failure to link business and manufacturing strategies.
- Inadequate assessment of the costs and benefits of investments in new technologies.
- Failure to understand customer requirements and to design and build products that customers will buy.
- Neglect of organization and people issues.

To succeed in the modern competitive environment is an enormous challenge. Many factors, for example rapid technological progress, environmental constraints and concerns are issues which we have little or no control over, and we must live with them. Others, such as the way we design products, are more controllable and these aspects can be shaped to improve our competitive performance.

There are, however, significant factors, *our traditions*, which can make success difficult and drive companies in the wrong direction. Tradition manifests itself in the form of our management accounting methods, the manufacturing goals we pursue, the way we use technology to achieve our goals, our design and management practices, the organizational structures we implement and our attitudes towards people. We often ignore this issue of tradition, or we only give it superficial attention. In many cases however, our traditions are so antiquated and inappropriate that they constitute a competitive liability.

We believe that many of the causes of our failure listed above can be traced to the question of tradition. For example, it has been our tradition to focus attention on technology to improve competitive position (usually through cost reduction). We have often taken the organization for granted, and accepted it as given. And we have ignored, or at best treated as secondary, the people issues. A further example is investment appraisal. New technologies such as computer-aided design (CAD) have company wide benefits that are not just related to reduced costs.

However, we have tended to justify CAD systems on the basis of labor cost savings in the drawing office, because this is our traditional way of justifying investments in new technology. We have justified investments in CAD on this basis, even though the benefits extend beyond the drawing office and cover issues such as quality.

However, an apparent success of an investment in advanced manufacturing technology cannot be taken as a sure sign of success. For example, we may be able to point to examples where a computer based technology has proved beneficial. The important issue however, is not the potential range of applications that might prove beneficial, but the range of applications for which the technology is well suited and useful. It is possible that the range is large, but the suitable and useful applications might be a smaller sub-set. If we achieve a successful implementation of a particular technology, this does not demonstrate that such an application is suited for the technology, only that it is possible with the technology. We can crack a nut with a sledge hammer, but the fact that we can use a sledge hammer in this way does not imply that it should be used in preference to a nut cracker.

We cannot regard a successful investment in technology as successful in any absolute sense. Alternative investments may well have produced an equivalent or even better result, and in a highly competitive environment, such missed opportunities are a source of competitive liability and must be seen as a failure.

Changes on the way

Manufacturing in the 21st century will not be based on the traditional concepts of high levels of vertical and horizontal division of labor, de-skilling, standardization and so on. Our new manufacturing paradigm, agile manufacturing, will not be dominated by technology, but by consideration of organization, people, and other issues, in parallel with technological issues.

In Chapter 2 we proposed that a more balanced approach was needed, which involves adopting an interdisciplinary view of manufacturing. The changes that this implies are profound, and affect us all. No one is exempt. None of our practices, methods or beliefs are sacred. To make the point clear we will illustrate some of the changes already being dealt with.

Our traditional strategic management thinking based on, for example, the model shown in Figure 3.1, is unlikely to fit well into

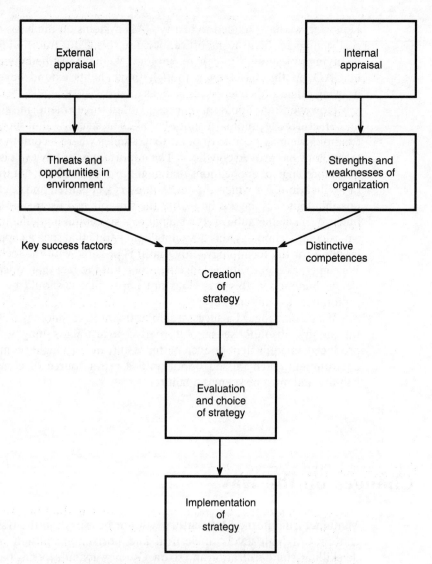

Figure 3.1 Traditional model of strategy development.

the competitive environment of the future, as this method is usually appropriate in circumstances where there is a high degree of stability (Mintzberg, 1990). In circumstances where market conditions are highly dynamic and risk is high, this approach needs to be replaced by a more evolutionary method of strategic management of the form shown

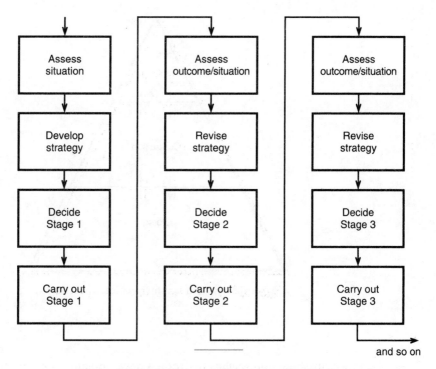

Figure 3.2   Adaptive model of strategy development.

in Figure 3.2, where we undertake strategy development within a framework of goals, but where the goals and impacts of decisions are re-assessed on a very short cycle basis, and where goals pursued and actions taken in one phase are dependent on the results of a previous phase. This style of strategic management is based on the integration of strategy development and implementation, and provides the information and the opportunity to abandon unfavorable lines of development before the sunk costs reach the level where the work becomes unstoppable.

Our traditional organizations, as depicted in Figure 3.3, are also largely redundant. In these organizations the thinking goes on at the top, and the doing takes place at the bottom. There is an army of controllers in the middle translating the decisions of the thinkers into actions for the doers, and trying to control these actions in detail. The fragmentation, centralization and steep hierarchies, functional layouts, horizontal and vertical division of labor and the de-skilling and the standardization of working methods that accompany our traditional organizations are all now mostly unnecessary and outdated. In place of our traditional organizations we are beginning to see the emergence of the high-involvement organization, where thinking, controlling and doing are, once again, reintegrated.

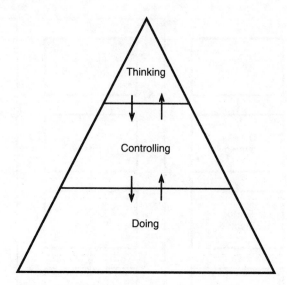

Figure 3.3 Traditional hierarchical organization.

Our serial approaches to product development shown in Figure 3.4 are also largely obsolete. This process is the direct cause of cost, poor quality products, manufacturing difficulties and so on. The integration of marketing, manufacturing, and field service into product development processes has been traditionally very poor, which has led to problems, not least of which are development time overrun, budget overrun, and products that do not meet customers' needs. This outdated way of doing things is being replaced by the concurrent engineering model shown in

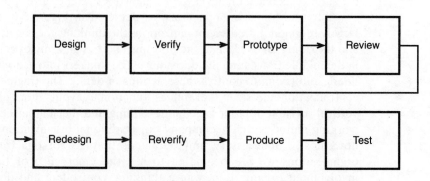

Figure 3.4 Serial engineering model of product development.

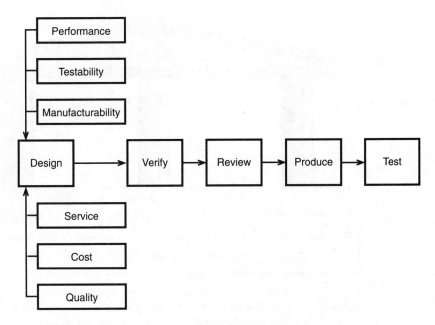

Figure 3.5 Concurrent engineering model of product development.

Figure 3.5 where issues such as product performance, manufacturability and so on will all be addressed in parallel, and marketing, design, field service and so forth will be integrated into product development teams.

Experience of manufacturing systems design and implementation suggests that no matter how sophisticated the technology, manufacturing systems do not operate effectively and yield expected benefits unless a whole range of issues is addressed. Traditionally, we have focused on the technology, and we have ignored or treated as secondary the organization and people issues. The resulting situation is imbalanced and mono-disciplinary. The design paradigm underlying our traditional view is largely based on breaking down complex systems into their component parts, which are then largely treated in isolation, the belief that task optimization leads to enterprise optimization, monodisciplinary professions, cost reduction and a single minded focus on technology.

In future, the traditional approach will be replaced by a more balanced and interdisciplinary approach. The underlying design paradigm will be based on a holistic systems approach, interdisciplinary design, balanced consideration of organization, people and technology, the creation of a learning environment and a focus on cost, quality and flexibility. The agile manufacturing enterprise will be supported by organization, people and technology as shown in Figure 3.6, but all these will be underpinned by an interdisciplinary design methodology.

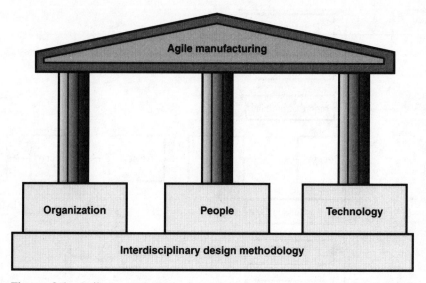

Figure 3.6 Agile manufacturing supported by organization, people and technology, and founded on an interdisciplinary design methodology. *Source:* Cheshire Henbury. © 1991. Published with permission.

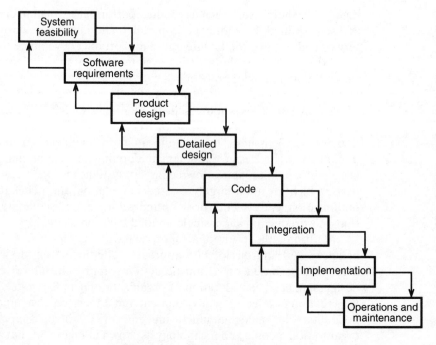

Figure 3.7 Waterfall life cycle model.

In the field of software development, the traditional waterfall life cycle model shown in Figure 3.7 is largely obsolete, except perhaps for a few specific classes of software projects. The problems associated with the use of this approach are now well documented, and given the high-risk nature of market conditions and the costs of failing to produce systems that meet the needs of customers and users, this stage-wise document driven process will be replaced more by the spiral life cycle model shown in Figure 3.8. This approach is a risk driven evolutionary approach, where we place our emphasis on reducing identified risks.

In the coming years, we will see a growing emphasis on what has been called idea transformation (Savage, 1992). During the industrial era, material transformation has been the dominant consideration, that is, the process of transforming materials into products. As we begin to enter the knowledge era, we will also become concerned with idea transformation. We will expect people to use knowledge to transform ideas into new products, better methods and improved processes. This is depicted in Figure 3.9.

The observations outlined above illustrate some of the changes to be faced. The point is that, as stated previously, the changes are profound and do affect us all. Moreover, the changes are such that we need new values with respect to our view of people, authority and control. We also need new processes through which to conduct our actions, work and activities.

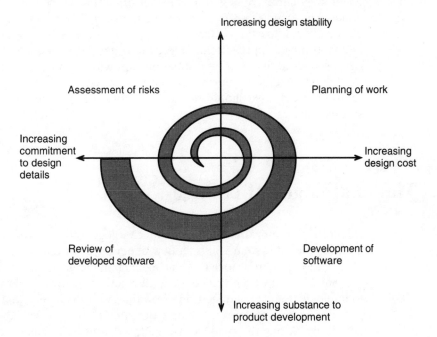

Figure 3.8 Spiral life cycle model.

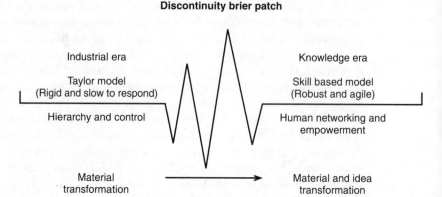

Figure 3.9 The discontinuity from the industrial era to the knowledge era. *Source:* Digital Equipment Corporation. © 1992. Published with permission.

The changes will also be painful for us. Savage (1992) refers to the pain aspects by referring to a discontinuity brier patch that lies between our traditional paradigm and the new paradigm of agile manufacturing.

Some companies have already started to change the way they use technology and have begun to consider organization, people and other issues. The changes needed are simple in principle, but in practice they can be difficult to achieve. Instead of looking for the technological fix, we need a broader approach that addresses organization, people, technology, product design processes, relationships with suppliers and so forth. We have to overcome our belief that technology provides the answers to all problems. We should not use technology to compensate for our shortcomings.

The challenges of change

Integrating organization, people and technology into a coordinated and interdependent system will be a new experience for all of us. It needs consideration in order to achieve an agile manufacturing enterprise.

This new approach will create quite a few problems. When we seek to implement agile manufacturing we will have to recognize that we are pursuing a moving target, because the state-of-the-art will always be advancing. Along the road we will be faced with hundreds of methods and techniques, as indicated in Figure 3.10.

Figure 3.10   The road to agile manufacturing is lined with panaceas.

These methods and techniques include just-in-time manufacturing, concurrent engineering, cellular manufacturing and CIM to name but a few. Many of these are useful techniques, but they are often oversold and presented as panaceas. We will have to learn that, while all methods and techniques are potentially useful, they are just part of the tool-kit of manufacturing. They are not panaceas.

We will have to start asking fundamental questions, not just about what to do, but also about why, when, and how to do these things. In other words, we will have to move away from panacea, prescription and platitude, towards carefully planned agile manufacturing. This will not be easy, given our tendencies in manufacturing to follow the herd, and to implement the latest fad or three-letter acronym.

We will also have to unlearn years of ingrained attitudes and practices. We need to start managing changes in company culture. Our present ideas of distinctions based upon employee groups, such as management and shop floor workers, need to be abandoned. We should only have one group, everybody part of one team. We also need to change our attitudes and develop the capability to design technologies and systems, taking account of human needs, such that better use is made of our people's skills and experience.

The economic and market factors outlined in Chapter 1 raise some important issues and questions. The first of these concerns the economic effectiveness of our manufacturing systems. If the change to economies of scope is less dependent on using automation as a means of achieving reduced costs, do we fully appreciate this change, and what is the new role for technology? Are we going to find ourselves designing manufacturing systems using concepts and financial appraisal methods that were largely, or only applicable to, economies of scale? Will the systems that we design give the expected return on investment?

The second issue is the under-utilization of human resources (human skill, judgment and creativity). Under economies of scale, we have almost come to accept as the norm that much factory work, especially on the shop floor, is tedious and without challenge. We have often regarded this situation as the price that we have to pay for economic prosperity. Economies of scope, however, would seem to demand a different type of workforce. One that is better trained, highly skilled and motivated, more adaptive and flexible, and less passive. And the way we organize manufacturing and the techniques we use to motivate people also need to be reconsidered.

If, as seems likely, the trends outlined in Chapter 1 continue, the importance of economies of scale will reduce, and economies of scope will become an important factor in economic growth. In other words, the opportunities for profit growth will not in future be derived from economies of scale, but from economies of scope, that is, competitive advantage will be derived from agility rather than from just trying to achieve low costs. The key business issues are therefore to reduce product development and manufacturing lead times, improve customer responsiveness and service, increase agility and reduce costs, against a background of highly variable customer demand patterns and changing specifications.

While it is clearly not possible or desirable to specify in detail the best way to achieve agile manufacturing, it is possible to distinguish between two fundamentally different responses. The first is based on the evolution of the traditional manufacturing paradigm, the other on the development of an entirely new and different paradigm, the one we have called agile manufacturing. Herein lies the problem.

Everyone in manufacturing has a set of core beliefs and assumptions specific and relevant to manufacturing, which are shared in common with colleagues in the industry. This is the essence of a paradigm: it is taken for granted and not seen as problematic by those who adhere to it. The paradigm defines how things are done and what is acceptable (Johnson, 1988).

A paradigm, however, is a double edged sword, because it is both helpful and unhelpful, depending on the circumstances. Associated with a paradigm is a mind-set, a way of thinking, which might become over-sensitized to some particular aspect of the manufacturing environment or available information, at the expense of other parts. This over-sensitizing is useful, because it helps us to become sensitized to important things, and this often serves us very well. For example, it helps to be over-sensitized to potential safety problems, or to design features in a product that can be regarded as gold plating (that is, expensive or unnecessary or both). Sensitization also occurs to patterns that remind us of a problem successfully solved.

We develop mind-sets slowly over a period of time. The subconscious mind gradually starts to exert more influence, and actions become more instinctive and intuitive, and detailed conscious thought about the right direction to go in becomes less evident. While this acquired instinctive and intuitive behavior is helpful to us in many situations, it is also extremely unhelpful in others where the assumptions about what constitutes the correct action are invalidated by changes in circumstances. At first inspection, the circumstances may appear to be like those experienced in the past (for example the need to introduce technology to maintain competitive advantage), and the paradigm leads us to accept the similarities, and act in the same way, until that is, we discovered the error.

It is well known that paradigms are difficult to change and to challenge because they are more than intellectual, they are also political, in the sense that they embody assumptions about power and authority. As a result, paradigms tend to evolve slowly as changing circumstances demand, or they are overturned by external agents, for example, people who have rejected the constructs of the existing paradigm.

Alternatively, paradigms can be changed in fundamental ways by internal agents if we feel confident enough to challenge our own beliefs and to make constructive criticisms of our own past history.

These three scenarios provide a very useful framework for examining the change problems that we are experiencing in manufacturing, with regard to strategy development techniques, new product development processes, manufacturing systems design methodology and the shift towards agile manufacturing. Before examining these three scenarios, however, it is useful to introduce an analogy that provides us with a simple way of looking at the situation.

Imagine a group of people who bake cakes for a living. These people use tried and tested methods and recipes, and are continually improving their recipes and baking new types of cakes. One day some people start complaining about the cakes. 'These cakes do not taste very nice', they say. The cake bakers say, 'but these cakes are good, and we know that they are good because we are cake experts'.

Many people, however, do not accept this argument, and remain unhappy. The cake bakers continue to innovate, developing the cake recipes. People continue to complain, and the cake bakers continue to ignore them. Slowly however, the cake bakers begin to realize that there is something wrong with the cakes. The cakes do not taste very good. They realize that the critics were right!

Given this new awareness, what can they do to improve the situation? There are three distinctive views; the evolutionary view, the rebellious view and the transitional view.

The evolutionary view is based on the belief that there is nothing fundamentally wrong with the way things are done at present, and that all that is required are some slight adjustments to compensate for the changed circumstances. In terms of our cake example, this amounts to saying 'OK, we accept that they don't taste too good, so in future we will add some icing to make them taste better'.

The rebellious view is based on the belief that the problems arise from a lack of *right thinking*. If left to us nothing will change. What is required is for an outside group to establish a new paradigm in keeping with the new situation. Back to the cake bakers. We would have a group of people external to cake baking who probably knew very little about it, setting up in business as cake bakers. What they would produce is unclear. With a bit of luck they might produce cakes, but they would be cake bakers on the fringes of mainstream cake baking, because their rebellion would always be seen as a threat. If they wanted to be taken more seriously, they would have to become bakers of distinction, which would mean acknowledging that, although faced with quite revolutionary changes, not everything that the mainstream cake bakers do is all bad.

The transitional scenario is one where we ourselves acknowledge that something fundamental needs to be done to improve the situation. We then begin an open minded quest for fundamentally better ways of doing things, which may also involve making some minor adjustments. In terms of cake baking this scenario represents the bakers making some fundamental changes to the recipes and the baking methods, as well as possibly adding icing to the cakes.

There appears to be far from universal agreement on the nature and scale of changes needed. There are people in manufacturing who do not accept the need for a new paradigm. There is a view that we should adopt the evolutionary scenario outlined above, all that is required are minor adjustments to the way things are done. For example, Majchrzak and Gasser (1992) consider the response obtained in manufacturing companies to the concept of interdisciplinary manufacturing systems design. They report that the idea of it, in which both the organization and the technology are designed simultaneously, was not considered, and many companies seemed genuinely skeptical that they would ever make different design decisions based on information about a mismatch between organizational and technological elements.

The belief that only slight adjustments are needed to our paradigm in order to bring the way we do things into line with new requirements has a technical name. In terms of change this view corresponds to a model known as **morphostatic change**. This simply means that the type of change we are faced with is incremental. We preserve the established order by treating disturbances as external noise requiring minor adjustments.

We are advocating a different view. It is our belief that major changes to our existing paradigm are needed. In terms of the theory of change we are advocating what is called **morphogenic change**. This simply means a type of change that produces a different order to that which existed previously. We treat disturbances as information about the inappropriateness of our established practices, and this leads us to make fundamental changes in methods and principles.

Our basic problem is not just how to manage change in manufacturing, but also how to distinguish between situations requiring morphogenic change and those requiring morphostatic change.

Our older models of change (Lewin, 1947) describe change as a process that consists of the unfreezing of a situation which is in a steady state, assisting the process of change through a stage of turbulence, and then refreezing at a new situation. An alternative model is to consider change as a continuous process, with transitional processes taking place at varying rates. Which is the most useful model?

It seems that the dynamic model of continuous change offers us the best way forward. Why? The reason is simple. Our older models of change imply that all that we have to do is identify our present position and then identify our desired steady state condition, somehow unfreeze the present situation, guide the system to a new state, and then refreeze it. This poses a number of problems.

First it assumes that it is possible to identify exactly in advance the desired steady state situation. This is unlikely to be possible because of the fluid and turbulent nature of the emerging competitive environment. Second, it assumes that once a change has been initiated, a steady state situation is desirable and that there will be little or no need for further change in the near future. This is also highly unlikely, because in the years ahead, product design competence, manufacturing systems design competence, manufacturing competence and so forth will all be competitive weapons. In order to remain competitive, we will have to apply continuous improvement in all these area, if we want to keep an edge over our competitors. Change, therefore, will be continuous.

Given a process of continuous change, how best should we initiate and manage it? This leads us to the idea of transitional systems suggested by Winnicott (1971) and later developed by Bridger (Trist, 1989). Transitional systems can be regarded as opportunities for tuning in (getting in touch with new situations to get a feel for their texture), working through (coming to understand the implications and facing up to the pain and emotion of upheaval) and designing (creating the new situation).

The concept of transitional systems can help to develop a new manufacturing paradigm. Clearly what is embedded in the idea of transitional systems is the concept that we should clearly understand the existing culture and the implications of proposed changes before embarking on the process of change. Only then should we begin to design new systems.

Concluding comments

In the Introduction, and in Chapters 1 and 2, material was presented which will help readers to tune into a new situation that we call agile manufacturing. In this chapter we have started to explore the change implications that arise from agile manufacturing. This brings us to the purpose of the following two chapters. We need to spend much more time looking at the nature and characteristics of our existing culture. Only when we truly understand what needs to change can we embark upon the process of designing the new situation.

Key points

- Agile manufacturing implies revolutionary changes to our enterprises. We should not be making small adjustments. We should reinvent our manufacturing enterprises.
- We should understand the reasons for past failures and make sure that we do not repeat these mistakes.
- A crucial factor underlying past failures has been outdated tradition. The methods and approaches used in the past have now largely outlived their usefulness and should be abandoned.

- We should understand the wide ranging nature of the changes that lie ahead, and also understand that we all have to change. Change is not just something that others have to go through.

- We need new methods, processes and values. We need to move beyond quick fixes, panaceas and prescriptions. We need to ask fundamental questions about what to do and why, how to do it, and when.

- Agile manufacturing implies a paradigm shift. The key to success lies in understanding change processes, and in professional and innovative management of change.

References

Browne J. (1992). Future integrated manufacturing systems: a business driven approach. In *Organisation, People and Technology in European Manufacturing* (Kidd P.T., ed.) pp. 17–30. Luxembourg: Commission of the European Communities

Browne J., Harhen J. and Shivnan J. (1988). *Production Management Systems: A CIM Perspective*. Wokingham: Addison-Wesley

Dertouzos M.L., Lester R.K. and Solow R.M. (1989). *Made in America. Regaining the Productive Edge*. Cambridge MA: MIT

Johnson G. (1988). Process of managing strategic change. *Management Research News*, **11**(4/5), 43–6

Lewin K. (1947). Frontiers in group dynamics. *Human Relations*, **1**, 5–41

Majchrzak A. and Gasser L. (1992). HITOP-A: A tool to facilitate interdisciplinary manufacturing systems design. *Int. J. Human Factors in Manufacturing*, **2**(3), 255–76

Mintzberg H. (1990). The design school: reconsidering the basic premises of strategic management. *Strategic Management J.*, **11**(5), 171–95

Savage C.M. (1992). *Knowledge Business Initiative*. Concord MA: Digital Equipment Corporation

Trist E. (1989). Psychoanalytic issues in organisational research and consultation. In *Working with Organisations* (Klein L., ed.), pp. 50–7. London: Tavistock

Voss C.A. (1988). Success and failure in advanced manufacturing technology. *Int. J. of Technology Management*, **3**(3), 285–97.

Winnicott D.W. (1971). *Playing and Reality*. London: Tavistock

4

The traditional management accounting paradigm

Introduction

The management accounting methods traditionally used in manufacturing industry were mostly developed during the age of labor intensive mass production. The business environment of this era was largely based on home consumption, secure export markets, stable demand and limited competition.

This environment is now changing. Much of manufacturing is no longer labor intensive, and high volume, low variety production has given way to high variety, low volume production. Markets have also become more global and dynamic, and the business environment is much more competitive. Moreover, manufacturing technology has become more sophisticated, and the benefits are no longer confined to the place of implementation and use. The technology can now bring company wide benefits, which are not only concerned with cost savings, but also with the potential for revenue generation (for example, as a result of increased customer responsiveness).

Against this background of change, one aspect of manufacturing has remained largely unchanged. The management accounting and investment appraisal methods used in today's manufacturing environment are much the same as those used 50 years ago (Johnson and Kaplan 1987; Kaplan, 1989). In fact, many of the basic ideas of management accounting can be traced back to the scientific management movement started by Frederick Taylor, in the US, in the late part of the 19th century (Kaplan, 1984, 1989).

There is now increasing criticism of these outdated methods in the accounting and management literature. A notable milestone in this critique was the publication in 1987 of *Relevance Lost: the Rise and Fall of Management Accounting* (Johnson and Kaplan, 1987). In the late 1980s and early 1990s activity based costing (ABC) emerged as an important alternative management accounting method (Brimson, 1991; Turney, 1992). We will return to ABC in Chapter 9.

In this chapter we wish to examine the criticisms of our traditional management accounting methods and consider some of the problems associated with the financial appraisal of **advanced manufacturing technologies** (AMT) such as **flexible manufacturing systems** (FMS) and **computer integrated manufacturing** (CIM) systems.

The reason why we wish to focus our attention on the management accounting paradigm is because management accounting forms a central part of any manufacturing business. Management accounting systems provide the financial information that helps to make business decisions. In this chapter we shall try to demonstrate that our traditional management accounting systems also provide the framework that supports and keeps alive many of our outdated manufacturing practices and beliefs. Our hypothesis is quite simple: if we want to change our traditional practices and beliefs, one of the first places to start is with our management accounting systems.

Management accounting is primarily concerned with three issues: product costing, performance measurement and control systems and investment appraisal. We shall briefly examine the basics of each of these areas. At each step, we will consider why our well established techniques are inappropriate to agile manufacturing environments.

Investment appraisal

definition

Capital investment appraisal is used to help to decide on the best possible way of investing the capital available for investment, or to compare competing investment proposals. Three techniques are widely used in manufacturing industry for investment appraisal. These are return on capital employed, payback period and discounted cash flow (DCF) analysis. All three are based on data such as generated revenue, operating costs and capital costs. For obvious reasons the data need to be fairly reliable.

The return on capital employed method involves calculating a percentage return on capital employed. This is done by taking the lifetime surplus and dividing it by the initial capital investment, and then multiplying the result by 100%. The yearly return is the return on capital divided by the life of the project. The best investment is the one that will yield the highest return on capital employed.

The payback period method seeks to quantify risk by establishing how long it would take a project to pay back the initial capital invested. The project that pays back its initial capital fastest is the best. The calculation of payback period is very straightforward. It starts with the amount of the initial investment, then subtracts yearly surpluses until there is no capital outstanding. This gives the payback period.

DCF is concerned with establishing how well a project performs in relation to the alternative of investing the initial capital at compound current interest rates. The calculations are performed in terms of discounting, which is the mathematical opposite of compounding. For example, compounding is concerned with finding out what $100 will be worth if invested at, say, 10% for five years. When discounting, the reverse question is asked, that is, what will money received in the future be worth, in terms of today's money (present value). The basis of the evaluation is that money received in the first year is of higher value than money received in the final year. The reason is that early money can be reinvested for a longer period.

The calculations start by determining the yearly cash inflows. They are then converted, using a chosen percentage rate of discount (for example, 10% or 12%), into discounted cash flows (that is, present values). These present values are then summed to give the present value of the project. The final step is to calculate the **net present value** (NPV), which is the present value minus the initial capital. The project with the highest NPV is the best because if compounded, the highest NPV is bound to give the highest end of project cash total.

Internal rate of return (IRR) is another DCF method that can be used as an alternative to the NPV method.

The case against traditional investment appraisal

Our traditional argument for investing in technologies that increase the level of automation and decrease the role of people in manufacturing has always been a straightforward one. A well known example illustrating the philosophy is described by Bradley (1972) in his book on the history of machine tools. In a dockyard during the first decade of the 19th century, new blockmaking machinery was installed, which resulted in 10 unskilled men performing work that had previously been done by 110 skilled men. The new machinery turned out 130,000 blocks annually with an estimated saving of $24,000.

For most of us this example illustrates what technological innovation has been all about; lowering skill requirements in order to reduce labor costs, and using less labor to achieve a given output, that is, increasing productivity. However, can we use such a simple argument to justify investments in new technology in agile manufacturing enterprises, which operate in a highly competitive environment and which involve much greater complexity and much greater amounts of information?

We now point out a few relevant facts that suggest a clear answer: that to rely on our conventional financial appraisal methods alone is ill advised.

Methodological problems

It has been argued in some of the published literature on AMT that our financial appraisal methods for new advanced manufacturing technologies are inadequate because they do not capture the strategic benefits (for example, increased customer responsiveness) that are vital to improving our competitiveness and profitability (Senker, 1983; Meredith and Suresh, 1986). The main appeal of our traditional financial *simple* investment appraisal methods is that they are reasonably simple to use. We tend to believe that they provide clear information about the effect on profits, and the data that is needed can be collected with relative ease. However, the claimed main disadvantage of these methods is that they do not capture non-financial and strategic benefits.

The payback method is probably the method that we use most widely *PB* for investment appraisal, because it is simple to use, and because we believe that it contains a built-in safeguard against risk. If we can recover *advantage* all the capital invested within two or three years, our risk is minimized. The method, however, suffers from the disadvantage that the time value of money is ignored. We completely ignore any returns that accrue after *disa* the end of the payback period, and we disregard the fact that projects may differ greatly with regard to the returns that occur after the payback period. It has been suggested (Mundy, 1984) that these disadvantages mean that the payback method is immediately biased against an investment in technologies such as FMS, where we may not realize the full benefits until long after the payback period.

For the purposes of capital investment appraisal, we should therefore only regard the payback period calculation as a first level assessment criterion. On its own, it does not offer us a very useful evaluation of the *DisA* investment, except perhaps in very simple situations. The primary reason for this is that the method makes no allowance for the profitability of our proposed investment. What it does provide us with is a safety-first measure of the value of our proposal, and it is because of this feature that we widely apply the method. In considering the profitability of a proposed investment we should also apply a DCF method (Watts *et al.*, 1982).

The return on capital method is, like the payback period technique, a simple one. As with the case of payback period, its main disadvantage is that it ignores the timings of returns. Consequently, if we use this method, we take no account of the fact that if one project makes a higher return in earlier years than another project, then these early returns can be reinvested. Because the return on capital method takes no account of the timing or implications of our investment, it has been suggested that this method is basically unsuitable for any type of investment appraisal (Mundy, 1984).

DCF methods are the only ones that are capable of coping adequately with differing time patterns of returns, differing project lives and reinvestment. DCF methods are, however, slightly more complex than the return on capital employed and payback period methods. However, although they have advantages over the other methods, it is claimed that DCF appraisal can sometimes lead us to reject investment proposals (Senker, 1983). This happens because DCF encourages us to focus on projects that yield quick returns. Returns anticipated to arise after several years are discounted. Consequently, if we have to choose between two broadly similar projects, where one yields quicker returns than the other, then DCF techniques will rate the project with the quicker returns more highly than the other projects, and based on DCF analysis alone, the most obvious project to implement is the one with the highest returns.

Another problem with DCF methods is the setting of too high a hurdle rate. Hurdle rates specify the minimum return that is expected from an investment. If our proposed investment does not satisfy the hurdle rate, then we will not be able to get it approved.

It has been argued (Senker, 1983) that some investments are of strategic importance. For example a project may be of a nature that would help us to get involved in a new technology on which our future could depend in a few years' time. In such cases it might be vitally important to invest in these strategic projects, even if the predicted DCF returns are relatively modest. It has also been argued (Mundy, 1984) that financial appraisal techniques are based on an analysis of cash flows resulting directly from the investment. For a single machine such as a machine tool we can quite easily obtain the required data. In these situations it is normally sufficient that we consider only the direct impact of the investment in terms of reduced unit costs, and this can be done over a relatively short period of time when the costs and benefits can be accurately estimated. However, this approach has a number of limitations when we try to apply it to the appraisal of system based technologies such as FMS and CIM.

It is claimed that we can identify and quantify with reasonable accuracy the costs and benefits of conventional equipment. However, it is also claimed that, when we have to justify an investment in FMS or

CIM, the costs and benefits associated with these technologies are far from obvious and are not always quantifiable. These intangible benefits may have a considerable effect on our business as a whole. Furthermore, it is also claimed that we can only estimate the tangible benefits of FMS and CIM with limited accuracy, particularly as the full benefits of these system based technologies may not become apparent until we have fully installed the system and operated it for a period of time. The claim is that, while the efficiency of our conventional machinery will decline with age, the efficiency of our FMS and CIM systems may well increase because of increased flexibility and operational experience (Mundy, 1984).

We can thus see that one of the main problems with all our financial appraisal methods is that they condense a complex situation into one sin- *too simple* gle number that cannot possibly be representative of the information needed for a decision (Meredith and Suresh, 1986). Moreover, all our financial appraisal methods are based on quantifiable costs and benefits. We can of course quantify such things as labor costs, material costs and so on, but it is not so easy to quantify the benefits of increased customer responsiveness. Indeed, it has been suggested that one should not attempt to quantify what is a condition for remaining in business (Meredith and Suresh, 1986).

The basic problem is that many of the advantages of new manufacturing technologies lie not in traditional cost reduction, but rather in strategic advantage and revenue generation. Our traditional financial *Conclusion* appraisal methods are well suited to appraisal of cost reduction or capacity expansion exercises, but are not particularly well suited to strategic and revenue generation investments (Meredith and Suresh, 1986).

Quantifying the benefits of CIM and FMS

One of the reported problems with the financial appraisal of FMS and CIM projects is our tendency to focus on improving efficiency by reducing direct labor costs, work-in-progress, and operating expenses. However, a feature of many FMS and CIM investments is the high *feature* capital cost, and many of us have experienced difficulty in making an appraisal based solely on direct costs. This has resulted in a tendency to overestimate any labor displacement effects of new technologies, in order to justify the investment.

A report of a study of the introduction of CAD into 34 companies (Senker, 1983) shows that, of the companies examined, 24 introduced CAD solely on the basis of savings in labor costs in the drawing office. Likewise, it has been suggested that the main benefit of robots is their cost advantage over manual labor (Watts *et al.*, 1982). Typical figures quoted are $6.05 per hour for manual labor costs, compared with $3.14 per hour for robot costs. These figures support the claim that robots lead to direct labor savings. However, the example presented by Watts *et al.* for the application of a robot, demonstrate that the economic benefits are not derived from savings in manual labor, but from reduced maintenance costs ($11,250 per year less spent on maintenance materials, and $350 per year less spent on maintenance labor) and improved quality resulting in a reduction of scrap rate from 20% to less than 3%. There is no mention whatsoever of cost reductions arising from any labor displacement.

Another feature of AMT is its ability to affect the total company operation (Senker, 1983) and often it is only when we view projects in this company wide context that we are able to assess them as being financially viable. Extra hidden costs may also be incurred, together with additional benefits that may arise from the need to integrate systems with the rest of the plant (Mundy, 1984). Thus we need to identify all project benefits and costs so that they can be included in a financial appraisal.

It has been suggested that traditional investment appraisal methods based on financial criteria (payback period, return on capital, DCF) cannot adequately capture the competitive advantage that can be derived from investments in AMT such as FMS and CIM. Consequently, it has been proposed (Meredith and Suresh, 1986) that financial appraisal should be accompanied by other forms of appraisal (analytic or strategic or both).

This position is not without its critics. Kaplan (1986) argues that, if for good strategic reasons, we consistently invest in projects where the financial returns are less than the capital invested, we will soon find that we are on the road to insolvency. Whatever special value we may advocate for CIM technology, we cannot override the basic logic that investments must produce a return.

Kaplan (1986) also believes that the trouble with the application of DCF to CIM appraisal does not lie in some gap between the logic of DCF and the nature of CIM, but in the very poor application of DCF to our CIM investment proposals. We do not need to, and should not, abandon the effort to justify CIM on financial grounds. Instead we should apply DCF analysis more appropriately, and be more aware of the special attributes of CIM.

If we examine CIM, we will find that a number of tangible benefits can be derived from our proposed CIM investment. These include inventory savings, less floor space and higher quality. Process flexibility, more orderly product flow, higher quality and better scheduling can result in less work-in-progress and a smaller finished goods inventory level. This reduction in average inventory level represents a cash inflow at the time the new process equipment becomes operational, and this one-off cash saving should be used in our DCF analysis.

CIM can potentially also cut floor space requirements. This saving arises because often we need fewer computer numerically controlled machine tools, because newer machines can do the work that was previously performed by a large number of conventional manual machine tools or older numerically controlled machine tools. The extra floor space might negate the need for extensions to plant and offices, or might allow the combination of operations from several plants into one. The redundant plant could then be sold or let. In either case more cash would be generated.

To take account of these reductions in floor space requirements in the investment analysis, the revenues generated as a result of floor space savings should be calculated, as well as the costs that might be saved. Typical cost savings might arise for example as a result of eliminating the transportation of semi-finished products or components between plants, or because of reduced plant running costs.

The potential for improved quality is another tangible benefit of CIM. When quality is improved there is less waste, scrap and rework and these benefits can be quantified and included in the cash flow analysis. However, improved quality also reduces the need for inspection and quality checks. This also results in quantifiable cost savings. Moreover, improved quality also leads to a reduction in warranty and in-field service costs. These savings should also be included in the analysis. It is also possible that better quality will also have an impact on reducing accounts receivable by eliminating the incidence of customers with-holding payments until problems have been resolved.

It is well known that there are a number of so called intangible benefits that can be derived from CIM. These include increased flexi-bility, faster response to market shifts and greatly reduced throughput and lead times. These intangible benefits are commonly believed to be as important as the tangible benefits, but, as is also well known, they are much harder to quantify. Often our investments in FMS and CIM have been justified on the basis of tangible benefits (often direct labor savings) but it has been found later that the real benefits arose from these intangibles.

The need to translate these intangible benefits into tangible benefits was recognized in the early phase of FMS development by Small (1983). Primrose (1991) has reported that we can quantify the intangible benefits by preparing a list of intangibles' benefits, such as flexibility of production, better quality products and such like, which can then be quantified by looking at the detailed implications of such general statements.

Although Primrose (1991) shows how the intangible benefits can be quantified, it may be the case that they may not always be quantifiable with any great accuracy. The difficulty in quantifying some of the intan-gibles arises because some of the benefits lead to generation of revenue rather than cost savings. It is fairly easy to estimate percentage reductions in costs that are already being incurred. However, it is much harder to quantify the magnitude of the revenue enhancement expected from features that are not already in place (Kaplan, 1986).

Good, bad or optimal investments?

In the preceding two sections we outlined some of the arguments that have taken place concerning the manner in which investments in AMT should be appraised. By way of conclusion, we will consider the basic underlying theoretical problem. To do this we turn to control theory and the principle of optimality. To explain this without recourse to mathematics, we shall consider a simple problem.

Consider the map of the continental US shown in Figure 4.1. Suppose we are on the west coast of the US in San Francisco and want to travel to an unspecified destination on the east coast. The objective is to travel to the coastal city on the eastern seaboard that is the shortest distance from San Francisco, but a constraint on our route is that we should travel through several other cities specified in Figure 4.1. The problem is illustrated in Figure 4.2. The distances shown are in miles, and are approximate based on straight line distances. How do we solve this problem?

One obvious way is to decide upon the details of our route as we go. At each city we will decide which city to visit next, by comparing the distance to the next cities, and taking the shortest distance. This way, we believe that we will take the shortest overall path. Thus, from San Francisco we would first travel to Salt Lake City, Utah (600 miles). From Salt Lake City we would travel to Denver, Colorado (400 miles), then to Tulsa, Oklahoma (540 miles), and then to our final destination, Norfolk, Virginia (1140 miles). The total distance is 2680 miles, which is not the optimal path! This is, in fact, San Francisco, Salt Lake City, Denver, Kansas City, New York, a total distance of 2640 miles.

To compute the optimal path we must work backwards. We start not at the final destination, but at the stage before. If the optimum path were to pass through Madison, then the final stage of the journey would be to Boston, which is 820 miles. Likewise, if Kansas City were on the optimum path, then the final stage would be to New York, a distance of 1040 miles. Similarly, if Tulsa were on the optimum path, then the final stage of the journey would be to Norfolk, which is 1140 miles away. Finally, if Dallas were on the optimum path, then the final destination would be 1140 miles away at Miami.

Now, the actual optimum path must pass through one of these four cities; Madison, Kansas City, Tulsa or Dallas, and the final stage of the journey is one of the four indicated. The question is, which of these cities is on the optimum path? To find this out we must move to next previous stage and repeat the procedure.

Starting at Cheyenne, we ask what is the shortest route to an east coast city. The distance from Cheyenne to Madison is 840 miles, plus the minimum from Madison to the coast, which has already been established as 820 miles, giving a total distance of 1660 miles. Alternatively, we could

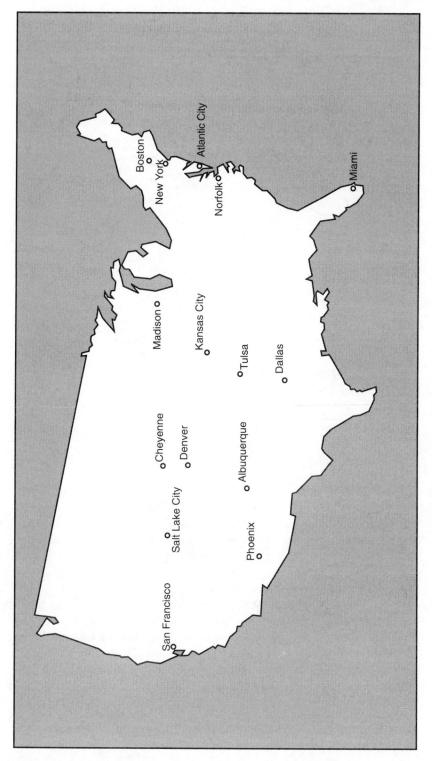

Figure 4.1 Continental United States and specified cities.

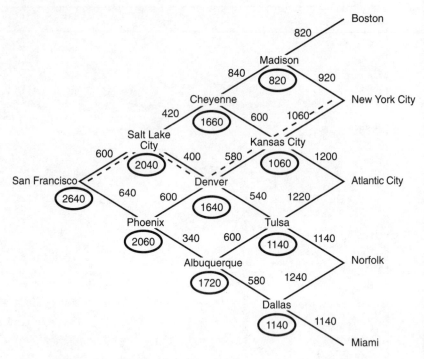

Figure 4.2 Finding the optimal path across the United States.

travel 600 miles to Kansas City, and then the minimum route of 1060 miles to New York, giving a total of 1660 miles again. This tells us that when travelling from Cheyenne, it makes no difference whether we go to Madison or Kansas City.

If Denver were on the optimum path, then the shortest route to the coast would be to New York via Kansas City, a distance of 1640 miles. The alternative route would be to Norfolk via Tulsa, a distance of 1680 miles, which is clearly not the shortest. Likewise, if Albuquerque were on the optimum path, then the two alternatives would be Albuquerque, Tulsa, Norfolk (1740 miles) or Albuquerque, Dallas, Miami (1720 miles), making the second alternative the one with the shortest path.

We are now in the following position. If we were in Cheyenne, then we would go to Boston via Madison, or New York via Kansas City. As both journeys are the same length, it makes no difference which one we choose, although we do end up at difference places. If we were in Denver we would go to New York, via Kansas City, and if we were in Albuquerque we would travel to Miami, via Dallas. The question is, which of these three cities; Cheyenne, Denver or Albuquerque is on the optimum path? To find out, it is necessary to move back to the next preceding stage, and find the shortest path to the coast.

If Salt Lake City were on the optimum path, then we could go to Cheyenne, so the total distance to the coast would be 1660 miles plus 420 miles from Salt Lake City to Cheyenne, making 2080 miles. Alternatively we could travel to Denver, and the total distance to the coast would be 1640 miles plus the 400 from Salt Lake City to Denver, making a total of 2040 miles. The optimum route from Salt Lake City to the coast is therefore via Denver and Kansas City to New York. In the same way we can consider the situation for Phoenix, where the shortest route is via Albuquerque and Dallas to Miami, a total of 2060 miles.

We can now find which of these two cities, Salt Lake City or Phoenix, is on the optimum route, by moving to San Francisco. From San Francisco to Salt Lake City is 600 miles, and thus the total distance to the coast via Salt Lake City is 2040 miles plus 600, which makes 2640 miles. The distance from San Francisco to Phoenix is 640 miles, plus the shortest distance from Phoenix to the coast, which is 2060 miles, making 2700 miles. Thus it follows that the optimum path from San Francisco to the coast is 2640 miles, via Salt Lake City, Denver, Kansas City, ending at New York.

What does this example show us? The most important lesson is that, at each step along the journey, if we take a decision which achieves a local optimization, that is, travelling eastward but to the city nearest to our present location, then this strategy does not guarantee that an overall optimum will be achieved. In terms of investment appraisal, if each time we make an investment decision we always seek to maximize return on investment (or some other criteria such as profit or cost savings), then we cannot guarantee that over a longer timescale, we will achieve an optimum.

The example also suggests that if we are designing a manufacturing system consisting of several subsystems, then there is no one best solution, as our traditional view of manufacturing might suggest. We can see that from Cheyenne to the coast we can go along one of two routes, both of equal length. This fact will be of importance when we come to consider questions of technological and organizational choice in later chapters. In the past, some of us have argued and claimed that there is no choice, but often this is not so.

The example also illustrates the problem with our traditional investment appraisal methods, such as return on capital, payback period and DCF. These consider the question of which is the most optimum investment at each particular step, not which sequence of steps leads to an overall optimum. The simple example demonstrates that finding the optimum investment is a much more difficult problem than it might have first appeared. The important point about this, however, is that under the competitive conditions that existed up to the 1980s, it may have been the case that it did not matter too much if we failed to make the optimum investment over the longer term. However, in the 21st century, achieving this optimum may well be a matter of crucial importance, given the highly competitive nature of markets and the complexity of modern system based technologies.

Consequently, it seems that there is some theoretical basis to the argument that pure financial investment appraisal methods, used on their own, do not provide a satisfactory guide to investment appraisal, when performance over the longer term is taken into account. This suggests that these financial methods should therefore be complemented with non-financial methods, or that a stronger link should be established between investment appraisal and strategic goals. We will return to these two points in Chapter 9.

Product costing

We will now turn our attention to product costing. The traditional approach to product costing is absorption costing, which can be sub-divided into three approaches; job costing, process costing and standard costing. Also contribution margin analysis in manufacturing has been used traditionally. This has been used to calculate break-even sales, whether to accept an order at a special price and such like. Contribution margin analysis, however, needs data derived from a variable costing system.

Absorption costing

The absorption cost of a product is the total costs divided by the number of items normally made in a period (for example, one year). The absorption cost has three components; direct labor, direct materials and overheads. It is possible to calculate exactly the direct labor cost and the direct material cost of a product, and it is also possible to calculate the total overheads of the plant. Traditionally, the allocation of each item of overhead to a product has not been considered a worthwhile exercise. Overheads have not been considered in the same precise way as direct labor costs and direct material costs. Thus each product is allocated overheads in proportion to the amount of productive capacity used up in making each item. Productive capacity can be defined in a number of ways. Direct labor hours and machine hours are two commonly used measures. Consequently, if we use 25% of productive capacity in the manufacture of a given product, then 25% of the plant overhead is allocated to this product.

It has been the tradition to organize manufacturing by functional department (for example, turning, milling, assembly). Overhead recovery is therefore related to the amount of productive capacity used in manufacturing each product in each department. This means that first the plant overheads must be distributed between each department. Each department is then allocated an **overhead recovery rate** (ORR), which is defined as departmental overhead divided by productive capacity. The ORR is the amount of overhead that is charged as a cost of using one hour's productive capacity (labor hour or machine hour).

Normally job costing systems are used where the products are of high value, but are also made-to-order, or are one-off non-standard products. The process of costing is based on establishing a selling price through estimates of the number of direct labor hours needed and the direct material costs, and by allocating overhead to the product on the basis of direct labor hours employed (or machine hours if more appropriate).

In situations where the products are of low value with identical features, it is not worth costing on an individual basis. Products of this kind include paint, nuts and bolts and screws. In these situations process costing techniques are used. This involves measuring the costs fed into a process over a period of time and the output from the process over the same period. Costs per unit are then calculated by dividing total costs by output, with adjustments being made for incomplete products (that is, work in progress).

Of more relevance to many traditional manufacturing enterprises is standard costing, which is used to cost high-value identical products such as consumer goods. Most consumer goods are relatively complex because they often consist of many thousands of components, and many processes are used in their manufacture. They are also manufactured in large numbers. In this type of situation, it can be very difficult to know how efficiently products are being manufactured. Standard costing provides a framework and the tools to help investigate manufacturing efficiency.

Standard costing involves working out, in great detail, how much it costs to make one item. This is known as the standard cost, which is the planned absorption cost of making one item. This investigation involves making detailed measurements of machine speeds, materials used, rejection percentages, direct labor time, overheads consumed based on planned production and so on. The standard cost of a product is presented in the usual terms of direct labor costs, direct material costs and fixed overheads.

When these detailed investigations are complete, it is necessary to calculate the master budget for the planned production. The master budget is the standard cost for making one product multiplied by the planned number of products to be produced in the period considered. The master budget, like the standard cost, is presented in terms of direct labor costs, direct material costs and overheads. When the master budget has been calculated, a flexible budget is then calculated. This is the expected costs for the actual quantity of products produced, because, in reality, the actual number of orders may be greater or less than the planned production. Both the direct labor cost and the direct material costs in the flexible budget will differ from the master budget, but the overhead is likely to remain unchanged. The flexible budget is the guide against which the actual costs can be measured to see if output costs have gone according to plan. The final step is therefore to measure the actual cost totals using the same breakdown as used in the standard cost.

Standard costing not only gives the cost of making a product, it also provides the framework for monitoring the performance of the manufacturing system, allowing the identification of problem areas. Standard costing also provides data on which investment decisions can be based. We have already examined the weaknesses of traditional investment appraisal techniques and we will return to this, and other aspects of traditional management accounting systems, later in this chapter.

Contribution margin analysis

The theory of contribution margin analysis assumes that every cost item can be classified as a variable cost or as a fixed cost. Costs that are output volume sensitive, such as direct materials, are variable. Costs that would be incurred regardless of output volume are fixed. In contribution margin analysis, fixed costs does not mean that costs cannot alter, only that they will not alter as a direct result of making one more item. The costs that are incurred in making a product, that is, direct labor, direct materials and overhead, can therefore be split into variable and fixed costs. It is likely that in the majority of cases the direct material costs will be totally variable.

We have tended to see contribution margin analysis as a powerful tool because it can provide us with important information to support decision-making. Contribution margin analysis allows the identification of the extra cost of making one more item and the resulting profit. This allows us to:

- Consider whether to take an order at a special price.
- Decide between alternative marketing strategies.
- Understand the cost-structure of a business and hence its ability to withstand a downturn in trade.
- Calculate the most profitable sales mix when a factor of production is limited.
- Understand the consequences of make or buy decisions on a business' total costs.

There are several important assumptions that must be satisfied when using contribution margin analysis, otherwise serious errors may be made and wrong conclusions reached. The assumptions are discussed in most management accounting textbooks (for example see Drury, 1988). The only assumption we will mention is that profits are calculated on a variable costing basis, not an absorption costing basis. This is to point out that the relevance of traditional absorption costing methods has been the subject of controversy for some time, especially with regard to whether variable costing is a better method than absorption costing.

The case against traditional product costing

Misleading information

The preceding overview of the basics of product costing leads us to draw some conclusions about the impact that traditional management accounting concepts have on decision-making, and hence on manufacturing design practice.

It can be seen from our simple overview that one way to make products more competitive is to reduce direct labor costs, or direct material costs, or overhead, or all three. However, the notion of profit is not that straightforward with respect to overhead.

The amount of overhead allocated to each department in manufacturing enterprise is a crucial decision, because it affects the cost of the products. However, there are certain elements of judgment that must be exercised in allocating overhead to each department, which has an effect on the profitability of products manufactured in these departments. In practice we have to base allocation on two things. First, we must consider the allocation of certain costs which are for things specific to departments. What is left over is then subject to judgment. However, our judgment must also take account of market factors. If allocation of overheads leads to product costs that are uncompetitive, then we need to do something to remedy this problem, for example, by reducing the allocation that we make to one department while increasing the allocation made elsewhere.

The fact that part of our allocation of overhead is subject to judgment, and that it is possible to redistribute overhead in order to influence the cost of making different products, should serve as a warning that management accounting is not an exact science, but more of an art. However, when dealing with numbers an illusion of accuracy and exactness can be created, and this can lead to too much confidence in the data, which is not justified.

Traditional management accounting methods also tell us that another way to improve competitiveness and profitability is to add extra productive capacity without increasing the overhead. This will result in a reduction in ORR. This is called diluting the overheads. ORR is governed by an estimate of productive capacity. The higher the productive capacity, the lower the ORR. This shows that we can, apparently, improve profitability by increasing machine utilization, or by doing things faster.

This fact is extremely important, and it is sometimes explicitly stated in management accounting textbooks that the speed with which things are made will affect their cost. Overheads are diluted if more things are made in a given time, and of course, the productivity of people employed as direct labor increases when things are made faster. It is said that if the word productivity has any meaning at all, it means the cost savings that can be achieved by making an item faster. This in turn means that its selling price can be more competitive.

In the early 1980s, it was pointed out by Ingersoll Engineers (1982) (also see Small, 1983) that time and skills have been inappropriately focused on reducing direct labor costs. We have given this cost element so much attention in the past, that it is now only a small part of the cost of sales. It is almost not worth worrying about, yet we still work away at this area of cost.

Direct labor costs in many of our manufacturing companies now range between 5–15% of total manufacturing costs. Often overhead costs reach 40% of total costs, with material making up around 50%. Yet, guided by traditional training, we have continued to work at reducing what has become a mere fraction of the difference between our own and our competitors' costs.

Tradition, of course, is a major factor in determining future actions and directions. What we have found to work well in the past continues to be used over and over again. But our adherence to traditional thinking is reinforced by our traditional management accounting methods, which indicate that we can make products more cheaply by reducing (often insignificant) direct labor costs. Moreover, as our traditional methods often allocate overhead to a product on the basis of the number of direct labor hours used in its manufacture, if we can reduce the number of direct labor hours we can also reduce the overhead allocated to the product. We can therefore make the product more cheaply!

The result of the traditional emphasis on unit costs is that management accounting systems become a constraint on what can be considered in the way of investment options. Management accounting systems provide the framework for the evaluation of investment projects. Anything that leads to benefits which cannot be identified within the framework of our management accounting systems, or which produces figures that are unacceptable within the framework of our traditional measurement systems will experience severe difficulties in being accepted, unless the rules of the system are changed, that is, we change the management accounting system.

An example of the potential problems can be seen with **manufacturing resource planning** (MRPII), **just-in-time manufacturing** (JIT) and **optimized production technology** (OPT). One claimed advantage of MRPII is that it is compatible with traditional management accounting systems. JIT and OPT are not so compatible. With JIT the aim is only to make things when they are required. JIT emphasizes one-off production as and when needed, zero defect production, continuing reductions in set-up and change-over times and elimination of work in progress.

Kaplan (1989) has highlighted the consequences of applying traditional management accounting methods to JIT manufacturing. Quoting figures for an integrated circuit testing facility over a three year period from 1986–88, he shows huge reductions in defects, throughput times, inventory and scrap. Yet for the same three year period the management accounting system recorded increasing unit and hourly costs for the test facility. As a result of this misleading information the company concerned opened a new test facility in a country with lower labor costs. This decision was eventually reversed, but only when it was demonstrated that inappropriate measurements were being derived from the traditional management accounting system.

Another consequence of using traditional methods based on allocation of overhead using direct labor hours arises in plants where there is a mixture of highly automated and labor intensive facilities. Highly automated systems usually result in an increase in overhead costs through the costs associated with programming, maintenance activities and such like. This can result in an increased overhead burden in the labor intensive facilities, as most of the overhead arising from the automated plant will be allocated elsewhere.

This can lead to the erroneous conclusion that there is a need to invest in more automation to reduce the costs incurred in labor intensive areas. This type of response can be compared with treating the symptoms of a disease, rather than treating the disease itself. What we should be doing in such situations is thinking about changing our management accounting systems, not further investing in automation that may not be required.

The important implication is that traditional management accounting leads us to the conclusion that improved competitiveness and profitability can be derived from reducing costs and doing things faster. Nothing else seems to matter. Intuitively we know this is not true, but the figures obtained from traditional management accounting systems do not show this! Moreover, it is now often the case that major costs lie in materials and overheads. Focusing upon and aiming to reduce our direct labor costs is relatively ineffective and often irrelevant, yet our traditional management accounting methods emphasize the importance of direct labor costs.

What is surprising is the small impact that these concerns about traditional management accounting systems have had on methods. Most companies still use traditional methods. Despite the fact that the number of people on the shop floor has shrunk dramatically with the advent of automation, a large percentage of plants still use costing methods devised half a century ago when plants were almost 100% labor intensive.

Cost distortions: cross-subsidization arising from customized products

It was pointed out in Chapter 1 that there is an increasing move towards tailoring products to meet customer requirements. In many plants this has led to a mixing of standard and customized products. This change has some important implications for traditional management accounting methods.

The traditional approach to allocating overheads to products is to use the amount of productive capacity (for example, direct labor hours or machine hours) used in making the product. This practice dates back to the 19th century, and in the days when products were relatively simple and overhead costs were very small relative to direct labor and direct material costs, it was quite reasonable to assume that each product accounted for the use of overheads according to how long it took to make the product. Today, however, this assumption is often not reasonable. As we have already pointed out, typically, direct labor accounts for no more than 15% of total manufacturing costs. Overhead costs typically account for about 55% and direct materials about 30% of total manufacturing costs.

Kaplan (1989) illustrates the problems that can arise when using traditional costing methods. He quotes the example of a company manufacturing electric motors. The company in question produces both standard and customized motors. Of the orders placed with the company, about 48% were for a single motor, and 75% were for five motors or less. However, the motors produced for these 75% orders accounted for only 25% of total volume. Orders for more than 100 motors accounted for about 2% of all orders, but these amounted to 44% of total plant output. The important thing to note however, is that the presence of customized motors results in increased overhead costs, because in this type of situation more people are needed for engineering design changes, scheduling, set-up changes, inspection and the like.

Traditional management accounting systems distribute the higher overhead costs arising from more customized production across all motors manufactured, whether they be standard or customized. It does not matter whether overhead costs are allocated on direct labor hours or machine hours, because in either situation a standard motor that represents 10% of the plant output would receive about 10% of the overhead.

A unique customized motor, however, that represents only 0.01% of the plant output has only 0.01% of the factory overhead allocated to it using traditional methods. This is the case, even though the motor might have required special design, purchasing, scheduling, handling and order processing and so on.

The result of this method of allocating overhead is that standard products are likely to be overpriced and as a result may be less competitive. The customized products, on the other hand, are likely to be underpriced, and as a result may be very competitive. This is known as cross-subsidization, which might result in the loss of profitable business through overpricing, and unprofitable business won through underpricing.

Johnson and Kaplan (1987) state that this sort of cross-subsidization happens because traditional product costing methods are primarily focused on allocating costs to products for the purpose of valuing stock, inventory and cost of goods sold. The primary criterion is for a method that performs allocations on a simple and easily measured basis. The cost distortions and cross-subsidization occur because (we believe) the resulting allocations bear some resemblance to actual product costs, and because we use the numbers generated by the system for product costing, rather than financial accounting, for which they are best suited.

Basically, Johnson and Kaplan (1987) have argued that, although 19th century costing techniques were aimed at cost management, costing systems lost their relevance as the emphasis shifted from cost management to cost accounting. This shift came about because the demands of the financial accounting system became dominant. External financial reporting demanded the inclusion of overhead in stock, and the main criteria for overhead allocation became consistency, objectivity and economy, rather than usefulness for decision-making.

Product selling price and limiting factors of production

It is possible to demonstrate, using contribution margin analysis, that product selling price must be changed to maximize profit under conditions when a factor of production is limited, as for example in the case of a bottleneck machine. We will now consider a simple problem to illustrate the point. Note that, in contribution margin analysis, profit equals contribution less fixed costs, and that contribution equals revenue less variable costs.

The objective of the exercise is to use contribution margin analysis to find the most profitable mix of products X and Y given that there are only 40 hours per week available on a particular machine, which we will call machine B, to produce both these products. The fixed costs we will assume to be $5000. Variable costs (materials) amount to $55 for product X and $50 for product Y. The first step is to find the unit contributions of products X and Y. The relevant information is as follows:

	Product X ($)		Product Y ($)
Unit revenue		100	110
Variable costs	55		50
		45	60
Unit contribution		$45	$60

From this calculation we can see that Product Y is the most profitable because it provides the largest contribution. However, there is a limit imposed by machine B, which means that we cannot meet the demand for X and Y. What mix of products is most profitable? To find out it is necessary to calculate the contribution per minute of limiting factor. That is, we need to find out which product makes the most contribution for each minute of the limiting machine time used.

Product X makes a contribution of $45 each, but let us assume that 15 minutes of the limiting machine time is used up to make this contribution. Therefore X's contribution per minute used = 45÷15 = $3 per minute. Product Y makes a contribution of $60 each, but let us assume that 30 minutes of the limiting machine time is used up to make this contribution. Therefore Y's contribution per minute used = 60÷30 = $2 per minute. Therefore product X makes more contribution per minute of machine B's time than Y. We should therefore make all the Xs we can sell and use the time left over to make Ys.

		Minutes
	Time available at Machine B (40×60)	2400
less	Time used up making 100 Xs (100×15)	1500
	Time left for making Ys	900

It takes 30 minutes of machine B's time to make Ys, so the number of Ys we can make will be:

900÷30 = 30 Ys

The profit we can make is now easy to calculate:

	Total contribution from X = 100 × $45 =	4500
	Total contribution from Y = 30 × $60 =	1800
	Total contribution	6300
less	Fixed costs	5000
	Profit under limiting factor	$1300

It is possible to draw a number of conclusions from this simple analysis. First, if we base our product mix on the contribution per unit, we will not achieve maximum profit. Why? The reason is very simple. Although product Y makes a larger per unit contribution than product X, this comparison ignores the time needed to make the two products. We can make two Xs for every Y that we make. It therefore follows that it is more profitable to make Xs because the contribution per minute for X is greater than that for Y.

Our second conclusion is that making extra Ys because of customer demand for Ys is not very profitable, unless the contribution per minute can be increased. In other words if a customer wants more than the 30 Ys that we can make per week, the contribution per minute of machine B's time must equal that obtained from X, that is, $3 per minute. This means that we need a unit contribution of $90 from Y. The selling price of Y must therefore be increased from $110 to $140 for each extra Y, beyond the initial 30 that we make, in order to compensate for the loss of production of Xs.

Note that we lose 2 Xs for every extra Y that we make. Thus, if we were only making 90 Xs in a particular week because of a change in demand, then we could make five extra Ys for $110 each in that week (although our profit would be less). Thus we can see that product price depends on demand for other products, not just on what it costs to make a product. Also, note that when we are making 100 Xs and 30 Ys and we are asked to make more Ys, then the price of extra Ys is more than the price of the 30 that we planned to produce. Management accounting based on absorption costing suggests that the price of extra items should be less than the price of the products that we planned to produce, because of overhead recovery. However, this ignores the fact that by making more Ys we have to make less Xs, which are more profitable than Ys.

Another issue worth mentioning at this point, because it is related to the above, is the question of the cost and pricing implications that arise from other forms of interactions between products. If we are asked to expedite an order, then this will usually result in a rescheduling exercise and possible delays to other orders. When we expedite it usually results in increased costs owing to the rescheduling, any additional material handling that may be required, increased set-up cost, possible overtime working and such like. With traditional management accounting methods these costs would be shown as being charged to the rescheduled orders, and would be reported as unfavorable variances in a standard costing system. However, these extra costs should really be charged to the expedited order, as this was the cause of all our additional costs in the first place. When we do this, the profitability of each order can be more accurately established, and decisions about whether to expedite orders or to charge extra for expediting can be taken in the light of the implications for the profitability of the order. Unfortunately, traditional management accounting systems do not provide this type of information (Brimson, 1991).

Performance measurement and control systems

Most of our financial performance measurement and control systems are based on variance analysis, that is, analysis of the differences between actual costs and planned costs. The purpose of variance analysis is to provide an explanation of why actual total costs are greater or less than planned. This involves us in analyzing major variances and sub-variances.

Variance analysis is based on using the master budget, the flexible budget and measurements of actual costs. By comparing the master budget total cost and the actual total cost we can establish the total variance. This is expressed either as unfavorable (meaning the actual cost was greater than planned) or as favorable (meaning the actual cost was less than planned). The purpose of variance analysis is to explain this total variance.

Usually there are several possible explanations for the total variance. The first is that we produced more or fewer items than the standard quantity. The flexible budget shows how much the actual quantity should cost. The difference between the master budget cost total and the flexible budget cost total will show the expected differences from the master budget as a result of actually making a different quantity. This is called the quantity variance, and is classified as a major variance.

Another possible explanation could be that we spent more or less than planned on direct labor. The direct labor major variance can be calculated by comparing the flexible budget direct labor with the actual direct labor cost. Another explanation could be that we spent more or less than planned on direct materials. The direct materials major variance can be found by comparing the flexible budget direct material with the actual direct material cost. The final explanation is that we spent more or less than planned on overheads. The overhead major variance is calculated by comparing the overheads in the flexible budget and the actual measurements.

Some of the major variances will be favorable and others unfavorable. Favorable variances offset unfavorable variances. Consequently, the total variance will be the sum of all four major variances. These four major variances explain the total variance, and indicate where we have made losses or gains.

Once major variances have been identified, the analysis moves on to consider the causes of the major variances, using sub-variance analysis. This next step in the analysis involves obtaining more detailed information from the flexible budget and the actual costs to establish direct labor hours sub-variance, direct labor rate sub-variance, direct material usage sub-variance, and direct material price sub-variance.

The overhead variance is a little more difficult to analyze, because in theory overheads should be independent of production volumes. In practice however, there are elements of overhead, such as plant hire costs, maintenance costs, energy costs and indirect material costs that do vary. The analysis of the overhead variance will provide an explanation of the difference between the actual amount of production overhead incurred and the amount which is charged to production, through the overhead absorption rates which have previously been determined.

For convenience of analysis and ease of understanding, it is better to divide overheads into fixed and variable components. Major variances for each can then be computed, and then analyzed in terms of their sub-variances.

The variable overhead major variance can be decomposed into variable expenditure sub-variance and variable overhead efficiency sub-variance. The variable expenditure sub-variance arises because of differences between actual and budgeted expenditure, and we need to further analyze this in terms of each individual item of variable overhead to discover the actual cause of the variance. The variable overhead efficiency sub-variance arises because the actual direct labor hours of input may be different from the direct labor hours of input that should have been used. The causes of this latter sub-variance are the same as those causing the labor hours sub-variance.

The fixed overhead major variance can be decomposed into fixed expenditure sub-variance and volume sub-variance. The fixed expenditure sub-variance arises because of differences between actual and budgeted expenditure, which needs further analysis in terms of each individual item of fixed overhead to discover the actual cause of the variance. The volume sub-variance arises because of differences between actual and budgeted production. Volume sub-variance is worth considering in a little more detail, as it is a point of criticism of the way we misuse information from traditional management accounting systems.

Over the short term, fixed overheads do not fluctuate with output. So when our actual production volumes are less than budgeted production volumes, the fixed overhead charged to production will be less than that budgeted, and our volume sub-variance will be adverse. In cases where actual production is greater than that budgeted, then the sub-variance will be favorable. The possible causes of volume sub-variances are changes in demand for products, poor production scheduling, labor efficiency, poor quality, labor disputes and such like. To discover more about the cause of the volume sub-variance, we can decompose this into two further sub-variances: volume efficiency sub-variance and capacity sub-variance.

The volume efficiency sub-variance will tell us about the efficiency of labor in the factory, and its causes are the same as those for the labor hours sub-variance, that is, it will provide a measure of the degree to which capacity is being efficiently utilized. The volume capacity sub-variance will provide information about the utilization of capacity itself. Failures to fully utilize capacity can arise for several reasons, as outlined above.

Perhaps the most important thing to note about fixed overhead variance analysis is this. Total fixed overhead variance analysis is equivalent to the under or over recovery of fixed overheads. The sub-variance analysis tells us the reasons for the over or under recovery of fixed overheads.

The final variance to mention is revenue variance, which is the difference between our actual and budgeted revenue. The difference between the master revenue budget and the actual revenue gives us the total revenue variance. We can explain this in terms of two variances, the revenue quantity variance and the price variance. The revenue quantity variance is the difference between the master and flexible budgets and shows the expected difference in revenue as a result of having sold a different number of products from that given in the master budget. The price variance is the difference between the flexible budget and the actual budget, and is the difference between the standard and the actual selling prices.

The total cost variance and the total revenue variance show the differences between actual and master budgeted costs and revenues. Both these will therefore reconcile with actual and master budgeted profits. It is thus possible to explain any favorable or unfavorable profit variance in terms of favorable or unfavorable revenue and cost variances.

The case against traditional performance measurement and control systems

The scope of management accounting

Kaplan (1988) has noted that management accounting systems need to address three different functions:

(1) Inventory valuation for financial accounting purposes, allocating periodic production costs between goods sold and goods in stock.
(2) Operational control, providing feedback to production and department managers on the resources consumed (labour, materials, energy, overhead) during an operational period.
(3) Individual product cost measurement.

Our traditional standard cost systems are not designed to measure product costs accurately or to provide timely information for operational control purposes. Their main purpose is to allow us to accurately value inventory.

Standard costs, it has been argued, often bear no relation to the resources consumed to design, produce, market and deliver our products. A product cost is only considered accurate when it mirrors the complete manufacturing process. Standard costing systems, in general, do not provide a mirror of the complete manufacturing process and may be sending inappropriate messages leading to incorrect decisions.

It has been argued by Kaplan (1989) that management accounting calculations (like the allocation of overhead to products and departments, or the computation of volume variances) should not be part of the control systems used for operational purposes, because these numbers will obscure the information needed to operate effectively.

For example, total fixed overhead variance is required for calculating product costs for stock valuations, but even undergraduate level textbooks (Drury, 1988) point out that its use for cost control purposes is questionable. Volume variances, however, also provide misleading information. If we make less products than budgeted for, the volume variance will be adverse and overheads will be under recovered, which means that profits will be reduced. If our volume variances are made favorable by making more than the budgeted volume, then overhead will be over recovered and profits will increase, even though the products are being made for stock and are just sitting in the warehouses.

Kaplan argues that no single system can adequately answer the demands made by the diverse functions of cost systems. While it is possible for one method to capture all the detailed transaction data, the processing of this information for diverse purposes and users demands separate, customized development. If we try to satisfy all our requirements with a single cost system, we will be unlikely to perform important managerial functions adequately.

Non-financial measures of performance

It is self evident that the systems used for performance measurement should be capable of providing information on efficiency and effectiveness of operations in a timely and accurate manner. However, existing traditional systems have problems with respect to these requirements. Most often relevant information is too aggregate and is received too late to take corrective actions. Moreover, the information received is usually distorted by unnecessary allocations, and excessive attention is devoted to financial measures of performance. Consequently we do not provide important non-financial operating measures of performance.

Timeliness is one of the most important criteria for a useful performance measurement system and we should relate the timing of information to our operating conditions. If we produce output continually then we should have at least daily reports. In some situations however, it may be more appropriate to produce information every hour or for each batch.

The information that we provide needs to summarize what and how much was produced, the unit costs, and the actual quantities of variable input resources used in manufacturing such as materials, labor, energy consumption, machine time used and such like. We also need to make available information about the quality of the output, along with other non-financial performance measures that we judge to be critical to achieving strategic goals.

Traditional management accounting, of course, stresses the adherence to standards that we, engineers and managers, determine. Any unfavorable variances are highlighted for explanation and correction. However, our traditional idea of undertaking variance analysis against a static standard is often not very useful in modern manufacturing.

What we need is information to support continuous improvement activities in relation to quality, yields, manufacturing times and efficiencies. When we are engaged in continuous improvement activities we all need information that will help us to detect problems quickly. And we need information that will guide our experimentation and learning activities. In traditional management accounting systems, knowledge exists centrally, and is imposed on other people and their operations. When we manage by continuous improvement, the improvements are suggested and made locally. The focus of performance measurement and control systems has therefore to shift away from adherence to centrally determined standards, to the provision of timely, accurate and relevant information for local experimentation, learning and improvement activities. Traditional management accounting systems do not provide this information.

Financial summaries of departmental spending, or actual batch costs, only provide partial indicators of the efficiency of operations. It is important that we use other, non-financial indicators, such as parts per million (ppm) defect rates, process yields, throughput times and so on.

Another problem with traditional management accounting systems, with their focus on financial measures and variances, is that they are unable to measure the skills, training and morale of our people. If they do not share our goals we cannot become a world class competitor. The attitudes, motivation, morale, skills and education of all our people is a valuable resource, and is just as important as any tangible assets.

Basically, the financial measures of performance generated by traditional management accounting systems provide an inadequate summary of our manufacturing operations. In today's global economy it is necessary to use non-financial measures of performance covering areas such as quality, inventory levels, productivity, flexibility, deliverability and employees. Without these measures we cannot hope to make any meaningful evaluation of our performance. If we achieve a satisfactory financial performance, but show stagnation or deterioration of performance against other, non-financial criteria, then it is highly unlikely that we will be able to become, or long remain, a world class manufacturing company.

Concluding comments

In this chapter we have tried to demonstrate that traditional management accounting techniques are severely flawed. The basis of the case is that they do not fully capture and describe a complex situation, and as a result they provide us with misleading information, which can lead to wrong investment decisions and a focus on issues that bear no relationship to strategic goals and away from issues of achievement and maintenance of an agile manufacturing enterprise. In Chapter 9 we will describe a framework for management accounting that better suits agile manufacturing.

Key points

- Understanding the limitations and applicability of the traditional management accounting techniques is crucial to success in agile manufacturing.
- Management accounting systems influence the behavior of people throughout the enterprise.
- Traditional management accounting systems help to preserve traditional approaches to manufacturing, our values and our beliefs.
- Management accounting systems are a key leverage point for long term changes. However, changing the management accounting system brings its own problems.
- The traditional investment appraisal methods, on their own, are not well suited to supporting investments in agile manufacturing. There are real difficulties in using these methods to make the strategic investments that are required for agile manufacturing.

- The fact that we face difficulties in trying to quantify investments in agile manufacturing does not mean that we should give up trying to quantify benefits. It implies that the traditional approaches need to be enhanced.

- The use of traditional absorption costing for management decision-making that involves using product cost information is often inappropriate, because of the cross-subsidizations introduced by this method.

- The traditional performance measurements and control systems, which are largely based on financial information, are inappropriate for agile manufacturing.

- One management accounting system is probably not sufficient for agile manufacturing. We need several management accounting systems for different purposes.

References

Bradley I. (1972). *A History of Machine Tools*. Hemel Hempstead: Model & Allied

Brimson J.A. (1991). *Activity Accounting. An Activity-Based Costing Approach*. New York: John Wiley

Drury C. (1988). *Management and Cost Accounting. 2nd edn*. London: Chapman & Hall

Ingersoll Engineers (1982). *It's Not So Much What the Japanese Do... ...It's What We Don't Do*. Rugby: Ingersoll Engineers

Johnson H.T. and Kaplan R.S. (1987). *Relevance Lost. The Rise and Fall of Management Accounting*. Cambridge MA: Harvard Business School

Kaplan R.S. (1984). Yesterday's accounting undermines production. *Harvard Business Review*, July–August, 95–101

Kaplan K.S. (1986). Must CIM be justified by faith alone? *Harvard Business Review*, March–April, 87–95

Kaplan R.S. (1988). One cost system isn't enough. *Harvard Business Review*, January–February, 61–66

Kaplan R.S. (1989). Management accounting for advanced technological environments. *Science*, **245**, 819–23

Meredith J.R. and Suresh N.C. (1986). Justification techniques for advanced manufacturing technologies. *Int. J. Production Research*, **24**(5), 1043–57

Mundy K. (1984). The financial justification of FMS. In *Proc. 1st Int. Machine Tool Conference* (Lane K.A., ed.), pp. 31–9. Kempston: IFS

Primrose P.L. (1991). *Investing in Manufacturing Technology*. London: Chapman & Hall

Senker P. (1983). Some problems in justifying CAD/CAM. In *Proc. 2nd European Conf. Automated Manufacturing* (Rooks B.W., ed.), pp. 59–66. Kempston: IFS

Small B.W. (1983). Paying for the technology – making the intangibles, tangible. In *Proc. 2nd European Conf. on Automated Manufacturing* (Rooks B.W., ed.), pp. 183–7. Kempston: IFS

Turney P.B.B. (1992). *Common Cents. The ABC Performance Breakthrough.* Hillsboro OR: Cost Technology

Watts P.L. Lewis A. and Nagpal B.K. (1982). Economic considerations in industrial robotics. In *Proc. 23rd Int. Machine Tool Design and Research Conf.* (Davies B.J., ed.), pp. 527–32. London: Macmillan

5

The traditional organizational, control, technological and design paradigms

Introduction

What we refer to in this book as traditional manufacturing has been developing over a long period of time since the start of the industrial revolution in the middle of the 18th century. It is our belief that traditional manufacturing can be characterized by five primary paradigms. The first paradigm is traditional management accounting practice, which we have discussed in Chapter 4. The four other paradigms are the organizational paradigm, the control paradigm, the technological paradigm and the technological design paradigm.

We treated the management accounting paradigm separately from the other four paradigms because we believe that it is the traditional management accounting paradigm that is largely responsible for maintaining the others. If we replace the traditional management accounting paradigm with one that matches the needs of agile manufacturing environments, then it is highly likely that this will enable the replacement of the remaining four.

What we will attempt to do in this chapter is describe these four paradigms, and show why they are now inappropriate and outdated. We will also try to demonstrate the relationships that exist between them. We will start by considering the organizational and control paradigms.

The traditional organizational and control paradigms

The main characteristics of traditional plants are centralization of control and decision-making, steep hierarchies, functional factory layout, horizontal and vertical division of labor, de-skilling, functional specialization and standardization of working methods.

Of course, many of our traditional organizational and control concepts are very old and can be traced back through history to the earliest civilizations. However, many of the concepts which we now associate with traditional plants only came to prominence during the Victorian period, especially towards the end of the 19th century, when these principles for organizing and controlling plants became established as normal practice. Since it was in this period that the application of these concepts, throughout manufacturing industry, started to become common place, we call the norm that is based upon these traditional concepts the **1890s model of plant organization and control**.

To a greater or lesser extent, many of our manufacturing enterprises still use these Victorian principles of organization and control. We typically have a pyramid shaped organizational structure of the form shown in Figure 5.1. Information flows upwards, and control is exercised from the top downwards. Six or seven levels of management are often the norm.

Our manufacturing facilities are also commonly arranged on a functional basis, with turning machines located in one part of the plant, milling machines in another, assembly work in another, and so on. Moreover, our control of these functions is often based on the hub and spoke model shown in Figure 5.2, with control and decision-making centralized in the planning office. We have also held a strong belief that shop floor people should leave their brains at home. Creativity, skill, experience and judgment are not required. It is management's job to solve any problems and to tell shop floor people what to do.

As a consequence of our beliefs, our pyramid structures can be divided into three layers, as shown in Figure 5.3, with thinkers at the top of the organization, and doers at the bottom. In between, there is an army of people who spend their time controlling and monitoring the work of those at the bottom. They translate the output from the thinkers into plans and instructions for the doers. And this army of controllers send reports back to the thinkers on how well things are going, usually within the framework of aggregated financial data that tells people at the top very little about how well the enterprise is really performing.

If we look at the details of the layers in the traditional organization, we will see that it is modelled along the lines of a military organization,

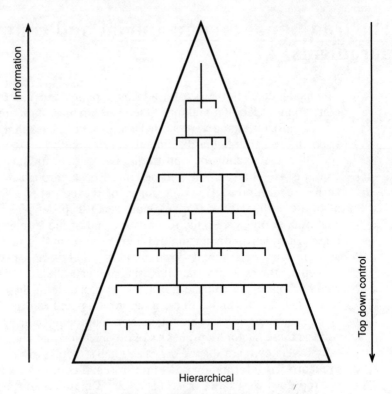

Figure 5.1 The 1890s model of organization.

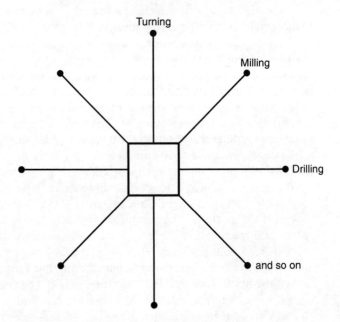

Figure 5.2 The 1890s model of control, centralized and process based.

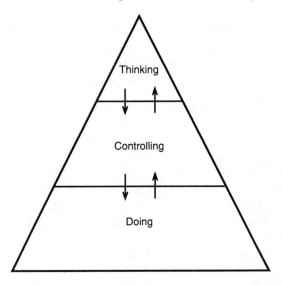

Figure 5.3   The traditional organization: separation of thinking, controlling and doing.

as illustrated in Figure 5.4. At the very top we have corporate officers (staff generals). Underneath them there are divisional managers or plant managers (field commanders). Reporting to the divisional or plant managers are departmental heads (commanding officers), who direct the work of section leaders (corps commanders). Within sections there are supervisors and foremen (company or platoon leaders), who give orders to shop floor people (front line troops). And of course, one's perception of the progress of the battle improves the further one moves away from the front line!

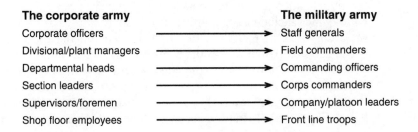

Figure 5.4   The military command and control structure of traditional organizations.

It is, of course, no accident that the organization of manufacturing enterprises mirrors that of the military organization. At the time when the first large industrial organizations were taking shape in the 19th century, the military provided the only fully developed model of organization known to work reasonably well, albeit under a set of rather special circumstances which do not exist in ordinary civilian life.

Several notable people in the 18th and 19th centuries exercised influence over the development of the 1890s model of plant organization and control. These include Adam Smith, Andrew Ure, Charles Babbage, Max Weber, Frederick Taylor, and during the early part of this century, Henri Fayol and Henry Ford, followed later by Alfred Sloan.

Max Weber, for example, was a 19th century sociologist. Although he was not involved in manufacturing industry, he has had an important influence over our views of what constitutes an effective organizational structure, through his concept of the bureaucratic organization. Weber argued that the most efficient type of organization was a bureaucratic one which displayed three important characteristics.

The first was that the duties and responsibilities of all members of the organization should be clearly defined. The second was that the various positions in the organization should be arranged hierarchically, with each person responsible to a superior and responsible for subordinates, with the exception, of course, of those at the top and bottom of the pyramid. The third was that an elaborate system of rules should govern the manner in which each person carried out his duties.

Government departments seem to be particularly prone to the bureaucratic model of organization. Weber's ideas are, however, also well established in both state-owned and private enterprises throughout the world, although the extent to which organizations are modelled along bureaucratic lines varies quite widely.

Henri Fayol, a French industrialist, writing in the early part of the 20th century, put forward ideas that we have come to regard as classic management wisdom. Fayol argued that the process of management was about planning, organizing, coordinating, commanding and controlling. And this process is something that we *exercise* over the personnel within the organization according to a clear and definitive set of guiding principles which include equity, unity of command and scalar chain. Within the framework of Fayol's school of management, the focus is on the organizational structure and the principles by which it is governed. The structure is carefully defined, the lines of authority and responsibility are delineated, and the rules of law, policy and protocol are established from the top management levels down to the personnel who work on the shop floor (Fayol, 1916). In this respect, Fayol's thinking mirrors that of Weber.

Frederick Taylor, a 19th century mechanical engineer, is another individual who has influenced our views on organization through the concept of so called **scientific management**. Taylor advocated a system of factory management, many aspects of which we still use today. This system is based on the vertical division of labor, with the separation of thinking and doing and the centralization of all decision-making. Taylor believed that all workers should be told exactly what to do and that their working methods should be standardized. He believed that there was only one best way of doing work that could be scientifically established. His system also prescribed functional specialization. The fundamental concept underlying Taylor's system of management is uniquely expressed in Taylor's own words (Taylor, 1907):

> 'Under our system of management the worker is told in minute detail what to do and how to do it and any improvement made upon the instructions given to him is fatal to success.'

Taylor became quite notorious for his principles of scientific management. Some of this notoriety stems from the fact that he promoted his views with missionary zeal. But he also appears to have been a person with a narrow outlook who was obsessed with the cause of scientific management. Taylor, however, was in many ways only expressing what many managers and engineers had been practicing, in perhaps less extreme form, since the beginning of the industrial revolution, notably, to use work organizational methods to firstly reduce manufacturing to a number of simple operations requiring little skill or initiative, and secondly to exercise detailed control over the manufacturing process.

Although many of Taylor's ideas about how to manage an organization were certainly not new at the time he was advocating them, they have, however, become associated with Taylor, hence the term Taylorism, which is now often used as a derogatory expression to brand people who still adhere to traditional concepts. Taylorism, therefore, for want of another label, is a term that is used to denote a traditional manufacturing strategy that is based on treating human beings in a narrow mechanistic way. It consists of a way of organizing work that aims to maximize control over all aspects of the work taking place within the enterprise. It is based on the imposition of hierarchical control, and one of the objectives is to minimize variety arising from unwanted human involvement in the manufacturing process.

It is true that most of us, to a greater or lesser extent, still commonly, and often unquestioningly, practice today, in our manufacturing organizations, concepts which are based on the Taylor model. However, we make a fundamental mistake if we assume that the Taylor model is nothing more than just a rather dated school of management. It is more than a management philosophy and more than a way of organizing plants. The Taylor Model also provides the foundations and principles on which we have based engineering disciplines (industrial engineering, production engineering, manufacturing systems engineering and so on).

This latter point in crucial. We can start to change organizations and management philosophies, and many manufacturing companies are doing just that. But we must understand that the Taylor Model is also a paradigm. It provides our managers and engineers with a set of principles that were established by Taylor and his associates.

It is commonly assumed that the essential elements of the model are separation of thinking and doing, the belief in the one best way, and a mechanistic model of human beings (that is people are machines that can be scientifically analyzed). However, this is only a partial picture. There are in fact several elements to the model, these being (Kidd, 1988; Gibson, 1992):

- *Reductionism*   The decomposition of systems into component parts or elements, which are then dealt with in isolation.
- *Optimization of components*   It is believed that optimizing each individual element of the system leads to optimization at the systems level.
- *One best way*   There is only one best way of doing something, which can be determined through analysis.
- *Absence of goal definition*   Problems and goals are taken as given, the task is to find a solution.
- *Mechanistic model of people*   Technology is addressed in a vacuum without regard for people. The assumption is that people are only motivated by financial reward and that they are nothing more than (complex) machines.
- *Hierarchical and centralizing style*   Everyone is an employee and employees should do what they are told. Employees are not expected to question decisions or to contribute their experience to the decision-making process. Decisions should be taken centrally by an elite few (Taylor's *esprit de corps*). The rest have to follow instructions and decisions.
- *Value free design*   Design is scientific and value free. It has no moral or ethical implications or effects on society or individuals. Preferences, bias, prejudice, politics and such like have no influence on the outcome.
- *Separation of thinking and doing*   Everything that needs to be done can be worked out through analysis. There is no need to pay attention to experience, tacit knowledge, intuition and so on. These are not required, and as a consequence of this, separation of thinking and doing is possible.
- *Individual reward for individual effort*   Reward people for what they do as individuals, not for what they do as part of a team.

In recent years we have begun to rename industrial engineers and production engineers as manufacturing systems engineers. However, we have not fundamentally changed the underlying principles of these professions. The reason is because we have failed to understand that not only are manufacturing enterprises built on the Taylor Model, but so are our minds. Many of us are convinced deep down that the model is the right way to do things. The essence of the job is still about getting ideas out of the heads of the thinkers and into the hands of the people on the shop floor, using mediators and controllers, or their technological substitutes.

The Taylor Model is so deep rooted and a part of our culture that we have often failed to recognize its existence or to accept that we have it in our own minds. It is so taken for granted that its assumptions are not questioned.

The case against using the Taylor Model in manufacturing

Within the organizational and management sciences the Taylor Model is often regarded as a set of simplistic and barbaric concepts (Nadworny, 1955; Rose, 1978; Peters and Waterman, 1982). However, although we are beginning to change, the model is still the dominant philosophy of work organization and the spirit that guides the development of our technologies. What we should realize however, is that the case against the model, and all other philosophies based on 19th century thinking, is irrefutable.

Business is now so complex and difficult, the survival of firms so hazardous and the environment so increasingly competitive and fraught with danger, that our continued existence depends on the day-to-day mobilization of every ounce of intelligence. The Taylor Model is therefore no longer relevant, as it only works in environments which are fairly static and stable. It is totally inappropriate for our modern competitive environment. Only if we can move beyond the model, and leave all its assumptions behind, can we hope to survive and prosper in the long term.

The Taylor Model also assumes that money is the only important factor that motivates work. This is well known to be an erroneous assumption. The model, therefore, tends to result in a working environment where we ignore many of the important factors that motivate people, and this can lead to a wide range of problems that can interfere with the achievement of our manufacturing objectives (Brown, 1954; Nadworny, 1955; Argyle, 1972; Rose, 1978). The model is based upon the social values of the Victorian era, which generally subsumed human considerations to those of monetary ones. Such an outlook is unacceptable in a modern society.

The Taylor Model tends to lead to the creation of jobs that require little skill or initiative. When our workforce was poorly educated we may have been able to justify this. However, since the time of Smith, Ure, Babbage, Taylor and Fayol, significant educational developments have taken place and the workforce of today is much better educated than the workforce of the 18th and 19th centuries. And with education comes higher aspirations.

There are compelling reasons why we should work to improve quality of working life. Significant differences often exist between the school environment and the working conditions which many school leavers may have to live with. Within the educational system, our children are educated most often in pleasant surroundings. Here they learn how to think and begin to develop the ability to make choices. Moving from this environment, some school leavers may well find a completely different type of situation in the working environment, where thinking and the ability to make choices have very little part to play. The Taylor Model creates a mismatch between personal work aspirations and actual job requirements. It has therefore become an anachronism.

It is also questionable whether the Taylor Model achieves what we have claimed it can achieve, because few people, if any, have ever fully implemented it. Also, we have never found it completely possible to eliminate the need for human skill and initiative. Very often therefore, people are expected to compensate for the inadequacies of our technologies and organizational practices, but they are often in a poor position to do so.

A further result of the Taylor Model is that it tends to result in a top-heavy management hierarchy, as the number of people involved in supervision and planning increases to compensate for the removal of initiative from the people at the bottom of the organizational pyramid. The result of the model is, therefore, ever increasing indirect labor costs.

In traditional manufacturing organizations, we have viewed people who we classified as direct labor as a cost to be minimized. These people are in fact a resource that we have under-utilized. In the long term, faced with increasing competition, we cannot afford to continue to waste our resources. The emerging business environment is characterized by intensive domestic and international competition that did not exist on the same scale in Taylor's time. The greatest scope for improvements in competitiveness lies in reducing indirect labor (overhead) costs and inventory and stock levels, and in increasing the rapidity of manufacture and the ability to respond quickly to customers' orders. This requires a fundamental shift towards a new model of organization if these required improvements are to be fully achieved.

Finally, we note that the Taylor Model is highly divisive because it divides people into two distinct groups, those who are subject to Taylor's methods and thinking (mostly shop floor people and some office people) and those who are not (management and other professionals). This tends to encourage the *us and them attitude* that has become synonymous with poor industrial relations. This type of attitude is outdated and counter-productive to the interests of all. As the Japanese have discovered to their profit, cooperation is commercially more beneficial than confrontation and opposition. The model helps to maintain the outdated distinctions between our so called blue and white collar employees, and keeps our industrial enterprises locked into a system of distrust and individualism.

The Taylor Model is a bottleneck on our progress towards new manufacturing paradigms. Its assumptions are at variance with those of approaches based on continuous improvements, where standards are not centrally determined and imposed from the top, but where all the people are involved in strategically driven efforts to improve various aspects of their work. The model stops us moving forward and keeps us locked into a framework where everything is judged by the values of the past. It constrains our thinking and leads us to reject, or to weaken, new ideas about how industrial enterprises need to be managed.

This is simultaneously an opportunity and a problem. It is an opportunity because in a world where many of us still adhere to the Taylor Model, those who can find the means to break free of the Taylor bottleneck can potentially gain tremendous competitive advantage. It is a problem because it is likely that many of our enterprises will not be able to face up to the transition away from the model, or will do so too slowly, and as a result, will see their competitive edge continuously erode, while those who do break free start to move ahead.

Traditional problems in the workplace

There has been an historical trend in the design and development of technological systems and work organizations towards division of labor, and the control, simplification and routinization of work. This general trend has had an impact on people's physical and mental wellbeing.

Professions such as industrial psychologists have been concerned for many years with problems in the workplace such as alienation and lack of job satisfaction. Even in today's competitive environment, where people provide one of the keys to improved competitive performance, we still have alienated people because they have no control over their work. The work of these people is meaningless to them, they feel that they do not belong to any community, and their work is not an important aspect of their personalities or lives.

If we create a work environment in which people feel alienated, it will have an important negative effect on their mental and physical health. It is known that high blood pressure, ulcers, heart disease, anxiety and mental stress can result directly from working in such environments. Östberg (1986) for example, mentions a study undertaken that showed a significantly elevated incidence of myocardial infarction for men in occupations involving work characterized by hectic activities (which can result, for example, from machine pacing) and few possibilities to learn new things.

Unfortunately it is still a fact of working life that much of the dissatisfaction arises most commonly at the lower levels of organizations, that is on the shop floor and in the lower echelons of office based work. It is also true that dissatisfaction is much greater in the more repetitive, machine paced work, and much lower in jobs involving variety and self control of the work process. The conclusion is that interesting jobs, involving the opportunity to use and develop one's own ideas and skills, are more satisfying than jobs where there is little or no scope for such things.

In the Taylor Model it is assumed that people only work for financial reward, and that other rewards are unimportant. There is no doubt that financial reward is a major motivating factor, but it is not the only return. There are also more intrinsic reasons. These include opportunities for socialization, for working in groups and working towards the fulfillment of group goals, and for making a contribution to our enterprises. Interesting work can also confer status and self respect. This comes from the feeling of having a useful role to play, and from the value that others attach to their ideas and skills. When we assume that financial reward is the only important reward that people seek from their work, we often create a situation where there is a significant lack of motivation, and financial incentive schemes will never be able to fully compensate for the loss or lack of intrinsic motivation.

The occurrence of people related difficulties in the workplace is not something that many of us would dispute; there is plenty of evidence in the management science literature, and in our own experience, to support the statement that such problems exist. Can the financial cost of such problems and the competitive implications be ignored?

It is known that people related problems in the workplace can contribute to absenteeism, low productivity, high labor turnover and a general lack of cooperation in relationships. In the more severe cases these types of problem can contribute to accident rates and also result in industrial relations difficulties, strikes and even sabotage. Apart from the obvious indirect costs incurred as a result of all these problems (for example, the indirect costs arising from the need to be continually recruiting and training new people), quality of working life problems can, in some situations, lead to the failure of people to respond satisfactorily in emergency situations which might affect safety, the environment, production plant and products. For example, Bainbridge (1983), in discussing the ironies of automation, refers to the fact that high levels of stress can actually lead to human errors.

The implications of these sorts of problems for current traditional practices are profound. Significant improvements towards achieving world class agile manufacturing performance cannot be achieved until we resolve these types of problem. When we attempt to implement concepts such as **total quality management** (TQM) and so on within the framework of a manufacturing system that creates people related problems, we will, and do, fail to achieve the sought after results.

However, we should clearly understand that these people related problems are not a problem in themselves, but are only a symptom of a much deeper rooted problem. The real problem is the way that we organize and deal with people. Until we address the root problem, our implementation of concepts such as TQM will continue to show disappointing results.

Organizational issues and benefits

We could argue that the description of traditional manufacturing enterprises that we gave in the first section of this chapter, are a gross caricature of the real situation. However, there is enough truth in the descriptions to warrant making the point that we can no longer afford to continue with these Victorian practices and to maintain our antiquated beliefs and cultures. We need new forms of organization, new work practices, new beliefs and a new culture.

Comparisons between Japanese and Western manufacturing enterprises (Burnes and Weekes, 1989) often show that the Japanese regard people as assets. In the West we typically regard our people as a cost to be minimized. In our traditional plants, shop floor people are often expected to leave their brains at home, or to think about only those issues that they are told to think about! Japanese companies, it is claimed, tap into the creativity of their shop floor people.

Of course, this is also a gross caricature of Japanese enterprises. Many of them are just as bad as our own manufacturing companies, but we only get to hear about the really good companies, while we tend to hear more about our own bad companies than our good ones.

It is also claimed that the organizational structure of many Japanese enterprises is generally more flexible and responsive than that of our own enterprises. The Japanese have fewer hierarchical levels, fewer specialists, fewer but more integrated departments and greater decentralization of decision-making. Again, these are claims that should not be taken as being general characteristics of all Japanese manufacturing companies.

With the implementation of new manufacturing technologies we have achieved a realization of the importance of organizational change. Many of our new technologies have highlighted the inappropriateness of our traditional organizational structures and work practices. In addition, techniques such as just-in-time manufacturing have demonstrated and reminded us that new technology is *not the sole source of improved competitiveness*.

The benefits of organizational change can include shorter throughput times, reduced inventory, improved product quality, more economic operating conditions and improved responsiveness. For example, by changing a plant to an organizational structure based on natural groups, it is possible to shorten throughput times by as much as 80% and to reduce in-process inventory by as much as 60%. The key point is that we can achieve these benefits without any investment in new technology (this of course does not mean that new technology is not needed or can be ignored). These benefits are solely the result of organizational changes. These organizational changes can also result in simplified material flows, easier production planning and control and improved job satisfaction, which can lead to more highly motivated people.

Some of our companies have already reorganized their plants from traditional process layouts to ones based on natural groups (Klingenberg and Kränzle, 1987). As a result of organizational and work practice changes, these companies are achieving reduced costs, improved due date performance, a high speed of response to quantitative and qualitative changes of demand, improved quality and a reduction in breakdowns. The improvements that are often claimed from such changes are summarized in Figure 5.5.

In these change situations, we can reduce costs because we usually achieve a net reduction in labor, and because less capital is needed to fund the business. Improvements in quality arise because people take responsibility for the quality of their work. Defects are therefore detected at an earlier stage or avoided altogether. This brings further cost savings through reduced rework and scrap.

Improvements in flexibility can be achieved because throughput times are reduced. Organizational factors which lengthen throughput times include too many levels in the hierarchy, too many functional departments, complex procedures and long signal processing times (Bolwijn *et al.*, 1986). Organizational changes that lead to reduced hierarchies, a smaller number of departments, simpler procedures and faster signal processing can therefore result in shorter throughput times.

Plant planning and control functions can also become much simpler as a result of organizational changes. If we are prepared to decentralize some planning activities such as detailed scheduling, we no longer need systems that attempt to organize the correct schedule of work for every

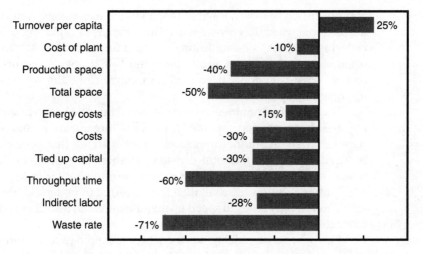

Figure 5.5   The benefits of organizational and work practice changes.

single operation on every single resource at every moment. Instead the system only needs to provide plant planners with information, allowing each natural group to be loaded with a sensible volume of work over a specified period. The detailed planning and scheduling can be done by people working within these natural groups. This can result in much simpler and cheaper computer systems, and the savings made on capital investments in computers can then be used to support other worthwhile projects, leading to better utilization of investment capital.

Organizational changes also provide the basis for achieving continuing improvement in manufacturing. For example, a rejected part, or a half finished item waiting for new tooling, or a part program that can be improved, or a design feature that leads to machining or assembly difficulties represent time and money wasted and competitive opportunities missed (Hayes, Wheelwright and Clark, 1988). Remedying these problems is partly what continuing improvement in manufacturing is about and is an issue for everyone. To tap into creativity we need new organizational structures and work practices.

The role of technology

One important characteristic of our traditional approaches to manufacturing has been the dominant role of technology, which we have relied upon to improve performance and to solve problems. In traditional manufacturing however, we have tended to use technology in the form of automation, which has provided us with a means of replacing people, or reducing their role, or diminishing the need for their skills. We have also often seen technology as a solution to most of, if not all, our problems, and we have commonly perceived technology to be the sole source of improved competitiveness.

The role of technology in our traditional approaches to manufacturing has been shaped by our traditional organization and control paradigm. Adam Smith, for example, demonstrated that costs could be reduced by using horizontal division of labor. This involves taking a whole work process and breaking it down into simpler tasks, each of which often requires less skill than that required to undertake the whole job. This not only tends to speed up manufacture, but also allows cheaper labor to be used.

This way of organizing work enables technology to be introduced more easily. While the whole work process may be relatively complex and thus difficult to automate, the simplified constituent tasks are usually much easier to automate. Economic and technical feasibility are usually then the only constraints on the introduction of technology to automate the relatively simple tasks created using horizontal division of labor.

The Taylor Model, which is based on vertical division of labor, has also influenced the role that we give to technology in manufacturing. A management system that is based on centralization of decision-making engenders the development of a technology with centralized characteristics. For example, numerical control with its emphasis on office based programming is based on the Taylor Model and its associated belief that all decision-making should be centralized.

Our technology has always had a dominant role in manufacturing and our faith in its role as the sole source of competitive advantage was perhaps at its height during the 1980s. During this period we believed that new advanced computer based technologies would provide the answer to the competitive problems that we faced. We believed that the technology would bring about improvements in both competitiveness and profitability. Research in advanced manufacturing technology was therefore encouraged and promoted throughout the industrialized world, often through government funded research programmes. Our orientation towards technology led us to develop advanced manufacturing concepts such as CIM, which we promoted heavily during the heyday of research policy based on technology push.

There has always been some disagreement over the definition of CIM. It is a term that has, unfortunately, been used to refer to the application of any type of computer based manufacturing technology. Thus for example, it has been known for people to claim that the use of CNC machine tools is a CIM application. It is our belief however, that CIM should not be confused with computer based technologies. Nor should it be seen as a question of linking computers in different departments. These are a part of CIM, but the most important aspects lie in what can be described as a business wide effort to integrate company activities such as design, sales and marketing, production planning, manufacture, research and development and financial management. Another important feature is the concern to link geographically separate sites within the business, and the electronic linking of a business with its customers and suppliers.

This question of integration is very important, and CIM is an important component of this integration, to which we will return later. In the meantime we note here that, within the framework imposed by traditional manufacturing concepts, we set about the development of CIM by focusing on the important technical considerations such as communication systems and protocols, databases, the development of data interface standards, computerized control systems and so on. We depicted CIM as a mixture of computers, software and communication systems which would allow us to remove duplication of data, provide up-to-date information and enable rapid transfer of data from one department to another. Because of our orientation towards using technology to automate, we also saw CIM as involving a high level of automation in design, production planning, manufacturing and warehousing. Above all, however, we saw CIM as providing us with the capability to achieve real-time centralized supervision and control of all operational processes.

In practice our vision of CIM has often been very functionally limited. Far from being a business wide concept that achieves integration between all aspects of a business, including marketing, R&D and such like, it is often primarily concerned with three functional areas; design, planning and manufacturing. When we referred to computer integrated manufacturing, we meant just that. The M in CIM really did mean manufacturing and nothing else, and our focus has been on using the technology to do more efficiently what we already do, even if the ways in which we do things are no longer appropriate.

Furthermore, most of us have failed to fully comprehend that the benefits of new computers and communication technologies lie in enabling things that we cannot easily do now. Such comprehension, however, requires some entrepreneurial and business flair, which most of us, whether we be technical specialists, government civil servants or academics, often do not possess. Those of us who have had responsibility as business leaders and managers, even when we understood the technologies, which has not been very often, have often failed to provide the direction, because we have not had the courage and the vision to recognize the potential and new opportunities created by the technologies.

The thinking of most of us who have been involved in the development of CIM has been shaped too much by the past. We too often apply past thinking to the new technologies, and thus miss the opportunities.

Our focus in CIM has been on centralized supervision and control. These issues are a recurrent theme in our traditional approach to manufacturing and these out-dated beliefs have had an unfortunate influence over the development of CIM, which we can, unfortunately, regard as the ultimate realization of the organizational concepts on which our traditional manufacturing is based.

In the past we have tended to treat people as an issue of secondary importance in the CIM development and implementation process, in accordance with normal practice. In the traditional approaches to manufacturing, we have commonly perceived people as a nuisance, a source of uncertainty and a necessary evil. We have tended to develop CIM to increase our control over people, using the mechanism of data collection systems and centralized computer control systems to achieve this goal.

The end of technological dominance

At the beginning of the 1980s many of us saw advanced manufacturing technology and information technology as a panacea for the lack of competitiveness in many of our manufacturing companies. It is now evident that our problems are more deep rooted than just simple overmanning or out-of-date technology. It now appears that we have placed too much faith in our technology. There is no doubt that technology is important, but it is only part of the story. Unfortunately we have tended to approach manufacturing as a set of technical problems, and sought technical solutions. Often the problems have not been technical, but have been organizational or derived from inappropriate work practices, or pursuit of the wrong objectives, for example.

Design for manufacture is one obvious example. This is not just a technical problem. In fact it is primarily an organizational one. It is possible for us to organize our design activities in a way that does not allow or encourage cooperation between design and manufacturing. We can train people to think within a narrow perspective, and we can provide rewards for empire building, turf defending and failure to cooperate. This what many manufacturing companies have done. And having done this, we propose that the problems that result can be resolved by using technology (often at great cost). A more imaginative approach would be to try to remove the problem by changing the organization and the working practices, introduce different reward systems, and then provide appropriate training. Only after these fundamental changes have been made should we be considering technology, to support, not just design for manufacture, but the whole new product introduction process, which is clearly a much wider issue than designing for manufacturability.

The latter approach is good business, management and engineering practice. It can achieve (possibly at a lower cost) what the former will probably never fully achieve. This is not to say that technology has no role to play. It does, but the philosophy of the latter approach is much broader than that of the first one, and because of this, technology may well be used in a completely different way, and may well be quite different.

This example of design for manufacture illustrates one of our common difficulties. Design for manufacture is not the problem. It is only the symptom of another problem. In the past we have not bothered to identify the problems, just addressed the symptoms, usually using technology.

When developing advanced manufacturing concepts such as CIM, we seem to have largely ignored this broader perspective. For example, we have implemented CIM systems in factories that are still laid out on a functional basis, without any consideration being given to whether or not a functional layout is still appropriate. We have done this in spite of the fact that we know that functional organizations create complex material flows, and lengthen manufacturing throughput times. Our response to problems such as complex material flows has often been quite stupid. We have installed complex computer systems to monitor and control material flows and we have made substantial investments in technologies to shorten throughput times. In other words, we have treated the symptoms of the problem, rather than addressing the root problems.

Having adopted this approach, we have then expected to be able to compete with other, more far sighted enterprises, who have done the obvious, that is, done away with functional organizations, and then applied computer systems if they are still needed, or applied them to other more appropriate applications.

CIM, as we practice the concept, should be more correctly described as computer interfaced manufacturing rather than computer integrated manufacturing. We have acquired an erroneous belief that the ills of our manufacturing companies can be resolved using this computer interfacing technology. Computers are a necessary requirement, but are not sufficient for agile manufacturing.

The design paradigm

Thus far we have outlined long established principles of organization and control and discussed the role of technology in manufacturing. We have seen that the role of technology is closely linked to our traditional model of organization and control. Associated with our traditional organization and control paradigm, and the role of technology, is an underlying design paradigm.

The relationship between the traditional design paradigm and traditional organization and control concepts, and the way we use technology, is mutually supportive. The design paradigm has fostered the development of concepts underlying traditional manufacturing, but at the same time, these traditional concepts have helped to reinforce the design paradigm.

We have already listed the characteristics of the Taylor Model. The design paradigm is largely based on these characteristics. There are however, a few important points which we should reiterate and expand upon.

The design paradigm on which traditional manufacturing is based is dominated by technological considerations. We have tended, in varying degrees, to treat people in a mechanistic way, and have regarded them, in most situations, as an issue of secondary importance. We have often viewed people as a nuisance, a source of uncertainty, a necessary evil, and this is reflected in our design paradigm. Tacitly, we often place an emphasis on reducing the role of people by designing technologies that automate and de-skill. We try to use technology, often without realizing it, to control people and to transfer decision-making to computers and ourselves.

Another important aspect of the design paradigm is the reductionist approach. Reductionism is based on the scientific method, and it has helped us to simplify and decompose problems so that they become manageable and solvable. However, related to this issue of reductionism is our belief that optimization at the task level leads to optimization at the enterprise level. Reductionism by itself is difficult to justify on the grounds that it allows problems to be more easily solved, if the resultant solutions are not economically satisfactory. So we have to assume that by using reductionism, we must also produce solutions that in turn lead to optimum performance at a higher level. Thus we must also believe that optimization of individual components and sub-systems leads to overall optimization.

This belief in the validity of optimizing each decision is of course theoretically incorrect (see Chapter 4), which can be mathematically proved. Nevertheless we have chosen to ignore this fact, and still believe, deep down, that complex systems can be broken down into components, and each component can be optimized in isolation from the other components. This very conveniently leads us to a monodisciplinary approach, or at best a multidisciplinary one.

However, the world of manufacturing is very complex. There are many interconnections between the components of a manufacturing enterprise. So complex is a manufacturing enterprise, that it is not surprising that we, in the past, have found it impossible to cope with its complexity, and have sought to reduce it to manageable areas, which we have tended to examine separately. And as a result, our knowledge of manufacturing is divided into well defined boxes which are entirely of our making and which are purely arbitrary. There is no natural law which states that the world should be divided into software engineering, psychology, organization and management science and so on. These subjects are man-made, and the divisions between them a matter of convenience.

What these divisions lead to however, is a monodisciplinary view of the world. Each of us views the world of manufacturing through our own system of values and narrow knowledge base. And in manufacturing the result of this monodisciplinary perspective has been a tendency to adopt a serial engineering approach, in both product design and manufacturing systems design.

In the case of product design, we have traditionally ignored manufacturing issues, which we have only dealt with once the product has been designed. In manufacturing systems design, we have ignored organization and people issues until the manufacturing technology has been designed, selected and installed, and then attempted to deal with the resulting difficulties. In both situations we have a common problem, and the reasons for the problem are the same. We have monodisciplinary professions, and we have these because we believe that the world can be reduced into sub-systems, which can largely be treated in isolation.

Finally we come to the matter of economics, which plays a central role in the design paradigm through the notion of cost efficiency. In manufacturing the attention paid to cost efficiency is largely seen in terms of the goals that we pursue when investing in new manufacturing technologies, that is, cost reductions and labor productivity. Cost efficiency also permeates traditional management accounting systems, that is, investment justification methods and performance measurement and control systems.

The main characteristics of the design paradigm underlying our traditional manufacturing can thus be summarized as:

- A reductionist approach.
- Monodisciplinary professions and views.
- Serial engineering.
- Optimization at the task level implies optimization at the enterprise level.
- Concentration on technology.
- Emphasis on cost reduction.

We should now consider what impact these characteristics have on people who have to work with the technologies and systems that we design and implement.

In a preceding section, we outlined some of the people related problems that we have commonly experienced in the workplace. Most of these problems arise from technology and organization. If we want to do something about these problems through the design of better technology and organization, then we need to understand the reasons why the problems arise in the first place.

For the purposes of the discussion in this section, it is convenient to consider three aspects of a technical system: the work organization, the human–machine interface and the actual technology which lies behind the human–machine interface (the technological form).

Typically when we talk about psychological and organizational input into the design of technical systems, the thing that most often comes into our minds is ergonomics. Ergonomics is most commonly understood as being concerned with the design of human–machine interfaces according to an understanding of the psychological and physiological characteristics of humans. We have a fairly comprehensive scientific understanding of the potential problems that can arise when people are faced with human–machine interfaces not conforming to good ergonomic design criteria. The fact that often we have chosen not to design human–machine interfaces according to good ergonomic practices is another matter.

Although the fields of hardware and software ergonomics are both reasonably well established, ergonomics in this sense is too narrow a perspective for dealing with the problems that arise in manufacturing. Human–machine interface design is an important aspect of design, but it is in fact only one dimension of a much larger problem. It is possible to have a well defined user interface, but still to experience many difficulties in the workplace. Ergonomics may help us to produce a user-friendly system, but the interface has very little to do with who we decide should control the work of the people, or with the skills and knowledge that are needed, or with how tightly we circumscribe the work, or whether people's full capabilities are being used to gain competitive advantage. It is the organization and the technological form that are important with respect to these particular attributes of a system.

In the past we have used techniques such as job expansion, job enrichment and job enlargement to help mitigate people related problems which can arise from technologies and organizations that lead to boring, simple and repetitive tasks. These job redesign techniques attempt to provide people with task variety, autonomous working conditions and additional responsibilities, within the constraints imposed by the technology that we previously designed without regard for the human factor. This is typical of our traditional serial engineering thinking.

We could design technologies and organizational structures that, for example, involve a lot of machine minding, where there are long periods of inaction. We can then set about improving the situation, to some degree, by giving the people extra tasks. These might involve quality control or minor repairs and maintenance of the system.

However, we could also design a technological system which provides the potential for skilled, interesting and satisfying work, but still end up with boring and mundane tasks. Studies by industrial psychologists (Burns, 1984; Kemp, Clegg and Wall, 1984) have shown that similar technological systems can be used in different ways by companies with similar characteristics in terms of products, customer requirements and so on. In the cases discussed in the above references, one company was using CNC machine tools that were under the full control of machinists, while in another company, similar machines were under the control of office-based specialists, and the machinists were machine minders.

We can thus see that there are two aspects to people related problems that are closely connected. On the one hand we use methods of organizing work that attempt to remove control and decision-making from people, and which can be applied to situations even when we produce a technology that has been designed to allow for user control. On the other hand, we can design technology such that the Taylor Model is incorporated into the design. This leads to technologies in which centralized control is built in, making it difficult to introduce alternative forms of organization.

The issue which we now need to address is why we design technology so as to produce unsatisfactory work for people, given that such work creates so many problems in the workplace, and given the value of making full use, throughout the enterprise, of people's abilities.

We can gain some insight into this problem by considering the example given by Rosenbrock (1982) of a robot carrying out continuous arc welding. He describes a system where the work is held in a jig on a rotating table with the robot doing the welding. The operator has the task of inserting a fresh workpiece into the jig and rotating the table towards the robot. The robot welds the component and, once it has finished, it withdraws. The table is then swung round and the operator removes the welded part, and the whole cycle begins again.

In earlier times we would have given the whole job to the welder, that is, mounting the workpiece in the jig, welding it, and then removing it. The welding would have required a certain degree of skill, and the loading and unloading of the part, relatively little skill. If we had asked the welder which component of the job was most satisfying and interesting, he would probably have said the welding. However, in our example, the task of welding has been given to a robot, leaving the human operator with the relatively unskilled work. In doing this we have made the job unskilled, trivial and machine paced.

We have here a rather absurd but all too common situation. The robot, which is flexible but of limited capability relative to the human operator, is doing the skilled work. The human, who is intelligent, flexible and has very wide capabilities, is undertaking the unskilled work.

Rosenbrock has suggested that examples like the robot welder (and there are many similar examples in all types of industries), highlight an attitude that we have towards people. If we found ourselves responsible, say, for the introduction of a computer system, we would be concerned to ensure that the full capabilities of the computer were utilized. However, as the robot welding example amply illustrates, we do not extend the same concern to people. The skills, ingenuity and creativity of people are precious assets, yet we treat people as a cost to be minimized, instead of a resource to be developed and utilized.

There is also a second absurdity evident in our robot welding example. In the development of this system, a repetitive and boring job has been created. A later generation of engineers may look at such a job and quite rightly say that this kind of work is quite unfit for people to perform, and then conclude that such a job should be done away with. Such a view seems very logical and, seen in this light, technological developments which allow such jobs to be eliminated seem to be entirely beneficial. The logic of our thinking is however, flawed. We created, using technology, a job that was unfit for people. We did this because we looked only at the economics at the task level, and concluded that it would be beneficial to implement the system described. The system is, however, only a small component of a much larger system, and it is unlikely that we would have achieved optimization of this larger system.

The robot example is a simple one, but it illustrates an important point. Before jobs can be taken over by machines they must first be fragmented and de-skilled. It is rare for any job requiring a distinct human skill to be taken over completely and entirely in one step by a machine. This is almost always done bit by bit, and at each stage the jobs left for humans are whatever remains over, when the job of the machine has been determined. Therefore, to apply the cure, namely to abolish a trivialized job, one first has to create the disease, a supply of trivialized jobs.

In pointing out some of the absurdities of the way we approach the design of systems, we are not advocating that technology such as the robot for welding should not be used. Rather what we are proposing is that the boundary of the system needs to be drawn much wider, so that, for example, the welding, the role of the welder and the organization of work are considered in a much broader context and judged against more comprehensive criteria.

The case against traditional design practices

The philosophy that underlies the development of many computer based systems appears to be largely based upon concepts of automation that are partly motivated by a vision of minimally manned, fully automated systems. The main difficulty with the idea of minimally manned systems has always been that they are brought about in an evolutionary manner extending over a large number of years, and not in one single step.

People, therefore, have always been expected to compensate for the inadequacies of technologies and system designs, and to do those jobs which we cannot automate, for technical and economic reasons, at any given point in time. Thus, the design of technical systems raises a number of other issues relating to ergonomics, work organization and social factors, in addition to the obvious technical and economic considerations.

Typically, the design of advanced manufacturing systems is undertaken by technical experts, and design objectives are usually expressed in terms such as low operation and unit costs, rapid response to changing demand, minimum throughput time, flexibility, reliability, minimum downtime and maximum spindle utilization time. If advanced manufacturing systems were purely technical artifacts, then this approach to their design would not raise any objections. However, the successful operation of the majority of systems depends upon people's abilities to compensate for the limitations of the technology, to respond to unforeseen events and to provide a high level of intelligent decision-making capability. Advanced manufacturing systems are, therefore, both social and technical systems.

Unfortunately, the technical perspective has shaped many of the developments in manufacturing technology that have led to boring, monotonous and machine paced jobs. These job characteristics have led to physical and mental health problems, increased labor turnover and absenteeism, industrial relations difficulties, accidents and mistakes (Brown, 1954; Oborne, 1987).

Problems such as these can be reduced by the application of human factors knowledge. For example, Murrell (1976) proposes that the machine pacing of people on a production line can be determined such that they can meet the requirements of the task without undue stress. However, we should contrast this approach with that adopted by the Swedish car manufacturer, Volvo, at their Kalmar factory. Here the production process was redesigned in an attempt to free people from machine pacing, to give them more autonomy and more task variety and to create a more pleasant working environment (Larsson, 1986).

The most obvious question raised by these two examples is concerned with the appropriateness of creating a technology that reduces people to mere mechanical components in the production process. Such a question raises social, technical and economic issues that are of direct relevance to the competitive position of manufacturing companies and the successful implementation and achievement of agile manufacturing.

Western democratic societies place a great emphasis on education. The aim has been to help individuals develop their personalities, aspirations and thinking abilities. In many traditional working environments the technology has left little room for the development of personality, for achieving personal aspirations or for exercising the thinking abilities cultivated during school years. This is an unnecessary situation that represents a waste of human resources, which are some of our most precious assets.

In our plants there are many activities where the skill and knowledge of people are required before the full benefit can be achieved from the technologies. The machining of metals is a good example. It is possible to construct a mathematical model of the machining process which can be used, given the availability of certain data, to calculate the optimum way of cutting metal.

This, however, is only a theoretical possibility. In practice, such a mathematical model is likely to cope with only the simplest and most carefully defined situations. The reality is that the data used in such models are subject to large degrees of uncertainty. The cutting process itself is not fully understood and cannot therefore be accurately modelled, and the work is subject to a large number of unpredictable disturbances.

This is a very simple example of the type of situation where the benefits of people's skills and experience can be used most effectively; we can combine people and computers to produce a result which is greater than the sum of the component parts. It is in these types of situation that we can use to good effect abilities so carefully developed by educators.

We have argued that we rely on people's skills and abilities. This is true, but often only in a tacit way. In practice we have not very often developed satisfactory facilities to enable people to achieve a human–machine symbiosis. Typically, we have seen the need for human skill as a defect, and we have often tried our best to 'eliminate' the people. In reality, however, we have left people to do the tasks which we could not think how to automate, and to provide support when the systems fail to function as we desire (Bainbridge, 1983).

Thus, determining people's tasks in this way, we have often fragmented and de-skilled their work. At some later stage we probably further fragmented and de-skilled the work, until what was left was stressful and boring. Having created these boring jobs, we would then have taken steps to eliminate them altogether using automation. However, as we pointed out above, before such cures can be applied, one first has to create the disease, the supply of trivial and machine paced jobs. In other words, ergonomics of the kind discussed by Murrell (1976) attempts to treat the symptoms of a disease – a better alternative would be to prevent the disease.

It is our belief that this process of job destruction is counter productive. It leads to alienation, lack of motivation and commitment, and an unwillingness to cooperate, to change and to improve. Thus we conclude that our traditional design practices are completely at variance with what we are trying to achieve in agile manufacturing.

But what of the economic issues? There has always been a question concerning economic losses arising from the failure of our conventional approach to automation to make full and better use of the human resources available within our enterprises. As mentioned earlier, we have been strongly influenced by the ideas of such people as Adam Smith, Charles Babbage and Frederick Taylor.

Many of the 18th and 19th century concepts associated with these people have been criticized for being mechanistic and inhuman. However, these concepts can also be criticized because they form the foundations of a manufacturing strategy that involves limited product variety and large production volumes (economies of scale), and are therefore highly inappropriate to agile manufacturing. In agile manufacturing the emphasis is on a competitive environment characterized by increasing product variety, decreasing production volumes, shortening product life cycles and reducing repeat orders.

Our most common justification for creating trivial and machine paced jobs has been an economic one; our Western societies have achieved economic prosperity through mass production and the associated division of labor, simplification of work and automation, and there is no other way that this prosperity can be achieved or maintained if we organize production differently and develop different forms of technology.

In today's competitive environment, where focus will be on agile manufacturing, traditional arguments are no longer relevant. In agile manufacturing there are good economic reasons for designing and developing technologies that collaborate with people's skills, rather than technologies that reject them.

We must therefore realize that our design paradigm is outdated, and that in agile manufacturing we cannot continue to waste human resources and to continue with the practices that have contributed to the creation of many of the people related problems that we have become so used to. We need to develop a more friendly technology that collaborates with people's skills. The question that remains to be answered is how do we set about designing this type of technology? We shall try to answer this question in later chapters.

Concluding comments

Traditional concepts of organization and control, and traditional technological and design paradigms were shaped by a different set of circumstances to those in an agile manufacturing enterprise. It is our contention that we must fundamentally change the way we do things if we are to succeed with agile manufacturing. In this chapter we have tried to describe the key characteristics of our traditional paradigms, so that we may better understand what we have to change. In the remaining chapters we will focus on what we should be doing in an agile manufacturing environment.

Key points

- Traditional manufacturing plants are built around organizational, control, technological and design paradigms that have ceased to be relevant.

- Principles of manufacturing organization and control are based on concepts first used in the 1890s.

- The Taylor Model is deep rooted in our management and engineering culture. It is in our heads. Before we can change this culture we need to fully understand the elements of the Taylor Model.

- The Taylor Model is not suited to modern manufacturing and competitive environments. It represents a barrier to achieving agility and it is in direct opposition to ideas such as continuous improvement.

- We must resolve the long-standing problems of alienation, lack of motivation and so on within our enterprises. The Taylor Model is the bottleneck that stands in the way of a successful resolution of these problems.

- The role of technology is shifting from automation of work to supporting complex decision-making. This requires new concepts.

- We need to develop a new technology design paradigm.

References

Argyle M. (1972). *The Social Psychology of Work*. Harmondsworth: Penguin

Bainbridge L. (1983). Ironies of automation. *Automatica*, **19**(6), 775–9

Bolwijn P.T., Boorsma J., van Breukelen Q.H., Brinkman S. and Kumpe T. (1986). *Flexible Manufacturing. Integrating Technological and Social Innovation*. Amsterdam: Elsevier

Brown J.A.C. (1954). *The Social Psychology of Industry*. Harmondsworth: Penguin

Burnes B. (1984). Factors affecting the introduction and use of CNC machine tools. In Proc. *1st Int. Conf. Human Factors in Manufacturing* (Lupton T. ed.). Kempston: IFS

Burnes B. and Weekes B. (1989). Success and failure with advanced manufacturing technology: the need for a broader perspective. *Advanced Manufacturing Engineering*, **1**, 88–94

Fayol H. (1916). *General and Industrial Management* 1984 edn. with revisions by Irwin Gray. New York: IEEE

Gibson J.E. (1992). Taylorism and professional education. In *Manufacturing Systems. Foundations of World Class Practice* (Heim J.A. and Compton W.D., eds.,), pp. 149–57. Washington DC: National Academy Press

Hayes R.H., Wheelwright S.C. and Clark K.B. (1988). *Dynamic Manufacturing. Creating the Learning Organisation*. New York: Free Press

Kemp N.J., Clegg C.W. and Wall T.D. (1984). Human aspects of computer-aided manufacture. In *Proc. IEE Int. Conf. Computer Aided Engineering,* Warwick, UK

Kidd P.T. (1988). Human and computer aided manufacturing: the end of Taylorism? In *Ergonomics of Hybrid Automated Systems I* (Karwowski W., Parsaei H.R. and Wilhelm M.R., eds.), pp. 145–52. Amsterdam: Elsevier

Klingenberg H. and Kränzle H. (1987). *Humanisation Pays: Practical Models. Vol. 2. Production and Production Control.* Eschborn: RKW

Larsson K.A. (1986). Car assembly at the Volvo Kalmar plant – ten years of experience. In *Human Factors* (Lupton T., ed.), pp. 129–36. Kempston: IFS

Murrell H. (1976). *Men and Machines.* London: Methuen

Nadworny M.J. (1955). *Scientific Management and the Unions 1900–1932.* Cambridge MA: Harvard University Press

Oborne D.J. (1987). *Ergonomics at Work* 2nd edn. Chichester: John Wiley

Östberg O. (1986). People factors of robotics and automation: European views. *Proc. IEEE Int. Conf. Robotics and Automation,* San Francisco, USA

Peters T.J. and Waterman R.H. (1982). *In Search of Excellence. Lessons from America's Best-Run Companies.* New York: Harper & Row

Rose M. (1978). *Industrial Behaviour. Theoretical Developments since Taylor.* Harmondsworth: Penguin

Rosenbrock H.H. (1982). Robots and people. *Measurement and Control,* **15**, 105–12

Taylor F.W. (1907). On the art of cutting metals. *Trans. American Society of Mechanical Engineers,* **28**, 31–350

PART THREE

Agile manufacturing enterprise design

6

Agile manufacturing enterprise design

Introduction

In Chapter 1 we referred to an agile manufacturing infrastructure proposed in the report *21st Century Manufacturing Enterprise Strategy* (Iacocca Institute, 1991). In this chapter we return to this infrastructure, and develop an approach for designing agile manufacturing enterprises. This approach is based on systems concepts.

The Iacocca Institute agile manufacturing infrastructure

The competitive foundations and characteristics of agile manufacturing enterprises were discussed in Chapter 1. It is proposed in the Iacocca Institute report that these enterprise characteristics should be supported by nine manufacturing enterprise elements.

These nine manufacturing enterprise elements are:

- Business metrics and procedures supportive of the development of agile manufacturing.
- A communications and information infrastructure which enables individuals and teams to rapidly interact, sometimes across large geographical distances, both within the enterprise and between companies.

- Cooperation and teaming mechanisms which enable and support cooperation.
- Enterprise flexibility to achieve rapid realization and response in an environment characterized by continuous change.
- Enterprise wide concurrency encompassing all aspects of the manufacturing enterprise, not just new product development and introduction.
- Environmental enhancement to meet increasing customer expectations and legal requirements for conservation of resources, protection of the environment and so on.
- Human elements that are supportive of human needs, human resource utilization and so on.
- Subcontractor and supplier support elements which will enable the many small to medium size companies with limited financial resources to integrate themselves into the computer networks of larger manufacturing companies.
- Technology deployment elements that will improve and accelerate the exploitation of new technologies.

It is then proposed that these nine elements imply 29 enabling sub-systems. These enabling sub-systems are:

- Continuous education and training.
- Customer interactive systems.
- Distributed databases.
- Empowered individuals and teams.
- Energy conservation.
- Enterprise integration.
- Evolving standards.
- Factory America net.
- Global broadband networks.
- Global dynamic multi-venturing.
- Groupware.
- Human–technology interface.
- Integration methodology.
- Intelligent control.
- Intelligent sensors.
- Knowledge-based Artificial Intelligence systems.
- Modular reconfigurable process hardware.
- Organizational practices.
- Performance metrics and benchmarks.
- Pre-qualified partnering.
- Rapid cooperation mechanisms.
- Representation methods.
- Simulation and modelling.
- Software prototyping and productivity.
- Streamlined legal systems.
- Supportive accounting metrics.
- Technology adaptation and transfer.
- Waste management and elimination.

This proposed infrastructure contains much wisdom on what constitutes good practice for the emerging competitive environment. However, there are several points of concern about this infrastructure.

First, the enabling sub-systems are somewhat arbitrary. For example, with respect to environmental aspects, the main enabling sub-systems are energy conservation, waste management and elimination, and zero accident methodology. These are supported by simulation and modelling, training, databases, improvements to manufacturing processes and so on. However, there is a whole range of environmental measures that manufacturing enterprises can be taking, such as predictive maintenance, improved housekeeping, process substitution, waste recycling, raw material substitution and so forth, which are all part of environmentally conscious manufacturing.

Second, the infrastructure appears to be a prescription for agile manufacturing, that is, implement all these and we will have an agile manufacturing enterprise. This is highly unlikely to be a successful way to achieve agile manufacturing, although it will appeal to our quick fix mentality.

Third, the infrastructure says nothing about how to set about designing an agile manufacturing enterprise, or about priorities, or how to manage change and so on. Few enterprises, if any, will have the resources to implement all these enabling sub-systems in one go and some of them may not be relevant in some situations, or may only become important later.

Finally, the infrastructure does not make explicit the complex web of relationships that exist between many of the enabling sub-systems. There is no framework which will lead us away from our traditional piecemeal approaches, and there is a danger that we will end up doing things in isolation within several sub-systems, and not be able to bring them all together as one coordinated and integrated whole.

The agile manufacturing enterprise design problem

One of the fundamental problems that we face today in the design of agile manufacturing enterprises is a lack of theoretical basis. In other engineering disciplines there is always some basic theory to work with, to provide insight and a conceptual framework. For example, electrical engineers have Ohm's law and other circuit theorems, and mechanical engineers have Hook's law, theories of bending, motion and so on. In the manufacturing engineering profession, all we have had in the past are the precepts of Frederick Taylor.

Manufacturing in todays' dynamic and competitive business environments can no longer be based on precepts, and in this chapter we will consider an approach to the design of agile manufacturing enterprises. We believe that this approach represents a first step towards achieving a more systematic and systemic approach to manufacturing enterprise design.

We have, in manufacturing, now achieved an awareness and recognition that the development of a world class manufacturing enterprise cannot be brought about by the application of new technology alone. We can only achieve competitive advantage from new technologies if our enterprise is designed and built on firm foundations. These foundations include goals and objectives, organization, people, technology, management approach, environmental issues and so on.

Manufacturing is highly complex, involving many interrelated issues, and covering several disciplines. What we need is a holistic methodology with supporting tools which will allow us to deal with all aspects of a manufacturing business, the interrelationships and the difficult process of planning and managing change.

The approach we have adopted in the past most often reduces to following a simple methodology or adopting a number of prescriptive *quick fix* solutions which focus on one, or a few particular aspects of manufacturing. We have approached things in a piecemeal fashion, doing something here, something else there, and have often found that things do not link together and work as a coordinated whole.

Our existing methodologies and tools to support the design and development of agile manufacturing enterprises offer only limited capability and coverage. These methodologies and tools are characterized by one or more of the following deficiencies:

- Often the underlying assumption is that of a simple, prescriptive, *quick fix* approach.
- Attention is focused on a limited number of issues.
- The methodologies are either entirely top-down or entirely bottom-up approaches.
- Often the methodologies are based on dated concepts that are only suitable for fairly static business conditions or stable mass production environments.
- There is an inherent separation of strategy formulation and implementation, as the interdependencies between the two are not acknowledged or accepted.
- The basis of the methodology is usually a stage-wise approach with feedback only between adjacent stages.
- The cycle time of the methodology is usually orders of magnitude greater than the dynamics of the business environment.
- Strategies are seen to result from a process of analysis and not as things that emerge and evolve.
- Analysis of the impact of strategies is commonly restricted to standard business measures of performance such as return on investment.

- Simulation tools to support the identification of the impact on a wide range of financial and non-financial performance metrics, of various strategies and various manufacturing techniques and technologies are not available.
- The organizational and people implications of new technologies are not explored and defined.
- Processes to support definition and prioritizing of projects and the systematic decomposition of high level goals into subordinate quantified objectives are not deployed.

The design, planning and implementation of an agile manufacturing enterprise is potentially very complex and difficult. Simple methods and solutions may provide us with short term gains and have a high comfort factor, but in the long term they are not likely to be very effective.

Furthermore, while the ingredients of agile manufacturing are available, we have as yet little guidance available with regard to how best to proceed. We have in the past adopted a narrow focus, with emphasis on tackling symptoms of problems, rather than the problems themselves. We have often tended to promote single focus prescriptive solutions. Often these solutions provide benefits, but they are limited in scope and may not be sustained, as illustrated in Figure 6.1.

Manufacturing industry has become very weary of the growing number of methods and techniques on offer which claim to provide magic solutions. While these methods and techniques have the potential to provide benefits, often these benefits remain illusive. As a result we tend to dismiss many methods and techniques as fads or flavors of the month.

It is now being suggested (Heim and Compton, 1992) that what is needed is a holistic approach which reflects the true complexity of the problem. Such a method, by its nature, will be complex. This cannot be avoided, and so, such a methodology needs to be supported by computer technology, so that it can be made practicable and usable. This is likely to be achieved by embedding the design theory and the methodology in a knowledge-based system, and providing computer based support tools.

It is our belief that in a global, dynamic and highly competitive environment, we can only design and develop a world class agile manufacturing enterprise if we adopt a holistic approach which acknowledges the true complexity of the changes needed. We believe that now is the time to move away from precepts, prescriptions and panaceas. We need to adopt a sound approach based on manufacturing theory. This theory should be focused on manufacturing enterprise design. Such a theory would need to be oriented to computer-aided design because of the complexity involved. However, we need to keep the computer-aided design process under the direction and control of our enterprise designers. This requirement therefore specifies the nature of the theory, because we are not talking here about synthesis oriented theory, but a design based theory.

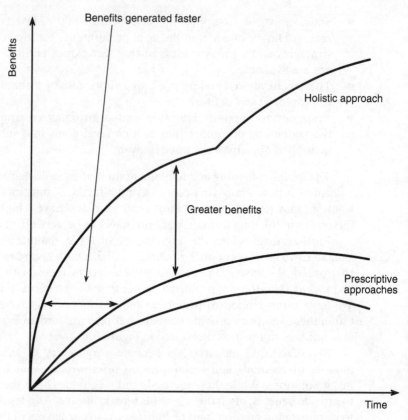

Figure 6.1 The rate at which benefits are generated. *Source:* Cheshire Henbury. © 1993. Published with permission.

Systems concepts as the basis of manufacturing theory

The main issues that we will address in this chapter are the nature and importance of systems concepts as the theoretical basis for agile manufacturing, and the implications of systems concepts for the design of agile manufacturing enterprises and the computer based technologies that we will use in agile manufacturing.

Before we address the theoretical framework, we should understand some important systems concepts. However, before we do this we should also understand what we mean by systems concepts.

If we examine the literature on systems concepts we will find two rather distinct interpretations. The first approach is what we might call true systems thinking, and the second we can describe as systems engineering. Although we might be tempted to see the two as synonymous, they are in fact two different things, based upon entirely different perspectives, but having some common features. We believe that the systems engineering approach is not appropriate to agile manufacturing enterprise design, and that we need to use true systems thinking.

In the following sections we will briefly discuss these two different approaches. We will then move on to state some of the underlying concepts of systems thinking, and then discuss the implications for the design of agile manufacturing enterprises.

The origin of systems thinking

Systems thinking has its roots in the belief, expressed by some biologists in the 1920s and 1930s, that the reductionism of natural science was probably not the best approach to the understanding of specifically biological phenomena. What was therefore proposed was a systems approach that was systemic, that is, concerned with understanding the whole (Checkland, 1981, 1983). The systems approach, as we practice it in engineering, often does not reflect this view, and thus we have something which we call systems engineering, which is based on reductionism rather than systemic thinking.

Checkland (1981) introduces the terms **hard systems** and **soft systems**. Systems engineering is a hard systems method, and it can be used to tackle problems in which objectives or goals can be taken as given, and a system designed to achieve the given objectives. Soft systems methods, on the other hand, are applied to situations where desirable ends cannot be taken as given.

According to King (1988), in hard systems thinking, the philosophy that informs the methodology is that:

- Needs can be clearly defined.
- Objectives can be set which are established by neutral scientific criteria.
- The engineering challenge is to design and select the best among possible alternative systems to achieve the scientific objectives.

Checkland has stated that the essence of hard systems thinking is the pursuit of the best solution; the belief in, and the search for, the optimum. Furthermore, Checkland has also argued that hard systems thinking is only applicable to systems which are characterized by interconnections which are part of the regularities of the universe, for example, electronic circuits, or by interconnections which derive from the logic of situations, for example, the manufacture of electronic circuit boards, where one operation must be preceded by another.

Checkland defines a third type of system, a human activity system, to which soft systems thinking must be applied, and for which the hard systems approach, on its own, will not work. Most real world system problems contain a human activity system. A manufacturing system is an example of such a real world system.

Manufacturing systems can be thought of as consisting of a designed physical system (that is, computers, machines, buildings and such like) which is designed to fulfill a human purpose (for example, to manufacture profitable and useful products). A manufacturing system also consists of a less tangible element, called the human activity system. This system consists of a set of linked activities undertaken by people. In addition however, other elements are also present, and these include: the social system which is a system of relationships between different groups, and individuals, the formal system of organization, the supplier system and so on.

Our understanding of an agile manufacturing enterprise, as a system, is not therefore restricted to considerations of the sub-system which we call the designed physical system, but to all the sub-systems. Furthermore, all these sub-systems cannot be viewed in isolation, but are interdependent. That is, what we determine in one sub-system, affects the others.

In systems engineering we have been exclusively concerned with the design of the physical sub-system, and we have usually disregarded the effect of the physical sub-system on the others. This tendency can be seen in technical publications in the area of manufacturing systems (Parnaby, 1981) where the concept of manufacturing system is seen largely in terms of hardware, processes, control systems, inputs and outputs and so on, and where social processes, for example human interaction, are outside the system. In fact what is considered is not the manufacturing system but the technical sub-system, because the overall manufacturing system also includes people, the social sub-systems and the like.

What we tend to do is focus our attention on the physical sub-system, because to be truthful, we are not very good at handling the other sub-systems. We find them too vague and undefinable, and we lack the understanding, skills and knowledge to address them.

Having focused our attention on the physical sub-system, and conveniently forgotten about the others, which eliminates the need to consider a whole array of sub-system interactions, we then proceed to break our physical sub-system down into component parts, thus avoiding having to think about the complex behavior of the overall sub-system. Having done this we feel comfortable with each individual component, and we then proceed to design the details of the physical sub-system, often convincing ourselves that, since we are using a systems methodology, everything will fit together and work well, and that by understanding the individual components, we will understand the whole of the physical sub-system.

Moreover, when we design the physical sub-system, we often follow the stage-wise analysis, synthesis, evaluation and implementation model.

The goals are assumed to be definable at the outset, and the task is to produce a system that satisfies the goals.

We should also contrast this Western view (for it is largely a Western view) of manufacturing systems with that of the Japanese view, as encapsulated in the concept of the Toyota production system, which is also the basis of the concept of lean manufacturing (Womack, Jones and Roos, 1990). An essential characteristic of the Toyota production system, and hence lean manufacturing systems, is that it is a system in the proper sense of the word.

Lean manufacturing consists of several interacting sub-systems; the product design system, the supply chain system, the sales system and the production system. It is not concerned solely with the technology of making automobiles, but also with the role of people, the organizing processes and the relationships and interactions. But it is also more than this, because underlying the concept is a breaking down of the barriers that exist between professions, departments, managers and shop floor employees, and between thinkers and doers. In other words, to able to think effectively, whether it be to formulate strategy, or to design engines, you must also be a doer. You must have experience of implementing strategy, or manufacturing automobile engines.

We now wish to demonstrate that our culture of systems engineering, with its focus on narrow isolated sub-systems and reductionism, and its adherence to separation, is inappropriate to the design of complex systems such as agile manufacturing enterprises.

We could at this point say that since the Japanese appear to have adopted a true systems approach we should too. This, of course, is an easy way out. The *me too* syndrome. However, this approach is not likely to be very appealing. We have been told, perhaps too often, how good the Japanese are, and how their methods should be adopted. It is important to first understand why these approaches should be adopted, before we adopt them. Many Japanese companies are good, but they are not all equally good. Some are better than others. Also, even though some Japanese companies are very good, it is not apparent that the Japanese fully understand the theoretical reasons why this is so.

We now address a number of issues that will help us to understand why the systems view is so important. First of all, however, we have to address some system concepts and explore their implications.

The importance of systems thinking: revelations of the true complexity of situations

Practical experience of applying systems concepts to real world problems often reveals unexpected effects. To illustrate this point, we will consider a simple example.

In urban areas suffering from traffic congestion, it would seem logical and intuitive to reduce congestion by increasing the use of public transport, such as buses. A logical and often promoted way of achieving this goal is to offer free or reduced fares, through local government subsidies of the local transport system.

The logic of the argument for fare subsidies is apparently irresistible. Lower fares will make public transport more economic in relation to private transport (automobiles) thus attracting more people to public transport and reducing the number of automobiles within urban areas. This will result in less congestion and hence a better bus service, because buses will be subject to fewer delays caused by traffic congestion. This is so intuitively obvious, that it is a surprise to find that it is not universal policy in all urban areas.

If we were to undertake a systems study, looking at the system wide effects of cheap fares, the resulting picture would be quite different. The first thing that happens when cheap fares are introduced is that those people in low income groups, who have previously limited their travelling for financial reasons, will be less constrained and the number of people from these social groups, using public transport, is likely to increase. Many of these low income people will not be owners of automobiles.

Those people in low income groups who do own an automobile may find the cheap fares attractive and transfer to public transport. However, people in higher income groups may actually value the convenience and comfort of automobile use, and may not, because of their financial position, be attracted by the economic benefits of cheap public transport.

Also, those in high income groups who do use public transport may be driven away by cheap fares, because the increase in passenger numbers will result in a deterioration in the quality of the service (measured in terms of seat availability, crowding and so on) at peak times. As there is always an imbalance in demand between peak and off-peak times, it may not be feasible to increase the number of buses or trains, owing to the increased costs and capital spending that this would imply. A further effect of cheap fares is that the resulting fall in the number of private automobiles using the roads as a result of lower income road users transferring to public transport may make it more attractive for those in high income groups to use automobiles in urban areas. So the most likely net effect of cheap fares would be to increase utilization of public transport while having minimal effect on the number of private automobiles in use.

What this example shows is that by undertaking a systems analysis a simple problem with a simple solution becomes a much more complex problem. Cheap fares taken on their own are unlikely to provide a solution to traffic congestion problems. What is needed is a range of measures, for example, integration of transport systems, park and ride schemes, toll systems to penalize certain users of automobiles, changes of attitude, road improvement activities, bus lanes, cycle facilities and so on, to make for an effective solution to traffic congestion problems.

Also note that in this example, our analysis was based on interactions between sub-systems. Our sub-systems were public transport, automobiles and people. We did not carry out a systems decomposition and study the details of the individual components. Instead we stayed at a very high level, looking at interactions. This, to a very large extent, is what systems analysis is all about, and this bears little resemblance to what is advocated in systems engineering textbooks.

This simple example really illustrates the whole point of the importance of taking a systems view, and building all factors into the systems model. This is an important issue. In complex situations, we are unlikely to develop successful solutions to problems if we do not adopt a systems approach. The systems analysis helps to reveal the true complexity of the situation, and also reveals the undesirable effects of proposed solutions. We cannot hope to understand the performance of a system if we try to break it down into its detailed component parts, and then look at the operation and performance of these components.

What we see also from this example is that the systems approach provides us with a powerful tool for revealing the true complexity of manufacturing problems and highlighting the potential difficulties that may arise as a result of proposed developments, new technologies and so on. In manufacturing systems design however, the focus of our systems approach has been on machines and the flow of products and information. Usually the boundary is drawn in a way that leaves people outside of the system, as part of the systems' environment. The system diagram ignores organizational problems that may result from new technologies. This is truly a systems engineering approach.

Some important systems concepts

It is not our intention to probe into the area of systems theory in great detail. Instead we wish to point to a few key concepts and to use these to make a number of points which have profound implications for the design of agile manufacturing enterprises and the way that we, in the industrialized world, should think about manufacturing.

Emergent properties: systems perform in unexpected ways!

One of the most important concepts of systems thinking is that of emergent properties and emergent behavior. In other words, when we put together some components to form a system, we obtain behavior that is a function of the components acting together. Often some of the emergent properties are undesirable ones. Most often with complex systems, they are extremely difficult to predict.

A simple example of emergent properties is when we take a simple single input, single output linear dynamical system and close a feedback loop between the output and the input. This introduces the possibility of system instability, and enormous efforts have been expended on understanding this phenomenon and devising design methods and compensation techniques so we can design stable closed loop systems.

If we increase the complexity of such a simple linear dynamic system, only slightly, by moving on to consider multiple input, multiple output linear dynamical systems, in which changes on one input affect more than one output (that is, we have cross-coupling or interaction in the system), then we notice new emergent properties. In this situation we may find it impossible to implement high feedback gains in one loop, without first reducing the gain in another loop. Alternatively we may find the apparently strange phenomenon of a system that is stable, but only when all feedback loops are open or when all loops are closed. If however, one loop for some reason is open (because, say, of some failure) then the system becomes unstable.

It should be stressed that we are only discussing systems that are relatively simple, that is, linear dynamical systems, which are in principle capable of being analyzed using powerful mathematical techniques. Most real world problems are non-linear. Moreover, not only are they non-linear, they are also stochastic (that is, subject to random noise and disturbances) and time varying (that is, the behavior changes with time).

If we find strange types of behavior emerging from relatively simple systems, which are capable of being analyzed, then our expectation is that more complex systems will behave in even stranger ways. And this has important implications for manufacturing, as manufacturing systems are, in general, complex non-linear, stochastic time varying systems. As such, they are likely to behave in unexpected and strange ways. If we concentrate our attention on only one part of the system, or try to treat different parts of the system as isolated sub-systems, ignoring the interactions between components and sub-systems, then it should not come as a surprise that the overall system does not function as we desire, or that it fails to live up to our expectations.

Open and closed systems

An important distinction can be made between open and closed systems. An open system is one in which there is an exchange between the system and the systems' environment. Information, energy, or materials, or all three, pass across the system boundary, into and out of the system. A closed system on the other hand is self contained, and there is no exchange with the systems' environment.

In practice all systems are open, but it is possible to regard some systems as closed, and to just concentrate on the internal operation. For example, many of the early management theories, such as those expounded by Frederick Taylor, are based on a closed systems perspective. People such as Taylor adopted approaches based on reductionist models taken from the scientific world. They concentrated on the internal operation of the factory, and assumed that the organization of a factory was sufficiently independent of the external environment to enable factory organization to be defined in terms of structure, tasks and formal relationships.

An important concept in systems theory is that closed systems have an inherent tendency, because of their unchanging nature, to settle into a state of static equilibrium. Moreover, closed systems can only move towards a condition of increasing entropy, that is, increasing disorder. Open systems, however, are in a dynamic relationship with their environment, offsetting the process of increasing entropy and thus maintaining a high degree of order.

An open system is not only open in relation to the environment, but also internally. That is, in an open system there is a dynamic relationship between sub-systems and components, and changes to one sub-system affects the others. Open systems adapt to changes in the environment by changing the structure and processes of the internal components.

Clearly a manufacturing enterprise, in the sense that we have defined above (physical, human activity, social and so on), is an open system. Materials and energy cross the system boundary, and information about the environment is used, through feedback mechanisms, to redirect the system and to restructure its internal composition. We can clearly see that if a manufacturing enterprise did not respond to the environment it would soon become inappropriate, and, in effect, it would die.

Our focus in manufacturing has been placed largely on the question of how to change and improve the physical system (the hardware and software) in response to changes in the environment. The problem with this approach is twofold. First, only one part of the system is being adapted to the changing environment. Second, because of internal dynamic relationships within the manufacturing enterprise, other sub-systems are reacting to this change, but not necessarily in a desirable or favorable way.

The net result of these reactions with the environment and internally may be to produce a misfit between sub-systems resulting in a manufacturing enterprise that is incapable of responding adequately to the environment. This might not be a problem when the environment is fairly stable, or competition is limited to price factors, or market demand is large enough to sustain inefficient systems. However, when the environment is dynamic and subject to rapid changes, or competition is based on more complex factors, and more competitors are chasing after limited market share, this inability to adequately respond may become a handicap to physical survival.

Equifinality

One key aspect of open systems theory is the principle of equifinality which states that a given final result may be achieved with different initial conditions and in different ways. The implication is that it is possible to achieve a given goal or objective by following any of several different options. There is no unique solution and no one best way.

This contrasts sharply with our conventional thinking in manufacturing. Manufacturing enterprise design, based on a closed systems view of the organization and people dimension, effectively isolates these elements from the technical sub-system and each other. Often our closed system approach is also based on a reductionist model which is founded on cause and effect relationships. This has led to our belief in a one best solution, or a one best way. Even when these rationalistic models give way to a more human and social orientation, the retention of the closed system approach still leads to the belief that sub-systems can be treated in isolation and a continued focus on a one best solution.

Equifinality suggests that there is considerable technical and organizational choice available in the development of agile manufacturing enterprises. A given set of objectives can be achieved in several different ways. There is no particular solution which can be regarded as optimal.

What we find here are theoretical concepts to support the points made in Chapter 3 about CIM, and its applicability. There are two points.

First, CIM as we have developed the concept is a closed system. Its development has largely only been concerned with technical issues. We have developed CIM in isolation from the other parts of the enterprise. The focus has been on design, production planning and control, robotics and so forth. Other parts of the manufacturing enterprise such as sales, marketing and management accounting have been ignored and treated as isolated sub-systems. The social, human activity and organizational sub-systems have likewise been ignored. When we have addressed them, it has usually been as though they were isolated sub-systems. Most often we have not considered the interactions between the various sub-systems.

In Europe and Scandinavia we have witnessed, in recent years, an effort to focus on some combination of technical, organizational, social and human activity sub-systems, but commonly these efforts are only focused on the shop floor, often because the people who have driven these developments have been primarily motivated by the humanization of work. Unfortunately, these approaches, while they rejected the rationalist model in favour of one based on a humanistic, social actor view, still leave the closed system, decomposition assumptions of the Taylor Model intact. The net effect has been, therefore, not the creation of a new manufacturing paradigm, but the development of a humanized form of the Taylor Model.

This is no doubt a laudable achievement, but the emphasis is still on optimization of components, the consideration of sub-systems in isolation and the pursuit of the one best humanized shop floor environment. This is not therefore an approach that can be recommended to the designers of agile manufacturing enterprises. We cannot say that the proponents of the humanized Taylor Model have overestimated the range of technical and organizational choice that is available; there usually have only been two basic choices available. We, in manufacturing, have generally chosen wrongly. The *correct* choice, their own, is in fact often a rigid prescription.

We can view our CIM systems, therefore, and the humanized versions, as being rooted in the classical Taylor Model; closed systems thinking, which assumes that one can develop sub-systems (for example, the technology, the shop floor working environment) without regard for the other sub-systems or the manufacturing enterprise as a whole.

The second point about CIM and its applicability is that a successful CIM application cannot be regarded as evidence that the application was suited to CIM, only that it was possible with CIM. Equifinality implies that several other possible solutions could have achieved similar results. Each one, of course, would have its own costs and implications associated with it.

Good, bad or optimal systems?

At this point we should now turn our attention to the issue of optimality. In systems engineering it is normal to seek an optimal solution. We now suggest that, in practical situations, an optimal solution is not necessarily desirable or realistic.

This statement might at first appear to be crazy. So we will ask ourselves a question. Is there any theoretical basis for such a view? To find an answer we shall turn to the theory of optimal control.

Our argument is based on work undertaken in the field of control systems on the topic of optimal control (Rosenbrock and McMorran, 1971). A common mathematical formulation of the closed loop optimal control problem is to seek a closed loop controller that minimizes the functional

$$J = \int_0^\infty (x^T Q x + u^T R u) \, dt$$

We need not concern ourselves with the details of this functional. All we need to say is that it can be proved, mathematically, that a unique controller exists which minimizes J provided that Q and R satisfy certain conditions.

What we do need to say, however, is that the closed loop system is only optimal in the special sense defined, namely that given a system, it is possible to find a controller that minimizes J. The word optimal, however, carries with it the suggestion that the system has desirable properties in general. Rosenbrock and McMorran have shown that this need not be the case. In particular, they demonstrated that the optimal system that they considered had properties that cannot usually be achieved in practice, and may have properties that are highly undesirable.

There are several reasons for this, some of which are highly technical. Some of the difficulties arise because of the difference between theory and practice. The optimal controller introduces something that control engineers call phase advance, which in an ideal theoretical system poses no problem. In a practical system, however, the presence of noise signals severely limits the amount of phase advance that can be introduced if actuator saturation and excessive wear are to be avoided. Also, because of the way the optimal control problem is formulated, the implementation requires that all system states be measured and used. In practice there are financial constraints on the number of measurements that can be made. There are, of course, ways of dealing with these problems, but they bring other problems in their wake.

Another point that Rosenbrock and McMorran made concerns the issue of conditional stability of the closed loop system. In complex situations where there is more than one system input and output (that is, a multivariable system) and where each input affects more than one output (that is, there is cross-coupling or interaction between inputs and outputs), then it is known that in these circumstances, a loop failure can result in an otherwise stable system, becoming unstable.

As Rosenbrock and McMorran pointed out, an essential requirement for most industrial control systems will be that changes in loop gains between zero (that is, an open loop resulting from a failure) and the design values, and in all combinations, should leave the system with an adequate stability margin. Rosenbrock and McMorran present a simple mathematical analysis of an optimal control problem which results in the minimization of the functional J, but which, when one loop fails, results in an unstable system. The example that they consider shows that optimality does not ensure this does not happen.

The implication of this simple analysis is that an optimal system is not necessarily a good system. It may in fact be quite bad, totally impractical and unusable. It is only optimal from a narrow theoretical point of view, in a very precisely defined sense. In practice, several unconsidered factors can combine to make it impracticable.

The implications for our conventional view, that of seeking an optimal manufacturing enterprise, are profound. Optimality is a very narrow and precise concept. Precision implies that we define the characteristic of the system and the optimization criteria exactly. The defined system is then only optimal in the precise sense defined. In practice, however, the system is not optimal because anything that is vague, or difficult to quantify or analyze is assumed be only a secondary effect and is left out of the system description. Thus the real system is not optimal. It is the model of the system that has been optimized.

If we believe that this precise concept is adequate and sufficient for the purposes of judging the performance of a manufacturing enterprise, then we have to accept that our belief rests on the assumption of a theoretical situation. In other words, it is quite legitimate to ignore the complexity that arises from the practicalities and constraints of real manufacturing enterprises. Moreover, our belief in an optimal solution implies that we believe that the system has some characteristics that make it desirable. Otherwise we would not use the terminology. But the point is, of course, that the complexities of real life situations, the things that we would prefer to ignore, can combine and act to make our so called optimal system a bad system. The implications are that it can be quite foolish to seek the optimal solution. The optimal solution in a complex situation only represents a theoretical ideal. It is the performance that we could achieve if the complexity and constraints of the real world did not interfere to produce a different outcome.

Ashby's law of requisite variety

Ashby's law of requisite variety states that continuing effective control in a changing environment requires a controller with a variety of responses which can match the variety of the environmental information (Ashby, 1956). Put another way, the variety within a system must be at least as great as the environmental variety against which it attempts to regulate itself. More succinctly, it means that only variety can regulate variety.

This law is part of a general theory of adaptive systems. A common example of its validity is found in aircraft control systems. The flight envelope of a modern aircraft covers a wide range of air speeds and altitudes which affects the system dynamics and behavior. Often it is not possible to design a single controller that can cope with the wide range of operating conditions, and control engineers have developed techniques called gain scheduling, which involves adapting the controller parameters or structure to suit the operating conditions. Thus, in other words, to control the aircraft over the complete range of operating conditions, a control system with variety designed into it is required.

What are the implications for manufacturing? The first is obvious. Manufacturing enterprises need an increased variety of responses to match the increasing variety of the environment. The second is also obvious. Unless the environmental conditions are fairly stable and well defined, as in the mass production environments of the past, then a highly automated manufacturing plant, where emphasis is placed on obtaining relatively limited variety from the flexibility of computer based manufacturing technology (programmable controls), may have insufficient variety to respond to the environment.

Third, but not so obviously, to survive in a highly dynamic environment, systems need to avoid becoming rigid, which will make them ineffective against external changes. Manufacturing enterprises need agility, and to achieve this goal, there is a need to be able to generate new ideas which can lead to new responses. This points to the central role of people and evolutionary concepts such as continuing improvement and incremental strategy development and so on, that is, the learning organization, responsive structures, adaptable people and flexible technologies.

A modern concept of manufacturing systems

The findings of the National Academy of Engineering's Committee on the Foundations of World Class Manufacturing (Heim and Compton, 1992) stress the importance of a system view in achieving the goal of a manufacturing system that is so efficient, responsive and effective that it will make the manufacturing enterprise that possesses such a system one of the most competitive in the world. The argument put forward is that a modern manufacturing company cannot be competitive if it continues to operate as a loosely coalesced group of independent elements whose identity rests on a particular discipline or a detailed job description.

It is argued in the study that there is a group of operating principles that must be recognized, understood and adopted by manufacturing organizations that aspire to be world class performers. Central to implementing these principles is the belief expressed by Gibson (1992) that our engineering practices, which are largely based on the Taylor Model, should be abandoned, in favour of more appropriate ones.

The argument presented here is similar. Although a systems view is essential, the concept of systems engineering, with its roots in the Taylor Model, is not appropriate. Systems engineering attempts to decompose manufacturing problems into sub-problems, which are then solved in isolation from each other. Often our goal is to achieve a one best solution by seeking to optimize fragments of the system or sub-system, in the belief that this will achieve optimization at the system level. Uncertainty should be reduced in order to make everything more predictable. All this is, quite simply, wrong.

Systems engineering does nothing to question or change the basic assumptions that underlie traditional manufacturing practices. Systems engineering as an approach is wrong for several reasons.

First, manufacturing enterprises are open systems, not closed systems, and as such, it is possible to reach the goal of agile manufacturing, from different initial starting conditions, in several ways. Second, it is not possible to take a systems view as recommended by Heim and Compton (1992), if major parts of the system are ignored or treated as isolated components or sub-systems. Third, unless a true systems perspective is adopted, it will not be possible to develop a true picture of the complexity of the system. Fourth, the traditional systems engineering view perpetuates the confusion between an optimal system and one that has desirable properties. Fifth, because of emergent properties, the behavior of the manufacturing enterprise will be more complex than expected. And sixth, the requirement of requisite variety demands that we should seek to create variety within the system, which implies accepting uncertainty.

There are two important points here, which reiterate and support issues raised in earlier chapters. First, response to changes in the environment should, in general, lead to changes in the whole of the manufacturing enterprise, not just to changes in the physical sub-system (hardware and software). Thus to increase competitiveness and profitability, it is necessary to consider system wide changes, not just technical improvements. This implies looking at new forms of organization, considering the utilization of human resources, looking at how technologies could be used to support human skills and knowledge and so forth.

Second, when changes are made in one part of the system, they have an effect elsewhere and these interactions should be considered during design. So, for example, while it is legitimate to foresee changes to technology as affecting skill requirements, it is equally legitimate to foresee desired changes to skills affecting the form of technology.

Joint technical and organizational design as a model for the design of agile manufacturing enterprises

That manufacturing systems consist of more than designed physical systems underlies the theory of joint technical and organizational design (Kidd *et al.*, 1991). The design approach is characterized by the idea that any manufacturing system is a combination of a technical sub-system

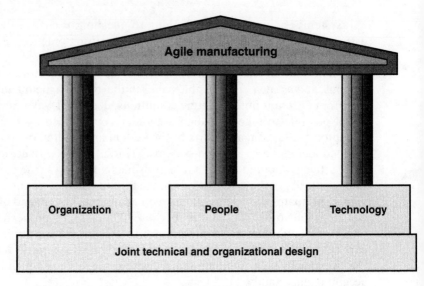

Figure 6.2   The basis of agile manufacturing. *Source:* Cheshire Henbury. © 1991. Published with permission.

(physical layout and equipment and so on), an organizational sub-system (a system of relationships among those who work in the manufacturing enterprise) and people. The technology, organization and people are sub-systems in mutual interaction with each other, and each influences the characteristics of the other sub-systems.

The joint technical and organizational design approach is concerned with integrating technical, human and organizational considerations in the design, development and implementation of manufacturing systems. The term has been interpreted in different ways, but most of these aim at some kind of joint optimization.

To achieve agile manufacturing it will be necessary to move beyond the Taylor Model, to go further than the humanized Taylor Model, and stop using technology-fix. Agile manufacturing needs to achieve integration of organization, people and technology, as illustrated in Figure 6.2. Underlying the three supporting pillars is the foundation, which is a design approach that deals with all three areas concurrently. This is joint technical and organizational design (Kidd *et al.*, 1991). The underlying principle is that all three pillars represent key sub-systems, which are interdependent.

The key feature of joint technical and organizational design is that it is a concurrent design method. This means that it is based on:

- Addressing organization, people and technology issues in parallel, with trade-offs made between all three areas.
- An interdisciplinary approach.

- Recognition that the organization and people issues within the design process itself, are as important as the organization and people issues that need to be addressed as part of the system design.

The benefits of joint technical and organizational design lie in the area of improved design and implementation processes, better system designs, more appropriate organizational structures, better matching of organization, people and technology and engaged and motivated people.

Design principles

To deal with the design of agile manufacturing enterprises, we need to adopt an approach based on the type of joint technical and organizational design principles formulated by Cherns (1976, 1987).

Originally Cherns (1976) formulated nine principles of joint technical and organizational design.

Compatibility

The design process by which we design agile manufacturing enterprises needs to be compatible with the objectives we are pursuing. We cannot, for example, bring about employee participation and empowerment by decree. Our objective is to design agile manufacturing enterprises, leading to systems which are capable of self-modification and adaptation, and where we derive competitive advantage from the people's inherent abilities. This requires that we develop some form of participatory organizational structure, but such a system must be designed by involving the people.

Minimum critical specification

This principle states that we should specify no more than is absolutely necessary, and this applies to all aspects of the system: tasks, jobs, roles and so on. We can be specific about what has to be done, but we should not over determine how things should be done. This implies a degree of flexibility and openness in job descriptions, group structures and technologies. This is exactly what is needed to achieve agility.

Variance control

Variances which cannot be eliminated should be controlled as near to the point of origin of the variance as possible. Variances are those events that are unexpected or unprogrammed. Some of these variances may be critical, in that they have an important effect on results. It is important that we should control variances at source because, not to do so, often introduces time delays which tend to lengthen throughput times and so on. In agile manufacturing, response time is a critical variable, which must be kept as short as possible.

The multifunctional principle – organism versus mechanism

Traditional organizations are based on a high level of specialization and fragmentation of work. This means that we can more easily replace people. The problem with this approach is that when we require a complex array of responses, as with agile manufacturing, it becomes easier to achieve this variety of responses when the system elements are capable of undertaking or performing several functions.

Boundary location

In traditional organizations we primarily organize around fragmented functions, and one result of this is that barriers arise which impede the sharing of data, information, knowledge and experience. Boundaries should be designed around a complete flow of information, knowledge and materials, so as to enable the sharing of all relevant data, information, knowledge and experience. In other words one should create natural groups. This is particulary crucial in agile manufacturing, because the sharing of these elements is very important to achieving rapid response, customer satisfaction and so on.

Information flow

We need to provide information at the place where decisions and actions will be taken based on the information. Many information systems are designed on the opposite principle. Information is usually provided to those distant from the point where decisions are taken, thus removing decision-making from those who are best placed to take decisions. Empowerment and continuing improvement, both key aspects of agile manufacturing, require that we provide everyone involved with information to support these activities.

Support congruence

This principle states that we should design our reward systems, performance measurement systems and so forth to reinforce the behaviors that we seek. For example, individual reward for individual effort is not appropriate if team behavior is required.

Design and human values

One of the objectives of manufacturing enterprises should be to provide a high quality of working life. This is particularly important in an agile manufacturing environment, where we will be faced with rapid changes, and where our aim is to use human abilities to gain competitive advantage. If we do not address the human factor, that is, issues of stress, motivation, personal development and so on, then agile manufacturing enterprises will be no more agile than our current manufacturing systems.

Incompletion

Design is never finished. As soon we complete implementation, its consequences, and on going changes arising from empowerment and continuing improvement activities, indicate the need for redesign.

In a later paper, Cherns (1987) introduced two further principles:

Power and authority

In agile manufacturing, when we assign responsibilities to people for tasks, we should make the resources that they need available to them, and give them the power and authority to secure these resources. In return we should expect people to accept responsibility for the proper use of the resources. We should also make sure that people have the knowledge and skills needed, but having provided our people with knowledge, skills and resources, we should avoid interfering, unless we are equally knowledgeable and skilled.

Transitional organization

We can be faced with two quite distinct problems when creating new organizations. We could be dealing with the design and start-up of plants on greenfield sites, or on brownfield sites (existing plants). The second is much more difficult. When we are designing agile manufacturing enterprises, we will be faced with both types of situation. We should, in both situations, view the design team, and the processes it uses, as a tool to support the transitions that we wish to see. In other words, the design team is an integral part of the process of managing change. As such it should embody the new values and culture and be diffusing them throughout the enterprise. The actions taken by the design teams will speak louder than any words embedded in mission statements. If we really want to see participation, empowerment, and all the other good things of which we have spoken, then we should start by ensuring that the design teams become the messengers of our new values and concepts.

HITOP™: A joint technical and organizational design tool

HITOP stands for the High Integration of Technology, Organization and People (Majchrzak et al., 1991). HITOP is a tool that helps to implement manufacturing and information technologies. The HITOP analysis process allows us to identify the organizational and job design implications of critical features of the proposed technologies. It then helps to identify key task and skill requirements so that we can properly plan and develop our human resources to meet operational needs.

HITOP comes in the form of a workbook, that is in effect, an easy to read analysis manual, providing step-by-step guidance, rationales for analysis, blank analysis forms and worked examples. It covers a wide range of issues and is based on a six stage methodology.

The first stage of the methodology involves making an assessment of our organizational readiness for change, which is followed in the second stage by an assessment of the technology that we have proposed, in order to identify its critical features. The third step is an analysis of the essential task requirements, which leads to the fourth step, an assessment of the skill requirements. The fifth step is concerned with determining how people should be rewarded. The final step is concerned with designing organizational changes which need to be achieved given the technology and people requirements, which leads to the generation of a specific implementation plan.

The HITOP design tool will therefore lead us through:

- An assessment of organizational readiness for change.
- A definition of the critical technical features of advanced technologies.
- The determination of essential job requirements, job design options, skills, training and selection requirements.
- The determination of requirements and options for pay, promotion and organizational structure.

The analysis thus provides a direct and ordered consideration of critical technology, organization and people factors, and helps to identify those factors which require in-depth attention. The analysis also gives an expanded insight into the total organizational and people impacts of specific technologies, going well beyond skills and training. Identification of people and organizational cost drivers in technology implementation is also another result of the analysis.

HITOP allows us to specify alternative organizations and different ways for managing people given specific technology plans. HITOP also provides guidance in determining the appropriate time for implementing technology plans, and helps to identify those equipment and system choices that are likely to create the greatest number of people and organizational problems, so that we may be better prepared to deal with them.

By performing HITOP analysis, we are guided by an iterative, systems based process in which all critical features of the organization, people and technology environment are systematically assessed and all implementable options are identified. This enables us to define the consequences of major decisions before they are implemented. As a result, surprises downstream will be reduced and necessary changes to the technology, organization or the people involved can be identified.

Total enterprise design

Joint technical and organizational design tools, such as HITOP, give us a means of dealing with organization, people and technology aspects of our manufacturing enterprise. But it is quite apparent that our manufacturing enterprises consist of more than just these three sub-systems. In our total enterprise system concept we also have customers, suppliers and so on, all important sub-systems.

In principle, however, there are no reasons why the type of approach we have discussed thus far, cannot be extended to consider the total enterprise. Instead of just using joint technical and organizational design to deal with organization, people and technology, we can address all aspects of the enterprise through total enterprise design.

A basis for total enterprise design can be found in what are called the foundations of world class manufacturing systems.

Foundations of world class manufacturing systems as a framework

The National Academy of Engineering has defined what are called the foundations of world class practice of manufacturing systems (Heim and Compton, 1992). It is argued that these foundations are as interrelated and overlapping as are the elements of the manufacturing system they are intended to improve. The foundations are, however, a system of action-oriented principles whose collective application can produce important improvements in the manufacturing enterprise. The foundations are ideally suited to agile manufacturing. Ten foundations have been proposed.

Goals and objectives

If we wish to become a world class agile manufacturing company, we must establish, as an operating goal, the objectives of becoming a world class agile manufacturing enterprise. We need to do two things. We need goals and objectives relating to the design and development of an infrastructure, and goals and objectives relating to the exploitation of the infrastructure. We have to assess our performance, across a wide range of metrics, by undertaking competitive benchmarking against our competitors and against other operations, functions, enterprises and so on. We should do this even in other industries, where there are organizations recognized as world class performers. The information that we collect through competitive benchmarking should be used to establish a wide range of goals and objectives. We should then make sure that these are communicated to all our people, and then obtain their commitment to achieving them. We should ensure that our performance is continuously measured and assessed against the objectives. In addition we should also continuously review the appropriateness of our goals and objectives and change them when necessary.

Customers

We must undertake to implement within the enterprise the concept that all parts of the system, and all our people, have a customer. Customers may be internal or external. We should seek to constantly strengthen this concept. All our people must know who their customers are, and must seek to understand and satisfy their needs. Customer focus should become a competitive foundation of our agile manufacturing enterprise. Understanding customer needs and the delivery of customer delight should permeate all our decision-making, actions and thinking.

Organization

All elements of our manufacturing enterprise should be integrated to satisfy the needs of our customers, both internal and external. This should be achieved in a way that is appropriate to the needs of each customer. We should eliminate the organizational barriers erected in the past, to enable and permit improved and effective communication and cooperation. Our organizations should be designed to improve the effectiveness of all aspects of our operations. We must keep our organizational practices and structures under constant review and keep a sharp look out for the emergence of wasteful procedures, bureaucracy, empires and turf defending. Our organization should be a competitive weapon and should assist us to provide our customers with high-quality products and services.

People

The involvement, commitment and empowerment of all the people in the manufacturing enterprise is critical to agile manufacturing. We need to make full use of our people's skills, knowledge, judgment, experience, creativity and intelligence. We must seek to use people in a process of continuous improvement in all elements of the manufacturing system, but in a way that is linked to our strategic goals. Our people must be trained, supported, committed and motivated. We must develop a new culture of concern about their welfare and wellbeing so that we avoid damaging attitudes and behavior. We must respect them and view them as a resource, and a source of competitive advantage.

Suppliers

In traditional manufacturing enterprises we have created an attitude of mistrust between ourselves and our suppliers. It is essential that the barriers should be tackled and eliminated in the same way that we must eliminate barriers between the elements in our manufacturing organization. We must share our goals with our suppliers, build long term partnership arrangements with them, exchange information, interchange our people, help our suppliers to improve and assist them to achieve a high degree of customer focus. We should achieve a high level of integration with our suppliers and share accrued benefits with them.

Management approach and philosophy

Management is ultimately responsible for creating a world class agile manufacturing enterprise, and for bringing about the change to a culture of customer focus and commitment. Management is also responsible for creating a system of values where people are seen as assets and resources. It is management that must bring about involvement and empowerment. And it is management that must implement infrastructure objectives such as continuous improvement. All this demands the personal commitment and involvement of all our managers. This is critical to success. We must help our managers to change their styles, values, beliefs and culture. Without these changes agile manufacturing will remain nothing more than an intellectual concept.

Metrics

Metrics, that is measures of performance, play a crucial role in helping to determine and monitor our performance. Metrics help to define goals and performance improvement targets. They are essential for carrying our competitive benchmarking. We need to develop a comprehensive set of appropriate metrics covering all aspects of the enterprise, including business performance, financial performance, operational performance and infrastructure matters. Our metrics should define, describe, and wherever possible, quantify the criteria used to measure the effectiveness of our manufacturing enterprise, all of the interrelated components and progress that we are making towards becoming a world class agile manufacturing enterprise. The information contained in our metrics should also be shared with all the people and used to support their continuous improvement activities.

Describing and understanding

In the past we have made a very poor job of improving our understanding of the characteristics of our enterprises. We have managed to create many depositories of knowledge, but never effectively coordinated it. We must now remedy this situation by seeking to describe and understand the interdependency of the many elements of the manufacturing system. Our goal should be to reveal new knowledge about relationships and to properly explore the consequences of alternative decisions. To do this we need to use modelling and simulation techniques, and bring together fragmented and partial understandings of the enterprise. We need to use the knowledge that we gain from our describing and understanding activities to improve the enterprise and to support all our communications.

Experimentation and learning

In a world where continuous change is the norm, we must specifically aim to undertake experimentation and learning activities, and then undertake an assessment and evaluation of the results. The knowledge and understanding that we develop and acquire through these experimentation and learning activities, once evaluated and accepted as beneficial, should, if appropriate, be transmitted throughout the enterprise. It should then be incorporated into the operating philosophy and procedures of the enterprise.

Technology

World class agile manufacturing companies will not use technology to compensate for inadequacies. We will use technology as a tool for achieving world class competitiveness. We will continuously search for technologies that offer the potential to create competitive advantage, and then adapt and implement these technologies at an appropriate time and in a way that will secure the potential advantages that we have identified. We will develop the skills necessary to bridge business orientation and technological awareness and capability, and focus our attention on building technology deployment capabilities as well as technology development skills.

In addition to these ten foundations, we include one more, which is of equal stature and importance:

Environment

An agile manufacturing enterprise will operate in a way that is environmentally conscious. We should, in all aspects of our decision-making and operations, seek to identify, address and resolve all the environmental aspects and issues. We should seek to do more than just comply with legal requirements, but should recognize environmental concerns as customer requirements and seek to deliver a high level of environmental responsiveness. We should seek to make environmental concern a factor that affects our customers' purchase decisions, and thus use environmental issues as a source of competitive advantage.

Using the foundations as a tool for total enterprise design

The eleven foundations that we have described above can be used as a theoretical framework for total enterprise design. Moreover, the framework is also suitable for embedding in a computer based tool to support total enterprise design.

To illustrate. Note that the foundations have been put forward as a set of interrelated elements. We can therefore represent them as a network as shown in Figure 6.3. The connections between each node (foundation) are not specified.

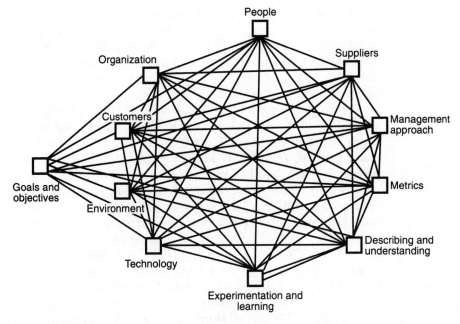

Figure 6.3 Network of interrelationships between manufacturing systems foundations. *Source:* Manufacturing Knowledge Inc. © 1993. Published with permission.

To understand the nature of these relationships we need to go down to a lower level. Consider a simple example.

Let us assume that environmentally conscious manufacturing is an enterprise goal. This specific goal might be decomposed into specific objectives which might be time dependent, for example reduce waste by 50% over the next 12 months, or eliminate 40% of solvent based cleaning fluids over the next 9 months. Thus, in order to implement our high level goal of environmentally conscious manufacturing we need to develop a set of metrics by which we can define and quantify our goal and also measure our level of achievement. Thus, the link between foundations, goals and objectives and metrics is a set of measures which we can use to plan changes and monitor progress.

It is possible to achieve our goal of environmentally conscious manufacturing through the application of several means, which involve either changing product designs, modifying processes and organizational structures, or improving manufacturing efficiency. Thus, under the foundation (environment) we can catalogue several specific methods and techniques to achieve environmentally conscious manufacturing. A number of methods and techniques are possible, including near shape forming, waste recycling, material substitution, housekeeping measures, predictive maintenance and training.

We can define links between each possible method and technique, and each metric. In some cases there will be no links between a particular method and technique and a metric. When a link does exist, then the nature of the link would need to be defined. For example, one particular method or technique might have a major impact on a given metric, while only a minor impact on another.

By using this type of information it becomes possible to define the methods and techniques most likely to achieve our sought after improvements. Thus the link between the foundation, metrics and the foundation environment is knowledge about the impact that each method and technique has on a particular environmental metric.

If we take a particular technique, say predictive maintenance, then this has links with other foundations. For example, to implement this we may need computer based support tools, hence a link to the foundation (technology). We would also need to train people, so we have a link with the foundation (people). Now, predictive maintenance might be split between maintenance personnel and production associates on the shop floor. So we have a link with the foundation (organization), and so on.

Thus, under each foundation heading, we can group many methods and techniques. We can also form links with other foundations, because to implement a specific method and technique in one foundation, we need also to do things in others. Using these principles we can model the relationships between foundations, making the high-level interrelationships shown in Figure 6.3 very specific. This enables us to begin to consider total enterprise design, and to consider and address the important interrelationships.

Concluding comments

We have tried to point out that a fundamental basis for the design of agile manufacturing enterprises is the systems view. However, this systems view is not the same as the one we have become familiar with. Our conventional systems thinking is actually reductionist and rather narrow. This is not really systems thinking. It is the exact opposite to what systems thinking is really all about.

The key message of this chapter is that it is not possible to develop a truly agile manufacturing enterprise using this out-dated approach. What we need is a design method that does not reduce the complexity of the problem through systems decomposition, but which allows us to work with the complexity. We need to fully understand and explore the complexity that arises from the interrelationships that exist between sub-systems, and to deal with the system as a whole, and not as isolated sub-systems and components.

Key points

- The basis of agile manufacturing enterprise design is systems theory, not to be confused with systems engineering.
- Our approach must be a holistic one, away from quick fixes and panaceas.
- We need to understand the key elements of systems theory, such as emergent properties and equifinality, before embarking on the application of systems theory to agile manufacturing enterprise design.
- We need to apply the concept of total enterprise design.
- Total enterprise design is based on the foundations for world class manufacturing systems. These foundations should be fully understood and seen as interacting sub-systems.
- The key to total enterprise design is keeping the full complexity of interactions in view while dealing with specific sub-systems.

References

Ashby W.R. (1956). *An Introduction to Cybernetics*. London: Chapman & Hall

Checkland P. (1981). *Systems Thinking, Systems Practice*. Chichester: John Wiley

Checkland P. (1983). OR and the systems movement: mappings and conflicts. *J. Operational Research Society*, **34**(8), 661–75

Cherns A. (1976). The principles of sociotechnical design. *Human Relations*, **29**(8), 783–92

Cherns A. (1987). Principles of sociotechnical design revisited. *Human Relations*, **40**(3), 153–62

Gibson J.E. (1992). Taylorism and professional education. In *Manufacturing Systems. Foundations of World Class Practice* (Heim J.A. and Compton W.D., eds.), pp. 149–57. Washington DC: National Academy

Heim J.A. and Compton W.D., eds. (1992). *Manufacturing Systems. Foundations of World Class Practice*. Washington DC: National Academy

Iacocca Institute (1991). *21st Century Manufacturing Enterprise Strategy. An Industry-Led View. Vols. 1 & 2*. Bethlehem PA: Iacocca Institute

Kidd P.T., Hamacher B., Lane G., Bolk H., Havn E., Klevers T. and Klein L. (1991). Joint technical and organizational design of CIM systems for SME's. In *Computer Integrated Manufacturing. Proc. 7th CIM-Europe Conference* (Vio R. and Van Puymbroeck W., eds.), 173–181. London: Springer-Verlag

King M.C. (1988). Interdisciplinarity and systems thinking: some implications for engineering education and education for industry. *European J. Engineering Education*, **13**(3), 235–244

Majchrzak A., Fleischer M., Roithman D. and Mokray J. (1991). *Reference Manual for Performing the HITOP Analysis*. Ann Arbor MI: Industrial Technology Institute

Parnaby J. (1981). Concept of manufacturing system. In *Systems Behaviour, 3rd edn.* pp. 131–41. London: Paul Chapman

Rosenbrock H.H. and McMorran P.D. (1971). Good, bad or optimal? *IEEE Trans. Automatic Control* (AC-16(6)), 552–4

Womack J.P., Jones D.T. and Roos D. (1990). *The Machine That Changed the World*. New York: Rawson

7

The enterprise design process

Introduction

In this chapter we will look closely at the nature of design processes. How we go about designing an agile manufacturing enterprise and the associated manufacturing systems and computer based technologies is fundamentally important, primarily for two reasons. First, certain assumptions are built into our systems design processes, and when we design systems and technologies we do so based on a set of norms and value judgments. Second, to achieve agile manufacturing, we need agile design processes. All traditional design processes are, however, far from agile. They are, in fact, extremely rigid, awkward and sluggish. They commit us to following actions often based on poor understanding of the problems, and they keep our attention focused on these actions, even when our reasons for pursuing them have altered, or even disappeared.

Insights into design processes

Research into design and design processes has mostly been addressed in a fragmented way. While the early 1960s saw the emergence of design as a generic research topic, with conferences being held covering a wide range of disciplines (Jones and Thornley, 1963; Gregory, 1966), generic design research did not flourish, and has now largely disappeared from academia. For the most part, design research is undertaken within the boundaries of individual disciplines and professions, largely without cross-reference to other disciplines, and most importantly, often without regard for the generic findings that are available. Thus, one finds references to architectural design (Lawson, 1980), joint technical and organizational design (Cherns 1976, 1987), man–machine systems design (Sage, 1987), software engineering design (Agresti, 1986; Boehm, 1976, 1988, 1989) and knowledged-based systems design (Hickman *et al.*, 1989) but the cross-fertilization between these areas is almost non-existent.

In some respects this is not surprising because as we have already observed, our knowledge of the world has been divided up into self contained boxes. Furthermore, there has been no tradition of combining these boxes and looking at the issues that lie in the areas between knowledge domains. Yet in other respects, this is a peculiar phenomenon, because through the 1980s and 1990s we have seen a tremendous growth in applications of computer-aided design (CAD). However, it would seem that it is possible to develop CAD systems without paying much attention to the insights generated by research into design processes (Kidd, 1990). In other words, it seems one can develop a CAD system by just concentrating on the technical tasks that designers undertake, and ignoring the process by which these tasks are undertaken. This is indeed a strange situation! Only with the growth of interest in concurrent engineering have we begun to consider our design processes in any detail.

Design: science, art or calculation?

Is design about science, art or calculation? Rosenbrock (1977), writing about engineering design, believes that it is an art rather than a science, implying a higher status for engineering design. Science is about systematic and formalized knowledge, while art implies judgment and the exercise of acquired human skills. In Rosenbrock's view, design, whether it be in mechanical engineering, architecture, control systems or ergonomics, is not just about systematic and formalized knowledge, but also skillful execution of tasks leading to a sought after result. This is not to say that scientific knowledge, methods and mathematical analysis do not enter into design in an important way. They do, but design cannot be wholly described as science or the application of scientific knowledge.

Jones (1981) made a very similar point. He observed that design should not be confused with art, science or mathematics. He argues that design is a hybrid activity which depends, for its successful execution, upon a proper blending of all three elements. Design is most unlikely to succeed if it is exclusively identified with any one element. Rosenbrock (1977) also commented that design contains elements of experience and judgment. These partly embody knowledge that is not expressible in exact and mathematical form, partly what Polanyi (1962) refers to as tacit knowledge (the things we know but cannot tell) and partly value judgments which are not amenable to the scientific method. Let us now examine the nature of design more closely.

Design problems, solutions and processes

Design is an area of great complexity. It is a human activity not fully understood, even by those who design. Lawson (1980) identified certain important characteristics of design problems, solutions and processes.

Considering design problems first, Lawson makes three important points.

(1) It is difficult to comprehensively state a design problem.
(2) Design problems are subject to subjective interpretation.
(3) There is a tendency for design problems to be organized hierarchically.

The difficulties of obtaining a comprehensive statement of the design problem arise because many aspects of design problems do not begin to emerge until attempts have been made to define solutions. Design problems are full of uncertainties about all sorts of issues, for example, constraints, objectives and priorities. Some aspects of design problems may never be fully exposed. As a consequence, a comprehensive and static formulation of design problems should not be expected. Rather it should be expected that design problems will become clearer as solutions are proposed and investigated.

The second point relates to the different way in which people view design problems. For example, an organizational scientist will take a different view of, say, operational problems with a machining center, than a technologist. People's views of design problems are value laden, and the definition of a problem is largely a matter of subjective assessment and judgment. Certain issues will be prominent in one person's perceptions, while other issues will be prominent in another's. As a result it is not possible to obtain an entirely objective formulation of a given problem.

The final point relates to the situation described in Chapter 5, where we noted the potential difficulties that could arise from using a robot to carry out arc welding, while leaving the operator with the more mundane tasks.

In Chapter 5 we also briefly discussed the serial approach to dealing with organization and people issues. We could install new technologies and then deal with any resultant difficulties afterwards in a sequential manner. We could then view these difficulties as design problems in their own right, and then try to resolve them within the given constraints.

Alternatively we could see the difficulties as symptoms of another, higher level problem, that is, our failure to address organization and people issues at the conceptual stage of the technical design. Since we have no objective way of determining the right level at which to address problems, Lawson points out that it makes sense to begin at the highest level that is reasonable and practically possible.

Moving on now to consider design solutions, Lawson highlights two important points:

(1) There is always a near inexhaustible number of different solutions.
(2) Optimal solutions to design problems do not exist.

Lawson argues that the first point stems as a logical conclusion from the observation that design problems cannot be comprehensively described. It would be more accurate to say, however, that this issue is a result, not just of our inability to fully describe design problems, but also because of our subjective interpretation and the hierarchical organization of design problems.

For example, in the case of the machining center, an organizational scientist and a technologist will both come up with different solutions to the operational problems. Likewise the solution of organization and people difficulties will be quite different depending on whether these are seen as problems in isolation, or as problems that arise from the way we approach the consideration of these issues, that is, serially rather than as parallel issues. However, there is another issue, and that is choice. It is extremely rare to come across a situation where there is only one design solution available for a given problem. For most problems there are several solutions, with many variations of each. All these diverse factors combine to produce a situation where there will be large number of different solutions for a given design problem.

Lawson's point about the lack of optimal solutions to design problems relates to the fact that to measure optimality one has to define a measure of performance against which the design solution can be measured. Design, however, involves trade-offs and compromises. Good performance in one area is usually achieved at the cost of performance in another and statements of objectives might be contradictory. Thus, Lawson argues that there are no optimal solutions, only a range of acceptable solutions. Appraisal and evaluation of solutions is largely a matter of judgment.

Finally, let us consider the design process. Lawson makes six important points:

(1) Design is an endless process.
(2) No process is infallible.
(3) Design involves problem finding as well as problem solving.
(4) Design involves subjective value judgments.
(5) Design is a prescriptive activity.
(6) Designers work in the context of a need for action.

The first point refers to the fact that, owing to resource (time, money, manpower) limitations, it is not possible to complete a design. Because of these resource constraints, design stops, even though we may not be entirely happy with the solution. The objectives will have been met, but not to our full satisfaction. However, we do not consider it to be worthwhile to proceed as the results would not justify the further resources needed. Of course, this does not imply that further design work will never be tackled. It will, but probably later.

With regard to the correct process by which design activity should be pursued, Lawson observes that we will never find an infallibly good way of designing. The point he is making is that there is no sequence of operations which will always guarantee a result. Design problems are all different, and solutions are not just a result of the problem definition, that is, what needs to be achieved or to be resolved. There are many other factors such as legal constraints, organizational politics, fashion and so on, which influence design problem solving. The search for a one best comprehensive design process is therefore like searching for the Holy Grail. It is a myth. There is no one best process.

We turn now to the intertwining of problem finding and problem solving. Lawson reports that during design, much time is spent identifying design problems. A central tenet of modern design thinking is that problems and solutions are seen as emerging together rather than one following logically on from the other. Therefore, problem and solution become clearer and more precise as the design process proceeds. This is an important point and we will return to it later in the chapter.

The fourth point that Lawson makes is that design is influenced by subjective value judgments. Design therefore is not solely concerned with logical and explicit criteria and objective assessment and decision-making. We are always taking decisions about which problems are the most important ones, and which solutions most successfully resolve these problems. Lawson argues that complete objectivity would demand total and dispassionate detachment. Human beings can never be wholly dispassionate or detached. On the contrary, we are usually deeply involved in the design problems that we address and often defensive about our solutions.

Lawson's fifth point is that design is a prescriptive activity. By this he means that, unlike in science, we are not primarily concerned with questions of *what is* and *why*, but with questions of *what might be*, *could be* and *should be*. We therefore prescribe and create the future, and because of this, Lawson believes that we should be subject to ethical and moral scrutiny.

Lawson's sixth and final point is that we work in the context of a need for action. In other words, our design activities are not an end, but a process by which we bring about some change in the world. As a result, we work with incomplete information and have to make compromises within defined constraints.

We can see that design is inherently subject to a large degree of uncertainty. It is often not possible to specify in an exact way what is required. There will be constraints on what we can achieve and we will have to make trade-offs between conflicting performance requirements. The solution to a particular design problem will therefore be a compromise, and we need to know a great deal about the relative advantages and disadvantages of the different design options before we can make a satisfactory choice.

We will also have to satisfy a large number of constraints and some of these will either be tacit, or will only be vaguely known. Furthermore, some constraints will only become explicit when we violate them. In addition, our knowledge of the system will always be limited and our system models will always be limited representations of reality, because some aspects of the real system will always be neglected and we will make simplifying assumptions in order to make the problem more tractable.

Design, therefore, is a skilled job calling for expert knowledge and judgment. It is carried out under conditions of uncertainty, and scientific knowledge and methods are used to support the activity. Design is also a creative activity in which we are continually learning new things, addressing new and unsolved problems and extending our skills and knowledge.

Divergence, transformation and convergence

It has been traditional to consider the design process as consisting of three distinct stages: analysis, synthesis and evaluation, as represented in Figure 7.1. Analysis involves decomposing problems into smaller ones. Synthesis involves a process of redefining the whole in a different way, and evaluation is the act of identifying the consequence of this new synthesis.

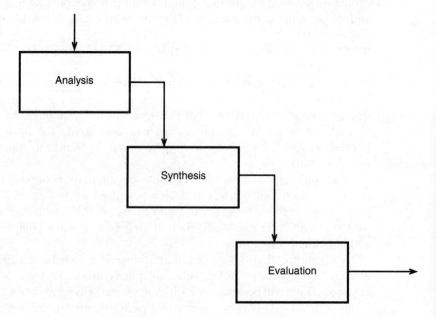

Figure 7.1   Model of a linear design strategy.

It is usual to iterate many times through these stages, so our simple linear model shown in Figure 7.1 becomes a more complex iterative model as shown in Figure 7.2. However, even this more complex model does not represent the true complexity of design, because it only shows iterations between successive stages, while in practice there will also be iterations across stages as shown in Figure 7.3. Even this more complex model does not convey the true complexity of the design process. If we think about the various phases that design projects pass through, that is, feasibility study, outline proposals, conceptual design, detailed design and so on, then within each of these phases we would also find elements of analysis, synthesis and evaluation, with several feedback paths within each. Thus our model is now as illustrated in Figure 7.4.

Jones (1981) presented a different classification structure of design which, he argues, is more relevant to systems designing than our traditional analysis, synthesis and evaluation model of engineering design. This more recent classification is based on three stages which he calls divergence, transformation and convergence. We will discuss each in turn.

Jones describes divergence as a stage in the design process where the boundary of a design situation is extended so as to create a search space that is large enough to enable us to undertake a fruitful search for a solution. The chief characteristics of the divergence stage are:

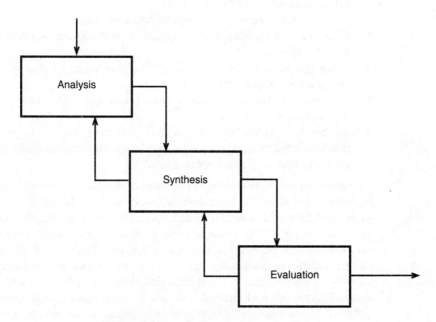

Figure 7.2   Model of an iterative design strategy.

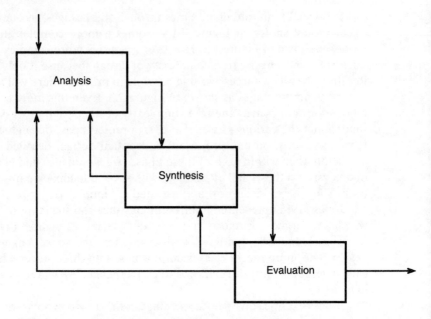

Figure 7.3 Model of an iterative design strategy with feedback across several stages.

- Objectives are unstable and tentative.
- The problem boundary is unstable and undefined.
- Deferment of evaluation and a retention of things that seem relevant to the problem.
- Investigations use the design brief as a starting point and over time this brief is revised and evolves.
- Actions are taken to increase uncertainty and to remove preconceived notions and solutions.
- Research is undertaken to evaluate reactions of users, sponsors, markets and producers, with the consequences of shifting the problem boundaries and objectives.

Jones reports that the divergent stage of design involves a lot of what he calls *leg-work* rather than armchair speculation. In Jones' view, it is important that this stage be based upon fact finding, and that critical decisions should not be taken until we have discovered what it is that we are looking for. We need to undertake this fact finding with the aim of de-structuring or destroying the original brief, while at the same time identifying the features of the design situation that will permit a valuable and feasible degree of change. The aim of divergence is also to rapidly achieve, at low cost, sufficient new experience to counteract any false assumptions that we, the designers, and our clients or customers, may hold.

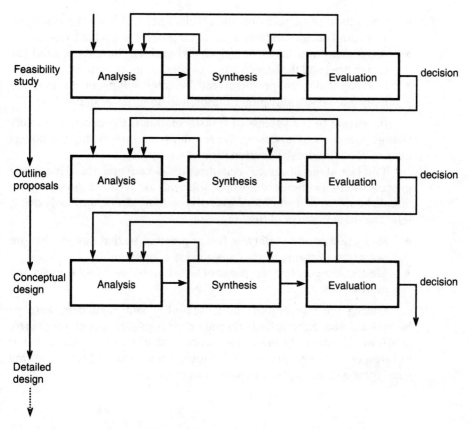

Figure 7.4   Model of a multiple phase design strategy.

Interestingly, Jones also points out that the skills necessary for this pre-design activity of divergence may not come readily to us as engineers and managers. Jones believes that researchers, writers and statisticians are more likely to possess the necessary skills needed for the divergent stage of the design process. We, as engineers and managers, may need to undertake a lot of unlearning before we reach a situation where we can maintain the degree of detachment, flexibility and breadth of view that is appropriate before we take design decisions.

After the divergent stage comes the stage that Jones has called transformation, which is the highly creative part of the design process. This involves elements of insight, pattern recognition and guesswork. It is in this stage that we find value judgments combining with technical issues to produce decisions which reflect the full reality of the design situation. The important characteristics of this stage are:

- Imposition of patterns on the results obtained from the divergent stage, and decisions about what to emphasize and what to ignore.
- Agreement and fixing of objectives, problem boundaries and the design brief and the identification of constraints and critical variables.
- Decomposition of problems into smaller sub-problems that are judged to be solvable either in isolation, in series or in parallel.

Important to the success of transformation is the ability to rapidly change sub-goals by assessing the feasibility and predicting the consequence of any particular combination of sub-goals.

The last stage in Jones' classification is convergence. This is the process where a number of possible solutions are reduced through more detailed analysis and considerations of secondary detail, until only one is left. The main features of this stage are:

- Reduction of uncertainty, as fast as possible, so that designs that are not worth pursuing further are quickly eliminated.
- Models representing the range of solutions become less abstract and more detailed.

During the convergent stage, flexibility and vagueness need to be avoided and the emphasis should be on providing detail. Of course, problems can arise during convergence, and if it should turn out that unforeseen problems prove to be critical, then there will be a resulting need for iteration, that is, a return to an early stage.

Designing computer based technologies

Now that we have gained some insight into the nature of design, and seen that simple linear models do not reflect the true complexity of design processes, we will examine some more complex models of the design process that are based on incremental processes. We will then argue that these incremental processes are more suited to the complex design situations that arise in the design of agile manufacturing enterprises and the computer based technologies we will use in agile manufacturing. In the next section we will consider how these design strategies can be adapted to agile manufacturing enterprise design.

Incremental and adaptive models

The literature on design is well stocked with models of the design process. One common model is the linear one, which assumes that work on one stage only begins when work on the preceding stage has been

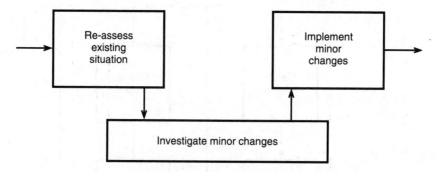

Figure 7.5 Model of an incremental design strategy.

completed. Because this rarely happens in practice, except perhaps for the simplest problems, iterative loops between the various stages are included to represent the interaction that takes place between stages. We do not need to adopt such rigid design strategies. There are other strategies we could adopt. We shall examine two of these, the incremental strategy and the adaptive strategy.

A model of an incremental strategy is shown in Figure 7.5. This is very similar to the traditional craft-based method of designing, which usually involved craftsmen making minor design changes or improvements to existing products. We have mentioned the need to implement a process of continuing improvement, and in effect what we were talking about was applying an incremental design strategy.

The incremental strategy is, however, a very modest one, and we can also adopt another approach, an adaptive one, a model of which is shown in Figure 7.6. With an adaptive strategy we decide only the first design action at the start of the process. Subsequent actions are determined later. The choice of each action is therefore influenced by the outcome of the preceding action. This allows design to proceed using the best available information. Unfortunately it becomes difficult to control cost and time scales and there is, of course, the risk that the design problem will not be addressed as a whole problem, but as a series of sub-problems. Once commitments have been made in the early stages they will be difficult, if not impossible, to reverse later, and this will constrain what follows. The risk is, therefore, that this may lead to inflexibility and an unsatisfactory overall solution in the longer term.

Software engineering life cycle models

We have seen from the preceding considerations that we do not have to confine ourselves to linear or iterative design strategies. The adaptive and incremental strategies that we could follow get us away from this

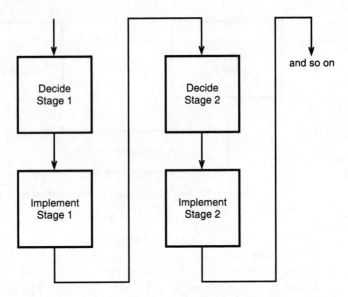

Figure 7.6   Model of an adaptive design strategy.

progression through hierarchical processes, where it is assumed that we more or less have to complete one stage, before starting another. With the incremental and adaptive strategies we have the possibility of taking small steps forward, seeing the effect and then either reversing what we have done, or moving on to another step. This opens up the possibility for experimentation and learning, or putting the design solution to the test of the real world before we move on to other problems. However, as we noted above, this has its dangers. How can these drawbacks be overcome? To answer this question we turn to software engineering life cycle models.

Boehm (1988) provides a brief overview and some background on the development of software engineering life cycle models. In the early days of software, the common approach adopted was what Boehm calls the code and fix model. Basically this involved two steps: writing some code and then fixing the problems in the code. Coding was done first, and then requirements, design, test and maintenance were considered later. This of course led to several difficulties, including poorly designed and structured code, poor correspondence with user needs and expensive maintenance.

To overcome the problems of this approach, linear design models were employed, but these were later improved upon, leading to the waterfall model shown in Figure 7.7. As Boehm reports, the waterfall life cycle model provided a recognition that feedback loops are required between stages. These loops need to be confined to successive stages to

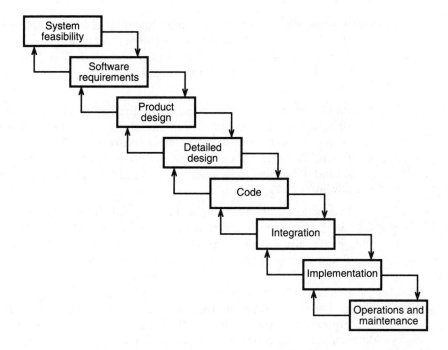

Figure 7.7 Waterfall life cycle model.

avoid expensive rework resulting from feedback across several stages. The waterfall model also allows the incorporation of prototyping in the life cycle, by a parallel step at the requirements and analysis phase.

Boehm reports that the basic waterfall life cycle model has become the norm for most software engineering projects, but that even with modifications to allow for such things as evolutionary developments and formal analysis methods the basic model has run into several difficulties. He states that the primary source of the difficulty with the waterfall model has been its emphasis on fully elaborated documents as completion criteria for the early phases of requirements and design. In other words, the waterfall model is a document or code driven process, and the start of a particular stage is triggered by the completion or sign-off of the preceding stage.

Boehm points out that this approach might well be appropriate for some software development projects, but there are many for which it is not. He highlights end-user interactive software as one example, pointing to the fact that document driven approaches have forced projects to write elaborate specifications of poorly understood applications, which has resulted in the design and development of unusable software. Furthermore, he also points out that for some applications such as fourth-generation languages and spreadsheet programs, it is unnecessary to write elaborate specifications before implementation.

Similar issues were raised by Floyd and Keil (1983), who have pointed out that our conventional stage-wise processes are based on the assumption that:

- Requirements for software can be determined and fixed in advance.
- Bulky documents formally describing software are sufficient as a primary means of communication between software developers and users.
- Essentially there is one system to produce and its initial design should determine the system's basic structure throughout its whole lifetime.

In practice, these assumptions have turned out to be problematic in situations where the software is embedded into work processes where people are also involved, that is, where there is a need for much user–computer interaction as part of the work that the people have to perform.

Boehm introduces what he calls the evolutionary development model. The stages of this approach consist of expanding increments of an operational software product, with the directions of evolutions being determined by operational experience. This approach provides a rapid operationalization of design concepts, provoking immediate user feedback, comments and direct operating experience, which can then be used to determine subsequent developments. Its disadvantage is its similarity to the code and fix model, its lack of structure and planning and its assumption that the chosen systems will allow for unplanned evolutionary paths.

We can see now that there is some similarity here with the design strategies already described. In the field of software engineering we see a sequence of models which are similar to the design strategies we outlined previously, these being: code and fix models (incremental design strategy), stage-wise models (linear design strategy), the waterfall model (iterative design strategy) and the evolutionary model (adaptive design strategy). We have noted that there are potential problems with each strategy. We turn now to one more model that may provide a way forward.

Spiral models

Gane and Sarson (1977), in their book on structured analysis methods for software development, outlined a design method based on what they call a spiral model, which permeates analysis, design, coding and testing. This spiral model can be represented diagrammatically as illustrated in Figure 7.8. The basis of this approach is that at each stage we build a skeleton of the system, which may be pictorial (a logical data flow diagram) or physi-

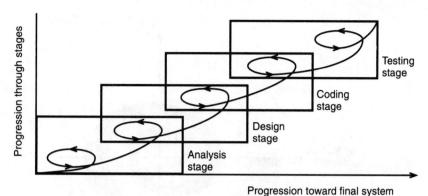

Figure 7.8   Model of a spiral design strategy.

cal (a partial implementation) depending on the stage, to see how well the skeleton works and to obtain user reactions and comments. After the skeleton is finished the process of adding flesh to the bones commences.

The analysis phase involves building models of the proposed system using logical data flow diagrams. Data flow diagrams are shown to, and discussed with, users, and this results in new insights and modifications. Then more detailed data flow diagrams are constructed, and again shown to users, and so on. This continues until the data flow diagrams capture the nature of the design problem and present it, not through verbal descriptions and requirements specifications, but through pictures.

The coding stage also involves users. The traditional bottom-up approach to software development is based on building programs and sub-systems as complete units, and then testing that they work together. The top-down approach, which is used in the spiral method, starts by producing a skeleton version of the system, which accepts some simple inputs, processes them in a limited way through as many sub-systems as possible and then creates simple output. After this skeleton version is working on the target application computer, more complexity and functionality is added to each sub-system. This is followed by more testing of the system. This process of increasing the complexity and functionality followed by testing continues until the full system is implemented.

What can be seen here are two important features. First, there is the use of models (logical data flow diagrams) that pictorially represent the design situation. We shall return to this later. Second, there is something in this process that takes us beyond the waterfall model, towards a more evolutionary approach without losing structure and planning.

Floyd and Keil (1983) introduced what they call a process-oriented approach to software development. This is a method in which software is developed through a sequence of cycles starting with initial design,

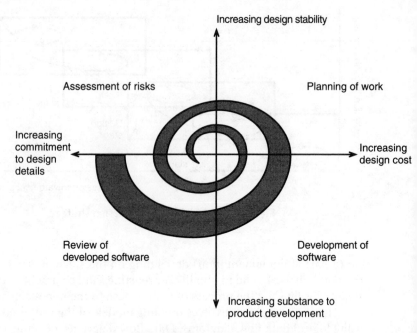

Figure 7.9 Spiral life cycle model.

implementation and evaluation, followed by several cycles involving redesign, reimplementation and re-evaluation. The method is designed to provide a mechanism for the users to contribute, with the designers, to the development of software.

The aim of the process-oriented approach is to provide:

- A foundation for generating well defined intermediate results which can be used in contractual agreements.
- Guidelines for planning, budgeting and supervising projects.
- A framework for discussing methods and tools for software development.

The spiral method has been developed further by Boehm (1988) into a full life cycle concept as shown in Figure 7.9, which accommodates most previous models as special cases. The model reflects the underlying concept that each cycle involves a progression that addresses the same sequence of steps for each portion of the product and for each of its levels of elaboration.

A development cycle starts with the identification of the objectives. These need to be related to the part of the system or product being elaborated. A statement of other means of implementation must then be generated, along with a definition of the constraints imposed on the application of these other means. The next step is an evaluation of the identified choices in relation to the objectives and constraints. This leads to the identification of uncertainties, which may represent significant sources of project risk. The identified potential risks are used to develop a strategy for reducing or eliminating the sources of risk.

Unlike the waterfall life cycle model, the spiral model is based on a risk driven approach, rather than a document or code driven one. As Boehm is concerned with reducing the risks associated with software development, he lists ten key software risk items:

- Limitations on the available skills.
- Schedules and budgets that are unrealistic.
- Development of inappropriate software functions.
- Gold plating in the form of unnecessary functionality and so on.
- Inappropriate and badly designed user interfaces.
- Changes to the requirements as the project proceeds.
- Problems with software supplied from external sources.
- Limitations on real-time operating performance.
- Problems with sub-contractors.
- Straining the capabilities of particular programming techniques and languages.

To deal with these risks, Boehm suggests a range of risk reducing activities, including prototyping, benchmarking, simulation, reference checking, user questionnaires, analytic modelling or combinations of these.

Of course, Boehm is not blind to the fact that the spiral approach has some difficulties. He points to two in particular. First, there is the problem of sub-contract software development for a client. These types of project are usually driven and controlled by the need to achieve project milestones, which are usually related to defined project deliverables such as the completion of stages and the production of fully defined specifications and fully completed and tested code.

Gane and Sarson (1977) have also addressed the problem of exercising management control over spiral activities. They point out that conventional methods are based on identifying project milestones in terms of completion of analysis, or completion of design. The production of interim reports requires an estimate of the degree of completion of an activity, for example, design is 40% complete. These criteria can mean little in practice, because such statements are vague. However, they have even less meaning in a spiral process, where management control must be exercised using more precisely defined deliverables such as planned versions of logical data flow diagrams, mock-ups, prototypes or partial implementations. In other words, what we need is a set of deliverables of increasing refinement, leading to final versions.

As a consequence of this requirement, deliverables must be much more tightly defined. Thus for example, project plans developed during the spiral process need to define what a particular version of a logical data flow diagram, mock-up or prototype will contain and when these will be completed. Thus when the due date arrives, if the defined deliverable cannot be demonstrated, then the project is behind schedule. We do not face the issue of something being 40% complete. The defined deliverable can either be demonstrated or not, and the length of time beyond the due date that it takes to deliver the deliverable provides a fairly good measure of how far the project is behind schedule.

The point is that we all, whether project managers, software developers or clients, need to be re-educated. Instead of monitoring projects by the completion of stages, we should monitor projects based on the completion of physical versions of logical data flow diagrams, mock-ups, prototypes and implementations.

The second difficulty that Boehm raises is the reliance on risk assessment expertise. Software developers must identify and manage sources of software risk. This leads to risk-driven specifications where the details of high-risk elements are worked out in great detail, but where the details of low-risk elements are left to be elaborated at a later stage.

There is a chance that we may use the spiral approach to develop the well understood low-risk elements in great detail, leaving the less well understood high-risk elements until later. We might think that we are making progress, but in reality our project may well be heading into problems. A more probable situation is the use of inexperienced developers who fail to adequately distinguish between high- and low-risk elements, leading to some high-risk elements being ignored.

Boehm's conclusion, therefore, is that some insightful review is required by experienced personnel in order to identify potential problems at an early stage.

Why is the spiral strategy preferable to stage-wise strategies?

According to Floyd and Keil (1983), one of the important assumptions underlying conventional approaches to software engineering is the belief that requirements for software can be determined and fixed in advance of its development. This belief is not unique to software engineering. It also permeates all branches of engineering. King (1988), for example, in writing about systems engineering, has noted that one of the key assumptions underlying the philosophy of what has become known as **hard systems thinking**, is that needs can be clearly defined.

We now return to the point that was made in Section 7.2.2 about the intertwining of problem finding and problem solving. As noted earlier, the central tenet of modern design thinking is that problem and solution are seen as emerging together rather than one following logically on from the other, which is the conventional view.

Of course, the conventional view was not an unreasonable assumption to make, given the relatively simple design situations that existed when the basic principles of engineering design were first laid down. And even today, the assumption is still valid for simple design problems. However, the characteristic of modern design problems is the trend towards ever increasing complexity, and our mistake has been the failure to recognize that assumptions that were valid in the past, when design problems were relatively simple, may no longer be valid today.

This is one reason why the spiral approach is an important design strategy. It acknowledges that problem finding and problem solving are intertwined concurrent activities. The definition of the problem becomes clearer as solutions are formulated.

One further reason why the spiral approach has become an important strategy is because of its potential to reintegrate users and designers. Specialization and division of labor in our society has increased as a result of increasing complexity and sophistication. Division of labor, however, has resulted in the separation of users from designers.

In the past, craftsmen often made their own tools, or would have been closely involved in their development, manufacture or both. For example, the people who in the 19th century made improvements and developments in machine tool technology, were often people with direct experience of using machine tools. However, the emergence of engineering professionals and increasing specialization eventually led to the creation of professional engineering designers who were often not themselves users of the products. This separation has resulted in the loss of the user's perspective on design problems and solutions. The spiral design strategy provides a basis for bringing users back into the design process, and it thus can assist with the reintegration of user and designer.

Adapting the spiral strategy to agile manufacturing enterprise design

In the preceding section a design strategy for the development of software using the spiral model was outlined. Clearly, if we were just concerned with software development, then the spiral strategy outlined above would suffice. However, enterprise design is rather different from software design and development, so we need to consider how the spiral model can be adapted. The first thing we need to do is to examine the enterprise design process.

The agile manufacturing enterprise design process

We could consider agile manufacturing enterprise design as a market driven, strategy based, systems design process. This design process typically might consist of four basic stages as shown in Figure 7.10. We can see that some of the important requirements are:

- The whole process is market driven.
- It is a continuing activity.
- Organization and people issues permeate all stages of the process.
- There are two distinct phases: audit and strategy development, and design and implementation.

In addition we should note that design and implementation would probably be broken down into smaller steps. These might include identifying the projects that are needed to implement the strategy

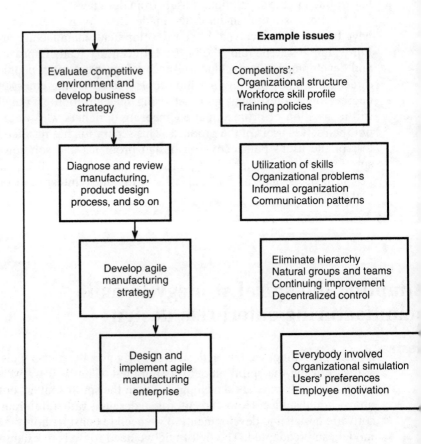

Figure 7.10 Outline strategic process.

developing an implementation plan that addresses the timing and funding of these projects and developing and implementing an information system architecture.

When designing an agile manufacturing enterprise we are specifying and making commitments to purchase proprietary equipment as well as developing or tailoring software. Some of this equipment is very expensive and we do not therefore have the option of buying a robot or a machine tool and then discarding it later if it proves to be inappropriate. We must structure the spiral approach in a way that does not violate constraints like these. Furthermore, we should note that it is unlikely that an agile manufacturing strategy will be implemented in one go. Projects are likely to be spread out over a period of time. Moreover the strategy itself must be continually adapted to changing conditions. It is not set in concrete, but is more like an evolving plan that is continuously changing.

We can see from the proposed model in Figure 7.10 that the process is linear and stage-wise. Thus the completion on one stage, for example development of business strategy, signals the start of the next stage, diagnosis and review of current situation. The model is also iterative, because at some stage it is necessary to reconsider business strategy (the business environment is not static). The assumption underlying this model, like the software engineering waterfall model, is that it is possible to determine and fix business requirements in advance of determining the agile manufacturing strategy, which in turn can be determined and fixed in advance of its implementation and so on.

Although it may be possible to foresee situations where this simple sequential process might be legitimate, it might be more realistic and practical to see the four primary phases as concurrent activities. Thus, is it not feasible to envisage a different kind of process, other than the conventional stage-wise one? Such a process would involve quickly developing initial business plans, followed by a rapid audit, and then the formulation of an initial strategy. Design and implementation issues would then be addressed, based upon identifying and dealing with high-risk and critical elements only, leaving less critical and low-risk aspects until later turns around the spiral.

A spiral based approach to agile manufacturing enterprise design

We will answer the preceding question by enumerating a process for achievement and highlighting the necessary tools. To do this we will refer to the spiral model shown in Figure 7.9, which is based on the model presented in Hickman *et al.* (1989). The vertical axis in the top half of the figure represents increasing stability of the design. The horizontal axis on the left side shows the increase in cost as the number of turns around the

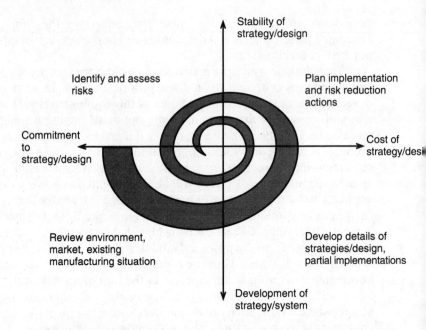

Figure 7.11   Agile manufacturing enterprise design spiral life cycle model.

spiral increases. The vertical axis in the bottom half represents the progress that is being made in the development towards a complete product. Finally, the horizontal axis in the left half represents the degree to which the commitment to the design increases as the number of turns around the spiral increases.

For enterprise design we need to relabel these axes because we are now considering strategies and systems. This leads to Figure 7.11. We can now consider typical turns around the spiral.

The first cycle around the spiral starts with the initial identification of the business objectives, opportunities, threats, competitors' performance and so on. There are likely to be several options available. The risks associated with each option should be established. This leads to an initial statement of several possible business strategies and their associated risks. For example these risks may include introducing new materials into products or pushing delivery performance beyond best practice for that industry.

An initial audit to establish the current situation is now undertaken. This is viewed from the perspective of critical areas and risks. From this can be drawn conclusions about strengths, weaknesses and deficiencies relating to these critical issues and risks. This audit can then be related to the business strategies, and so we arrive at requirements for the associated agile manufacturing strategies.

Thus far, we have established several possible business strategies, the associated critical areas and risks, and established what actions need to be taken to implement these strategies. We should have at this stage identified several possible ways of achieving each set of business objectives.

The next step is to take these strategies and undertake some preliminary design, planning, financial analysis and preliminary implementation activities. Of course, we do not do all this by spending a vast amount of money and time on each strategy. Nor do we buy new equipment. What we need to do is to collect and put together enough information to allow us to make an assessment of which of the business strategies we should be pursuing at this stage, while leaving open the possiblity of evolving the strategies later on, to take account of changing circumstances and new opportunities that may arise as we are in the process of implementing a chosen strategy.

How do we go about collecting this information? There are several ways, including workshops with employees to analyze and discuss the options, rough cut financial analysis to determine costs and benefits, logical data flow diagrams, mock-ups, simulation of factory layouts, the use of computers to emulate proprietary IT systems and software, organizational simulation to experiment with organizational options, job designs and so forth. We will say more about these tools in the final chapter.

The basis of this cycle around the spiral is to move rapidly from outline business strategy right through to considering details of manufacturing systems design and implementation, and then returning to consideration of business strategy. This corresponds to Jones' convergent phase. Decisions are delayed. We move rapidly to gather as much information as possible about critical areas and risks. We then get to the stage where we need to make plans for the next cycle. At this point we might expect to eliminate some of the options, and undertake a further cycle of the form described above. Alternatively, we might choose the business strategy, and then cycle around the spiral again, this time looking more closely at the manufacturing strategy options that are available so that we can start to converge on an appropriate strategy or strategies.

Once we have decided upon a particular manufacturing strategy, the speed at which we cycle around slows down and we move into the more detailed design and implementation. We are still on the spiral. The commitment to the strategies and designs is increasing. By this stage the strategies are, more or less, fixed, and we are in the phase of implementing projects to achieve these strategies. When designing there will be new risk areas to identify, and a need to keep applying tools to help identify risks and to help eliminate them.

However, there will come a time when it will be necessary to return to the start of the process and review the business strategy and if necessary devise a new one. So the whole process restarts.

So the spiral process can be adapted to the needs of enterprise design. Instead of determining and fixing upon a business strategy in its full detail without regard for its implications and risks, and then moving on to determine and fix upon a manufacturing strategy in full detail, we work on the basis of progressing items that are critical or which involve substantial risk. We seek to elaborate the implications of these critical areas and risks, so that we choose strategies in the light of this information. We also, in pushing forward these solutions, start to identify more about the problems, which may lead us to redefine our strategies.

Concluding comments

We conclude this chapter with the observation that the enterprise design process is a key component of agility. In adopting the spiral approach we not only seek to identify and eliminate risks, but also to achieve the intertwining of problem solving and problem seeking and the rapid adaptation of strategies and systems to the continuously changing needs of the market place.

But we can also achieve more than this. The spiral approach provides an opportunity of reintegrating designers and users, bringing the users' perspective back into the process. As we start to move around the spiral we can consult with the people affected by the implied changes. We can start to obtain their commitment. We can ask for their input. By this means we can start to show everybody affected that we value and trust them. In short, we can start the process of change, long before that process becomes evident in the form of new technologies, new machines, new organizational structures and new working practices.

Stage-wise models of design are hierarchical and rigid. They lead to an inherent lack of agility. To become agile, we must abandon these outdated design strategies and adopt more appropriate ones, without losing structure and discipline. The spiral approach, in principle, has the necessary structure and discipline built into it. What is primarily lacking are the tools to support an enterprise design process based on the spiral strategy. We will address this point in the final chapter.

Key points

- We need to focus attention on the processes by which we undertake the design of agile manufacturing enterprises.

- Traditional design processes are far from agile. They are extremely rigid, awkward and sluggish.

- Traditional design theory separates problem solving from problem finding. In more modern theories of design these two aspects are seen as intertwined.

- Many models of design process are based on stage-wise methods which do not correspond to the reality of complex design situations.

- In some situations, different types of design process are needed, such as incremental strategies, adaptive strategies or spiral strategies. These approaches are likely to be more relevant to agile manufacturing than stage-wise strategies.

- Spiral design strategies can form the basis of a very responsive agile manufacturing enterprise design process which is based on rapid evaluation, testing, experimentation and risk evaluation and reduction.

References

Agresti W.W., ed. (1986). *New Paradigms for Software Development*. Washington DC: IEEE Computer Society

Boehm B.W. (1976). Software engineering. *IEEE Trans. on Computers* (C-25(12)), 1226–41

Boehm B.W. (1988). A spiral model of software development and enhancement. *IEEE Computer Society Magazine*, May, 61–72

Boehm B.W. (1989). *Software Risk Management*. Washington DC: IEEE Computer Society

Cherns A. (1976). The principles of sociotechnical design. *Human Relations,* **29**(8), 783–92

Cherns A. (1987). Principles of sociotechnical design revisited. *Human Relations*, **40**(3), 153–62

Floyd C. and Keil R. (1983). Adapting software development for systems design with users. In *Systems Design For, With, and By the Users* (Briefs U., Ciborra C. and Schneider L., eds.). Amsterdam: North-Holland

Gane C. and Sarson T. (1977). *Structured Systems Analysis: Tools and Techniques*. Woking: McDonnel Douglas

Gregory S.A. ed. (1966). *The Design Method*. London: Butterworths

Hickman F.R., Killin J.L., Land L., Mulhall T., Porter D. and Taylor R.M. (1989). *Analysis for Knowledge-Based Systems. A Practical Guide to the KADS Methodology*. Chichester: Ellis Horwood

Jones J.C. and Thornley D.G., eds. (1963). *Conference on Design Methods*. Oxford: Pergamon

Jones J.C. (1981). *Design Methods. Seeds of Human Futures*. Chichester: John Wiley

Kidd P.T. (1990). Designing CAD systems: an open systems approach. In *Computer-Aided Ergonomics* (Karwowski W., Genaidy A.M. and Asfour S.S., eds.), pp. 512–24. London: Taylor & Francis

King M.C. (1988). Interdisciplinarity and systems thinking: some implications for engineering education and education for industry. *European J. Engineering Education*, **13**(3), 235–44

Lawson B. (1980). *How Designers Think*. London: Architectural Press

Polanyi M. (1962). Tacit knowing: its bearing on some problems of philosophy. *Review of Modern Physics*, **34**(4), 601–16

Rosenbrock H.H. (1977). The future of control. *Automatica*, **13**, 389–92

Sage A.P., ed. (1987). *Systems Design for Human Interaction*. New York: IEEE

8

Interdisciplinary design

Introduction

The aim of this chapter is to explore in some depth what we mean by interdisciplinary design, and how this relates to the enterprise design process. The concept of interdisciplinary design will be illustrated by means of a simple design study. Later, in Chapters 10 and 11, we will examine and address the interdisciplinary design of computer based technologies to illustrate the concept in detail. To begin with, we will consider why we should be interested in interdisciplinary design.

Success and failure in systems design

When beginning to explore the reasons why interdisciplinary design is important, it is necessary to consider what is meant by success and failure in systems design. In Chapter 3 we noted that a study undertaken by Voss (1988) had shown that 100% of the companies examined had reported technical success. This meant that they had all their technical systems working, with all operating problems resolved. Voss also noted that only 14% of these companies had managed to achieve business success by turning the technical success into improvements in competitiveness.

We can immediately see from these results is that the notions of success and failure are not straightforward. Ultimately, they have to be measured in terms of increased profitability and competitiveness, and technical success is no guarantee. However, let us now consider another issue. Apart from the obvious business criteria for success and failure, what criteria should be used at the design level? In short, what constitutes a successful design and what constitutes a design failure?

According to Voss (1988), technical success is achieved when technical systems are working and operating problems have been resolved. We suggest, however, that this does not necessarily constitute a design success. It may in fact be a design failure!

The reason why we make this remark lies in our understanding of the terms success and failure. For example, suppose we purchase and install a new CADCAM system. Eventually the system becomes operational, problems arise, and, to a greater or lesser extent, we address and deal with them. In the end, the system is doing what we wanted in the first place, and returning benefits in terms of reduced costs, shorter design lead times or whatever other criteria we considered important. The system is, therefore, successful. Or is it?

When we examine the new system from the perspective of whether or not we achieved the sought after benefits, then yes, we might conclude that the system is a success. However, when we start to understand the meaning of the word failure, we might not be so confident about our apparent success. Failure occurs when there is a disappointment or a shortfall between what is and what could have been (Bignall and Fortune, 1984).

In the case of our hypothetical CADCAM system, it may be that it achieved a cost saving of, say, $40,000 in the first year, but one of our competitors may have managed to achieve a much greater cost saving. Alternatively, it may have taken us 18 months to get the system installed and operational, while one of our competitors completed the same work in 12 months. Likewise, hidden problems like staff motivation may still be causing us difficulties, but our competitor has managed to achieve a very high level of commitment and motivation. Yet, according to the criteria of sought after benefits, our technology deployment exercise has been successful.

What we can see from this simple example is that whether a particular system design is deemed to be a success or a failure is a matter of judgment, which involves making a comparison between the actual output of the design process and some ideal, reference point or goal, or all three. Failure is judged to occur when this comparison shows a shortfall. The shortfall can, however, be assessed in several ways:

- Against a set of quantified benefits and costs.
- Through a detailed examination based on a wide set of criteria covering technical and human issues.
- With respect to impact on profitability and competitiveness.
- By reference to competitors' system design and implementation performance.

The first two are internal measures of performance. The third are business measures which are also largely internal with an element of external comparison. The fourth is entirely external, and provides a competitive benchmark. Ultimately, the competitive benchmark is the most important way to judge success and failure because developing and maintaining a competitive edge requires that we continually outperform our competitors in critical areas. And our systems design and implementation processes are a critical area. In fact, we could argue that this is one of the last remaining areas where we have yet to focus serious attention on improving our capabilities.

Basically, our philosophy is this. By using the first three measures of design performance, we treat the systems design and implementation process as a closed system, that is, it remains unaffected by inputs from the environment (our competitors' performance and practices). When we introduce the fourth measure of performance, then we convert the systems design and implementation process into an open system, that is, it responds to inputs from the environment (our competitors' performance and practices).

We considered the issue of open and closed systems, in detail, in Chapter 6. We now note that by improving the quality of our systems design and implementation processes, we can potentially achieve three important gains:

(1) A reduction in the time taken to design and implement new systems and a reduction in the time taken to pass through the initial learning phase, so that the full benefits arising from new systems can be achieved quickly.
(2) An increased capability to avoid systems design problems, latent defects and operational problems, leading to reduced costs over the full life cycle of our investments.
(3) Improved technology utilization capability in terms of satisfying business objectives.

In terms of success and failure, we therefore need to improve our systems design and implementation performance, as illustrated in Figure 8.1. Performance should be judged, not just against internal criteria, but also against those of our competitors. As long as our system design performance is below that of our competitors' best performance, then we should view the outputs of our systems design and implementation processes as failures. Basically, someone else can do it better, and these competitors therefore have the capability of deriving a competitive advantage.

Faced with this situation, we need to improve our systems design and implementation processes by implementing steps that will achieve a rapid improvement in design performance. Once we have achieved this rapid change, we also need to maintain our lead through a process of continuous improvement. Our competitors' performance should not be

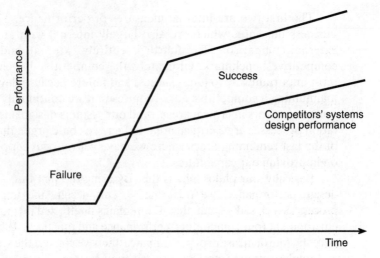

Figure 8.1 Success and failure in systems design.

viewed as a static target but as a moving one. If we stand still, then eventually we will fall behind again.

Of course, it could be said that this is very fanciful. It could be argued
that in practice, systems design and implementation performance is
not a competitive issue. And of course this might still be largely correct
in many companies. And that is exactly the point. If it is not now a
competitive issue, then someone will eventually make it one. So why wait
for someone else to start using their systems design and implementation
processes to gain competitive advantage? We should start thinking now
about what we can do to make it harder for our competitors to compete
with us.

What is interdisciplinary design?

In the following sections we describe the concept of interdisciplinary
design. Before getting down to the details it is necessary to understand the terminology. We need to clarify the differences between
monodisciplinary, multidisciplinary and interdisciplinary design.
Sometimes the terms multidisciplinary and interdisciplinary are used
in a very casual way, and are treated as interchangeable. They are not.
The following defines the context in which we use the three terms:

- *Monodisciplinary design* is concerned with only one discipline and the application of knowledge from this single discipline to the solution of design problems.
- *Multidisciplinary design* is concerned with using ideas from a range of disciplines, and the application of these ideas to the solution of design problems in a way that largely maintains the existing divisions between knowledge domains.
- *Interdisciplinary design* is concerned with the areas between disciplines and how insights from these areas can be applied to solve design problems, and how these insights lead to new visions, ideas and opportunities.

What we have here is a hierarchy of concepts. At the lowest and simplest level there is monodisciplinary design. Traditionally we have been trained to be monodisciplinary people. We are product designers, industrial engineers, mechanical engineers or whatever, trained to look at problems from our specialist perspective. In manufacturing this approach manifests itself, for example, in the serial engineering approach to product design, where products are designed without regard to manufacturing requirements.

At a higher level there is multidisciplinary design. In this case there are still monodisciplinary people around, but they are put together in multidisciplinary teams and asked to apply knowledge from a range of disciplines to design problems. Thus, in the case of product design, we are more likely in a multidisciplinary team to be using a concurrent engineering model, where in theory, we would address a wide range of constraints and issues, in parallel, from the early phases of design.

Finally, at the highest level, there is interdisciplinary design, where several knowledge domains are combined within several individuals so that they become multidisciplinary people who understand the judgment criteria used by several disciplines, so that eventually they begin to explore the areas between disciplines and seek out entirely new solutions.

In this hierarchy it can be seen that multidisciplinary design encompasses monodisciplinary design, but not vice versa. Clearly, monodisciplinary design activities are still needed, even within a multidisciplinary team. Likewise, interdisciplinary design encompasses multidisciplinary design (and hence monodisciplinary design), but not vice versa. Again, even within an interdisciplinary design activity, elements of multidisciplinary and monodisciplinary design still need to be undertaken.

Interdisciplinary design therefore means more than just the application of insights from other knowledge domains (for example, psychology and the organizational sciences) to the design of computer based technologies and systems. It also implies generating new insights and solutions based on a synthesis, within individuals, of different knowledge domains and insights.

The main issues

The design of manufacturing enterprises, systems and the computer aided technologies that we use in manufacturing, like much of engineering design, is largely based on a monodisciplinary approach. At best we manage to use a multidisciplinary method, but this is far from common practice. For example, we seem to design and implement systems and then to deal with any human or organizational problems afterwards, rather than designing systems in a way that avoids any potential organizational or people problems. This traditional approach is now outdated and often ineffective. The way forward lies in interdisciplinary design, where technical, organizational and people issues can be dealt with concurrently, and appropriate trade-offs made.

The time has come to start applying insights from other domains, such as psychology and the organizational sciences, to the design and development of manufacturing systems and new computer-aided technologies, and to consider the issues that lie between various relevant disciplines. We need to do this in order to achieve agile manufacturing and to make our technologies and systems more effective and to avoid any potential problems. This implies that we need to question how we design our systems, what these systems do and how they function.

For example, when we design new computer-aided technologies, we are faced with a choice. A machine such as a computer can collaborate with people's skills and knowledge making them more effective and more productive, and leaving room for the development of new skills and knowledge, in relation to new facilities and new theoretical insights. Alternatively, it is possible to use the computer in a way that rejects people's skills, knowledge and ability, and attempts to reduce their contribution to a minimum.

Later we will demonstrate how computers could be used to support and enhance human skills and knowledge. To achieve this goal, psychological and organizational insights and knowledge need to be used in a prospective rather than a retrospective way, to design new technology. This approach needs design methods and tools that will support this prospective use of psychological and organizational science knowledge.

The implication of this thinking is that technological developments should not just be evaluated for the impact that they have but rather that technological ideas should be shaped by psychological and organizational science insights in order to produce a better outcome.

A simple design example

To illustrate the concept of interdisciplinary design we shall consider the design of a robotics based manufacturing cell which is part of a larger manufacturing system. One requirement of interdisciplinary design is concurrency, which implies that organizational, people, technical and economic issues should be addressed in parallel.

It is the case that while the consideration of technical and economic matters poses few problems for us, the relevant organization and people considerations can often be difficult. The primary solution to the difficulty is to use psychological and organizational science insights and knowledge in a prospective way to form feasible design options. This requires development of a broad range of skills and knowledge in technical areas as well as in the psychological and organizational sciences. It is also necessary to internalize the judgment criteria used by psychological and organizational scientists.

As a consequence of these difficulties, we tend to focus on areas that are relatively easy. Examples of such areas are health and safety and human–robot interface technology.

Organizational and people issues are often more difficult to identify, and as a result they tend to be ignored, or only partially addressed, or they get left until after initial technical design options have been formulated. Unfortunately, this means that our initial design proposals are only influenced by economic and technical criteria, and little or no account is taken of relevant organizational or people related matters during the forming of these initial proposals.

When we are designing systems where robots are involved, what we tend to do is to place our emphasis, almost entirely, on the important issue of safety. Other matters such as skill requirements, decision authority and supervisory structure get left out, or are taken as given rather than being related to the true needs of the situation.

This, unfortunately, is the traditional approach. At best what might then happen is that we arrange for a retrospective evaluation, using psychological and organizational science criteria, but this usually has limited effect, because many design options will have been closed off by the time this evaluation takes place. Thus, retrospective evaluation is not very satisfactory if it should turn out that the evaluation shows a need for major design changes. We are unlikely to be willing to make major design changes if this involves a substantial amount of design effort, or we have already committed a substantial amount of time and money.

The example we shall now consider involves the prospective application of some basic knowledge from the psychological and organizational science domains to the design of a manufacturing cell, which is part of a larger manufacturing system. The cell consisted of a number of major elements, including robots, machine tools, computers and other forms of workhandling devices.

We shall now consider how we can use basic knowledge from the psychological and organizational science domains to influence our initial selection of robots and our proposals for the layout of the machines, robots and computers. We will also explore some of the important lessons that can be learnt from this design project. This analysis of the lessons will focus on the method that needs to be used to design the cell and the problems of interdisciplinary design. We will also examine some of the implications for human–robot interaction.

Description of the manufacturing cell

The cell that we are considering was intended for a plant manufacturing small gas-turbines. The culture within the plant was very strongly based on the Taylor Model, but the workforce was highly skilled. It was proposed that the cell would operate on a very different basis within this traditional environment. As a point of caution it should be noted that this in itself is often not a very wise move, as it can lead to the complete isolation of the alien manufacturing cell from the rest of the plant (Schott, 1990). On the other hand it is sometimes possible to use these small cells as pilot demonstrators to prove the feasibility of new concepts.

The proposed cell consisted of two computer numerically controlled turning centers, a system control computer, a work-bench for inspection of machined parts and other minor items of equipment. The use of robots and other types of workhandling systems was proposed as a means of automating certain tasks.

Rather than using semi-skilled machine minders, it was a requirement that the new cell would be manned by skilled personnel. The idea was that these skilled people should be given responsibility for programming the turning centers and other automated equipment, for example, the robots. Manufacturing targets would be set for the cell, and people would be given responsibility for meeting these targets. They would also be made responsible and accountable for the quality of their work.

These requirements had important implications for the design of the cell because it would be necessary for people to be able to work in close proximity to all the machines and computers during operation of the robot and the machine tools. For example, it would be necessary for the people working in the cell to gain access to control panels mounted on the machine tools both during programming and operation of the turning centers.

Method for the development of initial design proposals

A suitable method involves three steps. First, it is necessary to define the major design decisions. In this particular example this is not a difficult task. There are two major design decisions, these being the choice of robot type and the layout of the machines.

Second, it is necessary to identify the important psychological and organizational science considerations that relate to these design decisions before commencing any design work. Again this is not a difficult thing to do here. There are a number of important issues, for example, safety, provision of opportunities for socialization and allocation of functions between people and machines. Finally, a number of feasible design options need be to generated using the psychological and organizational science knowledge in a prospective way.

Once these steps have been completed, then more detailed design work is required in order to undertake an evaluation of the feasible options. In this later phase of the design process further, more detailed, design decisions can be made.

During technical design, we use many technical and financial criteria to guide our decision-making. However, we rarely explicitly state these criteria. We tend to absorb them through training and experience. They form part of our tacit knowledge base. Hence our decision-making during design involves a substantial amount of subjectivity and intuition.

When we are designing technical systems, we should also use psychological and organizational science knowledge in the same way as these subjective technical and economic criteria. It is not uncommon to find, during the course of design projects involving technologists and other professionals such as psychologists and organizational scientists, that we expect the latter to justify, in detail, everything they say or propose. But we do not expect our own economic and technical judgments to be detailed in the same way.

This practice is somewhat unfair and unreasonable. If we, as technologists, apply subjective criteria, then we should also allow other colleagues from non-technical professions the same liberty. This is one of the important aspects of the interdisciplinary design of technology. Psychological and organizational issues should have equality with economic and technical matters.

Identification of some of the relevant psychological and organizational science criteria

Safety is one of the most obvious considerations (Parsons, 1986; Rahimi, 1986; Rahimi and Hancock, 1986; Karwowski, Parsaei and Wilhelm, 1988; Karwowski *et al.*, 1988). In a growing number of countries, stringent legal requirements are beginning to be placed upon employers to provide a safe working environment. Often these legal requirements are enforced by some form of health and safety at work regulatory body. These organizations often have the power to shut down unsafe equipment, and can prosecute both employers and employees.

Safety requirements for industrial robots are very thorough and detailed in many countries because of concerns about the safety of employees. Consequently, robots in many plants operate within fenced off areas to prevent unauthorized access. Numerous safety devices, interlocks and so forth are installed to ensure that the robots are deactivated should anybody enter the fenced off area, and only appropriately trained and authorized people are allowed access.

Allocation of tasks between people and machines is another issue that we must consider. In the human factors literature there are many papers describing and discussing methods for task allocation. Typically it involves some form of assessment of the attributes of both people and robots with the aim of arriving at an optimum way of performing the tasks (Parsons and Kearsley, 1982; Kamall, Moodie and Salvendy, 1982). An alternative approach is to use a systems based method which takes into account anticipated tasks, product design, allocation between people and robots and iterative improvement in product design (Ghosh and Helander, 1986).

In our example, it is a requirement that much work will be done in the vicinity of the system by virtue of the fact that we have specified that the people working with the system will be responsible for programming, quality and planning their work. It therefore follows that the noise levels, in particular, the noise emanating from the workhandling system, will be important. We must therefore ensure that the noise levels are taken into account when we are deciding upon a robot.

The techniques that we will make available for human–robot interaction will also have to be considered. There are several options here, and these include robot teaching via force torque sensors (Hirzinger, 1982, 1983), computer based programming methods and teach pendants (Rahimi and Karwowski, 1990).

The considerations outlined above are all fairly standard design issues. It is possible to identify several more important issues by examining some basic textbooks on industrial psychology (Brown, 1954; Argyle, 1974).

Industrial psychologists have established that socialization is one of the most important things that people seek from their working environment. Since this is one of the key factors affecting quality of working life, we should make provision for opportunities for social interaction. This requirement should be taken into account as part of the system design with any potential barriers to social interaction identified. Clearly there is a link here with robot noise levels, as noise will act as a barrier to communication.

The control of stress must also be considered as an important issue. Stress control is a fairly broad ranging issue which covers several areas including physical environment, job content and control over the work process.

Stress control is linked to safety, but it is also related to socialization and hence to the opportunities that exist for receiving support from colleagues. Thus opportunities for colleagues to support each other is another issue.

Colleague support is also related to the structure of the work group. The question of group structures is primarily concerned with the size of work groups and communication and information structures. This therefore, is one more issue.

Finally, we note that in systems where robots are used, it is clearly important to provide appropriate training for the staff. Training is important in its own right, and also because it has an impact on safety and stress control. Furthermore, training is also important in relation to self development. Industrial psychology has identified self development as being important to the quality of working life. Thus training of personnel is an issue that we should address, but not just in terms of classroom teaching. We should also think about opportunities for on-the-job training and how our system design might hinder or support this.

Generation of feasible options

Issues to address when choosing a robot type

One of the objectives was to use the technology to support people's skills, knowledge and abilities and to make these more productive and effective. In our example, the reason for using a robot was to free people from the more routine tasks, so that they would have more time to undertake skilled work and management tasks. This objective had major implications for the type of robot used and the layout of the machines.

Of course, using a robot to free people from the more routine tasks such as loading and unloading the turning centers was not the only reason for introducing a robot. By automating the handling of workpieces we would also be able to contribute towards reducing manufacturing throughput times.

Often in the past we have normally used robots to try to minimize people's involvement in the work process or to replace them altogether. Here, our goal is not to replace people, or to minimize their involvement. In our proposed system, people might have to work in close proximity to the robots. This poses more severe safety problems than we would normally expect to encounter in situations where the role of people is being minimized.

We have several options with regard to workhandling devices. These include conveyors, use of dedicated workhandlers attached to each machine tool, fixed based anthropomorphic robots and gantry robots, or some combination of these. With each option, we can identify and deal with any hazards by performing a hazard analysis. From the safety perspective, conveyors are a potentially significant hazard, but one that we can easily deal with.

We can achieve transfer of components around the system by using a conveyor system. The cost of conveyor systems depends very much on the complexity designed into the system. For example we could install a simple manually controlled on/off type of conveyor, fairly cheaply. Alternatively, we could go for a high precision, computer controlled system. We could also use facilities for the merging and diverging of paths, reversing, 90° take off, stop control and precise presentation of items at desired speeds and time intervals and so on which would add further to the cost.

With regard to the loading and unloading of our turning centers, we can achieve this by using dedicated workhandlers attached to the machines. Dedicated workhandling devices usually only provide a limited number of movements. Thus, we have to ensure that components are positioned accurately within a target area, at the right time, otherwise the workhandlers will not function automatically and correctly.

On the safety side, since the movements of simple dedicated workhandling devices are restricted to a limited area of operation, and are cyclic and precisely timed, we can easily identify the hazards associated with their operation. The limitation on dedicated workhandlers is that their operational restrictions mean that they are less versatile than robots, but they are also cheaper.

The other options that we can choose from are various types of robots. Robots are much more versatile than conveyors and dedicated workhandlers. This means that we could use a robot for several operations including, in this case, loading and unloading the turning centers, and transferring parts around the system.

Our problem is what type of robot to use? We have several options, and in this example we considered gantry and fixed-base anthropomorphic robots. These two types of robot have different safety implications.

An important safety advantage of a gantry robot is that we can design the system so that the robot can only enter the working environment at specified locations. We can erect physical barriers at these entry points to prevent the loading arm on the gantry robot from entering the working area when there would be a danger to people.

A fixed-base anthropomorphic robot poses more severe safety problems because operations are performed within an envelope. This means that the robot needs to be fenced off to prevent any unauthorized access and to keep people away from the robot while it is carrying out its programmed operations. This type of robot places potentially severe restrictions on the movement of people within and around the system.

Allocation of tasks between people and machines

In our example, we have specified that one of our goals is to free people from the more routine work. In this case, this routine work includes loading and unloading the turning centers, and transferring materials around the system. This is essentially what we want the robot to do.

The role assigned to the robot has implications for the design of the robot's workhandling tools. We want the robot to be able to deal with all the loading and unloading of the turning centers, even those components which are rather difficult to handle. In our example, we were faced with machining metal rings of varying diameters. The thickness of these rings varies, but can be as thin as 2 mm. We were also dealing with a wide range of batch sizes, varying from tens to hundreds.

Many of the more flimsy rings are manufactured in larger batch sizes. It is important, if our robot is to relieve people from repetitive tasks such as loading and unloading, that it be capable of dealing with the full range of rings. This means designing grippers that can accommodate the complete part range.

Finally, we note that our requirement to keep robot noise level as low as possible eliminates the use of pneumatically activated robotic systems. The noise level resulting from venting air valves is unlikely to be acceptable in our proposed system, as we want people to work in close proximity to the robot. The noise emanating from the robot would act as a barrier to effective communication.

This need to avoid pneumatics is especially relevant to gantry systems, because most of the cheaper type of gantry robots are pneumatic. If we were to use a gantry robot then we should ensure that it is activated by an alternative type of drive, for example, by electric servo motors.

Socialization and associated issues

The next requirement to address is the question of communications between people. For this we must consider socialization and issues of stress control, colleague support, group structure and opportunities for on-the-job training.

These requirements suggest that we are talking about a system that is manned by more than one person. Two people would be the minimum manning level. But two people might not be enough because it is known that group size can have important effects. We need to ensure that our group is not too small, but we must be careful not to make the group too large.

If we have a large group, we will find a tendency for the group to become fragmented into smaller, less effective and cohesive sub-groups.

We would also be likely to find more absenteeism in a large group. Satisfaction might also be lower.

Smaller groups are therefore preferable. A group size between five and ten people is often recommended. In our example, a group size of five cannot be achieved because there would not be sufficient work for five people to undertake. This difficulty arises because issues of optimum group size were not taken into account when decisions were taken about the grouping of machines to form cells. Basically the formation of cells in our example is ill founded and it would have been better if the cells had been formed such that we would have been dealing with larger cells consisting, in our case, of more than just two turning centers.

The other matter which we need to address in relation to communications is that of group structure. We have three basic options here, a wheel network structure, a circle network structure or a multi-channel network structure (Figure 8.2). In simple problem-solving situations a highly centralized wheel network structure is better than circle network or multi-channel network structures. However, when we are faced with more complex situations, circle network or multi-channel network structures are better (Argyle, 1974).

In a system that is only manned by two people with relatively equal capabilities, there is no need for a supervisory figure. So called boundary management tasks, that is, dealing with the rest of the plant, can be shared. Given the size of the cell we are dealing with, and the number of people involved, group structure has no major importance. However, if we were to deal with a larger number of people, then we would have to define an appropriate group structure.

Human–robot interaction

When we introduce a robot, we have to decide upon a means of programming it. In our example, we have decided that robot programming will be done by the people on the shop floor. We therefore need to decide upon programming devices.

A teach pendant is one method. To use it, people would have to work in close proximity to the robot when programming. For safety reasons, however, it is desirable to keep people and robot apart as much as possible. Consequently, it is necessary to also provide robot programming facilities on the system computer. A secondary programming tool such as a teach pendant needs to be provided for use in situations where people need to be in close proximity to the robot in order to undertake the programming.

Layout of the cell

Since our cell has two skilled people working in it, and possibly one other person such as an apprentice, it is possible to satisfy our requirements for providing opportunities for socialization, stress control, colleague

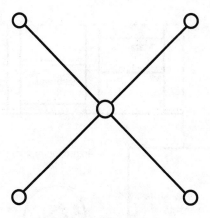

Wheel network structure

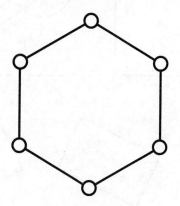

Circle network structure

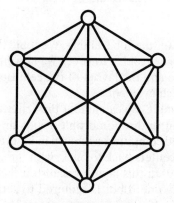

Multi-channel network structure

Figure 8.2   Group structures.

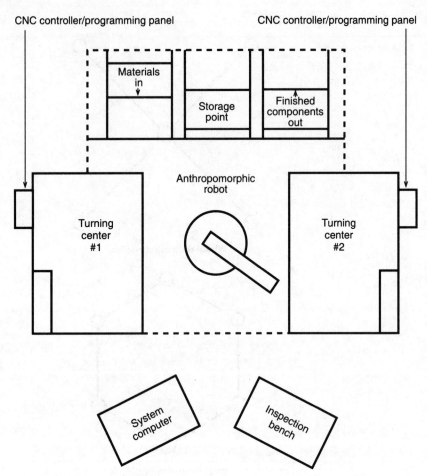

Figure 8.3 Manufacturing system layout: an infeasible design option.

support and on-the-job training. We could improve these aspects by using a slightly larger group. However, we now have to decide upon the type of robot we use and the layout of the cell. Both these decisions can hinder or support achievement.

For example, we can hinder the achievements of these requirements if we use an anthropomorphic robot and arrange the layout of the machines and computers as shown in Figure 8.3. Here we have positioned the turning centers back to back, with the robot sitting in between them. We have chosen this layout because it has cost advantages which arise because only one robot is required to serve both turning centers. The robot can also be used for parts transfer between these turning centers.

While the layout is cost effective, it is not ideal from the perspective of the people. Our two skilled machinists would be separated and would also be out of sight of each other for significant periods of time, and they might find it difficult to communicate while they were working. The only point, in this layout, where they would be in close proximity would be in the area around the inspection bench and the system computer. If our two people want to communicate while working at the turning centers, one or both would need to leave their work. In some situations this may not always be possible.

Our layout is also not very convenient for keeping an eye on what is happening, overall, in the system. A person standing at the controller mounted on Turning center 1, would not be able to easily see what was happening at Turning center 2, and vice versa. Our layout is also not very convenient if one of the people has to provide training for another person, for example a new recruit.

At first inspection, our proposed layout looks very good, but only from a technical and economic perspective. If we want to improve the situation for the people, then we need to take the human factors requirements into account. Thus, the arrangement shown in Figure 8.3 is a good example of an infeasible design option which need not be considered further.

We can improve the situation by adopting the layout shown in Figure 8.4. Here we now have two points in the cell, the system computer and the two turning centers, where the people are working in reasonably close proximity. Communication should therefore be much easier. In addition, the people will be able to keep an eye on what is going on at both turning centers, while working at one particular machine. Also, it will be much easier to achieve socialization, stress control, colleague support and on-the-job training.

Our new and improved layout does, however, have a disadvantage. To achieve the improvement for the people we have had to use two fixed-base anthropomorphic robots and a conveyor to service both the turning centers. This new layout is clearly going to be more expensive than our previous one. We might be able to reduce the capital cost, depending upon the price of the two anthropomorphic fixed-base robots used, by using a gantry robot, employing electric servo drives, as shown in Figure 8.5. With this layout we achieve the same benefits as outlined for the previous option, but without incurring the cost penalty of using two anthropomorphic robots.

Thus, we see that an initial, prospective application of psychological and organizational science considerations produces two feasible design options. Both systems provide a safe working environment, but most importantly, we can achieve this without undue restrictions on the movement of people in and around the system. They will be in close proximity and will be able to provide each other with support when required, and communications will not be hindered by machinery or the layout. We have also provided several locations where it will be easy for

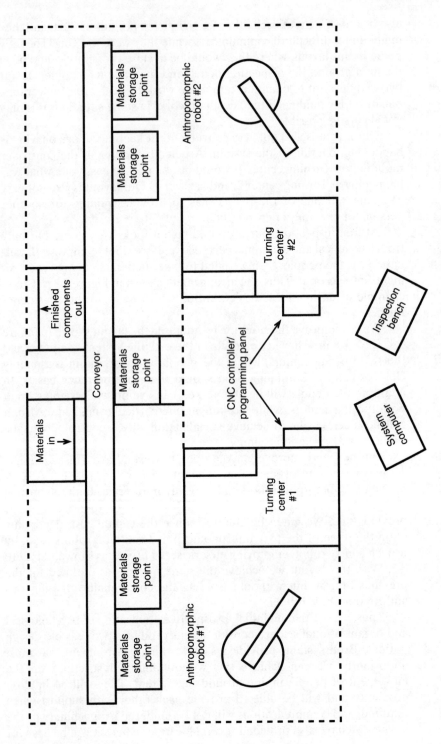

Figure 8.4 Manufacturing system layout: a feasible design using fixed base robots.

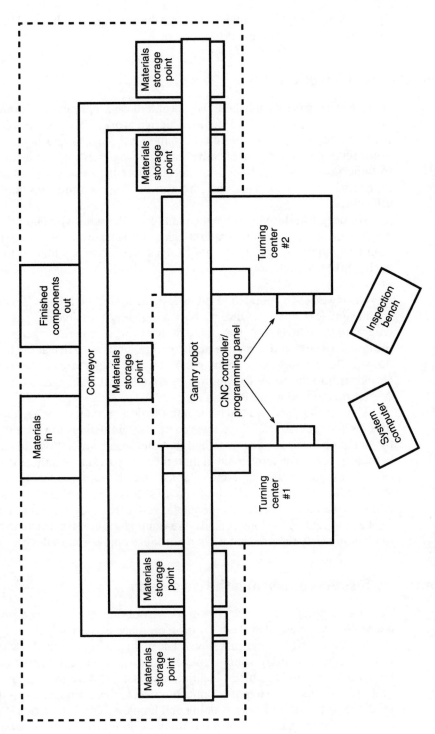

Figure 8.5   Manufacturing system layout: a feasible design using a gantry robot.

them to keep an eye on what is going on, which means that they will have more freedom to move about the system.

Detailed design work

Now that we have established two feasible design options we are in a position to undertake more detailed design work. This aspect is less problematic. We have taken into account psychological and organizational science issues in a prospective way, and what now remains is for us to undertake a more detailed technical, economic, psychological and organizational science analysis. This can be done without any major difficulties.

We need to internalize the judgment criteria used by psychological and organizational science experts. This is the essence of successful interdisciplinary design (Jones, 1981). This is much more difficult than asking other experts to make retrospective evaluations of our design proposals.

Once we have generated feasible designs, what then follows is more routine and less creative. Once we have a number of feasible designs, we enter into the convergent part of the design process, where we generate the design details, and eliminate many options, until we arrive at the final design. During this convergent phase we can make use of detailed checklists and the more conventional psychological and organizational science methods of analysis.

Thus, at this point we can bring into the design process a wide range of tools and techniques. We can use computer simulations to verify that the manning levels are adequate and that the people are not overloaded or underloaded. The movement of materials and parts around the system can be examined and mapped to establish that the layout is satisfactory and that the robots can fulfill the desired function. We can also examine and map the movements of the people to verify that they are not tied to the turning centers for long periods. We can undertake a hazard analysis to identify safety risks so that we can introduce appropriate safeguards.

Some conclusions concerning the case study

The methodology we used involved identifying the major design decisions. We then identified a range of relevant psychological and organizational science considerations. The main issues that we identified were: reasons for using robots, role of the robots, allocation of tasks between people and machines, health and safety, stress control, opportunities for colleague support, opportunities for socialization, group structure, robot noise levels, training and human–robot interaction. We then used these issues to inform our thinking about the problem, which led to the generation of feasible design options using the identified criteria in a prospective way. Having generated feasible design options, we could then proceed to undertake more detailed design work to evaluate the feasible options.

Our traditional approaches to designing the system would have been to come up with initial design proposals using technical and financial judgment criteria. We would then have proceeded to develop the detailed design. If we involved psychologists and organizational scientists it would be at this point that we would have presented our design proposals for their retrospective evaluation. Whether or not we would act on the results of the evaluation would depend on the implications of necessary design changes. If major changes were implied, it is likely that we would not implement them. It is unlikely that psychological and organizational science considerations will have a major impact on our designs, if we do not use this knowledge in a prospective way to guide our subconscious mental processes.

This leads us to an important point. The application of psychological and organizational science in a sequential way is often very unsatisfactory. When our design thinking is only influenced by technical and financial considerations, and the results are retrospectively evaluated for their psychological and organizational science implications, often the end result is unsatisfactory. When this type of approach is used there is a tendency for psychological and organizational science issues to become secondary ones. Most often major design changes are not made.

The reason why this happens is because it may be too difficult to change a design, or because the psychological and organizational science evaluation is nothing more than a critique of the proposed design, and no one has been able to operationalize the criticism into an alternative design. However, these points may in the end be only secondary. The main point seems to be this. If we do not use psychological and organizational science criteria in a prospective manner, in the same way that we use technical and economic judgment criteria, then what is not forthcoming are new ideas, unforeseen possibilities and new and original ways forward.

This last point is an extremely important one. For example, if we perceive robots to be reliable and faster replacements for people, then our vision of human–robot interaction is that of people serving the needs of robots and compensating for their technical inadequacies. If, on the other hand, we see robots as tools to support skilled people, as a kind of intelligent assistant, then human–robot interaction potentially becomes much richer and deeper. In the former case, we place our emphasis on producing a user friendly robot (Schulman and Olex, 1985), while in the latter case we place emphasis on developing a cooperating robot (Scibor-Rylski, 1986). The design of a cooperating robot would appear to be fundamentally different from designing a user friendly robot.

The example we have considered shows that it is not too difficult to find a wide range of psychological and organizational science issues that we should address when designing a robotics based manufacturing system.

Some interdisciplinary insights

Attempts at using insights from the psychological and organizational sciences in a prospective way to design new technology, and the consideration of issues that lie between technology and the psychological and organizational sciences, are very rare. The preceding example highlights some of the difficulties and the nature of the issues that need to be addressed. Based on this example and several other experiences of interdisciplinary design and related research finding (Jones, 1981; Kidd, 1992), it is possible to point out some important lessons.

Human intervention or involvement?

Experience suggests that it is both necessary and useful to draw a distinction between human intervention in a process and human involvement, and that this distinction has implications for skills, knowledge and working methods, and hence for technology. Many technical systems are designed on the basis that human skill and knowledge are still required and that the role of the people is to use their skills and knowledge to compensate for the inadequacies of the technology and to intervene in the system operation, when, for example, something goes wrong or the unexpected happens.

Research suggests that this was not a very satisfactory attitude to adopt towards people's skills and knowledge and the role that we expect people to play. When we take this view, we tend to see people largely as adjuncts to machines. They are needed to make the technology work, to plug the gaps in the design and to compensate for the deficiencies of the technology. A much better attitude is to regard people and their skills and knowledge as desirable. These human attributes should, therefore, be required, and our computers should be used to support the involvement of people in the work process.

But here, there is a clear divergence of philosophy concerning the issue of whether systems should be designed based on a belief that people's skills and knowledge are a necessity or on an understanding that skills and knowledge are desirable. The second of these encompasses the first, but not vice versa. Which option we pursue has fundamental implications for the technology that we develop, and for overall systems effectiveness and efficiency.

Design method alone is inadequate

Based on existing research it is possible to state that design method alone will not bring about interdisciplinary design. Jones (1981) reports that design methods have been singularly ineffective in bringing about interdisciplinary design. He points out that the invisible but troublesome barriers between professions and disciplines cannot be removed by methodology alone. Methodology can provide a framework and procedures, but the main requirement is that the persons concerned with interprofessional collaboration become so well acquainted with each other's criteria for judgment that the mutual misunderstandings of monoprofessional specialists are replaced by overlapping views.

It is clear, whether we be technologists or psychological and organizational scientists, that we are not well equipped by our training to achieve overlapping views. Most of us are largely ignorant of other people's professions, and such ignorance can lead to misunderstandings. For example, if a group of people were involved in a project aimed at using insights from psychology to design a technology that cooperates with the skill and knowledge of users, then it might well appear to outsiders who do not fully understand the project that the people working on it were focusing on the development of user friendly software. Such misunderstanding might well persist, because outsiders will interpret and relate the project to their existing understanding of human–computer interfaces.

Surface characteristics versus deep system characteristics

This last comment leads to another important observation. Rather than just applying ergonomic considerations to the design of human–computer interfaces, there is a need to apply psychological and organizational science insights to the design of the technology behind the interface.

Kidd (1988) describes a decision support system that was designed using this broader perspective. It is pointed out that the system characteristics were not achieved through the application of ergonomics to the design of the human–computer interface; the characteristics arose from the technology, not from the human–computer interface.

Later on in the paper it is reported that one must therefore make a distinction between the surface characteristics of a system, as determined by the human–computer interface, and the deeper characteristics of a system, as determined by the actual technology. The surface characteristics are strongly related to ergonomics, while the deeper characteristics relate more to the view of the user held by the designer.

The implication of this is that we have in our power the means to affect the nature of the skills and knowledge of people, through our work in designing technology. We can exercise this power to create a technology that rejects people's skills and knowledge, or we can use this power to design a technology that is better both for performance and for people. We will achieve a better result not just through improving the interface (surface) characteristics, but also by paying attention to the deep system characteristics, that is, the technology behind the human–computer interface. By technology we mean the algorithms, rule bases, databases, architectures and so on.

To a greater or lesser extent, human–computer interfaces are designed according to ergonomic guidelines. However, ultimately, the human–computer interface is of secondary importance with respect to making people's skills, knowledge and judgment more productive and effective. What really matters in this respect are the details of the technology behind the interface, and we have been singularly ineffective in addressing this issue.

Technology constrains organizational choice and job design

Research (Kidd, 1992) has highlighted the importance of technology in influencing organizational choice and job design. Conventional wisdom has always been that technology is of secondary importance with respect to job design and organizational choice. However, technology is clearly not neutral and can close off options and choice in the design of organizations and jobs. We have mentioned above that through computer-aided technology, we are able to affect the type and level of people's skills and knowledge. Most importantly however, we can use technology to closely circumscribe people's working methods, to limit their freedom of action and autonomy and to determine the degree of control that they have over the work process.

In effect, we are not only designing technology, but also organizations and jobs. And the technologies that result are often closed systems because they allow little or no choice over questions of organization and job design. Our CADCAM systems, for example, almost always centralize programming functions in a programming office, with DNC links being used to transfer the part programs to the machine tools. This is, without doubt, appropriate in some circumstances, but not in all circumstances. But anyone wanting to implement CADCAM will usually be forced to adopt this organizational form whether they want to or not.

The need for concurrency

A very important aspect of interdisciplinary design is the concurrent nature of the design process. We might suggest that what is needed is parallel design, in which organization and people issues are considered from the early stages of the design process, in parallel with the design of technology. Concurrency means more than just parallel design. In order to achieve interdisciplinary design, concurrency is needed, and parallel design is a requirement of concurrency. However, while parallel design is a necessary condition for concurrency, it is not a necessary and sufficient condition. In addition, we need to ensure that organization and people issues are integrated into the design process and that insights from these domains are used to shape the technology. Although parallel design combined with integration are necessary conditions, they are still not sufficient. More is needed.

What we also need is a proactive approach rather than a reactive one. Psychological and organizational science insights should not be used to retrospectively evaluate technical proposals. Rather they should be used to shape our design options so that these satisfy basic organizational and people criteria, as well as our more usual technical and economic criteria. This requires prospective application, and trade-offs between technical, organizational, human and economic factors. And the best way that we can achieve this is when the different knowledge domains and judgment criteria are combined within our own subconscious thought processes.

The problems of interdisciplinary design

Interdisciplinary design offers potential benefits in terms of computer-aided technologies and systems that are better for performance and people. Moreover, interdisciplinary design provides an opportunity to design computer-aided technologies and systems, such that the results can be more easily implemented in the workplace. This concept is called design for implementation and is comparable with design for manufacture. In addition, interdisciplinary design leads to the idea of developing computer based technologies that are skill and knowledge enhancing, rather than skill substituting.

Interdisciplinary design, however, as our simple design example has illustrated, is not easy. The main problems are discussed below.

The monodisciplinary tradition

Psychological and organizational scientists have criticized us for our lack of understanding and knowledge of their subjects, and our failure to adequately address them as issues in manufacturing. However, it would be equally valid for us to criticize psychological and organizational scientists for their lack of understanding and knowledge of technology and manufacturing.

Such criticism is, however, not very productive. It is not surprising that we are all somewhat ignorant of each other's work, culture, beliefs and so on, because in a very complex world it is impossible to cope with its full complexity and to know everything. Thus we must take steps to deal with the situation, and simplification is one way we have tackled this. It has therefore been traditional to divide knowledge of the world into boxes, but of course the divisions are man-made, mostly arbitrary and largely a matter of convenience.

It may now be that these divisions of knowledge have become problematic and are now acting as a barrier to progress. The essence of interdisciplinary design lies in removing these barriers and using insights from several disciplines, and the areas between these disciplines, to design manufacturing enterprises and computer-aided technologies that are better for performance and people.

Shaking off our monodisciplinary tradition is not going to be easy and we cannot achieve this overnight. The transition to an inter-disciplinary world will be a slow process and the change may well be both traumatic and challenging.

The implications of interdisciplinary design

One reason why interdisciplinary design is so important is that manufac-turing systems and the associated computer based technologies are not proving as effective as they should be. This is partly because the organizational and people dimensions have been ignored, or addressed in an inappropriate manner during design. Interdisciplinary design provides a way of dealing with organization and people issues, but this has implications for technology.

In Chapter 3 we made a simple analogy which helps to make the implications clear. We talked about baking cakes. If we see these cakes as technology and systems, then the same argument we applied to cake recipes also applies to technology and systems. If our technology and systems turn out to be unsuitable, we should consider changing the technology as well as improving the human–computer interface.

Our traditional monodisciplinary approaches do not lend themselves to introducing a process of questioning our established beliefs. They also make it difficult to see how to do things differently. An interdisciplinary approach not only provides the opportunity to question our technologies, and what we use them for, but also provides us with an opportunity to change our technologies.

Acceptance of interdisciplinary design

Experience suggests that, although interdisciplinary design is being recognized as an important design strategy, the division of knowledge into boxes hinders our acceptance of the idea.

Anyone who seeks to practice interdisciplinary design immediately enters into a no-mans land. There is a danger of identity loss, because a person engaged in interdisciplinary activities does not inhabit any well defined boxes.

Also, it seems that there is a kind of selective processing going on when people examine the results of interdisciplinary design. People with a technological background seem often to focus their attention on the technical results, and ignore the non-technical aspects (for example, how the results were achieved, or the non-technical goals such as making skills and knowledge more productive and effective). People with a psychological and organizational background, on the other hand, seem to focus their attention on the process, rather on the results.

As a result, everyone seems to be critical. For example, suppose a skill and knowledge enhancing computer based system has been developed. People with a technological background are not satisfied, probably because little value is placed on a technology that makes people's skills and knowledge more productive and effective. It may well be that what would make these people happier is a technology that allows them to do things faster, or which mimics human skills and knowledge.

On the other hand, it is highly likely that people with a psychological and organizational background will also be dissatisfied, probably because they do not value a technology that has been designed by technologists who have taken human needs into account. These people are more likely to prefer technologies that have been developed on a democratic basis with the users taking design decisions.

The problem is that we need to view and to judge the results of interdisciplinary design as a whole, taking into account how it was designed, as well as what it does and how it does it. So, not only must we change the way we think in order to undertake interdisciplinary design, but we must also modify the criteria by which we judge a design outcome to be a success or a failure.

A further problem is that we often do not see the need for interdisciplinary design. While there appears to be much recognition that organization and people issues need to be considered in the design and implementation of new technologies, we tend to adopt a very narrow view with regard to how these issues should be addressed. This view is often restricted to methods for overcoming resistance to change. We tend to assume that this resistance derives from people's reluctance to accept the technology, rather than from a mismatch between the organization, people and technology elements of our systems.

The notion of interdisciplinary design in which the organization, people and technology aspects of a system are designed simultaneously, seems not to have been considered. In one case, a researcher found that in 40 companies in the US, many people seemed genuinely skeptical that they would ever make different engineering design decisions based on information about a mismatch (Majchrzak and Gasser, 1992).

Job design and technological form

We will now consider in more detail the implications interdisciplinary design has on thinking in the area of job design. To address this issue it is useful to refer to Clegg (1984) who defines a job as consisting of two components, which he calls the role and the task respectively.

The role is seen by Clegg as being determined largely by the nature of the work organization (that is, the patterns of local control) and the task by the technology. Thus, according to Wall *et al.* (1984), the effects of the technology are seen in such job properties as repetitiveness, cycle time, pace, attentional demands and cognitive and manual skills. In relation to autonomy and control, however, the link with technology is seen as being less immediate and work organization is seen as the critical factor. This situation is represented in Figure 8.6.

It seems that there are two things wrong with this view. First, it is a convenient simplifying multidisciplinary assumption that allows professionals such as psychological and organizational scientists to avoid considering the details of the technology. It also allows us, as technologists, to avoid considering what insights from the psychological and organizational sciences we can use to design our technologies and systems. Although the actual work design of a system is not completely determined by its technological design, the range of possible work structures is limited by the view that we hold of the human–computer system. This view implicitly or explicitly influences our design thinking. Klein (1989) makes a similar point when she says that people cannot behave autonomously if they are technically constrained.

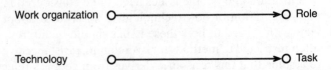

Figure 8.6 The multidisciplinary assumption of the relationship between role and task, and work organization and technology.

The second thing wrong with Clegg's model is that it assumes that our technologies can be considered as isolated systems (that is, as production machines) rather than as sub-systems of an integrated manufacturing enterprise. It has been pointed out by Kidd (1988), that numerically controlled (NC) technology has embodied in the hardware a view of the human–computer system that is based upon the separation of conception and execution. This particular view makes NC technology quite different from conventional manual machine tools, and means that our view of the human–computer system not only determines the task, but also has an important influence on the role.

We will find this to be even more true with CIM. The advent of CIM allows us to define, through computer architectures and software, the control and autonomy of people when using CADCAM systems and so on.

We will now consider the specific example of NC technology. First, however, we must take a brief look at its development. Our starting point is NC technology in the form originally conceived, with an office based programmer determining the machining strategy and a machinist on the shop floor loading and unloading the machine tool.

For several reasons, this concept does not normally work very well in practice (Kidd 1988, 1989). Machinists need to be able to modify the programmer's machining strategy on-line. However, are machinists in a good position to be able to undertake this work, given that they did not formulate the machining strategy and they may not be able to easily gain access to its details?

The machining process is difficult to define exactly in mathematical terms and is also subject to various disturbances. The development of a machining strategy therefore involves choice-uncertainty. This simply means that any attempt to determine the machining parameters mathematically, using equations or empirical data or both, will normally fail, unless knowledge, in the form that develops from direct experience of the machining process, is used to modify results.

A person who is not directly involved in the machining process is unlikely to acquire sufficient skills and knowledge to do this effectively (Bainbridge, 1983). Thus an office based programmer is unlikely to be able to effectively undertake this work, either because he does not have enough practical machining experience, or because his practical skills and experience decay and become outdated with time.

We will now demonstrate that machinists face similar problems, but for different reasons. First, it is necessary to examine the situation faced by machinists using a conventional manual machine. Such people, working with full autonomy and control, can determine an appropriate machining strategy by selecting appropriate workholding devices and cutting tools, and by selecting the most appropriate sequence of operations and the associated cutting parameters. They can put this strategy into effect by manipulating the hand wheels on the machine tool. Using the feedback parameters that are available (visual, audible, tactile and so on) the machinists can monitor the efficacy of the strategy and modify it as necessary.

The key feature of this situation is that the machinists have strong control over the process and receive a high level of feedback, which allows self monitoring of performance and development of the skills and knowledge required for successful strategy formulation and for dealing with unforeseen events.

It is possible to organize work around this conventional machine along the lines suggested by the Taylor Model, that is, to separate conception and execution, although in practice, this may be difficult to achieve. Such a situation would involve removing many of the control parameters from the machinists, but would not affect to any great extent the feedback parameters. This situation would correspond to weak control and a high level of feedback, and is likely to be very frustrating and annoying for a skilled person.

In the case of NC machines, we have managed to create a totally different situation. Here the machinists can only exercise limited control by means of manual overrides. However, we have also affected the feedback parameters. The machinists now have no hand wheels to manipulate, so tactile feedback has been eliminated. The cutting process takes place behind a sliding screen, which needs to be closed for safety reasons before machining can commence, and normally the workpiece will be obliterated from view because of the volume of cutting fluid needed for cooling. So the amount of visual feedback is severely restricted. Audible feedback is also reduced. The situation corresponds to weak control and low levels of feedback.

In this situation it is very difficult to change the work organization to increase the machinists' autonomy and control. The nature of the technology has imposed severe constraints on what is possible, because we developed this form of NC technology to support a centralized form of organization and control.

We can remedy the situation by changing the technology. Indeed this has happened with the arrival of shop floor programmable CNC technology. This form of NC technology clearly does allow considerable organizational choice because we can use it in a number of different ways. This choice has been observed by a number of psychological and organizational scientists (Wilkinson, 1983; Burnes, 1984).

In parallel with the emergence of shop floor programmable CNC systems, we have also been further developing the centralized systems based on the Taylor Model. We have now achieved a degree of integration between design and manufacturing with the development of CAD-CAM systems. These not only achieve a technically integrated system which allows the part programming to be done direct from the design geometry, but also allow us to introduce knowledge-based software to improve the model of the machining process such that, in theory at least, the probability of developing a correct NC program is significantly improved.

To summarize this situation, we clearly see that it is possible to design technology, as in the case of NC technology and CADCAM, in a way that leaves little room for organizational choice. It is also possible to design technology, as in the case of shop floor programmable CNC, in a way that does leave room for organizational choice.

Furthermore, we can see that NC technology does not place machinists in a good position to exercise control over the machining process because of the weak control and low levels of feedback. So attempts to increase their autonomy and control in this particular area will not be satisfactory if these organizational changes are not also accompanied by changes to the technology. We could achieve a much better situation if we designed the technology with user control and autonomy in mind. Of course, by giving the user other work (for example, maintenance tasks) it is possible to provide more autonomy and control, but this is a reactive strategy.

The assumption that the task is primarily determined by the technology, and the role by the work organization is not therefore wholly correct. It is a simplifying assumption that leads us down a multidisciplinary path. Its message is that we, the technologists, should design technology without any regard to organization and people issues, and then invite psychological and organizational scientists to design the organization and jobs around the technology.

Here we are stating that since the role is not just determined by the work organization, but also by the technology, we should design the technology to reflect this situation.

The role of allocation of functions in interdisciplinary design

Allocation of functions between people and machines, that is, deciding what people will do and what machines will do, is a traditional research area for the human factors community. Few researchers or practitioners, however, seem to have asked the question whether allocation of functions is a useful concept that has significant relevance to design. This question should be considered, because a case can be made in industrial design situations, as opposed to military and safety critical design situations (for example, air traffic control), that the concept has little relevance.

The detailed history of the development of allocation of functions is not of concern. The literature is full of papers addressing the topic (Brennan, 1984; Chapanis, 1965; Chu and Rouse, 1979; Greenstein and Lam, 1985; Jordan, 1963; Kamall, Moodie and Salvendy, 1982). What we need to address is whether these methods are useful and relevant.

Chapanis (1965) points to a number of issues that are often ignored in the allocation of functions area. These include the following:

- To make general human–machine comparisons is frequently the wrong thing to do. For example, although computers may be good at undertaking calculations, this is not a good reason for always using a computer to do them.
- Deciding whether a person or a machine can do a particular task better is not always important as all that may be necessary is to use that component which is adequate.
- When we make general comparisons between people and machines we give no consideration to trade-offs.

Chapanis also mentions a number of other important points. First, allocation of functions in human–machine systems is determined in part by social, economic and political values, which may vary from one country to another. Thus, a design that works in one country may not work in another. Second, assignment of functions must be continually re-evaluated, because technology is forever changing and what is not possible now may well be in the near future. Third, many of the difficulties experienced in making allocation decisions arise from engineering uncertainties. We tend to often make changes throughout the design and we sometimes work on the basis of trial and error.

Chapanis' recommendation is that we approach allocation of functions by first preparing a complete and detailed specification. We should follow this step with an analysis of all system functions. We can then make some tentative assignments. We should follow this by an evaluation of the total functions allocated to people in order to make sure that there is neither overloading nor underloading of the people.

What is wrong with this recommendation? It seems that there are a number of points that make the concept of formal allocation of function procedures unrealistic in practical design situations.

First, design experience suggests that it is almost impossible to write a complete and detailed specification. Some constraints and goals are difficult to formulate and often cannot be clearly expressed until a model, mock-up or prototype system has been built. If a specification is written and presented to a client, it is likely that he will accept it. When the system is built it is likely that he will say that it is not exactly what he wanted or was expecting. The reason for this is that some goals and constraints remain tacit and only become explicit when the goals have not been met or the constraints have been violated.

Second, design is not an orderly process proceeding from specification to implementation. It is highly iterative and much more complex than is often portrayed by simple linear or even iterative models. Specifications are also often changed as the design proceeds, as it becomes apparent that some things may not be feasible or because someone comes up with a better idea. These changes are of course subject to formal controls, but a design specification is often not a static document.

Third, many aspects of design are subconscious processes involving creative activity. People may suddenly come up with new ideas. These are explored and discussed. Some experimentation is undertaken. The ideas get modified, and so on. As this creative process takes place, allocation of function decisions are being taken, not explicitly, but in a more implicit way.

Fourth, technological innovations often start in a research laboratory. This process might involve elements of curiosity driven research; for example, what can we do with expert system technology? Some research ideas may then find their way into products, which are then bought by customers who add them to their existing systems. Thus, even when starting from a greenfield site, much software and hardware is bought in off-the-shelf, and is not customized. Control over allocation of functions is therefore restricted because detailed design is in effect undertaken by several third parties, who may have been more concerned with achieving technological innovation, than with addressing issues of human–machine interaction.

Fifth, allocation of functions only determines what people and the machines will do. It says nothing about how the machines operate. In modern language this means that allocation of functions has little influence on computer architectures and the detailed operation of software, that is, what the algorithms do and how this functionality is achieved via procedures and different programming paradigms.

Sixth, allocation of functions says nothing about the goals of the system, which are often a dominant factor in determining what people are expected to do. For example, knowledge-based systems can be used in a generative mode in an attempt to achieve automated shop floor scheduling, possibly in real time. Alternatively, knowledge-based systems can be used in a more passive way to act as a system to expand the users' understanding of the characteristics of scheduling algorithms and rules. When we adopt the goal of using knowledge-based systems to achieve automated scheduling, we place constraints on what people are expected to do. Allocation of function methods make no cognizance of this fact, and could be said to be concerned with the secondary, more detailed allocation decisions that stem from the major design decisions, which we have already taken long before allocation of functions becomes a design issue.

Finally, design is a mixture of art and science, rather than being just pure science. It involves a mixture of formal and informal methods, analysis, mathematics and elements of judgment and experience. We often know from experience that we have to do certain things in order to achieve a given result. With experience it should not be necessary to undertake detailed analysis of tasks in order to create satisfactory work for people.

From this picture we can see that design is not a straightforward process. Simple models which depict a process of clearly defined stages, starting with the development of a requirement specification and ending with the testing of the built system, do not represent the full complexity of design.

Design is also a dynamic and evolutionary process. It involves a lot of creative thought, which is followed by a process of elimination and the build up of the fine design detail. All the time, prototyping, simulation and experimentation may be going on. As the process of building up the detail continues, there are bursts of more creative activity as unexpected problems arise which need to be resolved.

Our designs, therefore, take shape over a long period. In this complex process there is no specific point at which tasks are allocated, either to people or to machines, unless the design process is made very formal and over restrictive. The process of allocation of functions happens somewhere along the road but nobody can pinpoint the moment, because it does not exist. It happened on a continuing basis and it involved trade-offs between various aspects of the design.

Allocation of functions might be seen as a vehicle for introducing psychological considerations into technical design. However, as in the case of job design, it allows our psychological and organizational scientists to avoid getting to grips with our technology, and allows us to avoid asking what psychological and organizational knowledge we should be using to design the details of our technologies. Allocation of functions is largely therefore a multidisciplinary idea. It is of some use, but is a tool with many limitations.

However, perhaps the most important issues concerning the relevance of allocation of functions are raised by Jordan (1963) who clearly believes that allocation of functions is not very relevant. In his paper he points out that the term allocation of tasks to people and machines is meaningless because this assumes that people and machines are comparable. Jordan argues that they are not, but rather that they are complementary. The problem is not therefore one of deciding what each should do, but of designing a system so that the work is done by people and machines.

According to Jordan this requires new formats for systems analysis and design. Jordan suggests that designing from a tool perspective will be part of this new approach. This idea is in fact taken up in later chapters of this book. Jordan also indirectly mentions that interdisciplinary design will form part of this new approach, by suggesting that machines should be designed to take account of people's need for motivation, that is, insights from psychology should be used in the design of machines.

It is these points that are the most interesting. Instead of allocating functions between people and machines, we should be considering ways in which machines (and systems) can be designed as tools according to psychological and organizational criteria. This does not involve explicit allocation of functions. Rather it involves designing technology in a way that achieves certain desirable psychological and organizational results, as well as the more normal technical and economic benefits.

This approach also addresses some of the points raised by Chapanis. It avoids task allocation. It does not assume that design decisions are independent of the culture of the society in which the technology is to be used. And, it involves trade-offs between technical, economic, organizational and psychological considerations.

Some theoretical insights

Because of the way we have structured knowledge into professions, and the traditional emphasis in manufacturing on using technology to increase competitiveness and profitability, we have noted that technology has become dominant, and that organization and people issues have often been treated as secondary. The situation that has prevailed in manufacturing could therefore be described as imbalanced and monodisciplinary as illustrated in Figure 8.7. It could be argued that what is required is just the removal of this imbalance and giving psychologists and organizational scientists more say in the design of manufacturing enterprises, systems and technologies.

We believe that agile manufacturing requires more than just a redressing of the balance. The way forward lies, not just in redressing the imbalance, or addressing the problem from a multidisciplinary perspective, but in an interdisciplinary approach as illustrated in Figure 8.8. It is in the areas between disciplines (where the discs overlap) that our attention should be focused.

Although we hear the phrase interdisciplinary design used more and more, there appears to be very little in the way of a theoretical framework for interdisciplinary design. We might well ask the question why?

What seems to be happening is that because of the difficulties of working between disciplines, which are engendered by our traditional knowledge boundaries, and the significant amount of new learning that we need in order to grasp sufficient knowledge from other domains, we are largely staying within our own areas. Often, therefore, significant

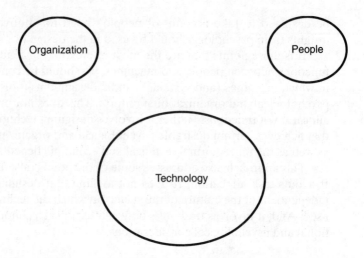

Figure 8.7   The prevailing situation in manufacturing: imbalanced and monodisciplinary.

interdisciplinary design does not take place. The basic fact is that the road to interdisciplinary working is a long and hard one, and it will take us a long time to get anywhere.

We now offer a number of theoretical insights concerning the impact of the psychological and organizational science knowledge on the design of technology, which provides a basis for such a theoretical framework (Kidd, 1992).

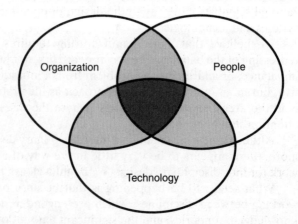

Figure 8.8   The desired situation in manufacturing: balanced and interdisciplinary.

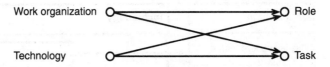

Figure 8.9   The interdisciplinary assumption of the relationship between role and task, and work organization and technology.

The first issue that we need to clarify concerns the influence of technology and organizational choice on task and role. The multidisciplinary perspective has already been described. The interdisciplinary perspective is illustrated in Figure 8.9, which indicates that task and role are both influenced by work organization and technology. The nature of the interactions can be understood by referring to the case of NC technology that we considered earlier. A number of observations can be made.

First, significant organizational choice in the way a technology is used can only exist if we design the technology to allow for different organizational structures. If the technology has been designed to support one form of organization, for example one based on the Taylor Model, then significant organizational choice is unlikely to exist. Thus, our technical designs can render certain forms of organization impossible or extremely difficult to achieve. The corollary of this is that technology can be designed to reflect organizational criteria.

Second, if we design our technology to offer organizational choice in the way that it is used, then our technology must also be designed to reflect the needs, preferences and existing skills of potential users, as well as any new skills that we may deem to be desirable given the need to use certain technologies or to develop new roles. It is not enough to specify an organizational structure based on autonomous work groups, say, and then to ignore the development of the details of the technologies. Our technology can determine the skills, knowledge and working methods of users, including the need and opportunities for interaction with other groups. The corollary of this is that the details of our technology can be shaped by psychological and organizational considerations, as well as technical and economic considerations.

In the light of these observations, the second issue is therefore concerned with the impact of organization and people issues on the detailed design of our technology. Broadly this means that issues from the psychological perspective, for example, personal development, learning and motivation and from the organizational perspective, for example, creation of a social environment in which people act together as part of a group, group structures and decentralization can be used to influence the detailed design of computer based technologies. This framework is presented in Figure 8.10 (Kidd, 1992).

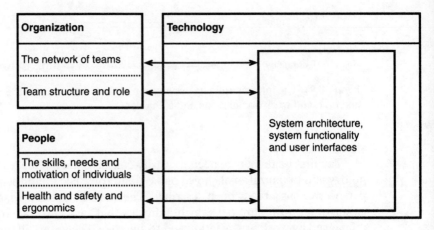

Figure 8.10   A framework for interdisciplinary design. *Source:* Cheshire Henbury. © 1990. Published with permission.

The psychological perspective is represented by the 'people' box. This broadly covers two areas. The first is health and safety and interface and work space ergonomics, and the second is the skills, knowledge, needs and motivation of individuals. The organizational perspective is represented by the 'organization' box. This again broadly covers two areas. The first is the structure and role of teams, and the second is the network of teams covering relationships and interaction between teams, which includes those from outside the plant or the company, as in the case of supply chain considerations.

The direction of the arrows from the 'organization' and 'people' boxes to the 'technology' box is important. They are shown as a two way relationship between organization and people on the one hand and technology on the other. The two way relationship shows that organization and people considerations can be used to shape the technology, and vice versa. In practical design situations there will be a trade-off between organizational, people and technical considerations.

The state-of-the-art of the impact of the psychological and organizational sciences on technology is almost exclusively restricted to the area of the impact of health and safety and ergonomics. The impact of networks of teams, team structures and roles, and the skills, knowledge, needs and motivation of individual users have been largely ignored.

The exact nature of the impact of organization and people considerations on the technology (that is, the architectures, the detailed functioning and the human–computer interfaces) will be further investigated through design studies presented in Chapter 11. However, at this stage it is possible to state that the prime influence of organizational considerations will be on the architectures of computer systems, that is the distribution of computers throughout the plant, networking, the form and integration of databases and the functional distribution of software. However, organizational considerations may also influence the detailed design of the software. The people considerations will have their main impact on the detailed design of the software, and well as the user interfaces.

Concluding comments

We have endeavored in this chapter to explore one of the fundamental requirements for achieving agile manufacturing – an ability to design manufacturing enterprises, systems and technologies in an interdisciplinary manner. The benefits that can be obtained from such an approach include improved systems design leading to faster implementation and avoidance of potential problems through addressing all relevant issues. Of equal importance, however, are the opportunities that are opened up for developing new ideas and new solutions by exploring the areas that lie between disciplines. However, achieving interdisciplinary design is not easy and will take a long time to become normal practice.

Key points

- Success and failure in systems design activities has to be judged against external benchmarks, as well as by internal criteria.
- Systems design processes are a competitive weapon. If we can improve them, and develop capabilities which our competitors do not possess, or will find hard to imitate, then we can make life harder for them.
- The complexity of agile manufacturing design problems necessitates an interdisciplinary approach to design.
- Interdisciplinary design should not be confused with multidisciplinary design. The two terms are not synonymous.
- The aims should be to apply insights and knowledge from several domains, but also to explore the areas that lie between disciplines. It is in these areas that we are likely to find new ideas and new and original ways forward.

- Design is affected by the values that people hold. It is not a purely rational process. Therefore design method alone cannot lead to improvements in design process.
- We should understand the differences between the surface characteristics of computer based technologies and their deeper characteristics.
- Technologies can constrain organizational choice. When we design technologies we are designing organizations and jobs.

References

Argyle M. (1974). *The Social Psychology of Work*. Harmondsworth: Penguin

Bainbridge L. (1983). Ironies of automation. *Automatica*, **19**, 775–79

Bignall V. and Fortune J. (1984). *Understanding Systems Failures*. Manchester: Manchester University

Brennan L. (1984). The influence of new technology on the allocation of function decision. In Proc. *1st Int. Conf. Human Factors in Manufacturing* (Lupton T., ed.). Kempston: IFS

Brown J.A.C. (1954). *The Social Psychology of Industry*. Harmondsworth: Penguin

Burnes B. (1984). Factors affecting the introduction and use of CNC machine tools. In Proc. *1st Int. Conf. Human Factors in Manufacturing* (Lupton T., ed.). Kempston: IFS

Chapanis A. (1965). On the allocation of functions between men and machines. *Occupational Psychology*, **39**(1), 1–11

Chu Y-Y. and Rouse W.B. (1979). Adaptive allocation of decision-making responsibility between humans and computer in multitask situations. *IEEE Trans. Systems, Man, and Cybernetics* (SMC-9, (12)), 76978, IEEE

Clegg C.W. (1984). The derivation of job design. *J. Occupational Behaviour*, **5**, 131–46

Ghosh B.M. and Helander M.G. (1986). A systems approach to task allocation of human–robot interaction in manufacturing. *J. Manufacturing Systems*, **5**(1), 41–9

Greenstein J.S. and Lam S.T. (1985). An experimental study of dialogue-based communication for dynamic human-computer task allocation. *Int. J. Man-Machine Studies*, **23**, 605–21

Hirzinger G. (1982). Robot teaching via force-torque sensors. In *Cybernetics and Systems Research, Proc. 6th European Meeting on Cybernetics and Systems Research* (Trappl R., ed.). Amsterdam: North-Holland

Hirzinger G. (1983). Direct digital robot control using a force-torque sensor. *Proc. IFAC Symposium on Real Time Digital Control Applications*, Guadalajara, Mexico

Jones J.C. (1981). *Design Methods. Seeds of Human Futures*. Chichester: John Wiley

Jordan N. (1963). Allocation of functions between man and machine in automated systems. *J. Applied Psychology*, **47**(3), 161–5

Kamall J., Moodie C.L. and Salvendy G. (1982). A framework for integrated assembly systems: humans, automation and robots. *Inter. J. Production Research*, **20**, 431–48

Karwowski W., Parsaei H.R. and Wilhelm M.R., eds. (1988). *Ergonomics of Hybrid Automated Systems I*. Amsterdam: Elsevier

Karwowski W., Rahimi M., Nash D.L. and Parsaei H.R. (1988). Perception of safety zone around an industrial robot. In *Proc. Human Factors Soc. 32nd Annual Meeting*, Santa Monica: Human Factors Society

Kidd P.T. (1988). The social shaping of technology: the case of a CNC lathe. *Behaviour and Information Technology*, **7**(2), 193–204

Kidd P.T. (1989). The social and engineering design of computer numerically controlled technology. In *Designing Human-centred Technology: A Cross-disciplinary Project in Computer-aided Manufacturing* (Rosenbrock H.H. ed.). London: Springer-Verlag, 51–64

Kidd P.T. (1992). Interdisciplinary design of skill based computer aided technologies: interfacing in depth. *Int. J. Human Factors in Manufacturing*, **2**(3), 209–28

Klein L. (1989). Inside and outside – a struggle for integration. In *Working with Organizations* (Klein L., ed.), pp. 58–69. London: Tavistock Institute

Majchrzak A. and Gasser L. (1992). HITOP-A: a tool to facilitate interdisciplinary manufacturing systems design. *Int. J. Human Factors in Manufacturing*, **2**(3), 255–76

Parsons H.M. (1986). Human factors in industrial robot safety. *J. Occupational Accidents*, **8**, 25–47

Parsons H.M. and Kearsley G.P. (1982). Robotics and human factors: current status and future prospects. *Human Factors*. **24**(5), 535–52

Rahimi M. (1986). Systems safety for robots: an energy barrier analysis. *J. Occupational Accidents*, **8**, 127–38

Rahimi M. and Hancock P.A. (1986). Perception-decision and action processes in operator collision avoidance with robots. In *Proc. 19th Annual Conf. Human Factors Assoc. Canada*, Richmond (Vancouver), Canada

Rahimi M. and Karwowski W. (1990). A research paradigm in human–robot interaction. *Int. J. Industrial Ergonomics*, **5**(1), 59–71

Rosenbrock H.H. ed. (1989). *Designing Human-centred Technology: A Cross-disciplinary Project in Computer-aided Manufacturing*. London: Springer-Verlag

Scibor-Rylski M. (1986). 'Yes-man' – A cooperative robot workstation. In *Human Factors* (Lupton T., ed.). Kempston: IFS

Schott E.S. (1990). Flexible work practices for flexible manufacturing systems. In *Proc IEE Colloquium on The Human Factor in CIM,* London: IEE

Schulman H.G. and Olex M.B. (1985). Designing the user-friendly robot: a case history. *Human factors* **27**(1), 91–8

Voss C.A. (1988). Success and failure in advanced manufacturing technology. *Int. J. Technology Management*, **3**(3), 285–97

Wall T.D., Burnes B., Clegg C.W. and Kemp N.J. (1984). New technology, old jobs? *Work and People,* **10**(2)

Wilkinson B. (1983). *The Shopfloor Politics of New Technology*. London: Heinemann

9

Management accounting and investment appraisal

Introduction

In Chapter 4 we examined and highlighted the problems associated with the traditional management accounting paradigm. A number of important difficulties and methodological issues have arisen in relation to the traditional methods, which will need to be addressed and resolved in agile manufacturing environments. These are:

- Investment decisions have been taken based only on financial appraisal.
- The aim of most investment has been to reduce costs. Technologies tend to be justified using cost reduction even when the goal is increased flexibility or quality.
- Traditional management accounting methods encourage a cost driven approach and support the view that people are a cost rather than an asset.
- Overhead allocation based on the amount of productive capacity used in the manufacture of a product is often an inappropriate way to allocate overheads, especially when a significant amount of customized work is mixed with standard work.
- Traditional methods do not highlight the true cost drivers.
- The emphasis is on financial performance measurement and control systems, which can lead to erroneous conclusions.
- Difficulties in justifying investments in FMS and CIM because they lead to revenue generation that is difficult to quantify, and because the full benefits may not be realized until some time after implementation.

The traditional management accounting and investment appraisal methods in use today are inadequate for the complexities of agile manufacturing. New methods, such as activity based costing, are being implemented, but a number of issues need to be addressed. The purpose in this chapter is to consider these issues and form the outline framework of a management accounting system suitable for agile manufacturing environments.

Central issues

Before we enter into details, several issues need to be highlighted and discussed. First, the relevance of more recent management accounting innovations has not been considered, in detail, in relation to agile manufacturing. Most often the discussion has centered around the inappropriateness of traditional management accounting methods in relation to accurate product costing and the justification of advanced manufacturing technologies such as FMS and CIM.

We suggest that most investments in agile manufacturing, whether in organization, people or advanced manufacturing technologies, are likely to bring company wide and strategic benefits. However, the continuing use of traditional methods that tend to focus attention on cost reduction exercises, does not provide a framework supportive of agile manufacturing environments, and as a result, many necessary investments may not appear to be financially viable options. We should, therefore, consider the new management accounting approaches.

Second, no clear investment appraisal method has been developed to support the adoption of agile manufacturing. Examples of best practice and guidelines do not exist. The basic problem is not that the development of such a method poses inherent difficulties, but more a case that no one has yet fully developed and tested one. A method is outlined in the following pages.

Third, it is not clear from the recent literature on management accounting, if the available tools for investment appraisal are wholly adequate to the task of evaluating investments in agile manufacturing. We will demonstrate that, for the most part, they are suitable if used appropriately.

Basically, our argument is that the design of agile manufacturing enterprises, in which the skills, knowledge and judgment of people are used to achieve increased competitiveness and profitability, needs a more broadly based investment appraisal approach. This should involve financial assessment and other forms of evaluation. It is also our contention that new management accounting and investment appraisal methods are needed. We believe that some of the investments required will only appear economically valid if new management accounting methods are introduced to replace the traditional methods, which have their roots in the scientific management movement.

This, of course, implies that financial appraisal will remain an essential feature of decision-making. We are not suggesting that investments should be made on the basis of faith alone, or upon financially misguided and simplistic concepts which focus only on one limited aspect of the enterprise. The point is that financial appraisal should be done within an appropriate supportive framework, not one based on an outdated concept of manufacturing.

In developing this framework, it is necessary to acknowledge that, given the company specific nature of management accounting systems, it is not feasible or desirable to rigidly specify what sort of management accounting regime should replace the traditional methods. All we can do is highlight some of the underlying foundations of a new management accounting paradigm. We do not claim that these principles are new. The critique of traditional management accounting (Johnson and Kaplan, 1987) has reached a state where it is now feasible to point to the areas of weakness, and suggest how they should be overcome. This is new: we have related these concepts to a new manufacturing paradigm, rather than to a more technically sophisticated version of our old paradigm. The weaknesses that are referred to above are outlined in Chapter 4. Here we concentrate on stating the requirements. There are several.

First, because in an agile manufacturing environment we will place our emphasis on cost, quality and flexibility, rather than on cost alone, our traditional practice of justifying investments based on cost savings needs to be enhanced via considerations of quality and flexibility. It therefore becomes necessary to find ways of translating quality and flexibility into financial terms, both in terms of savings and revenue enhancement.

Second, traditional product costing techniques handle overheads in a way that results in inappropriate allocations. It is necessary therefore to introduce management accounting techniques that will result in appropriate allocations between customized and standard products. We also need to avoid the problem of shifting overhead allocation from automated production systems to labor intensive activities. Such problems arise because our overhead allocation is often based on an inappropriate measure of direct labor hours.

Third, our traditional sole emphasis on financial measures of performance is no longer appropriate. New metrics are needed which focus attention on both financial and non-financial measures, which should be both timely and presentable as information rather than as data. This information should not be centralized, but distributed for use by the people who will be engaged in processes of continuous improvement.

Activity based costing

The traditional approach to allocating overheads to products, is to use the amount of productive capacity (direct labor or machine hours) in making the product. This practice dates back to the 19th century. In the days when products were relatively simple and overheads costs were very small relative to the direct labor and material costs, it was probably reasonable to assume that each product accounted for the use of overheads according to how long it took to make it. Today this is not regarded as a reasonable assumption. Typically, direct labor accounts for between 5–15% of total manufacturing costs. Overhead costs typically account for about 55%, and direct materials about 30% of total manufacturing costs.

Activity based costing (ABC) systems were developed to deal with the shortcomings of traditional management accounting systems highlighted in Chapter 4. ABC, among other things, provides a more appropriate way of dealing with overhead costs, and relating these to products.

Basic principles

The details of activity based costing are presented in several texts (Berliner and Brimson, 1988; Brimson, 1991; Turney, 1992a). The basic principles of activity based costing are:

- Costs are traced to cost objectives (that is, products, customers and other cost objectives).
- No distinctions are made between direct and indirect (overhead) costs.
- Costs are either traceable or non-traceable to cost objectives. As a rule of thumb, 80–90% of all costs are traceable. Non-traceable costs are not allocated to cost objectives. They are incurred within organizational units (for example departments), and are allocated to that organizational unit's primary activities. These non-traceable costs are not allocated on a company wide basis.
- Costs are traceable when it is possible to establish a causal relationship between a factor of production and a specific activity.
- ABC is not just a product costing method. It can also be used as a cost management tool, without using the information to cost products. It is also used for budgeting and to support activity based management.
- Unlike conventional costing approaches, ABC acknowledges that in a modern manufacturing environment there are significant costs which are not volume related. These costs should not be treated as volume related costs. A bill of activities does not require a distinction between volume or non-volume related costs. Both are traced according to actual usage, rather than allocated.

- ABC is a resource consumption model not a spending model. Products consume activities, and activities consume resources. A change in production volume results in a change in activity, which leads to a change in resources required (under or over capacity in terms of resources). An immediate change in spending does not necessarily result because it takes time to acquire or dispose of resources.

- As a resource consumption model, ABC will highlight the effect that day-to-day decisions will have on medium to long term consumption of resources. It will also highlight the cost implications of these day-to-day decisions. However, it will not highlight immediate effects on cash flows.

- Activities form the foundation of activity based cost management systems. Activities should not be confused with tasks, since several tasks combine to form an activity. It is necessary to determine the cost of activities in relation to some activity measure (that is, the cost per unit output).

- Activities are classified as primary and secondary, repetitive and non-repetitive, discretionary and non-discretionary. Other useful classes of activities are high market leverage activities and non-value added activities.

- ABC involves creating a bill of activities for each product. There are two widely used methods of generating a bill of activities. These are the CAM-I method and the output measure method. The CAM-I method is best used in situations where products consistently use the same activities. The output measure method is particularly suitable for job shop environments where the activities used to build a product are in constant flux.

- The development of an activity based costing system requires some trade-off between accuracy and complexity. For example, it is unlikely in practice that the assumed linear relationship between activity cost and activity volume will exist. The relationship is only linear within certain bounds and conditions, but to introduce non-linear relationships would introduce more complexity. Thus in practice the ABC model needs to be updated to reflect changes in resources deployed.

- The implementation and operation of an activity based costing system involves identifying and understanding cost drivers. A cost driver is a factor that creates or influences cost. In practice there will be very few really important cost drivers. Typical examples of cost drivers are plant layout and product designs.

- Activities are subjected to a life cycle analysis. Costs of activities where the benefits are only relevant to the current cost period are dealt with in the current cost period. Any costs associated with activities where the benefits extend beyond the current cost period are apportioned over the life of the product.

- Activities are described in terms of both financial and non-financial measures of performance. The financial and non-financial performance information is considered as attributes of activities. The key to effective cost management is to implement changes that improve multiple dimensions of performance simultaneously, which is only possible when the financial and non-financial measures are tightly coupled.

- A distinction is made between absolute profitability and profitability per unit of production time, through the concept of profit velocity. This is based on the observation that company profitability is both a function of the absolute profitability and the number of products that can be produced during any given period of time.

Activity based costing, if implemented and used properly, will provide a foundation for achieving enterprise excellence. It is capable of supporting our efforts in this direction because it will help to eliminate distortions and cross-subsidization caused by our traditional cost allocations. It will thus provide a baseline for our efforts in improving cost and performance. When we implement activity based costing, we will be provided with a clear view of how the mix of our diverse products, services and activities contribute, in the medium to long term, to our profitability.

With ABC we can combine non-financial information and activity cost information. This will provide us with the information that we require to operate effectively. Activity information is the key to continual improvement to our profitability. There are several reasons why activity accounting is important to agile manufacturing.

First, activity accounting has the capability to help improve make or buy, estimating and pricing decisions, because the product cost information that we obtain from ABC mirrors the manufacturing process. This mirroring is a requirement for accurate product costing and informed decision-making. Activity accounting also facilitates elimination of waste by providing visibility of non-value added activities. By highlighting the cost drivers, it also helps to identify the true source of costs.

Second, is the facility that ABC provides to link strategies to operational decision-making, thus enabling us to identify core competencies, capitalize on activities that are our strength and restructure or eliminate activities that do not contribute to the achievement of our objectives. ABC also provides us with feedback on whether the results we anticipated are being achieved so that we can take corrective action. Time, quality, flexibility and conformance to schedule goals are set by linking performance measures to strategies.

Third, continuous improvement and total quality management are encouraged, because our planning and control activities are focused at the process level. Continual evaluation of the effectiveness of activities, through the means of externally set performance and cost goals at the activity level, leads to the identification of potential investment opportunities.

Fourth, the effectiveness of budgeting is improved by identifying the cost–performance relationship of different service levels. Profitability can also be improved by monitoring total life cycle cost and performance.

Fifth, activity accounting provides us with insight into our fastest growing and least visible element of cost, that is, all the activities such as sales, programming, maintenance, administration and such like that support and surround manufacturing.

We should note that any cost management system based on activity based costing cannot do more than identify potential problems. What we do with this information is crucial to the success of ABC and our cost management systems. The importance of activity based costing is that it allows us to expand beyond our traditional and rather narrow direct labor cost monitoring, to include the monitoring of all our costs, simultaneously providing a more accurate tracing of costs to products. It also allows the elimination of the tracking of direct labor by assembly and product and replacement with monitoring of activities, in terms of both financial and non-financial measures of performance.

The CAM-I ABC model

One fundamental aspect of ABC is the linking that it provides between strategy and operational decision-making. This enables us to focus on those activities that are crucial to the success of our strategies, and to restructure or eliminate those activities that are non-critical or do not contribute to the achievement of our objectives.

Another fundamental feature of ABC is that activities are described in terms of both financial and non-financial measures of performance. The financial and non-financial performance information is considered as attributes of activities. The key to effective cost management is to implement changes that improve multiple dimensions of performance simultaneously, which is only possible when financial and non-financial measures are tightly coupled.

These financial and non-financial measures of performance provide a framework for continuous improvement which is linked to our strategies. To achieve continuous improvement, people need accurate and timely information about what is happening. This is what ABC can provide. ABC is not just a more accurate means of tracing overhead costs to products. ABC also provides the means by which people can focus on improvements which will lead to improved business performance. The information that ABC provides can also be used to improve and help set our strategies.

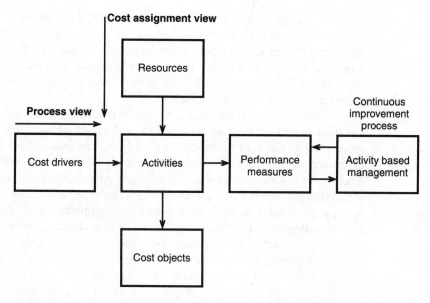

Figure 9.1   CAM-I ABC model. *Source:* CAM-I. © 1990. Published with permission.

When we use the information generated by ABC in this way, we are undertaking what is called **activity based management** (ABM). ABC provides the information, while ABM uses the information in various ways to help us to achieve continuous improvement (Turney, 1992b). This is why financial and non-financial measures of performance need to be tightly coupled. When we achieve this tight coupling, it becomes possible to generate plans that lead to improvements in multiple dimensions of performance, simultaneously. In today's competitive environment, a purely cost driven approach to manufacturing is no longer acceptable and does not work in the long term. We must also seek to improve the non-financial measures of performance. Traditional cost systems do not support this approach, which is one of the main reasons why we need ABC.

CAM-I have developed a model of ABC which has two components as illustrated in Figure 9.1 (Raffish and Turney, 1991). The first component of the model is called the cost assignment view. This reflects the need to assign the cost of resources to activities and then the cost of activities to cost objects (such as customers and products). This cost assignment information will allow us to undertake analysis to support a wide range of decisions. These include product pricing, component sourcing, make or buy, product design decisions and the setting of priorities for improvement efforts.

The second component of the model is called the process view. It reflects the need for information about the performance of activities. This information shows what causes work, that is the cost drivers, and how well the work is done, that is, performance measures. Activity information helps us to identify opportunities for improvement and the means by which we can make them.

Cost drivers are factors that influence or determine cost. Cost drivers are the causes of the effort required to perform an activity. These cost drivers tell us why an activity is performed and how much effort must be expended to carry out the work. For example, if we have a method of working or a process that leads to a large number of defects, then this method or process is a cost driver which increases the effort that we need to expend to carry out an activity. We implement performance measures such that they will describe for us the work that is being undertaken as part of an activity. We can then use these performance measures to provide information about how well an activity is performed and what factors are influencing the consumption of resources.

The example shown in Figure 9.2 (Raffish and Turney, 1991) will serve to illustrate the operation of this model. To start with, it is necessary to consider the cost assignment view. The total procurement cost is $6m. Of this, $450,000 is spent on the purchasing activity. We need to find a causal relationship to trace these costs to products. A good measure of the purchasing activity is the number of purchase orders issued. There are 6000 purchase orders issued each year. So the cost of each purchase order is $75. Thus the cost of this activity can be directly traced to each product based on the number of purchase orders that each product requires.

At this point we could stop, and just say that for cost control purposes the number of purchase orders is the cost driver, and to control cost we should find a way of reducing this number, or actually reducing the total amount spent on the purchasing activity, or both. However, if we just focus attention on the cost assignment view, then all we achieve is a means of tracing the cost of purchasing to each product and a financial measure of performance to use for cost control purposes. We have still to address the development of a comprehensive set of performance measures that encompasses important non-financial measures of performance.

The next step is, therefore, to address the process view, which indicates the flow of information and transactions. What triggers the purchasing activity is the arrival of a requisition, and 8000 of these are generated each year. However, what causes the generation of requisitions is the requirement for materials. It is this requirement that is the cost driver. If we want to look at fundamental problems, rather than at symptoms of problems, that is, the cost and number of purchase orders, then we have to go right back and look at the nature of the process that leads

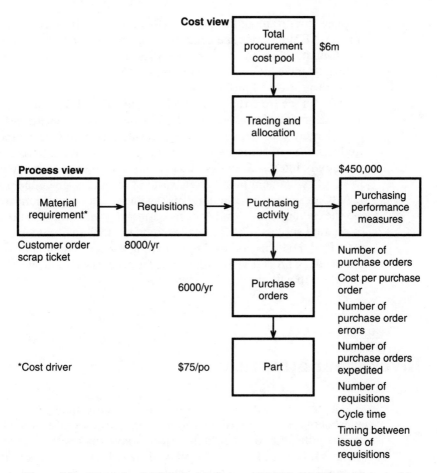

Figure 9.2 Example of ABC model. *Source:* CAM-I. © 1990. Published with permission.

to requirements for materials. In other words, we need to discover what it is about the way the material requirements arise, or are generated, that leads us to have to spend what we do on issuing purchase orders.

We therefore need to establish a performance measurement system that will generate insight into the nature of any problems, rather than just performance measures that focus attention on the symptoms, that is the cost incurred. So we start to build, and perhaps from time to time add to, a set of financial and non-financial measures of performance that will help identify where improvements can be made. The performance measures that could be used in this case are cost per purchase order, number of purchase order errors, number of purchase orders expedited, number of purchase orders issued, number of requisitions, cycle time, timing between the issue of requisitions and so on.

The important point is that ABC provides the information that enables ABM to guide the continuous improvement process. It helps to focus our attention and resources on those activities that are strategically important and which will yield the greatest benefits in terms of improved competitiveness and profitability.

We can see from the CAM-I ABC model that ABC is not just about cost assignment. However, ABC is often only associated with cost assignment, largely with respect to more accurate assignment of overheads to products. It is, of course, not necessary to implement the process view if one is only interested in cost assignment, but to implement ABC with only cost assignment in mind is a waste of resources, given the potential of ABC to support total quality management, continuous improvement and the linking of day-to-day decision-making with strategic objectives. To operate successfully in an agile manufacturing environment, we cannot afford the luxury of just implementing the cost assignment view. We also need the process view, and in fact, the process view may well be more important than the cost assignment view.

Investment appraisal

In Chapter 4 we outlined the techniques used for financial appraisal of investments and discussed the problems that arise from their application and the difficulties of using them to justify investments in advanced technologies such as FMS and CIM. We will now examine some non-financial appraisal techniques that we can use to complement our traditional financial appraisal methods (Meredith and Suresh, 1986).

Analytic appraisal methods

Analytic appraisal techniques are largely quantitative but they are more complex than the traditional financial approaches. They also allow us to capture more information and they frequently enable us to consider uncertainty and multiple measures and effects. The advantage of analytic appraisal methods is that they are more realistic, allowing us to take more factors and subjective judgments into account. The disadvantage is that they require more data, and the analysis that we have to undertake can be considerably complex and time consuming. Basically we have two analytic appraisal methods; value analysis and portfolio analysis.

Value analysis   R& D

With this approach we use a two stage process. In the first stage we undertake a pilot project which we treat as an R&D investment rather than as a capital investment. We take our decision on whether to proceed with our pilot project based on an assessment of the expected benefits. These expected benefits are not necessarily quantified at this stage, as we may well be using the pilot project to help us to quantify the expected benefits.

The pilot project will involve a small-scale system with limited functional capability that will allow us to assess a few of the expected benefits. When the pilot stage is over, we evaluate the benefits to the enterprise. Once we have established the value predicted from the pilot project, we can estimate the cost of the pilot. If the cost is acceptable in relation to the predicted benefits, then we can more confidently proceed to the second stage, which is where we develop the full system. First, we need to cost the full system and then to evaluate the expected value of the benefits. After comparing costs and benefits we can see if it is justifiable to proceed with the implementation of the full system. If the value is acceptable then the development of the full system can proceed.

The importance of value analysis is that it can help us to approach the proposed manufacturing projects with more understanding and less risk. The essence of value analysis is to separate the cost and the value that we derive, which allows us to ascertain if the value of the benefits obtained is worth the cost. Value analysis also provides us with an incremental approach to manufacturing projects that allows us to more easily control costs. This helps us to avoid risks getting out of control.

Portfolio analysis

When we are faced with a situation where we have a number of projects competing for the available capital, we have to choose a set of projects for implementation. We can make selection a little easier by creating a portfolio of projects and then ranking them according to specified criteria. There are a number of ways we can set about ranking our projects.

A very simple method is to use non-numeric models. Here we justify projects on the basis of some important characteristic that makes them exceptions to the general appraisal process.

One way we can achieve this ranking is to classify some projects as being immune from any criticism or evaluation. This usually means projects that have been suggested by someone very senior and powerful in our company. Projects like these are pursued until they are successful or until they are terminated. We can get these projects terminated only if we can convince the person who suggested the project, or that person recognizes for himself, that the project is either a failure or not worthwhile. The second way we can achieve the ranking is to classify projects as an operating necessity. Basically, these are projects that are required to keep the manufacturing enterprise operating, or to keep the company in business.

Another, more analytic approach, is to use scoring models. There are several options to choose from. The simplest scoring model is the **unweighed 0–1 factor model**. With this method, we select a set of relevant factors and ask several people to score each project on each factor depending on whether or not it qualifies for that criterion. The total number of qualifying factors are summed for each project and this then serves to rank the projects.

If we use a simple linear scale measure to denote the degree to which one of our projects meets a specific criterion, say on a 10 point scale, then we have an unweighed factor scoring model. We use the total score that we obtain for each project to rank the projects. We can extend this idea further by placing weights on each of the factors to indicate the importance that we attach to a particular criterion. This achieves a weighted factor scoring model.

Strategic appraisal approaches

The strategic approaches that are available are less technical than the financial and analytic methods. Strategic methods do however have one important advantage, and that is their direct link with the goals we have set for our enterprise. The disadvantage is that when we use them, we may end up ignoring the financial impacts. It is therefore necessary to use strategic methods in conjunction with financial and analytic approaches. Basically there are four main strategic approaches.

Technical importance

With this method we take a strategic view of projects by considering whether these projects are necessary in the sense of enabling us to meet our goals and objectives. In other words, we will be unable to attain a desired end unless we undertake certain projects first. The implementation of open systems may well fall into this category, because it will more easily enable integration of our systems both within our own enterprise and with our customers and suppliers.

Thus, when we appraise projects under the heading of technical importance, we are implying that projects are a prerequisite for follow-on activities. The returns generated from the projects may be negligible, or even disadvantageous, but more desirable and advantageous projects cannot be implemented without the completion of these technically important projects.

Business importance

When we justify a project on the grounds of business importance, we select projects on the basis that they will directly help us to achieve our business goals. For example, a project may lead to significant improvements in customer responsiveness. This is often a key business objective. Thus, projects that lead us to the attainment of our business goals will probably need to be implemented even if they do not generate any cost savings.

Competitive advantage

With this approach we recognize that some of our projects may need to be undertaken because they provide opportunities for us to gain significant competitive advantages over our competitors. Projects such as these are not necessarily directly relevant to our business goals. The opportunity to sell new product or to use new materials requiring new manufacturing processes are examples of projects that may offer competitive advantage.

Research and development

Some of the projects that we want to undertake may offer the promise of a return, but associated with the projects are certain risks. These risks make it difficult to justify the required investment. The problems, difficulties, costs and benefits of such projects can be investigated and analyzed by setting up R&D projects. If the results of our R&D projects indicate that the ideas are likely to be successful or beneficial, then this provides a case for justifying the larger investment that we will need in order to take the projects through to completion and implementation.

Relevance of new management accounting thinking

We will now consider how the concepts that we have outlined above relate to the problem of appraising investments in agile manufacturing.

It is possible to argue about the worth of activity based costing in relation to the more accurate tracing of overheads to products that this approach offers. However, the real importance of the activity based costing approach lies in several areas: its potential to refocus our attention away from direct labor costs towards the real cost drivers, the emphasis on both financial and non-financial measures of performance, the support that it provides for continuing improvement and the information that it generates for investment appraisal.

As discussed in Chapters 1 and 4, we have in the past sought to reduce direct labor costs. This emphasis on direct labor costs, as we have already seen, is built into the traditional management accounting paradigm. Now, if we fail to understand what the real cost drivers are in our plants, then our enterprises will not flourish. This in itself is reason for us to change our approaches. However, unless we also change our traditional values, then it will be extremely difficult to foster an environment in which our skilled people become an important element of our competitive advantage.

Moreover, once we have begun to seriously develop our human resources, the last thing we should be doing is trying to justify capital investments on the basis of how much of our human capital we can dispose of. When we go down the road to agile manufacturing, the people become a fixed cost. We would have to be in a difficult situation indeed, before contemplating letting the people go.

So, in order to foster the development of agile manufacturing, and to keep it alive, we do need to rethink some of our accepted management accounting fundamentals. Activity based costing offers the opportunity for a change of approach. This is where its value lies. We may well be able to cost our products more accurately using ABC, but this is not ABC's main strength. This lies in the information that it can provide to support our efforts to change our cultures and foster empowerment of the people.

The importance of including non-financial metrics in performance measurement systems is now becoming more widely accepted. We saw in Chapter 4 the consequences of failing to consider non-financial metrics. The importance of non-financial measures of performance have a twofold impact on agile manufacturing. Not only are they important because they avoid the pitfalls of a pure, financial based approach, but they also help to foster the creation and development of an environment where we begin to value and respect people's skills and knowledge.

But non-financial measures of performance do more than this, they also provide a framework for predicting potential benefits and improvements which we can often translate into financial measures for the purpose of financial appraisal, as we shall see later.

Finally, we turn to the question of investment appraisal methods. In brief, we have no fundamental disagreement with the concepts of combining financial, analytic and strategic approaches, as long as they are combined in an appropriate way, and that the financial aspects are not subsumed to the analytic and strategic aspects. We say this, not because we think that one is more important than another, but because any one of these, taken on their own, does not provide an adequate basis for appraisal in an agile manufacturing environment, and because in the end manufacturing is about making profits, and any approach that ignores this aspect will not be successful.

Appraisal of agile manufacturing

Appraisal method

Any methodology that we use when undertaking an appraisal of any investment in agile manufacturing should be based around five principles: χ

(1) Metrics must be established that will enable appropriate measures of performance to be quantified.

(2) A broad based investment appraisal approach must be used, involving elements of financial, analytic and strategic justification. Reliance on a single approach should be avoided, unless there is a good reason for adopting only one approach.

(3) It is necessary to work backwards from aggregated performance metrics which are proxy measures, to direct metrics in terms of such things as products, systems and people.

(4) As many as possible of the non-financial direct metrics should be converted into quantified financial costs, savings and revenue generation potential. These should be classified as recurrent or one-off.

(5) It is necessary to know which direct metrics to emphasize. What is appropriate for a technical investment in a new robot for example, may not be appropriate for an investment in an organizational concept such as natural groups.

When undertaking an investment appraisal it is wise to consider the following points:

(1) Most investments are unlikely to lead to costs and benefits confined only to the point of implementation. It is important, therefore, to identify the company wide costs and benefits. The sought after benefits must be clearly defined and prioritized by relating them to business strategies and opportunities.

(2) Identify the interfacing and integration issues, potential benefits and costs of integration. Pay particular attention to the costs associated with clashes that might arise later on, and remember that interfacing and integration are not only technical areas, interfacing between people and departments is also relevant. With computer equipment don't forget upgrade costs. For example, can the same data be transferred and used without modification?

(3) Do not try to quantify the costs and benefits in great detail at the very start. Use rough-cut analysis to get a feel for the financial implications of the proposed investments. This means that it is necessary to avoid getting bogged down in particular technologies, vendor's solutions, detailed organizational structures and so on.

(4) Pay particular attention to the learning curve costs. When new systems and organizational structures are implemented, people spend a lot of time learning and may not, as a consequence, be very productive. As a result, it may be necessary to take on extra staff on a temporary basis, which brings additional costs. Don't underestimate training costs.

(5) Be aware that the more complex the proposed systems, the longer may take to pass through the learning curve. Full benefits may not be achieved until much later than might be considered normal. This might involve setting lower financial hurdles than has been normal practice in the past, as the timing of the returns may be much slower but nevertheless, just as important to competitiveness.

There are two ways in which we can address the question of financial appraisal. The first is traditional. Work through the stages and then decide which investments to pursue. The alternative is the spiral approach. Although in this book the spiral approach is preferred for reasons already explored, we will examine the stage-wise process first and then adapt it to the spiral method. The proposed method is based on that presented by Bontadelli (1992) which is a standard procedure. There are seven steps in the process:

(1) Formulation of problem or improvement opportunity.
(2) Develop feasible options.
(3) Develop net cash flow for each feasible option.
(4) Select financial criteria.
(5) Analyze and compare feasible options.
(6) Select one option.
(7) Post evaluation of results.

Bontadelli's method is purely concerned with financial analysis. First we will consider the basics of his approach and then consider how it can be modified to include analytic and strategic methods as well as a spiral approach.

The first step addresses formulation of the problem, that is, stating clearly and explicitly what is required, so that projects are well defined and clearly understood. In effect, we are, at this stage, defining strategic goals, but in addition, we are also looking to define other information such as time scales, budget and specific goals for the project, or project and expected results.

Since there are always several ways of achieving a set of goals, the second step involves defining several feasible options. Of course, what constitutes a feasible option is largely based on our experience, judgment, values and bias. As Bontadelli points out, however, this step is fraught with problems. In order to establish feasible options, we must have sufficient knowledge to understand what technologies organizational concepts and management philosophies are relevant. If this knowledge is inadequate, then the feasible options will be limited and more appropriate ones will not be explored.

Step 3 of the method is concerned with developing net cash flows for each of the options we have identified. This involves determining the length of the analysis period, which should be related to either expected life of the equipment or the expected life of the products served by the equipment. The estimating baseline should also be determined, either on a total cost and revenue approach, or a differential approach. Care should be exercised to avoid overestimating revenues from continuation of the current situation (if considered as a feasible option), underestimating time and costs to implement advanced manufacturing systems and setting too high a hurdle rate which can introduce a bias against advanced manufacturing projects owing to the potential late timings of returns.

The fourth step is selection of a financial criterion for evaluation. Minimum attractive rate of return (hurdle rate) is normally the one we would use. Other possibilities are payback period, return on investment and marginal or weighted cost of capital. Comparison of the feasible options takes place in Step 5 using the well established financial appraisal methods, that is, DCF methods such as net present value, and so on.

Selection of a feasible option takes place in Step 6. The results of the financial appraisal obtained from the preceding step will be used to support this decision. Other factors, for example political issues, may also influence the decision. The final step in the analysis is undertaken after the proposed system has been implemented to establish if the actual results from the selected option actually achieve the estimated results, with the view of establishing if and where we have made any errors, so that our future appraisals can benefit from the experience gained.

In Chapter 7 we proposed that strategy development should not be divorced or separated from implementation. We proposed a spiral approach with elements of implementation being used to generate information and experience which we then feed back to guide strategy development. As a result of this proposed integration between the two aspects of strategic management, that is, strategy development and strategy implementation, it is obvious that any investment appraisals that we perform will be a more integrated activity repeated on many occasions.

Investment appraisal is a part of the process of implementation and evaluation which feeds back to development. In other words, investment appraisal is not the last step, a final hurdle to overcome, but one of the tools used in design, development and implementation.

To describe a single cycle around the spiral we need to refer back to what we described in Chapter 7 and elaborate in more detail on the appraisal aspects of the spiral method. We proposed that we start with several strategy options developed in outline form, and then proceed to cycle around the spiral several times, looking at various aspects of the

strategies such as financial appraisal and implementation experience. A
the end of each cycle we return to the strategies, and either eliminat
some, modify them or add new ones, or all three, depending on th
experiential and analytic information that we gather. As a consequenc
of the spiral approach we are making several attempts at appraisal. It i
not just a one-off sequential activity, perhaps only to be repeated agai
when a new project comes up for evaluation or when a new strategy ha
to be implemented.

In examining the seven steps discussed above, we shall discuss thei
relevance to the spiral method. Starting with Step 1, formulation of prob
lem or improvement opportunity, we see that this step becomes redun
dant, as it is already an inherent part of the spiral method, one of the aim
of which is to improve the process of problem definition by integratin
problem finding with problem solving. Likewise with Step 2, developmen
of feasible options. This is also an inherent part of the spiral approach.

If we now move on to consider Step 3, development of net cash flo
for each feasible option, then clearly we need to undertake this activit
as part of any financial appraisal. But financial appraisal is clearly also
part of the process of gathering information on proposed options, includ
ing non-financial data. Also, in the early cycles around the spiral, we ma
only wish to make rough-cut estimates of cash flows, reserving mor
detailed and accurate data gathering for later turns around the spira
when a number of options have been eliminated.

In Step 4, we are asked to select financial criteria. Usually, only on
criterion is chosen. This we discourage, and recommend that a numbe
of criteria be selected, for example, payback period, net present valu
and internal rate of return. This might seem a burden, but there is no rea
reason not to do this, given that we are looking for information t
support decision-making, not a single parameter on which a go or no-g
decision will be based. Furthermore, we can, if we wish, change th
criteria as we make several turns around the spiral. For example, on th
first turn we may simply look at payback period to make a rough assess
ment of the risk associated with a particular option. On a subsequen
pass, we may use a more sophisticated measurement such as NPV.

In Step 5, we analyze and compare feasible options. Bontadelli advo
cates the use only of a financial appraisal method in this step. Howeve
at this point the analytic and strategic tools should be introduced t
complement the financial analysis. Again we will be making severa
passes through this stage, so early turns, which will be based on rough cu
data, may indicate that simple financial analysis is required along wit
some analytic appraisal. Later turns will involve more accurate an
detailed data, thus indicating that DCF type analysis may be required.

In Step 6, the task is to select one option based on the results of th
financial analysis. In the spiral approach we are of course interested i
selecting from a number of options, but also modifying options in th

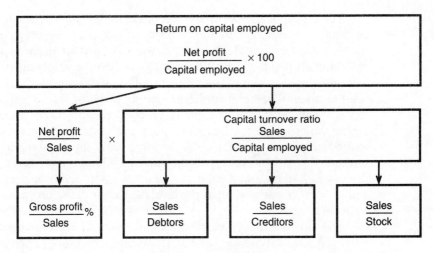

Figure 9.3   Relationship between financial ratios.

light of experience and analysis. This emphasis on experience and analysis is important. Once we have made several turns round the spiral we will be in a good position to make a decision about what to do, not just based on relatively simple financial analysis, but on a detailed picture of the implications of each option.

Finally, to Step 7, post evaluation of results. Again this is an inherent part of the never ending process of turns around the spiral. Of course, we must undertake post implementation evaluation and then feed the information back, not just to improve the financial appraisal method, but to guide the continuing evaluation of strategy and search for new directions and opportunities.

Thus we see that the appraisal method is nothing more than a part of the spiral process outlined in Chapter 7. However, in undertaking appraisal, we have underscored the importance of appropriate metrics, both direct and aggregated. Let us now consider the question of which metrics to consider. What we need is a broad range of metrics at both levels. We shall deal first with the aggregated metrics.

Traditional aggregated business metrics are based on several inter-related financial ratios, shown in Figure 9.3, such as return on capital employed, operating profit as a percentage of sales and capital turnover. Taken together they provide a picture of the profitability and liquidity of a business. The central metric in Figure 9.3 is return on capital employed, which is profit for the year divided by the capital employed multiplied by 100%. This provides a measure of the profitability of a business, that is the return on the amount invested in the business, and allows a comparison to be made to see if the investment might be bettered elsewhere by making an alternative investment.

The return on capital metric can be derived by multiplying together two other metrics, namely the operating profit as a percentage of sales metric, and the capital turnover metric. The first of these metrics is calculated by dividing operating profit by sales and multiplying by 100%. This gives the amount of operating profit earned from sales and can be used to assess whether a sufficient amount of profit is being generated from the sales arising from a given level of overheads (cost of goods sold, selling expenses, general expenses and administrative expenses). The second metric is calculated by dividing sales by capital employed multiplied by 100%. This gives the value of sales generated from every dollar invested in capital employed (current assets and fixed assets) and can be used to assess whether the level of sales or the selling price needs to be increased.

The capital turnover metric described above is related to three lower level financial ratios. The first is stock turnover ratio, which is sales divided by stock. This provides a measure of the number of times stock turns over per annum. The second is average credit given, which is sales divided by debtors. This is a measure of the speed of collecting from debtors. Finally, the third ratio is average credit taken. This is sales divided by creditors and is a measurement of the speed of payment to creditors.

The question arises whether these financial ratios, taken on their own, provide an adequate framework for assessing the performance of a manufacturing company. What other aggregated metrics could we use? Several have been suggested. Two important ones are (Compton, 1992):

- *Flexibility* is the capability to respond to changes in the market, ability to incorporate and exploit new technology and the ability to adopt new work practices.
- *Complexity* is a property that results from the number of dysfunctional units, the flow of information, decision hierarchies and so on.

The problem with both these metrics is that they are not easy to quantify. Another problem is how they relate to financial metrics.

If we take flexibility as an example, we could expect that it would have some impact upon sales. If we are capable of responding more rapidly than our competitors to changes in markets, then we should be more able to satisfy market demand and gain a sales advantage over them. This may well eventually translate into an increased return on capital employed. Likewise, if our complexity in terms of flow of information and decision processes is high, then this may imply an increased proportion of sales revenue consumed and less profit obtained. However in both cases, while the connection with return on capital employed can be made, it is not as direct and obvious as parameters such as sales revenue and profits. This suggests that we should not be looking at aggregated metrics such as complexity and flexibility, which are difficult to

Table 9.1   Non-financial performance metrics.

Distance travelled by parts within factory	Part counts
Number of material types used	Production space per product
Material utilization in each component	Buffer sizes per process
Number of processes used in production	Level of exploratory activities
Fraction of sales to repeat customers	Number of layers in organization
Responsiveness to service requests	Number of departments
Time required to accomplish a unit process	Ratio of direct to indirect labor
Manufacturing cycle efficiency	Number of patents applied for
Number of defects identified per employee	Change-over times
Machine reliability	System productivity
Yield and quality of processes	Units produced per labor hour
Machine utilization	Number of field repairs
Amount of scrap	Customer returns
Amount of rework	Inventory turns
Labor hours per unit process	Throughput times
Energy consumption per unit process	New product introduction time
Fraction of workforce with degrees	Turnover of employees
Fraction of workforce with advanced degrees	Absenteeism
On-time delivery performance	Fraction of people training in SPC and such like
Number and frequency of customer complaints	Fraction of people trained in team working

quantify, but at a whole range of direct metrics which can then be translated into figures which enhance sales revenues and increase profits.

The question arises of which direct metrics to use. We have suggested that these should be related to such things as products, systems and people. We could in principle list tens of metrics which we could record and monitor. Some of the possible metrics that have been suggested in the literature (Kaplan, 1990; Heim and Compton, 1992) are listed in Table 9.1. The problem is that there are too many. We do not know how important each is to a particular business. If we measure them all, we will accumulate a mass of data. Meaning will be lost. The information that is present in the data will never be extracted. What should we do?

First, we should only concentrate on key metrics because there is no need to measure every single thing that happens in a manufacturing enterprise. When we are controlling a chemical plant or an aircraft, we do not attempt to measure and control every variable. The cost would be prohibitive, and to achieve good control we do not need to do so. Likewise with a manufacturing enterprise. Only a handful of variables need to be closely monitored and controlled. The question is, which ones?

We answer this by tracing backwards from what we are trying to achieve. If our goal is to increase return on capital employed, then we must increase the capital turnover or the operating profit as a percentage of sales, or both. We can achieve this in several ways, including increasing sales revenues, reducing the cost of sales and expenses and reducing the total capital deployed in the business.

We can increase the sales revenue by being more competitive: offering customers greater choice, better service, improved product quality and so on. We can reduce the cost of sales by reducing overheads, selling expenses and the cost of goods sold. The amount of capital deployed in running the business can be reduced by reducing inventories and improving the speed with which payments are made by our creditors. Of course, none of these variables can be treated in isolation. They are all highly interactive. They do, however, suggest a range of metrics which one should measure and control. These can be categorized as:

- *Time metrics*   Key parameters which affect delivery times and new product introduction times.
- *Quality metrics*   Key parameters which affect the quality of a product.
- *Innovation metrics*   Key parameters which affect companies' capability to innovate and improve.

Notice that we do not have any explicit cost metrics. Why? The reason is simple. Each of these three groups of metrics, time, quality and innovation, have associated costs. For example, one quality metric could be scrap rates. A high quality process should produce extremely low or zero scrap levels. Scrap is a cost which should be reduced by improving the quality of the process. One can achieve this in several ways; through organizational changes, by making better use of people and through technological means.

One may well ask, what about direct labor costs? Surely this is a cost metric that should be measured? To answer this question we should consider two things. Yes, direct labor is a cost, but in modern manufacturing environments it is a small percentage of total costs which might therefore be better regarded as a fixed cost, especially in an agile manufacturing environment where the goal is to tap into the skills and knowledge of the people.

Furthermore, we should see labor costs in the light of a quality metric. For example, if a process involves a high level of manual interaction with a product, but with a low level of skill requirement, then we should regard this as a low quality process with associated cost. We say that it is a low quality process because, first, there is scope for human error if the work is mundane, and second because the human element could be better employed to improve the innovation metrics or to undertake more highly skilled work with a greater added value.

What then are the direct metrics that we associate with time, quality and innovation? Several are suggested in Table 9.2. We do not claim that this set of metrics is complete, nor that it is suitable for all manufacturing enterprises. What we do claim is that each one can be translated, either into a value of sales gained or lost, or into costs and benefits, or both. In terms of investment appraisal this is exactly what we

Table 9.2   Some key time, quality and innovation metrics.

Time related metrics	Quality related metrics	Innovation metrics
Responsiveness to service requests	Number of defects identified per employee	Number of exploratory activities
Manufacturing cycle efficiency	Number of field repairs	Number of patents applied for
Change-over times	Amount of scrap	Ratio of unsuccessful to successful product introductions
New product introduction time	Customer returns	Parts count trend
Distance traveled by parts within plant	Number and frequency of customer complaints	Fraction of workforce with degrees and advanced degrees
On-time delivery performance	Turnover of employees	Fraction of people participating in suggestion schemes, continuous improvement
Ratio of direct to indirect labor	Fraction of people trained in SPC, TQM	Fraction of people trained in team working
Throughput times	Fraction of sales to repeat customers	Number of suggestions per employee
		Material types usage trend

need. We want to be able to translate improvements, for example in time metrics, into financial figures so that we can combine them with other financial data such as system costs, to produce a financial appraisal. We shall now consider a way of translating metrics into financial figures.

Supporting tools

Catton (1986) demonstrated that it is possible to turn what are termed intangible benefits into tangible ones. This is done by exploring in detail the implications of a proposed action, in the same way we might use cause and effect or fault tree analysis, to trace the root causes of a problem or fault.

We wish to turn non-financial metrics into quantified costs, benefits and savings. We can achieve this goal by repeatedly asking what the implications are of achieving an improvement in non-financial metrics. We will consider some examples to illustrate the use of this technique.

The justification of CAD systems is often based purely on the expected reduction in the number of draughtsmen we believe will result from introducing CAD. However, post project evaluation seldom demonstrates the expected reductions. Frequently, intangible benefits are included to support our justification. So the statement is often made that implementing a CAD system will allow us to halve design lead times. We then ask ourselves what are the detailed implications of this statement.

We find that it is likely that we would have time to order material, instead of holding it in stock, which would generate a tangible benefit in the form of stock reduction. Also, we will improve our capability to deliver on time instead of late, so we have another tangible benefit, in that we can issue invoices more quickly and get paid earlier, leading to a reduction in working capital. We would also receive more orders because we would be competitive on delivery, so again we would have a tangible benefit in the form of increased sales.

Another example is to investigate whether or not to delegate scheduling and CNC programming to the skilled people working on the shop floor with the aim of improving their job satisfaction, motivation and commitment within a team oriented, decentralized, organizational structure. We might have proposed this step because improvements in job satisfaction, motivation and commitment can result from allowing the shop floor people to undertake scheduling and CNC programming tasks within a team oriented, decentralized organization.

Again we explore the detailed implications. In this example we find that motivated people, supported by appropriate technology, who are part of a team and who feel committed, are more likely to be concerned with the quality of their work and to be responsive to the need to complete work on time. This contributes to on-time delivery, so we have a tangible benefit because we can issue invoices more quickly and get paid earlier, leading to better control of working capital. We would also have less scrap and less rework, which gives a tangible benefit because we will spend less money on materials and reworking faulty parts. Furthermore, we would be able to generate more orders because we would be competitive on delivery performance, so again we would have a tangible benefit in the form of more sales.

Catton (1986) also described a number of other ways in which benefits can be quantified. The first is comparative estimating. This involves estimating improvements by making comparisons with similar companies who have implemented similar changes. By using this information as a benchmark, along with our own company information (for example, our own material usage) it is possible to estimate the benefits that we might obtain. The advantage of this approach is its simplicity. The disadvantage lies in the accuracy of the comparison and in evaluating any differences between the starting points of our own company and the benchmark enterprises. This approach is therefore best used in high-level comparisons to evaluate overall strategies.

A second method is analytic estimating. This involves recording existing parameters, obtaining details of proposed parameters (for example, from machine specifications or national data) and then financially evaluating the changes. For example, the effect of reducing set-up time by introducing automated tool changing technology can be demonstrated by comparing the technology vendor's estimated times with our own recorded historical times and frequencies. From this we could, for example, compute new economic batch quantities, and hence we could estimate reductions in finished stock and work in progress, which would lead us to quantify inventory savings, space savings, and perhaps indirect labor savings.

A third approach is in-house estimating, which is a useful way of quantifying the most intangible of benefits, that is, those which arise from increased sales resulting from reduced tendering and delivery time. This involves asking our colleagues to estimate anticipated benefits in a way that overcomes their natural reluctance to risk making predictions about the future. It is suggested that the effect of reduced delivery time, for example, can be obtained by asking our colleagues what the effect on sales would be, of increasing and decreasing delivery times by increments of 20%. Most of our colleagues would be keen to point out that sales could be lost owing to poor delivery performance, and once having demonstrated this, must logically be able to show improved sales for improved delivery.

This approach works best if similar information can be obtained from several independent sources to verify accuracy. Alternatively, if an individual does not wish to give a firm prediction, he can be asked to provide best, most likely and worst outcomes. The results can then be averaged using some appropriate formula.

Catton (1986) also points out the need to undertake risk analysis when evaluating benefits. One way to do this is to undertake sensitivity analysis. This is a simple technique which involves analyzing each of the factors affecting the return to determine how much each factor can change before the project becomes unacceptable (that is, a zero or negative NPV). Thus the importance of success in each of these factors will be clearly defined.

Sensitivity analysis also demonstrates factors for which alternative solutions should be tried. For example, Catton (1986) points to a capital equipment manufacturer that bought in most of its components. This policy was reviewed and compared with the benefits of in-house manufacture. The resultant strategy proposal was to acquire CNC machining centers and associated equipment. In applying sensitivity analysis to the proposal, the results showed that the project remained viable at various optimistic and pessimistic levels of throughput. However, the strategy was sensitive to the current component suppliers' selling prices. In this respect, if the current suppliers of components reduced their prices then the investment in an AMT strategy would be less attractive. As a result, rather than reducing costs by adopting the AMT strategy, the company persuaded their component suppliers to reduce their selling prices and thus achieved the desired cost saving objectives.

Another approach to risk evaluation is probability analysis, which is an extension of sensitivity analysis and estimating likely outcomes. For each of the key elements identified in the sensitivity analysis we need to provide probabilities of success for each outcome. Thus by reducing delivery times by half, increases in sales can be quoted as zero increase –

10% probability, 10% increase – 60% probability and 20% increase – 30% probability.

By using the variations and probabilities for each main factor it is possible to arrive at probabilities of achieving different DCF returns.

Concluding comments

We have tried in this chapter to outline an approach to management accounting and investment appraisal suitable for agile manufacturing environments. It is important that the approach adopted be broad, and that investment appraisal be seen as an analysis tool to support design of agile manufacturing enterprises. Investment appraisal is not a final hurdle, something to be overcome. The analysis techniques used for investment appraisal should be deployed concurrently with design, to help shape our designs and to help with design choices. The serial approach that is most commonly used today is no longer appropriate.

In addition we have discussed the concept of activity based costing. This has tremendous potential as a tool to support decision-making. Regrettably, its potential is not fully exploited. ABC often appears to be used as a way of increasing the accuracy of the arbitrariness of allocating overheads to products, rather than as a way of eliminating the artificial distinctions between overhead and direct costs. What ABC provides is a whole new approach to management accounting, one that is better described as cost management. Such an approach is ideally suited to agile manufacturing environments, where we not only wish to undertake product costing, but we also wish to have information, financial and non-financial, to guide innovation, learning, experimentation and continuing improvement activities.

Key points

- We need to develop new management accounting and investment appraisal techniques for agile manufacturing, using new concepts such as ABC.
- We need to improve our capabilities at quantifying so called intangibles, but also our capabilities to deal with softer issues such as motivation and skill base.

- We need an investment appraisal approach that is more balanced and broader with respect to the issues addressed.

- Focusing on cost reduction alone is inappropriate. We need also to look at revenue generation enhancement through the development of agile manufacturing capabilities.

- Activity based costing provides a powerful framework for a management accounting system that is appropriate to agile manufacturing. However, ABC should be examined in light of its ability to support activity based management, continuous improvement and so on, not for its claimed ability to more accurately cost products.

- There is a danger of overselling the benefits of ABC. ABC is not just for management accountants. It needs to be seen as a competitive weapon, not just a replacement for absorption costing. It should be used for more than just product costing or cost management.

- Analytic and strategic appraisal methods should be used to complement financial appraisal methods in a spiral approach. The aim is to use the techniques to support design. Investment appraisal should not be viewed as a hurdle to clear, once the design options have been fully developed.

References

Berliner C. and Brimson J.A., eds. (1988). *Cost Management for Today's Advanced Manufacturing. The CAM-I Conceptual Design.* Cambridge MA: Harvard Business School

Brimson J.A. (1991). *Activity Accounting. An Activity-Based Costing Approach.* New York: John Wiley

Bontadelli J.A. (1992). Application of the engineering economic analysis process and life cycle concepts to advanced production and manufacturing systems. In *Economics of Advanced Manufacturing Systems* (Parsaei H.R. and Mital A., eds.), pp. 91–110. London: Chapman & Hall

Catton P.G. (1986). Advanced manufacturing technology – evaluating the intangible benefits. In *Proc. Conf. on Planning for Automated Manufacture*, Coventry, UK, September 1971

Compton P.D. (1992). Benchmarking. In *Manufacturing Systems. Foundations of World-Class Practice* (Heim J.A. and Compton P.D., eds.), pp. 100–6. Washington DC: National Academy

Johnson H.T. and Kaplan R.S. (1987). *Relevance Lost. The Rise and Fall of Management Accounting.* Cambridge MA: Harvard Business School

Heim J.A. and Compton P.D., eds. (1992). *Manufacturing Systems. Foundations of World-Class Practice.* Washington DC: National Academy

Kaplan R.S., ed. (1990). *Measures for Manufacturing Excellence.* Cambridge MA: Harvard Business School

Meredith J.R. and Suresh N.C. (1986). Justification techniques for advanced manufacturing technologies. *Int. J. Production Research*, **24**(5), 1043–57

Raffish N. and Turney P.B.B. (1991). *The CAM-I Glossary of Activity Based Management.* Arlington TX: CAM-I

Turney P.B.B. (1992a). *Common Cents. The ABC Performance Breakthrough.* Hillsboro OR: Cost Technology

Turney P.B.B. (1992b). Activity based management. ABM puts ABC information to work. *Management Accounting (USA)*, January, 20–5

PART FOUR

Skill and knowledge enhancing technologies for agile manufacturing

10

Skill and knowledge enhancing technologies

Introduction

In preceding chapters we raised the issue of what we termed skill and knowledge enhancing technologies. These have been defined as computer based technologies that help to make human skills and knowledge more productive and effective, allowing these human attributes to evolve and develop into new skills and knowledge in relation to new insights and new techniques. What we do in this chapter is consider these technologies in more detail, applying some of the concepts that we defined in earlier chapters, considering the conceptual framework for the design of these technologies. In Chapter 11 we will consider, in some detail, an example which will help to illustrate the points that we are making in this chapter.

Rosenbrock (1977) suggested that technology can be designed in one of two ways. A machine such as a computer can collaborate with people's skill and knowledge, making them more effective and productive, and allowing them to evolve in relation to new facilities and theoretical insights. Alternatively it is possible to use the computer in a way that rejects people's skills and knowledge, reducing to a minimum the contribution that they make to decision processes.

This chapter is concerned with the application of the first approach to the development of computer based systems. We discuss a systems design method which we call the **skill oriented design paradigm**, in which organizational and psychological, as well as technical and financial considerations, are addressed concurrently in the systems design process. Emphasis is placed upon designing the deep system characteristics of the technology rather than just the usual surface characteristics (that is, the human–computer interface) of the organization. Organization and people issues should be considered in a proactive manner and not in a reactive way. The emphasis of the design philosophy is, therefore, on developing the deep system characteristics of the technology to fit people, rather than just designing user friendly surface characteristics (that is, interfaces).

General design principles will be presented, and we will use developments in lathe technology to help develop a conceptual framework for the skill oriented design paradigm. Implications for the systems design process and for the role and values of our systems designers will also be discussed. In Chapter 11 we will describe a system that has been designed using the skill oriented design paradigm. First, however, the nature of our more traditional technology oriented design strategies will be considered in some detail. An example of computer based scheduling will be used to highlight the problems of this approach. We will try to demonstrate, using insights from other disciplines, why technology oriented strategies are often inappropriate.

Scheduling – an example of a technology oriented approach

To make our point, we will examine the results of two European ESPRIT (European Strategic Programme for Research and Development in Information Technology) projects which are representative of the type of technology oriented projects that we tend to pursue in the US and Europe. The two projects in question are ESPRIT Projects 932 and 2434.

Both these projects were concerned with applying knowledge-based systems to achieve real-time automated scheduling. The scheduling systems developed in these projects are based on a combination of operations research (OR) algorithms and knowledge-based systems. Both projects were largely technology oriented, and show little evidence of a broad approach or a strong orientation towards users. This has resulted in complex and technically sophisticated systems, which, nevertheless, still do not provide real-time automated scheduling.

ESPRIT Projects 932 and 2434

Work on ESPRIT Project 932, which was called *Knowledge-Based Real-Time Supervision in CIM*, started in January 1986 and was completed in 1990. There were 15 organizations in the project consortium, including some very large manufacturing companies. The objectives of the project were to:

- Develop a dynamic scheduling system using knowledge-based system (KBS) techniques. The aim was to develop a system that could bridge the time gap between the large planning horizons of logistics systems such as Communications Oriented Production Information and Control Systems (COPICS) and Manufacturing Resource Planning (MRP II) systems, and the real-time conditions on the shop floor (microplanning).
- Develop generic shells covering: knowledge acquisition for plant analysis and plant operation, user interface modules for different types of users based on KBS techniques and windows and expert systems for production planning, preventative maintenance and quality control.
- Construction of the above modules followed by implementation in two plants (an electronic appliances plant and a tire manufacturing plant), to test the applicability of the generic shell to the different applications.

A number of demonstrations of project results were undertaken at industrial user and academic sites during the course of the project. The industrial user site demonstrations involved:

- Testing of a work cell controller for scheduling.
- AI-based simulation of a FMS.
- Use of a diagnosis KBS.
- Testing of a planning KBS.

There are many publications arising from this project including (Isenberg, 1987; Meyer, Isenberg and Hübner, 1988; Meye, 1989; Meyer and Walters, 1990), and a book by Meyer (1990) entitled *Expert Systems in Factory Management: Knowledge-Based CIM*. This book provides a useful source of material for evaluating the approach and the degree of success in achieving the goal of real-time automated scheduling.

Work on ESPRIT Project 2434, which was called *Knowledge-Based Real-Time CIM Controllers for Distributed Factory Supervision* started in January 1989 and was completed at the end of 1991. There were 19 organizations in the project consortium, including several large manufacturing companies, some of which were involved in ESPRIT Project 932. The objective was to make operational, on the shop floor, modern production philosophies such as optimized production technology (OPT), just-in-time (JIT) and load oriented production (LOP). This was to be achieved by delivering knowledge-based systems to each relevant function of the plant. The main goals were:

- Development of a CIM-Shell: adapting architectures and AI methods suitable for CIM.

- Development of a distributed CIM controller network: building expert systems and design tools for workcell and shop controller realization.
- Plant implementation: testing CIM controllers for small, medium and large batch manufacturing in electronics, tire, cable and integrated circuit industries.
- Development of CIM products: controllers and tools into marketable products including dedicated controller chips.

A dynamic scheduling and planning system was proposed to bridge the time gap between high-level planning systems such as COPICS and the real-time conditions on the shop floor, which was also an objective of the preceding ESPRIT Project 932. It was proposed that the system should generate manufacturing schedules, in real time, based on both higher and lower level constraints, as they became apparent. Expert systems and CIM modules were to be tested at three large-scale manufacturing plants, as follows:

- Car radio plant (small batch, large product range, discrete production).
- Tire manufacturing plant (large batch, mixed discrete production).
- Cable manufacturing plant (partly continuous, partly discrete production).

It was intended that the results from these plant tests would be used to produce a generalized expert system development shell for the optimization of internal production.

In comparison to the number of publications arising from ESPRIT Project 932, less has been published about ESPRIT Project 2434. The main source of information has been Ulfsby (1990), several papers (Isenberg, 1990; Guida and Basaglia, 1990; Walters, 1990; Zumegen and Dohr, 1990) published in the proceedings of an ESPRIT workshop (ESPRIT CIM-Europe 1990) held in Saarbrücken in 1990, and Basaglia, Saraiva and Guida (1992).

Both ESPRIT Project 932 and Project 2434 addressed scheduling. The main aim of both projects was the development of real-time closed loop CIM controllers for automated scheduling. The intention was to produce controllers that could respond to changes in the environment (availability of machines, production demands and so on). The basis of the proposed real-time automated scheduling system was knowledge-based systems technology. Both projects addressed the design and development of a CIM/AI Shell and expert systems to achieve this concept of real-time automated scheduling.

The final report (Meyer and Walters, 1990) for ESPRIT Project 932 provides some insights into the results of this particular project. The claimed project results include 55 knowledge-based systems, applicable, it is said, to production planning (including scheduling), quality or maintenance functions. It is claimed in the report that project results are at the stage of prototyping and internal exploitation. Of these 55 knowledge-based results 9% relate to standards (that is generally applicable methodologies), 47% are described as prototypes that have been demonstrated in laboratory trials, 42% are classified as internally exploited results used directly by a partner or an associated company and 2% are marketed products used by external companies. The three functional areas addressed by ESPRIT Project 932 were production planning, quality control and machine maintenance. Just under half of the results (49%) are applications in the production planning area.

A comparison of the project synopses indicates that Project 2434 is more than a continuation of Project 932, that is, a project that takes the work further on. One of the objectives of Project 932 was to implement modules at two very different user sites and to test the applicability of one generic shell to the two different applications. At best this appears to have been a limited success, for it would appear that Project 2434 is partly concerned with completing this work.

The clearly stated aim of both projects was to achieve real-time automated scheduling. However, there is no evidence in any of the publications relating to ESPRIT Project 932 that real-time automated scheduling was achieved. In fact it is clear from Meyer (1990) that the scheduling systems are not interfaced with any real-time data collection system, and no mention is made of the benefits obtained from this type of real-time approach. Evaluations are only presented for computer based versus manual scheduling, and the results, not surprisingly, show improvements using a computer. There is no comparison with computer based methods employing more traditional OR methods such as despatching rules, which would have been a more realistic and valuable comparison to have made.

We must conclude, therefore, that the goal of achieving real-time automated scheduling was not achieved in ESPRIT Project 932. The results of Project 2434 appear to be little better. Basaglia, Saraiva and Guida (1992) report that a third ESPRIT project has been set up, starting in 1992, with the goal of achieving real-time automated scheduling. Clearly, this goal is more elusive and difficult to achieve than those working on these projects imagined. We shall see later that this is indeed the case, and that research results that have been available for several years (see Section 10.3) suggest that the manner in which projects such as ESPRIT Projects 932 and 2434 have set about trying to achieve these goals is entirely wrong and leads to self inflicted problems.

Both these ESPRIT projects are founded on the idea of combining OR and AI. Many scheduling systems are based upon the use of a number of scheduling heuristics called despatching rules. There are many such despatching rules. Typically they are based upon batch size (for example, largest first or smallest first), number of operations (for example, largest first or smallest first), operation time (for example, largest first or smallest first) and so on. Some of the commonly used despatching rules are shortest processing time first, earliest due date first and shortest set-up time first.

It is also possible, using computers, to implement optimization algorithms that will search for the minimum value of total set-up time. A common way of formulating the optimization problem is known as the traveling salesman problem (TSP), which involves finding the shortest round tour between a number of cities, subject to the constraint that each city is only visited once.

ESPRIT Project 932 used the TSP formulated to achieve the minimal cost (that is, minimum set-up time) round tour in a given production sequence. This is the cyclic formulation of the TSP, which of course is not generic, because the start and end jobs are generally not the same, especially in the sort of dynamic manufacturing environments that exist today. To deal with this situation one can use the acyclic formulation of the TSP, which is based on finding the optimal sequence that minimizes the total set-up time or cost in scheduling n different components (or families) starting at component one and finishing at the nth component. This however, is not addressed in the published literature arising from Project 932.

If we take a closer look at the way the TSP has been solved, we find that the algorithms used are approximation algorithms. These are implemented in the workcell controller, known as AIPLANNER. This is described by Meyer (1990). The workcell controller constitutes a flexible decision support based on heuristic rules and approximation algorithms. The main planning strategy is to determine the bottleneck workstation, optimize order sequence and throughput for the bottleneck workstation and consider realistic process parameters (machine breakdowns, set-up times, maintenance times and so on).

The optimization goal is to minimize work in progress (WIP) and simultaneously maximize the probability of meeting due dates. The planning parameters which can be adjusted to reach this goal are planning window, time buffer, batch size and product mix. Due dates, planning horizon, maintenance intervals and product quantities are fixed. Set-up times are minimized. The planning steps are:

(1) Determine the planning horizon and planning windows (normally one week and one shift respectively).
(2) Assign the orders for the bottleneck workstation to the appropriate planning windows (it is assumed that each order can be started and finished in the window).
(3) Derive an optimal sequence of all bottleneck workstation orders per window (that is, minimize set-up times on the bottleneck workstations).

(4) Derive the load of the bottleneck workstation per window using the computed sequence, and carry orders to the previous window if the capacity is exhausted.

(5) Schedule the orders starting at the bottleneck workstation backward and forward to all other workstations involved.

(6) Test the derived plan: are the capacities available?

(7) Validate the derived plan: perform a simulation.

(8) Change parameters of the planning model (for example, time buffer, batch size and so on) and restart at Step 1.

The problem-solving heuristics of the planning problem are partly implicitly contained in approximation algorithms, and partly made explicit by rules. Some rules are:

(1) Prefer orders which need little set-up time at current workstation.

(2) Prefer small orders.

(3) Prefer late orders.

(4) Finish orders first with high WIP content.

(5) Finish orders first with high added value.

(6) Prefer specific product types.

(7) Keep bottlenecks busy.

(8) Sequence orders according to due dates (earliest due date rule) and many other well known sequencing rules.

AIPLANNER's optimization (minimize set-up time) is based on the TSP formulated with triangular inequality. A great number of graph search methods and approximation algorithms are available to solve the TSP. AIPLANNER employs two of them: the Greedy algorithm (Papadimitriou and Steiglitz, 1982) and the Christofides algorithm (Christofides, 1975).

The aim is to find an order sequence with minimum cost (that is, total set-up time). This is achieved by using one of the approximation algorithms to generate a sequence which minimizes total set-up time. This solution is then further processed using heuristics (for example, start with the product that leads to the smallest set-up time when changing over to the next product, or take largest order first, or take most urgent order first).

The partners in Project 2434 have also been developing scheduling systems based upon combining AI and OR. One of the partners in this project has been developing scheduling systems based upon bottleneck scheduling. This works by scheduling jobs on the bottleneck resource first. The remaining jobs on other resources are then synchronized with the bottleneck resource to reduce lead times.

The system is based on:

• A bottleneck scheduler which makes an optimum schedule for the bottleneck resource.

- A forward scheduler which schedules the jobs after the bottleneck.
- A backward scheduler which schedules the jobs before the bottleneck.

The forward and backward schedulers are implemented by heuristic search methods taken from OR using priority dispatching rules such as shortest processing time first. It is reported that the bottleneck scheduler uses a hill climbing method from AI which is described in Hanan and Kurtzberg (1972).

Hanan and Kurtzberg (1972) consider the physical design of back-planes for computers. This involves optimal placement of circuit modules on a printed circuit board. Because of the complexity and magnitude of most practical problems, no methods exist which guarantee an optimal solution. As a result, methods based upon heuristic rationales are employed. Several approximation algorithms are discussed by Hanan and Kurtzberg. It is not clear from Ulfsby which of these approximation algorithms has been used in ESPRIT Project 2434. It is also not clear why Ulfsby has referred to the algorithm as a hill climbing method from AI. The use of heuristic methods and approximation algorithms is well established as a means of solving optimization problems, and these concepts were developed independently of AI, which is why Hanan and Kurtzberg make no reference to AI techniques. Heuristics and approximation algorithms are part of the basics of optimization theory (Burley, 1974).

Issues raised by ESPRIT Projects 932 and 2434

A number of important questions can be posed about these two ESPRIT projects. First, how generic are the results? Second, are the results too complex for widespread use in manufacturing industry? Third, how beneficial will the real-time automated scheduling prove to be? It is not possible, of course, to provide definitive answers, but what can be done is to point out some issues which suggest that the results of these two projects have serious limitations.

First, we will address the issue of generality. It seems that both projects have centered around three user sites: a car radio plant, a tire manufacturing plant and a cable plant. There is no description, or even mention in the published literature, of any work that has been undertaken to consider issues of generality so that the CIM controllers and the concepts of real-time automated scheduling can be applied, not just in all three plants considered, but more generally in manufacturing.

The book by Meyer (1990) is solely concerned with the car radio plant, and makes no reference to the manufacturing problems within a tire or cable plant. Ulfsby (1990) reports that the partners in Project 2434 are developing their own software systems. The project cooperation therefore appears to be limited to exchanging methodologies rather than on trying to make a common software system. There must, therefore, be some concern about the generic nature of the results, given the failure to identify issues of generality.

A further point is that all three plants are large manufacturing facilities, producing relatively large batches, and owned by large companies. These are not typical examples of manufacturing enterprises in the US and Europe, which are mostly small to medium size companies. It is hard to imagine technical systems developed by large companies for large manufacturing facilities being used by many of our smaller enterprises. Most of these companies do not have the technical know-how, the hardware platforms or the financial resources to support real-time automated scheduling using KBS techniques.

This, in fact, is a more general problem with our CIM technologies. On the whole, the development work on CIM seems to have been mainly confined to large manufacturing enterprises. The whole process of CIM development has largely been driven by the needs of larger manufacturing companies. Moreover, because the development of CIM architectures and CIM components based on AI is a complex and challenging task, many of our small to medium size manufacturing companies have been unable to participate in the development work.

Many large manufacturing companies have research and development departments, and the financial strength and manpower to invest in the development of CIM. However, many of our small to medium size manufacturing companies do not have the capabilities to invest in long term CIM research and development projects. CIM concepts, therefore, seem mostly to be developed and influenced by our larger manufacturing companies, and are then later adopted (and possibly adapted) by our smaller manufacturing companies.

Furthermore, as we have already pointed out, in the past the development of CIM has been largely dominated by technological considerations. We have normally neglected the human and organizational dimension during CIM research and development projects. We have considered these issues as matters relevant only to the deployment of the technology, and not considered, as part of our R&D brief, how technology deployment can be improved by making CIM technologies easier to implement. This is rather silly, as once we have determined the technology, we have to live with any inherent deployment difficulties. Such difficulties might have been avoided if we had thought about the deployment while we were developing the technology.

We should ask ourselves whether this technology oriented development of CIM is likely to produce results that best suit the needs and capabilities of our small to medium size manufacturing companies. We commonly assume that technologies suitable for larger manufacturing enterprises can be used by smaller companies. This assumption is questionable and may well be a false one, but it is one which is characteristic of our technology oriented perspective.

The approach adopted by ESPRIT Projects 932 and 2434 seems to be one that inherently belongs in the realms of big companies with big development budgets, and with the large technical resources needed to keep complex systems working. But even our large companies should think twice before getting involved with such technologies. They might find the cost of maintaining these sophisticated systems prohibitively expensive, and that the benefits generated might need to be considerable, before such technology oriented approaches become justifiable. For a significant number of companies, this approach might prove to be problematic. What we need to do is to find better ways of developing and deploying these advanced technologies.

It is often the case that adequate scheduling can be achieved using an open loop approach and by allowing people to use their judgment and experience to compensate for changes in the environment. The success of this approach has already been demonstrated, as we shall see later, and it therefore seems that the closed loop real-time approach, as developed within these two ESPRIT projects, is unlikely to find wide application in industry. This is not to say that these technical advances should not be pursued. They should, but within a framework that provides a broader picture of the problems. A more successful strategy to follow might be to start with fairly simple human–computer based open loop scheduling, and then to take more evolutionary steps towards improving the overall system performance, rather than adopting this big-bang technology development approach, which ignores infrastructure issues, and which may be a bridge too far in terms of manufacturing industry's capabilities to support and exploit these technologies.

Thus, if we want to consider moving towards exploiting real-time scheduling, which does not necessarily have to be automatic, in our small to medium size companies, assuming that it might bring some benefits if used properly, then a more evolutionary approach would seem to be more appropriate. Such an approach should also take the other aspects of the scheduling problem into account. We will address some of these issues in the next section.

An interdisciplinary view of scheduling

In the preceding section we identified that real-time automated scheduling, which was the stated goal in ESPRIT Projects 932 and 2434, was not achieved. The scarcity of detailed descriptions of the problems and characteristics of operation, and the lack of results from such systems, clearly suggest that the project aims in this area were not achieved. What we will do now is show that this outcome is not unexpected, and that an interdisciplinary approach strongly indicates this outcome should be expected. Such an interdisciplinary view also provides the framework for developing a different approach to the development of technology.

As a first step we will look at the nature of scheduling problems and the relevance of OR and AI to them.

The relevance of OR and AI to scheduling

McKay, Safayeni and Buzacott (1988) have argued that the approach of OR and AI to scheduling is theoretical and thus is often not applicable to the dynamic characteristics of the actual situation found in complex manufacturing environments such as job-shops. Although not all manufacturing environments are job-shops, the trend towards greater product variety, smaller batches, customized production and one-of-a-kind manufacturing is actually moving many companies towards job-shop characteristics. It is therefore important that we should take note of research such as that undertaken by McKay and his co-workers.

McKay, Safayeni and Buzacott (1988) report the results of a preliminary field study which illustrates that the basic theoretical approach does not represent the reality of open job-shop scheduling. They thus concluded that the applicability of OR and AI is limited to those situations that are fundamentally static and behave like the models.

The problems that schedulers face is how to schedule and despatch work in a way that satisfies many conflicting goals that may be both explicitly stated and unstated, using hard and soft information that may possibly be incomplete, ambiguous, biased, outdated and erroneous. Moreover, job-shop environments are seldom stable for longer than half an hour. There are many sources of variability, and unexpected events occur all the time with the effects being longer lasting than the batch processing times for the work in progress in the areas affected.

Schedulers use many tools to deal with variability and constraints. Also, they use intuition to provide a picture of what is happening, what can happen and what will happen. This insight involves using a great amount of sensory data and a mental model of the process to gain insight into aspects of operation that are not contained in reports and computer systems.

The scheduling situation is characterized by many constraints and issues that can affect the scheduling of different parts of the shop at different times for different reasons. When scheduling, some issues will be paramount while others will be ignored. These sub-sets will change with time, date, mood, climate and so on.

Scheduling and control is difficult because of:

- Set-up and processing time variability which makes prediction and forecasting difficult.
- The practice of preempting jobs and pushing sensitive jobs through which causes other jobs to be late.
- Senior management accepting orders and guaranteed results without consulting shop floor schedulers.
- Arrival of materials which cannot be predicted accurately.
- Shortages of skilled manpower. Often there is enough for normal demand, but not enough to recover backlog.

In real world scheduling, individual events might happen quite rapidly, but outcomes may not be clear for hours or even days. It is hard to get a sense of how individual events combine to produce an eventual outcome. There is also a need to observe several things simultaneously and mentally integrate their locally independent states in order to estimate overall system state. There are many multiply-determined distinct events, which are difficult to view, and trends are difficult to determine because of the discrete nature of the processes. The problem is made worse by the fact that often system components are tightly coupled and interactive. System states do not stand for the whole, so sub-goals have no privileged perceptual relationship to the overall goal. These factors make it hard to determine the effect of a single action and to learn cause–effect relationships.

These are just a few aspects of the real world of job-shop scheduling. Very few aspects of the real world problem have been noted in the academic literature. The theory of job-shop scheduling is very restricted, and is far removed from the reality of the problem. Furthermore, it is often the case that what technologists end up doing, like those people involved in the two ESPRIT projects we discussed earlier, is dealing, not with scheduling problems, but with the symptoms of problems that actually exist upstream of the plant.

An example of an upstream problem is the sales function. If sales personnel make due date promises to customers without any regard for plant load, capacity or the feasibility of due dates, which is not uncommon in our fragmented world of traditional manufacturing, it is not surprising that there will be scheduling problems. All computers can do in such circumstances is to slightly ameliorate these problems by dealing with the symptoms. To really resolve the problem we must take a much broader perspective and deal with the source of the problem, not with the symptoms.

Another problem with OR is that it tries too hard to be scientific (Grant, 1986). This leads to a technique oriented approach that discounts the value of subjective judgment, and in a subjective world, OR can be dismissed as being unrealistic. Grant also notes that the heuristics used in scheduling can be very simple. He reports that an extensive survey of the scheduling literature shows that the work of the scheduler is based on heuristics at three levels:

(1) Loading rules can be constructed to take account of the job-processing time, the due date for the job and the state of congestion in the shop.
(2) Heuristics for improving schedules, for example, alternate operation, look ahead, re-do.
(3) Heuristics about the applicability of the loading rules and of the schedule improvement heuristics for a given objective.

According to Grant, only the loading rules have been studied thoroughly by OR workers.

Despite the difficulties and the complexities of scheduling, experienced schedulers often achieve acceptable levels of performance. This naturally leads many of us to the conclusion that an approach based on AI might be more appealing, since this would take account of subjective judgment and other heuristics. However, it has been argued by McKay, Safayeni and Buzacott (1988) that AI has not fared much better than OR, largely because the problem formulation used by AI researchers is essentially the same as that used by OR people.

AI researchers appear to use the same limitations and assumptions in investigating how AI can be applied. Selective information is still used. Even though AI uses far more domain information than the heuristics documented in the OR literature, representation and scheduling logic is oriented towards the process planning problem in an automated plant, and not the constraints encountered in a dynamic job-shop. A common approach is to use expert systems which identify rules, priorities and weights for the scheduling algorithm.

It is suggested by McKay, Safayeni and Buzacott (1988) that for AI to be useful, the problem would have to exhibit a number of deterministic characteristics that would reduce the need for subjective scheduling, such as:

- Stable and well understood simple manufacturing processes.
- Simple manufacturing goals which are not affected by hidden agendas.
- Short cycle times so that work can start and finish without interruption.
- Predictable and reliable set-up and processing times.
- Known delivery quantities, times and quality.
- Long times between failures relative to cycle times, and short repair times.
- Accurate and complete information in the computer on processing times and the status of jobs.

The more attributes from this list that a job-shop possesses, the better the chances of being able to use job-shop scheduling theory directly.

Such shops require little predicting and intuition. It is unlikely that there are many shops satisfying even a small portion of these characteristics.

This analysis also tends to confirm the conclusions that derive from the failures of ESPRIT Projects 932 and 2434. In these projects, the environment would appear to be highly automated with large batch sizes. It is very unlikely that many of the criteria, as specified above, were satisfied. As a consequence, the probability of being able to achieve a realistic real-time automated scheduling system would appear to have been quite small.

Another problem with AI is that a lack of contextual knowledge severely limits capability, and it is also difficult to handle a broad domain. In other words, problems must be well defined, and it is in these situations that successful systems are most likely to be achieved. This is occasionally reported in literature that has been more specific about the nature of the manufacturing environment. Usually, however, the characteristics of the manufacturing environment are not described in any detail, if at all. This makes it almost impossible to attach any scientific reliability to the results claimed by researchers developing AI based scheduling systems. Basically, the results are compromised by the failure on the part of researchers to define, explicitly and in detail, the characteristics of the manufacturing environment with which they are dealing.

As AI people know, knowledge is central to intelligent behavior. The problem with the real world, unlike that of research experiments and development projects, is that the real world keeps changing, and keeping knowledge bases up to date is a challenging task, and clearly one that has not yet been successfully achieved.

It is reported (Fox, Allen and Strohm, 1982) that human schedulers typically spend about 80–90% of their time determining the constraints of the environment that will affect their schedules. Only 10–20% of their time is actually spent on the construction and modification of schedules. Most OR and AI based computer scheduling systems are targeted at generating schedules, that is, dealing with 10–20% of the scheduling task. We seem to have largely ignored the remaining 80% of the tasks that our schedulers undertake and have offered them very little in the way of computer support for these other tasks.

Human scheduling behavior

Many of us may share the belief expressed by Roth and Watt (1991) that people are not very good at handling scheduling, even for fairly small problems. Yet, Roth and Watts also state that it is worth looking at the way people solve scheduling problems, because even though they cannot attempt to investigate all possibilities, they can often achieve a fairly good solution, which would seem to contradict their belief that people are not very good at handling scheduling! We will now examine some research results concerning the evaluation of human performance when scheduling.

Sanderson and Moray (1990) have undertaken a survey of research into human scheduling performance. From their survey of the research literature they report a number of general findings. These are:

- It has been claimed that human schedulers often (but not invariably) perform better than job-shop despatch rules because people are more flexible.
- Human–computer interactive scheduling can be better than using a person or computer alone.
- People seem to be able to exploit opportunities for action that emerge when system parameters are highly variable, although the effects of system variability are not clear cut.
- Humans use predictive scheduling aids to a limited degree, preferring to look no more than three steps into the future.
- Field researchers have characterized expert human schedulers as having mental look-up tables of uneven granularity for making decisions and choosing actions.

There are, however, many unanswered questions. For example, under what conditions will humans show better scheduling performance than algorithms? What is the expected relative performance of humans given certain plant set-ups and information management and display systems? What features of scheduling tasks might pose insurmountable obstacles for humans?

Behavior under time pressure and distraction

Research into human behavior under conditions of time pressure and distraction supports the intuitive conclusions that such behavior is different from the behavior that prevails under more leisurely circumstances. Wright (1974), for example, reports that for conditions of high time pressure and moderate distraction, experimental evidence supports the hypothesis that people tend to accentuate negative evidence and use fewer attributes to assess the situation. In other words the harassed decision-maker becomes extremely alert to discrediting evidence on a few salient dimensions.

The picture this presents is of people making simplifications when operating under heavy information overload arising from increasing amounts of data to be assessed, or decreasing time available for assessment. Thus, faced with a decision task of considerable complexity, people will try to restructure the task into a simpler one. If the ability to restructure the task by controlling the time pressure or distractions is limited, then this restructuring might well involve restricting attention to certain portions of the available information. Data about less relevant dimensions might be excluded from consideration, even though under less taxing conditions this data might well be considered important. Alternatively, attention might be focused on data in certain regions of each dimension.

Thus in effect, decision-makers accept some distortion of their ideal assessment and judgment strategy under conditions of pressure. If entire dimensions of information are ignored, then choices are made in ignorance of what outcomes to expect on those dimensions, and the dimensions that are attended to will, as a result, have relatively greater impact on judgments than would normally be the case. When negative evidence is highlighted, awareness of the positive outcomes is sacrificed, and when positive evidence is focused on, the awareness of negative outcomes is sacrificed.

Of course the two strategies are not mutually exclusive. However, which strategy dominates may be determined by external factors such as appraisal, rewards and punishment. It is possible that when people are heavily penalized for making mistakes and identifying false benefits, and have their successes ignored, they will adopt a negative strategy, focusing all their attention on negative evidence.

Sanderson and Moray (1990) have examined situations of time pressure, where humans have to complete a number of given tasks by specified due dates. In this type of situation it has been demonstrated that knowledge of the optimal rule for completing the tasks does not improve human performance significantly, and under conditions of strong time pressure, knowledge of the optimal rule can actually interfere with completing the tasks on time. The reason for this is straightforward and is related to the information processing demands of the tasks. Under conditions of strong time pressure humans cannot make use of scheduling rules and they perform better using their intuition, especially when the optimal rule is complex. Thus when they are told what the optimal rule is, and then spend time working out the results of the scheduling rule, there is insufficient time left to process the tasks.

The above seems to be a general result as it agrees with other research. In situations where correct planning and scheduling would be advantageous, but time pressure increases, humans abandon the optimal approach and adopt a simpler policy such as first come first served, or earliest due date first, even when these are not optimal. Decision-making becomes simpler and less compensatory under time pressure.

The above results are concerned with humans who are involved in scheduling their own time to complete tasks which they themselves are undertaking. The results indicate that, in this type of situation, under conditions of time pressure, a great deal of assistance in the form of a scheduling decision aid is needed. This type of situation is not so normal in manufacturing, where people are more usually involved in working out a schedule for a group of resources (for example, a FMS or a manufacturing cell).

Behavior when scheduling resources

Sanderson and Moray (1990) mention a number of factors which are properties of the system, as experienced by the human, which influence the processes of recognition, decision and action. These factors are called **subjective factors of the scheduling situation**, which are a function not of people or the manufacturing system alone, but of the interaction between the two, given various scheduling policies, as the system moves towards its goals. Subjective parameters are not plant specific, although their values might be, and are relevant to many scheduling situations.

Subjective parameters influencing recognition of system state include the:

- time available to examine the system;
- inherent observability of the system;
- number of features to be contemplated simultaneously;
- uncertainty of sub-system states;
- familiarity of the system state;
- degree to which system state conforms to a known pattern or schema;
- ease of projecting to future states.

Those subjective parameters influencing decisions include the:

- number of possible and plausible action alternatives, their similarity, and whether they can all be held in working memory;
- presence in long term memory of previously successful decisions and the complexity of judging whether a possible decision will satisfy system goals.

Finally, subjective parameters influencing the successful execution of action include the:

- time available to act;
- number of sub-actions in the plan;
- familiarity of the actions to be carried out;
- possibility of state change during actions;
- potential for interference with memory by new events.

Sanderson and Moray (1990) also discuss human intervention in computer based scheduling. They suggest that people intervene either when the present or future state of the system is seen to deviate from a goal, or whenever humans see a window of opportunity for intervention. Indications of the need for intervention requiring recognition include present or predicted system states which appear to be contrary to current scheduling goals. These include such things as congested queues, uneven distribution of load over machines, delayed jobs and missed due dates, low output rates and opportunities presented by unexpected slack time. An important question is how easy will it be for human schedulers to see that these things are happening. This depends on the quality of information display and the degree to which the human must project into the future or mentally integrate over past states.

Types of human intervention which necessitate decision and action include changing or preempting the current scheduling rule, improving upon a computer produced schedule, changing scheduling criteria and changing such features as job weights or priorities.

Scheduling systems need to support decision and action in all four decision and actions areas identified above. However, it is also clear from the preceding discussion that a scheduling system should not just improve the quality of decisions, but should also improve recognition of system state and the successful execution of actions.

The issue of subjective system parameters should be considered when attempting to achieve these objectives. The development of scheduling systems should take into account these subjective system parameters. The implication is that an ideal scheduling system should contribute towards:

- improving system observability;
- limiting or controlling the number of features to be contemplated simultaneously;
- uncertainty reduction concerning sub-system states;
- improving user familiarity with the system state;
- improving the degree to which system state conforms to a known pattern or schema;
- easing the projection of future states;
- generating a number of possible and plausible action alternatives and assessing their similarity;
- storage and recovery of previously successful decisions and means of supporting complex judgments about whether a possible decision will satisfy system goals.

Clearly these are a complex set of requirements which may be difficult to achieve in a particular system design. The research undertaken by Sanderson and Moray does not suggest how these requirements could be fulfilled, so these should, therefore, be seen as a set of requirements which designers of scheduling systems should attempt to satisfy. Basically, these requirements are issues which should be addressed during the design of any scheduling system.

Human–computer interactive scheduling

All computer based systems for scheduling involve some form of human intervention and monitoring. Few of our systems, however, are designed on the basis of any understanding of human behavior in scheduling systems, or with a view to making effective use of people's skills and knowledge. As Sanderson (1989) reports, there are several reasons why it is important that we should consider the human planning and scheduling role in advanced manufacturing.

First, planning and shop floor control and scheduling have a major impact on the performance of our production systems. People are involved in the control of scheduling, and their performance is critical and just as important as the computers and software that are used for planning, control and scheduling. Second, the algorithmic and heuristic methods that we use to automate such systems always have inherent limitations. People are invariably needed, therefore, to back up the systems when these limitations threaten production. Third, when an advanced manufacturing system fails or malfunctions we expect people to reschedule and to reroute work.

In all situations, including those where we find it necessary to implement a high level of automation, it is important to know how people can best be supported. This requires that we develop an adequate understanding of the strengths and limitations of people's planning and scheduling abilities. Such understanding is not evident in most of our technology oriented projects.

There are also several drawbacks to the algorithms and expert systems used in production planning and scheduling. First, no analytic model can fully represent the behavior of a manufacturing system. Second, many of our simplifying assumptions are violated, making the presence of people crucial to success. Third, our expert systems are only as powerful as the rule and knowledge bases and inference engines that we implement. When situations arise where our expert systems lack rules, they will be prone to inferior inferences. Fourth, our knowledge and rule bases may quickly become out of date as we make continuous changes to the plant and products. So, the conclusion is that people on the shop floor are still required to intervene in such situations.

The type of drawbacks and limitations of algorithms and expert systems mentioned above have led many people to conclude, not only that people are needed in advanced manufacturing systems, but that people should be active and engaged. Thus, these human–computer interactive planning and scheduling systems are needed for several reasons:

- There is normally potential for significant downtime in advanced manufacturing systems, and people are needed to troubleshoot and to get the system operational again when failures occur.
- There are dangers that people will become too remote from the system and the processes. They may not develop, or may lose, their mental model of the system functioning and structure.

- A number of research studies and industrial applications suggest that human–computer interactive systems often outperform systems in which either people, or computers, dominate the scheduling process.

This last point is perhaps a key one. It is easy to show that humans can outperform computers, and vice versa, by selecting appropriate experimental conditions. This proves nothing. Comparison of human and computer performance assumes that the two are comparable, but as we have already indicated, this view is limited. If we view them as complementary, then the question becomes one of how to design the system on the basis of complementary elements, and this leads to a different view of people and the technology needed to support them.

We always make a tacit assumption that people will be around monitoring the system in case something goes wrong, as no scheduling and control system will be able to handle all system abnormalities or changes in production requirements. We should design our systems with this assumption explicitly stated, and provide the support that people require.

Godin (1978) reported that there has never been any widespread effort to do work in the area of interactive scheduling in a manner similar to the way in which job-shop despatching rules have been studied. That situation has still not changed significantly. Most computer based systems require some form of human input, intervention and involvement. But this aspect of the system is seen purely as an interface issue, not one about cognitive processes and the effective sharing of tasks between human and computer, making appropriate use of each.

It is unfortunate that this is so. Research undertaken in the field of human–computer interactive scheduling shows promising results (Ferguson and Jones, 1969; Krolak, Felts and Marble, 1971; Haider, Moodie and Buck, 1981). However, as Sanderson (1989) points out, merely noting that humans enhance system performance does not provide a solid basis for the design of human–computer interactive scheduling systems.

Although it is desirable and useful to use people in this way, it is not appropriate to develop such systems without first understanding the issues involved in their design. For example, it might reasonably be thought that it would be desirable to provide graphical user interfaces, rather than alphanumeric interfaces. However, research has shown that graphical displays do not guarantee better performance (Sharit, 1985). Furthermore, it is important to understand under what circumstances humans enhance scheduling performance, and to establish those situations where scheduling is best left to the computer.

The areas where computer support should be provided should also be addressed. Given that human schedulers only spend about 10% of their time actually scheduling, to focus attention largely on this particular aspect would seem to be inappropriate. Finally, we should consider our values and attitudes. Are we talking about computers solving problems with the help of people, or people solving problems with the help of computers, or some strategy in between? All these strategies seem to be fundamentally different approaches, leading to different kinds of systems.

The above issues lead us on to consider questions of design strategy, design principles, conceptual frameworks for the design of such systems and design concepts.

Technology design strategies

Many if not most technological systems are designed such that people who use them undertake only those tasks which we have found too difficult or expensive to automate. In this type of situation it is also often the case that we have given little thought to the facilities and support that the people require in order to satisfactorily undertake these tasks (Bainbridge, 1983). This approach to systems design can be referred to as a **technology oriented design paradigm** because it is primarily concerned with technology and technical functionality.

There is however, another systems design approach, which we will call the **human factors design paradigm**. This strategy is also largely based upon automating only those tasks that are not technically too difficult or expensive to automate. This approach involves using ergonomics, cognitive psychology, job design principles and so on to develop appropriate human–machine interfaces, organizational structures and so forth with the aim of improving ease of system use and operation, and providing a better quality of working life for the people. This approach may sometimes question the validity of automating some functions (Hwang *et al.,* 1984) even if it is possible to automate them, although the difficulties that human factors experts face when working with many of our technologists make this type of consideration a very rare event (Meister 1987; Perrow 1983).

Although this human factors design paradigm is better than the technology oriented design paradigm, human factors experts on the whole have not sought to question the form of our technology. They have tended to accept what the technologists have proposed, and then tried to make the best of a highly imperfect situation. There is, therefore, usually no human factors input provided in the design of the technology that lies behind the human–computer interface. The main focus is placed, instead, on the interfaces and people's work environment. The probable reason why this has happened is that there has been an underlying belief that it is possible to design and optimize sub-systems (that is, the technology, the human–computer interface and work organization) in isolation, in the belief that this will lead to optimization of the overall human–machine system.

There is also a third design approach, called the **skill oriented design paradigm** where we seek to design the overall system using organizational, psychological, technical and financial considerations jointly, in such a way that insights from the organizational and psychological sciences are used to shape the technology, as well as the human–computer interface and the organization. The aim of this skill oriented design paradigm is to develop technology that allows people's skills and knowledge to become more effective and productive, that is, to achieve skills leverage, allows the evolution of people's skill and knowledge and provides people with effective and satisfactory tools that will support and enhance their skills and knowledge.

There are numerous examples of technological systems that have been designed using the technological paradigm, for example, the early types of numerically controlled (NC) machine tools. These machines are controlled by programs which normally have to be written by a specialist programmer who is based in an office. Thus, the only way that the machine operators can influence the machining process is through the use of overrides located on the machine tool's control panel.

In recent years there has been a move towards designing NC machine tools using the human factors paradigm. Thus the new generation of NC machines, which go by the name of computer numerically controlled (CNC) machine tools, are provided with facilities for operator programming, and usually have color graphic displays, tool path simulation facilities, and other types of user friendly programming aids, although the quality of these displays and facilities is very variable.

Although this shift away from the technology oriented paradigm is something that is long overdue, those of us adopting the human factors approach have not really considered whether traditional ergonomics and job design, which just tend to accept the technology as given, provide adequate tools to deal with complex technologies and systems which are still largely designed on the basis of technical and financial considerations alone.

It is well documented (Braverman, 1974) that many of the technologies used on the shop floor have been developed over a long period, effectively de-skilling and impoverishing the working lives of the people who have had to use and work with the technology. Although in the past this trend was most evident on the shop floor, it is now becoming evident in office and professional systems. One reason why this has happened is because **technological form** affects people's skills and knowledge. But just as important, technological form can also be used to closely circumscribe people's working methods, limit their freedom of action and autonomy and determine the degree of control that they have over their work.

We might well ask, in what way does traditional ergonomics and job design provide the tools and techniques to ensure that the technology is designed to enable people to use systems according to each individual's personal preference or according to the method that each person finds most appropriate and acceptable? Surely it is necessary, given the potential that computers provide to **over-determine** and control people's working methods, for our human factors experts to be closely involved in the design of the technology that lies beyond the human–computer interface?

The skill oriented design paradigm provides the basis for a systems design process in which these issues can be considered, and for taking into account organizational and psychological considerations in the design of our technology. Unfortunately however, there is one major problem that can prevent the skill oriented design paradigm from becoming the dominant design method, and this difficulty arises from our values and attitudes.

Within both the technical and the human factors design paradigms, automation of tasks is primarily driven by technical and financial considerations. We rely, however, either tacitly or explicitly, upon people to intervene to ensure that the systems continue to work in unforeseen situations. And we expect people to cope with events that cannot be dealt with via automatic devices. The implication of this is that we hold a set of values and attitudes which are derived from a belief that the skills, knowledge and judgment of our people are *still* required.

The skill oriented design paradigm however, is based upon the concept that the skills, knowledge and judgment of the people are desirable attributes which should not be designed out of the systems. Technology should therefore be designed so that people's attributes, such as their skills and knowledge, are encouraged to expand and develop, and this demands that we think of these human attributes as things which *should* be required.

This concept has major implications for future technological developments. What we are suggesting is that new technologies should not de-skill people, or fragment their work. This implies a fundamental change in the path of technological development.

In the following sections we will consider the conceptual framework that underlies the skill oriented design paradigm.

Design issues

Major design issues are user acceptance and the usability of new technologies. This is not just a question of user friendly interfaces. It involves a range of design issues that are connected with the functionality of systems and people's relationship with technology. It has been noted by Bainbridge (1983) that automated systems are often designed so that people undertake only those tasks that we find too difficult or expensive to automate. People's work is, therefore, largely concerned with compensating for the inadequacies of the systems. Often the role of people is reduced to intervention when something goes wrong, or when the unexpected occurs.

Bainbridge has attempted to demonstrate that this is an unsatisfactory situation. It can often lead to stressful working conditions. Also, most often, it does not provide many opportunities to develop an understanding of the system. Moreover, it does not provide opportunities for people to test the validity of any understanding of the system that they might develop. Furthermore, this type of situation does not provide the opportunities that are needed to develop the experience and skills that are important for successful intervention.

Traditionally, this has been the point where we have invited human factors specialists to address problems that we have created with our technology. Typically, we have asked them to improve the situation, not by changing the technology, but by designing better human–machine interfaces and redesigning jobs with the aim of reducing stress and improving people's job satisfaction. Occasionally the human factors people have questioned the validity of automating some functions, but the actual form of the technology has usually been left unchanged. The human factors specialists have tended to accept our technology as given. They have influenced the surface characteristics of the technology (the human–computer interfaces) and the environment (the working conditions and the organization), but have left the deeper characteristics of the technology unchanged.

We also note here that there is often a change management problem associated with the introduction of new technologies, and that we have not adequately addressed these problems. For example, new technologies can create a demand for skills and knowledge that do not exist and which are unrelated to existing skills. Experience of introducing new technologies suggests that older people often have the greatest difficulties in adapting to new technologies. Young people seem to adapt quite well. However, with the falling number of school leavers, we cannot rely on a supply of young people, and our attention will have to shift towards overcoming the change problems experienced by older people.

We have noted previously that computer based technologies provide us with the ability to affect the type and level of skills needed by people. This also allows us to closely circumscribe people's working methods, limit their freedom of action and autonomy and determine the degree of control that they have over their work (Kidd, 1988). This characteristic of the technology raises the question about who controls people's working methods, and the question of whether their personal preferences, as users of our systems, should be accommodated.

All these issues point to one conclusion. The way we design computer based systems is largely outdated and often inappropriate. There is a strong tendency for us to design systems that act as a substitute for people's skills and knowledge. Possibly as a consequence of this, we place too much emphasis on functionality, and do not pay enough attention to usability issues.

Human factors attempts to deal with this emphasis on functionality by improving surface characteristics and organization. It is necessary to address these matters, but this approach to design is only a response to the symptoms of the core problem. What is really needed is to solve the core problem, and this means changing the technology and the design methods. The need is for a changed approach, one that seeks to satisfy human as well as technical and economic needs.

Design and technical implications

The traditional approach to design has been to place technical functionality above questions of usability. We need to change this approach. Questions of usability must not be secondary, but must be placed on an equal footing with technical functionality. Instead of design being driven by technical and economic criteria, equal attention must be paid to human, technical and economic considerations. The method that we use to address human issues is important.

Often the technology is designed first, and then the human issues have to be dealt with around a fixed technology. Attention is usually focused on surface characteristics and organization. We should replace this reactive design method by a proactive approach. Psychological considerations need to be used, along with the usual technical and economic considerations, in a proactive manner, to generate design solutions that satisfy psychological, technical and economic criteria.

This is not just a question of considering human issues in parallel with technical and economic issues. This only leads to a multidisciplinary method. What we need to do is more a question of integrating the three areas into an interdisciplinary design approach. In terms of design method, this primarily means we need to internalize the knowledge and values of psychologists and other non-technical experts. This, more than design methods, is the key to successful interdisciplinary design (Jones, 1981). It also implies generating feasible design options that have been shaped by psychological and organizational considerations. This is quite different to using psychological and organizational criteria to retrospectively evaluate design proposals that have been shaped only by technical and economic considerations.

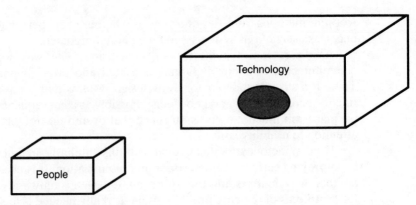

Figure 10.1   Technical change: the traditional approach. *Source:* Cheshire Henbury. © 1990. Published with permission.

Some design principles

Good design is not something that can be achieved by following a set of prescriptive criteria. It is, however, possible to indicate some general principles. Three principles are given below. These principles are derived from practical experiences of attempting to change technology. They appear to represent the most important experiences of the work undertaken thus far.

The first principle is to try to develop computer systems that are in some way related to people's existing skills. This principle can be demonstrated by means of the simple analogy of trying to fit square pegs into round holes, as illustrated in Figure 10.1.

A better approach might be to design systems to leave room for the exercise of existing skills, but also to allow these skills to evolve into new skills. This is illustrated by Figure 10.2. This approach should result in systems that will allow people to make use of a system using techniques and skills that they will find familiar, but it also allows them to develop new skills. Of course, in some situations it is not possible to design systems based on existing skills. Some systems of this kind are discussed in Chapter 12. The point of this design principle is, however, not to be prescriptive about this issue, but only to highlight the potential importance and need to analyze the existing situation (see Chapter 11).

The second principle is to design systems as learning systems. Continuing improvement in operating practices cannot be achieved if technologies do not allow skilled users to learn how to use systems in appropriate ways. People should be free to adapt their work strategies to each situation and to suit their own preferences. Room should be left, therefore, for people to develop their own working methods and to experiment with systems. This should not of course be done in a way that exposes them and the systems to danger (see Chapter 12).

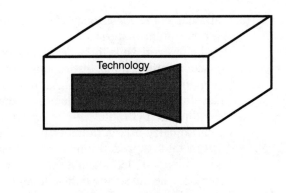

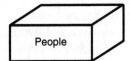

Figure 10.2   Technical change: another strategy. *Source:* Cheshire Henbury. © 1990. Published with permission.

This safety consideration leads us to the third design principle (the guardian angel principle). Design systems to act as a guardian angel which will provide passive monitoring that can call attention to illegal or dangerous actions or decisions. The system should advise people of the consequences of their actions (Kidd, 1990a).

A conceptual framework for the design of skill and knowledge enhancing technologies

In this section we will consider a conceptual framework for the design of skill and knowledge enhancing technologies. We will develop the framework by using a practical example of lathe technology. In Chapter 11 we will present a detailed case study based on machine tools.

The manually operated lathe developed into its present form during the 18th and 19th centuries (Rolt, 1965; Steeds, 1969). During this period the features and technical capabilities of lathes underwent considerable changes. The construction of lathes, the way they were powered, the types of cutting tools used, the size of workpieces that could be accommodated, the materials that could be machined, the type of cutting operations performed and the range of workpiece holding devices were all significantly changed, developed and improved.

Early 18th century lathes had very poor accuracy and considerable skill would have been required to obtain any satisfactory results (Steeds, 1969). Most of the technological developments that have taken place (Rolt, 1965; Steeds, 1969) were aimed at improving the accuracy attainable, the consistency of results and the range of facilities available for machining materials.

However, while these developments in the manual lathe were taking place, another, quite distinct path of technological development was beginning to emerge. Around about the 1850s the capstan lathe was developed and in the final quarter of the 19th century the automatic lathe was invented (Bradley, 1972). A capstan lathe is a machine tool that is able to carry a large number of cutting tools. These are then used to cut metal in a predetermined way. This sort of lathe would normally be set up by a skilled machine setter, and then operated by an unskilled person. The automatic lathe contains further technical refinements that allow the motion of the cutting tools to be controlled by means of cams and levers.

These early developments in semi-automated machining were followed in the 1940s by the development of a much more sophisticated automatic machine tool known as a numerically controlled lathe. With this type of lathe the motions of the cutting tools are controlled by means of closed loop position control systems. The information required to drive the control loops is fed into the system by means of programs, which are normally stored as a set of coded instructions on a punched paper tape or a magnetic tape. There is a detailed account of the development of NC technology given in Noble (1984).

NC technology allows decision-making and the formulation of a machining strategy, that is, deciding how a component is to be made, what feeds, speeds and depths of cut to use, which tools to use and so on to be separated from the execution of the machining strategy. This means that these two jobs could be undertaken by different people. Usually the machining strategy would be developed by a programmer in an office, while the implementation would be handled by a machine operator.

In practice it turned out that separation of thinking and doing proved difficult to achieve. So it became necessary to allow the machine operator to override the feeds and speeds determined by the office based programmer, using devices fitted to the machine tool control panel.

Hazelhurst et al. (1969) have undertaken a comparison of the skills of machinists working with NC and conventional manual machines. To do this comparison, they defined the extent to which operators need and use motor, perceptual, conceptual and discretionary skills when setting up, operating and checking a conventional lathe. These investigations show that a large amount of all these types of skills are required and indicate why we regard the operation of a conventional lathe as a highly skilled occupation.

However, it is also the case that the operation of very early lathes from the period around 1700 was also a highly skilled occupation. In the time span from 1700 to the 1970s, a large number of developments took place in lathe technology. We might well ask ourselves if, in this same period, there was also a process of de-skilling going on, which accompanied the changes in lathe technology?

Hazelhurst *et al.* (1969) noted that the nature of the organization affects the skill requirements of NC machinists. For example, when the Taylor Model is used to organize the plant (Taylor, 1902, 1907), the role of the machinists is usually very restricted and little skill is required. When we move away from the Taylor Model the role of the machinists will usually involve much greater control and responsibility, and hence the machinists will need more skills. Similar observations have also been made by Burnes (1984) in connection with the use of CNC machines.

An aim of developing NC machines was to enable the machining of the complex geometries occurring in the aircraft industry. However, NC technology (like the capstan lathe) possesses one important characteristic that is not embodied in conventional lathe technology. The NC machine tool is a formalization, in technology, of one of the principal objectives of the Taylor Model (Taylor, 1902, 1907), and that is, the separation of decision-making and planning from the actual execution of work.

The way we organize, therefore, can be seen as an important factor in determining the skills that people require to operate a machine tool. Organization also determines the degree of control that people can exert over machines. We can see NC technology, therefore, as a technological way of restricting people's control, and of determining their skill requirements.

We can therefore summarize the historical situation as follows. Developments have taken place in both organization and technology, and technological innovations have followed two quite different paths. The organizational developments are applicable to both types of technology. However, certain types of technology tend to be associated with particular forms of organization (Woodward, 1958).

Now that we have briefly outlined the historical background, we can consider how developments in lathe technology have affected the skills of the machinists. In particular, we will consider whether or not de-skilling has resulted from the various developments in conventional lathe technology.

Our proposition is that, in general, developments in conventional lathe technology have not resulted in the de-skilling of the machinists, but that developments such as the capstan lathe and NC technology have enabled their de-skilling. In these latter cases, organizational choice is an important determining factor. We are not implying that the actual form of technology does not have any effect upon people's skills. What we are making is a statement of a fact. NC technology and a capstan lathe make it much easier to introduce the Taylor Model of organization.

The suggestion that developments in automation technology result in de-skilling is controversial. There is a disagreement between those who argue that automation has a de-skilling effect (Bright, 1958) and those who argue a more positive impact of automation on people's skills (Taylor, 1971).

We base our proposition concerning the relationship between changes in lathe technology and the effect that these changes have had upon machinists' skills upon a historical understanding of innovations in lathe technology.

First, we have used a definition of skill proposed by Cavestro (1986). Cavestro states that skill is seen as the ability to control both the work process and the machines involved. Second, we have viewed the way in which developments in the technology have affected the skills of machinists using the conceptual framework proposed by Jordan (1963). This framework is based on the observation that machines can serve man in two ways: as tools and production machines. A tool extends our abilities, both sensory and motor, while production machines attempt to replace the people.

We arrive at the conclusion that most of the innovations in conventional lathe technology can be classified as the development of tools which have allowed machinists to retain control over their work. The changes in the technology have assisted machinists in their work, and helped to make difficult jobs easier, and impossible jobs possible.

However, it also seems that the development of the capstan lathe marked a change and departure from the development of tools, and was the beginning of a process concerned with the development of production machines. This new line of development eventually led to the invention of the automatic lathe and then the NC lathe. A characteristic of production machines is that it has led to a significant reduction in machinists' control over their work.

We noted that NC technology usually results in the separation of the planning and decision-making from execution. With a conventional machine tool, the technology in itself does not result in the separation of planning and execution. To achieve this we must use the mechanism of organizational structure. Thus, NC technology results in a significant reduction in the control that machinists have over their work.

A further example concerns the way in which we achieve motion of the cutting tool. With NC technology we use a program to store instructions; the movement of the cutting tool. This program supplies instructions to closed loop position control systems. With a conventional machine, machinists determine the motion of the cutting tool using mechanical hand-wheels. Sometimes, however, they use an automatic feed facility. Automatic feeds were developed to assist machinists. To some degree, automatic feed facilities automate the motion of the cutting tool.

Thus, NC technology has eliminated the need for machinists to physically move the cutting tool. The motion of the tool is determined by a program which drives closed loop control systems. This not only replaces this aspect of the machinists' work, but also reduces their control. On the other hand, a conventional lathe fitted with an automatic feed facility can be used either manually or semi-automatically. The main thing to note is that the choice of operating mode is determined by the machinists. The people, therefore, retain control over their work. Our NC technology offers no such choice to the machinists.

Our conclusion, therefore, is that developments in conventional lathe technology have not resulted in de-skilling people. Rather these developments have resulted in the evolution of the machinists' skills. As the technology developed, the old skills developed into new skills in relation to the new technology. The challenge we face, therefore, is to find a way of continuing this evolutionary process using modern (computer) technology and applying a skill oriented approach in all areas where we deploy technology.

A necessary step in facing up to this challenge would appear to be to shift our perspective. We need to change our philosophy from the development of computer based technologies as production machines, to a philosophy that views computers as tools. Our design effort needs to be focused on what Kammersgaard (1985) has termed the tool perspective. With the tool perspective, we reject the concept of human–computer comparability, and we aim instead at the development of computer based tools for use by skilled users of the technology. In place of the concept of human–machine comparability is substituted the idea of human–machine complementarity (Jordan, 1963).

We should point out that designing from a tool perspective does not imply the rejection of NC technology. Clearly, NC machines do help to make the machining of complex geometric shapes easier and can thus be said to extend motor abilities. But they can only be regarded as tools if, at the same time, machinists' control over their work is not reduced.

There is also some trade-off needed between technical and economic requirements on the one hand, and the needs of people on the other. To adopt a polarized view based on a perspective of people versus machines is not appropriate or very helpful. There is an old saying that total abstinence is easier than perfect moderation. So while it might be much simpler to adopt a polarized view, rather than to face up to the complexities of design problems, such a view is not likely to lead to much progress.

Sometimes it will be necessary to automate aspects of people's work and take away certain aspects of their control. But we should not do this without first thinking through the implications and fully examining other options which might lead to a better result, both for the people and for performance and overall effectiveness.

Design concepts

The HCIM reference model

In an agile manufacturing environment no person works alone. Likewise, no computer-aided technology is likely to be an island. Computer-aided technologies need to be designed as part of an integrated manufacturing enterprise. However, first it is necessary to fully understand what integration means. A typical dictionary definition is *to combine parts into a whole*. The way we have approached computer integrated manufacturing in the past seems largely to have been concerned with combining technical artifacts (computers and software) into a whole, according to criteria that are largely technical in nature.

For the purpose of agile manufacturing, we need a much broader vision of integration. Such a vision is embedded in the concept of human and computer integrated manufacturing (HCIM) developed by Kidd (1991). The HCIM concept of integration is based on three dimensions, that is people integration, human–computer integration and technological integration. When we design any computer-aided technology, it is necessary to address these three. More specifically, whether we be working in a research laboratory of an information technology vendor company, or in a manufacturing company, there is a need to attempt to develop technologies that enhance the three types of integration.

Referring to the HCIM architecture shown in Figure 10.3, we need to address the overall system architecture when designing technology. This system design should consider the network of groups, the structure of each group, the interaction between groups, the nature of the supporting software and the technical communication and integration needs between supporting software modules. Groups can be both internal to the plant or enterprise, or external (for example, suppliers or customers as users of our products).

These architectures should enable our enterprises to implement appropriate natural groups, both in their offices and plants. These natural groups should ideally be designed around complete material or information flows, not around individual functions, which can lead to inefficiencies and time delays. We should also seek to provide technologies that will enhance and support teaming, communications between people and so on by providing a human communications bus as shown in Figure 10.3. We need to avoid technical barriers to communication, and seek opportunities for using technology to bring about cooperation. This, for example, means using technology to support cooperative working, and experimentation, learning and innovation. More is said about these issues in Chapter 12.

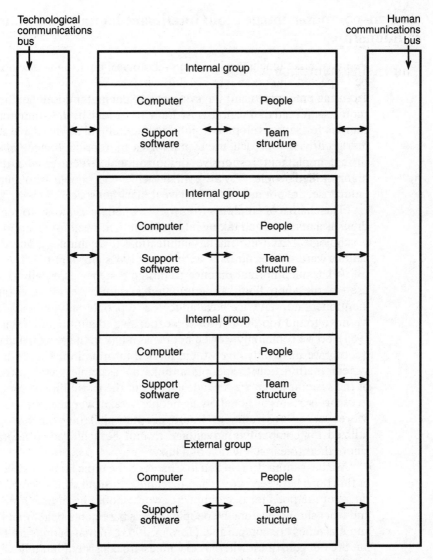

Figure 10.3 Human and computer integrated manufacturing reference model. *Source:* Cheshire Henbury. © 1989. Published with permission.

There is also a need to undertake input–output analysis to establish how a given computer-aided technology interacts with the other sub-systems. This, however, is not just a question of technical analysis, for example data links and identification of variables but also a question of organizational analysis, for example, who will undertake NC program-ming, and how can tasks be shared between the teams or natural groups to ensure efficient and effective completion of them.

Human–computer integration: intelligent human–computer relationships

People, unlike machines, have a psychological environment which must be respected and taken into account when we are designing agile manufacturing enterprises and the systems and computer based technologies required. We need to seriously address issues such as motivation, opportunities for self development, job satisfaction and so on. If we adopt a market driven approach, use technologies appropriate to agile manufacturing, implement responsive organizational structures and develop highly skilled people, very little will be achieved if people, throughout the enterprise, are not motivated and treated with respect.

The change of emphasis from viewing people as a cost, to regarding them as a resource and taking into account their need for an appropriate psychological environment, has implications for technology. These implications were seen as far back as the early 1960s (Jordan, 1963).

It has been normal practice to design systems, especially those for use on the shop floor, as automated systems. As we have already mentioned, normally we have allocated to people only those tasks that we have found too difficult or too expensive to automate (Bainbridge, 1983). So we commonly viewed people as a link in the system and consequently we have only given them limited information. Thus, when our systems malfunction, the people, as links, are as helpless as any other part of the system. Often we have designed out the possibility of continuing to use the systems by not allowing people to take over in an effective way. Moreover, an environment where people's skills and knowledge are utilized for competitive advantage cannot be achieved in a situation where their role is solely that of a link.

We have already discussed in Chapter 8 the topic known as allocation of functions between people and machines. Basically this encompasses a range of methods for deciding what work should be done by machines and what should be done by people. This is based on a belief that people and machines are comparable (Jordan, 1963), in that people are flexible but are not consistent whereas machines are consistent but inflexible.

This concept of comparability is wrong, because people and machines are complementary. Rather than trying to compare them and then allocating tasks and designing the technology on this basis, the design problem becomes one of thinking how people can be complemented by machines and vice versa.

This line of thought leads to the conclusion introduced in Chapter 8, that the term *allocation of functions* between people and machines is a meaningless one in many situations. Rather, the issue is one of thinking about how a task can be done by people and by machines.

When we design a machine we always take into account the physical environment, that is, we consider the power supply, maintenance requirements, the physical operating environment, mechanical protection and so on. We also take into account, to some degree, people's physical environment, including illumination, ventilation, noise levels, human–computer interface characteristics, working hours, safety and so on. However, a fundamental difference between people and machines is that people have a psychological environment. Creating an adequate physical environment is necessary and important, but it is of secondary importance with regard to the psychological environment.

People's psychological environment is concerned with motivation, job satisfaction, attitudes, and using their distinctive attributes for competitive advantage. We have largely ignored the problems associated with the psychological environment with respect to the detailed design of technologies.

Unless we motivate people we are unlikely to be able to ask them to complement our technologies, and the motivation to work as a complement to the technology must be considered as a criterion in technology design. Unless people's work represents a challenge, they will not use their skills, knowledge, flexibility, experience and judgment. They will not be interested in learning or in changing when change is needed, nor will they take on the responsibilities associated with their work. When we design technology such that people do the least possible, we eliminate all challenge. We must therefore build challenge into our technology, otherwise people may start to behave just like machines.

And here we have a very important conclusion to draw. People differ very significantly from machines in one very important respect. When people are forced to behave like machines they know that they are being used inefficiently and are not trusted. They will, either overtly or covertly, resist and rebel against such a regime. So in the long term, nothing could be more inefficient and self defeating than to design technology which results in rebellious people.

Here lies the future challenge. The need to consider people and their motivation is likely to become a major design issue. We need to overcome the Victorian 'Hell Hole' image of many manufacturing plants if we are going to attract more people to work on the shop floor. However, it is also sometimes argued that the shortage of skilled people will mean that more automation will be needed.

On the one hand, we have a desire to motivate people, to introduce greater flexibility, to manage change and to make better use of people. Yet we still believe that technology can be introduced as a substitute for people's skills, without having damaging consequences on their motivation.

This is not an argument against automation. The major issue here is one of motivation and the question of people's acceptance of technology, and the usability of new technologies. If we want to tap into people's creativity and make better use of their skills, we cannot ignore these questions.

Too often the normal procedure is not to take any account of people's methods of working, existing skills or personal feelings. Typically, new technologies start life in our research laboratories and then arrive in our plants and offices, demanding new skills and working methods. This, as we have already mentioned in Section 10.5.2, is like trying to fit square pegs into round holes.

There is nothing wrong with new skills and working methods, but we should take account of the existing situation, for the simple reason that it is more likely that new technology will be accepted if it provides a familiar starting point. This is especially true for older people, who sometimes find accepting new technology a more difficult process than their younger colleagues.

The open systems concept

The term open system comes from general systems theory and is used to describe a system that receives inputs from and sends outputs to the systems environment. The term is very much associated in manufacturing with system architectures based on the International Standards Organization Open Systems Interconnection model (ESPRIT Consortium AMICE, 1989).

The concept of an open system is, however, also used in management science to describe organizational structures that take into account and respond to the environment. The idea can, however, have a much broader application. It can be applied not only to system architectures and organizational structures, but also to work practices, human–computer interfaces and the relationship between people and technologies such as scheduling and control systems and decision support systems (Kidd 1990b, 1990c).

The requirement in agile manufacturing for flexibility, adaptation, responsiveness, and the need to motivate people and to make better use of their skills, judgment and experience, suggests that organizations, work practices and technologies need to be developed so that what we end up with will allow highly trained people, throughout the company, to adapt their work strategies to the variety of situations that they will have to face. This implies that our organizations, work practices and technologies will have to be designed to be open systems (Kidd, 1989).

In this context we define an open system as one that allows people a large degree of freedom to define the mode of operation of the system, the nature and form of the interaction between the sub-systems and between the system and its environment. The term basically implies a system which is extremely responsive and adaptive.

Open systems applied to human–computer integration

The aim when designing skill and knowledge enhancing technologies is not to use computers to substitute for, or to eliminate the skills and knowledge of, people, but rather to enhance their skills and knowledge and to make these more productive and effective. In other words we wish to use the technology to lever skills and knowledge. Thus our goal could be seen as seeking to combine the power, speed and accuracy of computers with the skills, knowledge, judgment and creativity of people.

Unfortunately, this goal is not easily achieved because the concept of skill and knowledge enhancing computer-aided technology is subject to wide interpretation. The following example, taken from computer-aided control systems design (CACSD), will serve to illustrate the problem.

A common problem

MacFarlane (1982) observed that a synthesis approach to design reduces our scope, as designers, to exercise skill and judgment. This is because a synthesis method requires us to specify, usually in detail and in mathematical form, the system constraints and the required performance. The computer then uses this data, within an algorithm, to produce a design solution.

MacFarlane goes on to say that a CACSD system should provide skilled designers with a set of manipulative and interpretative tools which will enable designers to build up, modify and assess a design put together on the basis of physical reasoning within guidelines laid down by people's engineering experience. When we design a CACSD system, therefore, we need to consider the way in which the burden of the design work is shared between skilled people and the computer. The aim, he argues, should be to achieve a situation such that each makes an appropriate contribution to the overall solution, and this involves developing techniques which will lead to a fruitful and effective symbiotic relationship between the computer and the user.

He then observes that the computer is conventionally used for calculation, manipulation and optimization. He then proposes, by way of an example of his thinking, that in any fully developed CACSD system, the tuning of controller parameters during simulations is best done by a systematic use of appropriate optimization techniques.

Although this sounds like an appropriate sharing of design tasks between people and the computer, the idea does have a number of problems that are not immediately evident. To understand the nature of these problems we need to compare two possible approaches to tuning controllers during simulations.

The first is a manual approach which involves a skilled control systems designer making the adjustments to the controller parameters.

The second approach is an automatic method, as suggested by MacFarlane, and involves using an optimization algorithm.

This manual approach can result in a very good learning situation. We can experiment with different controller parameters and observe results, and the process of making these adjustments can give us more insight into the system's performance characteristics, and can give us a feel for the system. This approach also requires the use of knowledge and the exercise of skill and judgment. The prime disadvantage of this approach is the time taken to achieve a satisfactory performance (for a complex system this can be several weeks of effort).

The optimization method is, by comparison with the manual approach, very fast. However, since the computer is doing all the work there is no real learning situation. Furthermore, we will not develop much of a feel for the system, or extend our understanding about the system, and little or no knowledge, skill or judgment is needed. Moreover, if the optimization algorithm fails to produce a satisfactory result, there is usually no indication from the computer why this has happened, and we will have gained little or no insight which we could make use of when trying to resolve the problem.

Although a superficial examination of the optimization approach suggests that the power, speed, and accuracy of the computer are being used to support people, what in actual fact exists is our classic human–computer relationship. The computer is doing all the work, and when it fails, people are left to cope as best they can.

The problems with this optimization based approach arise from two sources. First, the selection and use of the optimization approach as an appropriate way to tune controllers during simulations is based solely on the criterion of the amount of time taken to produce a result. The manual method is slow, and since the computer is better at examining a large number of options, and can do so very quickly, we conclude that controller tuning is best done by a computer. This is an example of what Jordan (1963) has referred to as **man-machine comparability**. Unfortunately, this man-machine comparability perspective ignores the needs of the people who will use the computer. In this particular case these needs are related to learning and the opportunity to exercise skills and judgment.

Second, the selection of the optimization approach ignores the fact that the algorithm may fail to achieve a satisfactory result. If a tool sometimes fails, then we need to understand under what conditions it will fail and should have access to alternative tools. But the problem with automatic techniques is that they place people in a passive role. The understanding and insights that are required for effective intervention are not developed when people are not actively engaged in a task, and all or most of the work associated with a task is being done by a computer.

The example considered refers to CACSD, but it is not unusual, as the same situation is found elsewhere. MacFarlane is sympathetic to the idea that people, as computer users, should be in control of their work. He believes that the computer should support their work, rather than just automating tasks. However, he finds it extremely difficult to break away from our conventional approach of designing computer systems on the basis that either something is done by the computer or it is done by people.

It appears to be almost a universal fact that there is no new vision of any other way of tackling the human–computer relationship. It is now becoming more common for researchers to state that people and computers are complementary rather than comparable. But this statement is typically followed by an illustrative example of the form, 'computers are fast and consistent but lack flexible reasoning, while human information processing is slower but can handle events which are ill-defined'. An example of this type of statement can be found in Hwang *et al.* (1984).

The problem with such examples is that they are based on the principle of human–machine comparability, not on the principle of complementarity, because they make comparisons between people and computers. In other words comparability still prevails, even when complementarity is preached.

There is one way out of this dilemma – leave people to determine their own relationship with the computer.

User defined human–computer relationships

The situation discussed above illustrates a class of system that we can describe as a closed system. Essentially, a closed system is one where we determine, through the system design, the actions of people to a degree that is more than required, say, by hardware, or software or performance constraints. In other words, a closed system is one in which we overdetermined the user-computer relationship.

A simple example of a closed system is the human–computer interfaces found on most CNC machine tools. We determine these when the systems are designed. Kidd (1990c) demonstrated the concept of an open systems human–computer interface for workshop-oriented CNC systems. This allows machinists to customize the interface to their own personal preferences. This involves changing the dialogue, the screen layout and so on.

Thus a closed system will typically restrict people's freedom of action, or force them to use the technical system in a particular way that is of our choosing. In the closed system approach, when we attempt to automate a particular task, and the system fails, people are left without any computer based decision support.

An open systems approach leads to a different type of system. With an open system, people are not unnecessarily restricted in what they can do. For example, if they wanted to violate some constraint, they could. Of course appropriate warnings would need to be given, and a design decision whether to allow this would be subject to considerations such as safety and the consequences of potential system failure. In some circumstances, this unrestricted approach could not be allowed.

More fundamentally, however, an open system is not characterized by the situation that we described earlier in relation to controller tuning. In our example, controller tuning was either done by the computer acting alone, or by the control systems designer largely acting alone. However, between these two extremes there are an infinite number of possibilities. An open system would allow people to make use of any of them.

In essence therefore, an open system is one where the relationship between people and computers is determined by each individual user, and not by the designers of the technical system. The role of the designers of the technical system is to create a system that will satisfy people's personal preferences, and allow them to work in ways that they find most appropriate.

Perhaps of greatest importance, however, the open systems philosophy helps to prevent designers of technical systems from imposing their own views on what computers should do and what people should do. Design is influenced by subjective value judgments (Lawson, 1980), and a good way to minimize the effect of our value judgments is to eliminate, as far as possible, the opportunities for us to make them. The open systems concept is one way of achieving this.

It therefore follows that computer based systems should not be designed as closed systems, but as open systems. This means avoiding restrictions, using decision support systems in a way that is highly interactive and which allows sharing of the decision-making process in a way that is unique to each person and problem situation.

Evaluative and generative systems

To more fully understand how an open systems approach can be used to design a human–computer relationship, it is necessary to introduce the concepts of evaluative and generative decision support systems (Gershwin *et al.*, 1986). An evaluative decision support system is one that takes a set of proposed decisions and evaluates and predicts the results of these decisions. A generative decision support system is one that takes a set of criteria and constraints and generates a set of decisions.

Thus, in the example from CACSD, the use of a computer algorithm to undertake controller tuning is a generative approach. The manual tuning method is an evaluative approach. Simulation is also an evaluative approach. Automated decision-making using artificial intelligence, or computer algorithms, or both, is a generative approach.

The problem that we seem to face is that we cannot break out of the evaluative versus generative dichotomy. There is no logical reason for this, because there is no reason why a system cannot be designed to be both evaluative and generative. Between these two opposite modes of operation there is a continuum of operating possibilities. The only problem is that we do not design systems to operate within this continuum, because we insist on defining the mode of operation of the system in great detail, and exclude the possibility of people determining their own operating modes. Often there is no need for this. It is just a matter of tradition. The existence of this continuum has important implications for the computer based systems that we design, as we will illustrate in Chapter 11.

The role of knowledge-based systems

The question of using knowledge-based systems (for example, expert systems, fuzzy logic) in decision support tools would seem to be more problematic than using conventional programming techniques because these knowledge-based technologies are commonly used in a skill and knowledge substituting role. Our conventional wisdom would suggest that the rules which experts use, say for example, when scheduling machines in a plant, should be elicited from the people involved and then incorporated into an expert system rule base. The expert system could then be used to generate a schedule.

Östberg (1988) has described five possible ways that expert systems can be used. The first is the **transactional mode** where an expert system takes over all responsibilities and performs all the tasks, and people just act as human facilitators. The second is an **interactive mode** where people perform tasks with the help of an expert system and remain in charge during the dialogue. The third is the **commentary mode** where people perform tasks independently of the expert system, which is used only when people need a second opinion. The fourth mode is the **teaching mode** where an expert system teaches people until they have reached task proficiency. Alternatively, an expert system may act as a manual for the infrequent task performer. The fifth and final mode is the **supervisory mode**, where an expert system is a passive supervisor and only calls attention to illegal actions, or decisions likely to interfere with other tasks and decisions and so on.

The conventional approach to expert systems development is almost exclusively concerned with developing systems that operate in a transactional mode. This is the approach associated with our closed system thinking. Essentially, we try to produce systems that attempt to mimic people's expert knowledge. If people are experts already, the computer tells them what they already know, and does things which they can already do. Thus, people have to deal with a system that contains expert knowledge from the domain of their own expertise. All they have to do is to specify the problem and then the computer will attempt to solve that problem.

The open systems philosophy, however, involves a different approach, which is based on the idea of using knowledge-based techniques, not necessarily to just solve problems, but also to give advice, expand understanding, help people deal with complexity and support decision-making and learning. A knowledge-based system should not be telling people what they already know, or doing things which they themselves can do, but should instead be making their work more productive by giving advice and reminding them of the possible consequences of their decisions. This, of course, is far more difficult than just attempting to mimic actions.

Coombs and Alty (1984) argued that human experts are rarely required to solve well defined problems, which is what our traditional expert systems, operating in the transactional mode, have been designed to do. Instead, people work on problems which involve several knowledge domains. What is required, therefore, is for an expert in one knowledge domain to receive advice from experts in other knowledge domains. This involves using knowledge-based systems which contain knowledge and expertise from these other domains.

By adopting an open systems approach we would aim to use expert systems to support people, rather than trying to replace them. This would involve establishing what extra skills and knowledge people require in order to do their jobs more effectively. We also need to choose an operational mode that leaves people free to act, and of course, this may include the transactional mode if this is what a particular user wants.

When we undertake an analysis of the skills and knowledge used in people's work, we will usually be able to reveal a number of possibilities for developing expert systems. For example, many computer based systems make use of algorithms that are often numerically unreliable, or there may be a number of procedures that could be used for a given task, each having its own characteristics and range of applicability. The expertise concerning these issues lies in the domain of numerical analysis or operations research and people who use computers often do not possess this knowledge.

Our people, for example, may be concerned with scheduling a batch of components in a way that minimizes set-up times. As they work towards producing a satisfactory schedule, they can use different algorithms. Each algorithm is likely to give different answers, and each has different characteristics. Do they know what these characteristics are? Do they know how to match these characteristics with particular scheduling problems? Which algorithm will work best for the particular mix of products to be scheduled? Some of the knowledge and expertise that could help the people to understand the problem and to answer these questions, and thus assist them to make more effective use of their time, lies elsewhere, outside their area of knowledge.

Knowledge-based systems containing knowledge from a number of knowledge domains could thus be used to assist people with their work. These systems however, would not only provide a transactional operating mode, if this mode was considered appropriate, but would also be capable of operating in supervisory, commentary and learning modes. Such systems would be advising people about the consequences of their decisions, and adding to their knowledge, that is, enhancing their skills.

Concluding comments

In this chapter we outlined a conceptual framework for the development of skill and knowledge enhancing technologies. In the next chapter we will describe, in detail, an example. We will use the design of a machine tool system to illustrate the concepts. Of course, the ideas have wider application, beyond the shop floor, and also beyond what can be regarded as process oriented skills, that is skills required to manufacture a product. In Chapter 12 we will turn our attention to future developments, and deal with non-process oriented skills, that is innovation skills.

Key points

- Skill and knowledge enhancing technologies represent a new paradigm for the application of computers in manufacturing. These technologies are a key component in agile manufacturing.

- Traditional technology development projects in manufacturing tend to be technology oriented, are often over complex and are commonly based on an inadequate understanding of the problems.

- Many technology development projects are focused on a limited sub-set of problems, and often deal with the symptoms of the problems, rather than the root causes.

- An interdisciplinary view of manufacturing problems often sheds a completely new light on what needs to be done and provides insights into different applications for technology.

- Technology oriented design strategies are not suitable for developing skill and knowledge enhancing technologies. We need to use a skill oriented design strategy.

- Skill and knowledge enhancing technologies make people's skills more effective and productive. The objective is not to replace their skills and knowledge, which has been the traditional approach.

- Technologies need to be designed taking into account the psychological environment of the people who will use them.

References

Bainbridge L. (1983). Ironies of automation. *Automatica*, **19**, 775–9

Basaglia G., Saraiva F.C. and Guida M. (1992). Increasing effectiveness of scheduling systems through integration with the factory environment: The Pirelli experience. In *Computer Integrated Manufacturing. Proc. 8th CIM-Europe Conf.* (O'Brian C., MacConaill P. and Van Puymbroeck W., eds.), pp. 325–36. London: Springer-Verlag

Bradley I. (1972). *A History of Machine Tools.* Hemel Hempstead: Model and Allied Publications

Braverman H. (1974). *Labour and Monopoly Capital.* New York: Monthly Review Press

Bright J. (1958). Does automation raise skill requirements? *Harvard Business Review*, July–August, 85–98

Burley D.M. (1974). *Studies in Optimisation.* Leighton Buzzard: International Textbook Company

Burnes B. (1984). Factors affecting the introduction and use of CNC machine tools. In Proc. *1st Int. Conf. Human Factors in Manufacturing* (Lupton T., ed.). Kempston: IFS

Cavestro W. (1986). Automation, work organization and skills: the case of numerical control. *Automatica*, **22**, 739–43

Christofides N. (1975). *Graph Theory: An Algorithmic Approach.* London: Academic Press

Coombs M. and Alty J. (1984). Expert systems: An alternative paradigm. In *Developments in Expert Systems* (Coombs M., ed.), pp. 135–57. London: Academic Press

ESPRIT CIM-Europe (1990). Proc. *CIM-Europe Workshop on Implementing CIM*, Saarbrücken. Brussels: ESPRIT CIM-Europe

ESPRIT Consortium AMICE, eds. (1989). *Open Systems Architecture for CIM.* Berlin: Springer-Verlag

Ferguson R.L. and Jones C.H. (1969). A computer aided decision support system. *Management Science*, **15**(10), B550–61

Fox M.S., Allen B.P. and Strohm G.A. (1982). Job-shop scheduling: an investigation in constraint-directed reasoning. In *Proc. AAAI-82*, Carnegie-Mellon University, Pittsburgh PA

Gershwin S.B., Hildebrant R.R., Suri R. and Mitter S.K. (1986). A control perspective on recent trends in manufacturing systems. *IEEE Control Systems Society*, **6**(2), 3–15

Godin V.B. (1978). Interactive scheduling. Historical survey and state of the art. *AIIE Trans.*, **10**, 331–37

Grant T.J. (1986). Lessons for OR from AI: a scheduling case study. *J. Operational Research Soc.*, **37**(1), 41–57

Guida M. and Basaglia G. (1990). An experience in the integration of OR and AI to dynamically schedule a tyre factory. In *Proc. CIM-Europe Workshop Implementing CIM*, Saarbrücken. Brussels: ESPRIT CIM-Europe

Haider S.W., Moodie C.L. and Buck J.R. (1981). An investigation of the advantages of using a man–computer interactive scheduling methodology for job shops. *Int. J. Production Research*, **19**(4), 381–92

Hanan M. and Kurtzberg J.M. (1972). Placement techniques. In *Design Automation of Digital Systems: Theory and Techniques* (Breuer M.A., ed.), pp. 213–82. New Jersey: Prentice-Hall

Hazelhurst R.J., Bradbury R.J. and Corlett E.N. (1969). A comparison of the skills of machinists on numerically controlled and conventional machines. *Occupational Psychology*, **43**, 169–82

Hwang S.L., Barfield W., Chang T.C. and Salvendy G. (1984). Integration of humans and computers in the operation and control of flexible manufacturing systems. *Int. J. Production Research*, **22**, 841–56

Isenberg R. (1987). Comparison of BB1 and KEE for building a production planning expert system. In *Proc. 3rd Int. Expert Systems Conf.*, London

Isenberg R. (1990). CIM-controller: an overview. In *Proc. CIM-Europe Workshop on Implementing CIM*, Saarbrücken. Brussels: ESPRIT CIM-Europe

Jones J.C. (1981). *Design Methods. Seeds of Human Futures*. Chichester: John Wiley

Jordan N. (1963). Allocation of functions between man and machines in automated systems. *J. Applied Psychology*, **47**, 161–5

Kammersgaard J. (1985). *Four Different Perspectives on Human–Computer Interaction*. Report DAIMI PB-203, Aarhus University, Denmark

Kidd P.T. (1988). The social shaping of technology: the case of a CNC lathe. *Behaviour and Information Technology*, **7**(2), 192–204

Kidd P.T. (1989). Systems based approaches to CIM: questions of method, competitiveness and profitability. In *Proc. IEE Seminar Systems Engineering Contribution to Increased Profitability*, London, UK

Kidd P.T. (1990a). Information technology: design for human involvement or human intervention? In *Ergonomics of Hybrid Automated Systems II* (Karwowski W. and Rahimi M., eds.), pp. 417–24. Amsterdam: Elsevier

Kidd P.T. (1990b). Designing CAD systems: an open systems approach. In *Computer-Aided Ergonomics* (Karwowski W., Genaidy A.M. and Asfour S.S., eds.), pp. 512–25. London: Taylor & Francis

Kidd P.T. (1990c). An open systems human–computer interface for a workshop-oriented CNC lathe. In *Ergonomics of Hybrid Automated Systems II* (Karwowski W. and Rahimi M., eds.), pp. 537–44. Amsterdam: Elsevier

Kidd P.T. (1991). Human and computer integrated manufacturing: A manufacturing strategy based on organization people and technology. *Int. J. Human Factors in Manufacturing*, **1**(1), 17–32

Krolak P., Felts W. and Marble G. (1971). A man–machine approach toward solving the travelling salesman problem. *Comms ACM*, **14**(5), 327–334

Lawson B. (1980). *How Designers Think*. London: Architectural Press

MacFarlane A.G.J. (1982). Conceptual frameworks for control systems CAD. In *Proc. 21st IEEE Conf. Decision and Control*, Orlando FL, December 1982

McKay K.N., Safayeni F.R. and Buzacott J.A. (1988). Job-shop scheduling theory: what is relevant? *Interfaces*, **18**(4), 84–90

Meister D. (1987). Systems design, development and testing. In *Handbook of Human Factors* (Salvendy G. ed.). New York: John Wiley

Meyer W., Isenberg R. and Hübner M. (1988). Knowledge-based factory supervision: the CIM shell. *Int. J. Computer Integrated Manufacturing*, **1**, 31-43

Meyer W. (1989). Cooperating expert systems as CIM modules. In *ESPRIT '89 Conference Proc.* (Commission of the European Communities ed.). Dordrecht: Kluwer

Meyer W. and Walters H. (1990). *EP932 Final Results: CIM/AI Value Analysis*. ESPRIT Project 932 Report, Philips Research Laboratories, Hamburg

Meyer W. (1990). *Expert Systems in Factory Management. Knowledge-Based CIM*. Chichester: Ellis Horwood

Noble D.F. (1984). *Forces of Production*. New York: A. A. Knopf

Östberg O. (1988). Applying expert systems technology: division of labour and division of knowledge. In *Knowledge, Skill and Artificial Intelligence* (Göranzon B. and Josefson I., eds.), pp. 169–83. London: Springer-Verlag

Papadimitriou C.H. and Steiglitz K. (1982). *Combinatorial Optimisation: Algorithms and Complexity*. London: Prentice-Hall

Perrow C. (1983). The organizational context of human factors engineering. *Administrative Science Q.*, **28**, 521–41

Rolt L.T.C. (1965). *Tools for the Job: A Short History of Machine Tools*. London: Batsford

Roth A. and Watt S. (1991). All constraint is not evil. *EXE* **6**(2), 21–7

Rosenbrock H.H. (1977). The future of control. *Automatica*, **13**, 389–392

Sanderson P.M. (1989). The human planning and scheduling role in advanced manufacturing systems: an emerging human factors domain. *Human Factors*, **31**(6), 635–66

Sanderson P.M. and Moray N. (1990). The human factors of scheduling behaviour. In *Ergonomics of Hybrid Automated Systems II* (Karwowski W. and Rahimi M., eds.), pp. 399–406. Amsterdam: Elsevier

Sharit J. (1985). Supervisory control of a flexible manufacturing system. *Human Factors*, **27**(1), 47–59

Steeds W. (1969). *A History of Machine Tools 1700–1910*. Oxford: Oxford University Press

Taylor F.W. (1902). Shop management. *Trans. American Soc. Mech. Eng.*, **24**, 1334–480

Taylor F.W. (1907). On the art of cutting metals. *Trans. American Society of Mech. Eng.*, **28**, 31–350

Taylor J.C. (1971). Some effects of technology on organizational change. *Human Relations*, **24**(2), 105–23

Ulfsby S. (1990). Dynamic production scheduling. In *Computer Integrated Manufacturing. Proc. 6th CIM-Europe Conf.* (Faria L. and Van Puymbroeck W., eds.), pp. 153–69. London: Springer-Verlag

Walters H. (1990). Knowledge based scheduling in batch manufacturing: cost benefits. In *Proc. CIM-Europe Workshop Implementing CIM*, Saarbrücken. Brussels: ESPRIT CIM-Europe

Woodward J. (1958). *Management and Technology*. London: HMSO

Wright P. (1974). The harassed decision maker: time pressures, distractions, and the use of evidence. *J. Applied Psychology*, **59**(5), 555–61

Zumegen P. and Dohr H.-W. (1990). Uniformly structured knowledge bases in intelligent CIM-controllers for quality assurance and maintenance. In *Proc. CIM-Europe Workshop Implementing CIM*, Saarbrücken. Brussels: ESPRIT CIM-Europe

11

Design of skill and knowledge enhancing technologies for machine tool systems

Introduction

In this chapter we examine skill and knowledge enhancing technologies in more detail. Attention will be focused on machine tool systems. We begin by providing an overview of some historical developments of the design problem as seen from the skill oriented design paradigm. We also compare this perspective to the more common view derived from the technology oriented design paradigm.

Attention will then be focused on the organizational and psychological criteria that are judged to be relevant to the design problem. We will then undertake a skills and knowledge analysis to establish areas where computer based technologies might be applied, and then look at some designs developed using the skill oriented perspective.

We confine attention to one particular type of machine tool, the lathe. What we say, however, can be extended in principle to other types of machine tools.

Historical overview

As already pointed out, the production of components on a manually operated lathe is a highly skilled job. Success depends upon the skills of the machinists in two important and interrelated areas, which we call planning and execution. The first is the planning of the work, which involves deciding the sequence of machining operations and determining the cutting parameters, the depth of cut, the feed and the speed. The second area is the execution of the plans. This requires an ability to recognize and respond to potential problems. It also requires, to some degree, manual dexterity in setting up the machine tool and manipulating handwheels.

Numerous technical and organizational developments have taken place which have led to an increased separation of planning and execution. Automatic feeds have removed the need for machinists to continuously manipulate handwheels, and capstan lathes have allowed planning activities to be shifted away from the machinists. The development of NC technology has further contributed towards this separation of thinking and doing, and this has had a major impact in reducing machinists' control over their work.

NC technology allowed the handwheels and autofeeds of the manual lathe to be replaced by closed loop servo motor drives. But the technology was also developed according to the prevailing paradigm. This was dominated by the Taylor Model notion of separating the functions of planning and execution, and removing responsibility for decision-making from the machinists.

The NC approach specified that planning activities were to be dealt with in a planning office by programmers. Programmers determine the sequence of machining operations and the cutting parameters. With early NC systems the information was stored as a program on punched paper tape, which was used to provide the NC controller on the machine tool with the instructions required to drive the closed loop servo controls, which in turn drove the cutting tools. When the program was complete, the paper tape was taken to the machine tool for testing and proving-out. If the program was incorrect, which was often the case, it was returned to the office for correction.

The role of the machinists was, in theory, confined to loading the lathe with raw material, running the prepared program, removing the machined component for the machine tool and cleaning away metal cuttings. In practice, however, the machinists' role was usually somewhat different.

The NC method assumes that a machining strategy can be determined by someone located away from the machine tool, who does not necessarily have any direct or day-to-day experience of machining.

Scientific knowledge and empirical rules can be used to develop the program, and any problems that may arise can be dealt with at the proving and testing stage.

However, the machining process is not well defined or predictable, and hence it is also necessary, in practice, to rely on the machinists' skills and knowledge to cope with unforeseen problems and unpredicted disturbances, in order to ensure that machining is completed successfully. Consequently, most NC controllers were fitted with overrides which allowed the machinists to adjust the feeds and speeds. If unexpected problems were very severe, then the machine tool would have to be stopped and the office based programmer would deal with the problems by changing the program.

NC technology is an example of a technology designed using the technology oriented design paradigm. This paradigm often results in separation of thinking and doing, which is a goal that we have specifically pursued. It concentrates on technical functionality and ignores the roles and needs of people. It rejects, and seeks to replace, people's skills and knowledge, while often relying on these skills to overcome the deficiencies of the technology.

So what? Is this really an important issue? The answer depends upon whether one thinks that these old Taylor Model ideas are still relevant in agile manufacturing. If you believe they are no longer relevant, you have probably recognized the fallacy of the Taylor Model resulting in an effective manufacturing enterprise.

The basic problem is that the model assumes nothing is lost when thinking and doing are separated. Scientific knowledge enables this division of labor. However, the problem is that this view is only correct in very simple situations of the type that may have existed in Taylor's time. The more complex the situation, then the more likely that scientific knowledge will be restricted and of limited value. In these situations scientific knowledge needs to be combined with practical knowledge and experience, in such a way that each complements the other. However, by removing the planning work from the machinists, the opportunities available for developing, exercising and practicing skills and knowledge have been significantly diminished. We will find it extremely difficult to achieve this complementary situation.

Moreover, original NC technology has placed machinists in a position where, with the machining information in a form that is suitable only for a machine to read, it has become difficult to know what the machine will do. Responses to unsatisfactory machining conditions are therefore purely reactive. Machinists have to wait for events to happen before they can do anything about them. The possibility of using skills, knowledge and experience in a proactive way has been designed out, and machinists cannot, therefore, easily foresee problems and take action to avoid them.

Of course, the technology that we have just described is an old one. In recent years shop floor programmable CNC technology has started to replace it. CNC machine tools usually have facilities that allow programming to be done on the shop floor, and also provide tool path simulation facilities to support the testing and proving of the programs. This newer technology, therefore, allows the programming to be done on the machine rather than in an office, although they can be used in the more conventional way too.

CNC potentially allows planning and execution to be recombined into one job, thus reversing one of our main objectives of original developments in NC technology. Implicit in this change in the technology is an acknowledgement that there are large areas of overlap between planning and execution activities. To achieve successful execution one needs to be part of the planning activity, and to undertake satisfactory planning one must have experience of execution. In other words the two things are interdependent, and to succeed, one must have experience of both. Thus, in short, to separate these activities is to create an inefficient, ineffective and inflexible method of working.

A shop floor programmable CNC lathe can be seen as an important improvement over the more conventional NC technology, since it allows a return to more flexible modes of working associated with the operation of a manually operated lathe. Is it now possible to take this favorable technological change further, and develop tools which will help to make machinists' skills and knowledge more productive and effective? It is necessary to retain simultaneously the technologically derived advantages that can be obtained from CADCAM integration, and the benefits from the development and application of scientific knowledge and theory. In the remaining parts of this chapter we will describe some developments that have been driven by these objectives.

Description of design requirements

In this section we outline some of the design requirements for skill and knowledge enhancing technologies for machine tool systems. We address technical, organizational and psychological requirements.

Clearly, one important requirement is that we should aim to combine planning and execution activities, or achieve a satisfactory level of integration when situations demand a degree of separation. What other requirements are relevant? To answer this question we can undertake a number of analysis activities. We can look at existing shop floor CNC systems, undertake control and feedback analysis and undertake a skills, knowledge and task analysis.

Existing systems: workshop-oriented programming

There is a long tradition, dating back to the first NC machine tools developed in the late 1940s, of supporting office based programming of these machines. There has also been a vigorous debate over the effectiveness of this approach, and there are people who believe that, in many cases, a more effective way to program these machines is to undertake this work on the shop floor using skilled machinists.

A survey of 584 US manufacturing plants provides evidence to support this belief; showing that programming costs of CNC machines are lower when people on the shop floor do the programming! It seems that the reasons why we prefer to adopt office based programming often have more to do with our desire to exert control than with efficiency and cost (Kelly and Lan, 1990).

During the 1980s a concept known as workshop-oriented programming (WOP) technology was developed in Europe. This technology can be regarded as a first step towards the development of skill and knowledge enhancing (as opposed to skill and knowledge substituting) technologies.

A number of machine tool manufacturers have developed WOP systems. One in particular is worth referring to (Hekeler 1989a, 1990) because it has a number of interesting characteristics derived from specific design considerations which focused on the skills and knowledge of the machinists and the application of insights from human factors experts.

Many machinists are capable of programming in abstract programming languages such as EXAPT, or can be taught to do so. This is not, however, the area in which the primary skills and knowledge of the machinists lie. These are concerned with metals, the machining process and how to make things. The WOP system in question was developed to make the machinists' primary skills and knowledge more productive and more effective, and to avoid the need to develop programming skills which were seen as secondary and less important. The way this aim was achieved was through the development of programming techniques which resemble the way that machinists would produce a component or a conventional manual machine tool using their customary thinking and working methods. At the same time the degree of flexibility and freedom of action that a programming language can provide was retained.

The claimed benefits of this approach are quite impressive (Hekeler 1989b). Evaluation trials undertaken in a plant manufacturing diesel engines and aircraft turbines suggest that a skilled machinist with no NC experience whatsoever, can use the system without aid after 15 minutes of instruction. Within one week it is claimed that these machinists were performing as well as their more experienced colleagues did at the beginning of the trials. The trials also compared the cost of programming and testing for a range of components varying from simple to complex. It is

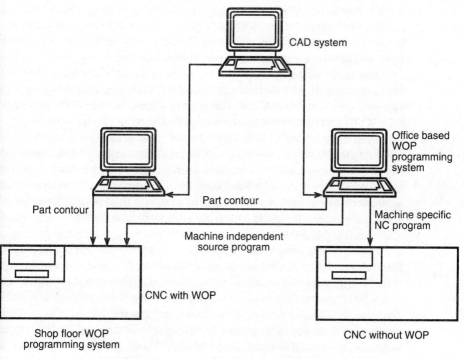

Figure 11.1   Architecture of a WOP system.

claimed that the results demonstrate that this particular WOP system was far more economic than any other type of office or shop floor based programming method.

The WOP system was also designed to provide a standardized programming environment for skilled people, regardless of whether programming directly on a machine, in a supervisor's office or in a planning and programming office. This is an important organizational aspect of the design because it has implications for team working. By using technology familiar to both shop floor and planning office people, it is much easier to bring about cooperation between these parties when a team effort is called for. There are no artificial barriers created by application of different programming technologies, to hinder the creation of a team to tackle a specific job. This example clearly illustrates how it is possible to assist team working by shaping the technology in an appropriate way.

The system also includes a CADCAM link so that CAD geometry can be transferred, through an interface which converts the drawing into a suitable NC-compatible geometric contour, to the CNC programming system. The architecture (see Figure 11.1) of this CADCAM system provides for choice in organization and job design. Unlike many of our

CADCAM systems, which assume that NC programming will be done in an office, it also provides facilities to transfer the CAD geometry directly to the shop floor where it is converted into a NC-compatible geometric contour for direct programming on the machine tool.

The success of this WOP system has encouraged other manufacturers to produce their own systems. However, there are reports that some systems are not very flexible. The reason seems to be that they are not true WOP systems. What appears to have happened is that some manufacturers have added user friendly graphical interfaces to their abstract EXAPT programming languages. The result is that they have restricted the freedom of action of the machinists, which has caused frustration and given WOP a bad image on the shop floor (Kidd, 1992). This illustrates an important point. There is more to developing skill and knowledge enhancing technologies than simply adding user friendly interfaces to technically oriented systems.

From this example we can start to derive some requirements. First, the techniques that we develop should bear some resemblance, if possible, to people's existing skills, so that the technology provides some familiar starting point. Second, the system should not introduce artificial technical barriers to cooperation, communication and team working. Third, the system should be capable of being used in a stand alone mode, as well as integrated with CAD systems. Finally, the system should provide organizational flexibility so that organization, working practices and job designs are not over constrained by the technology.

Skills, knowledge and task analysis

Before proceeding to design skill and knowledge enhancing computer-aided technologies, we should gain some understanding of machinists' skills and knowledge and the tasks that they undertake, so that it becomes possible to decide where computer support can be usefully applied.

If we examine the work that machinists undertake, we will find several tasks relevant to the work. These are:

- setting up the machine tool;
- developing a machining strategy;
- implementing the strategy;
- problem finding and solving;
- housekeeping activities;
- communications and recording activities.

The above list can be further divided into more detailed task descriptions. Also, some of the above tasks are interrelated. For example, before one can set up the machine tool, one needs to have worked out a machining strategy so that one knows which tools to use and what sort of workholding devices are required. However, the selection of a machining strategy is dependent on knowing what workholding devices and tools are available. So the above set of tasks are not things that are independent of one another, and it is likely that the machinists will be undertaking several tasks concurrently.

Central to the machinists work are the tasks of developing and implementing a machining strategy, and problem finding and solving activities related to development and implementation of the machining strategy. Typically, we have directed our attention towards finding ways of developing skill and knowledge substituting technologies to automate these core activities.

From the perspective of demonstrating the concept of skill and knowledge enhancing technologies, there are two reasons why it is useful to address these two areas. First, this will allow readers to make a comparison with more conventional skill substituting technologies. Second, as development of a machining strategy and the implementation of that strategy are core activities, they provide a challenge to develop technologies which achieve the goal of making skills and knowledge more productive and effective, while at the same time taking into account broader design issues such as user acceptance, user motivation and other organization and people issues which are usually disregarded.

There are several areas where computer support could be provided. These are:

- tool selection;
- determining the sequence of cuts;
- selection of cutting parameters;
- changing cutting parameters;
- predicting the consequences of decisions;
- monitoring the machining process.

From this list, we can start to understand the sorts of skills and knowledge that machinists need in order to fulfill their tasks. Starting with knowledge first, we can see that important areas are:

- materials, their properties and how they behave when cut;
- the cutting process, including the forces at play and potential problems;
- the characteristics and limitations of the machine tool including workholding devices;
- relationships between cutting parameters;
- tool characteristics and their operating ranges.

Much of this knowledge is experiential. Some of it is formalized and can be found in textbooks and handbooks, but much of it is gained from experience. Some of it may also be tacit, in that it resides in the subconscious mind rather than in the conscious mind, and cannot therefore be easily expressed. People may not be aware of this type of knowledge, but it influences some of their actions without them having to consciously think. Some of this knowledge may only become apparent when something happens to violate the conditions which the knowledge represents.

From the above, we can start to propose areas where we might combine codified knowledge, in the form that is available in textbooks, with this extensive body of experiential knowledge that machinists possess.

The most obvious area is that of the cutting process, where there is a body of theoretical and empirical research which could be used to support machinists with the selection of cutting parameters, taking into account tool characteristics, machine tools characteristics, material properties and so on. The other areas where computer support might be provided are more difficult to deal with. For example, working out the sequence of cutting operations is largely a matter of experience. There may be some requirements which might be derived from the logic of a particular situation, machining requirements, product finish or accuracy requirements, but on the whole, this is an area where judgment and experience are more important than codified knowledge.

Now that we have a basic picture of the sort of tasks that machinists undertake, we should consider the associated skills. A scheme for categorizing the skills associated with machining has been developed by Hazelhurst *et al.* (1969). These skills are:

- *Motor skills* These are manual skills requiring the coordination of hand and eye, and involve control actions such as manipulating handwheels, and other adjusting and checking activities which require precision of movement.
- *Perceptual skills* These are sensing, measuring and judging. Effectively this means using the perceptual senses of sight, hearing, touch and smell to interpret how a system is running.
- *Conceptual skills* These are concerned with abstracting, calculating and inferring. For example, deriving information from drawings about what tools to use and what depths of cut, feeds and speeds to use.
- *Discretionary skills* These are skills that are required to make decisions, take independent action and exercise resourcefulness.

According to the research results presented by Hazelhurst *et al.* (1969), the setting up, operation and checking of an NC machine tool requires very little in the way of motor skills in comparison to those required to operate a manual lathe. This is not a surprising result, given that the need to manipulate handwheels has been eliminated. Also they found that discretionary skills were similarly reduced, largely because decision-making is undertaken by office based programmers.

However, they noted from their work that the perceptual load placed upon machinists increases because a large amount of vigilance and machine monitoring is required. As Bainbridge (1983) has pointed out, this is not necessarily a good thing, as it can lead to stress and boredom. This suggests that the role of computer based technologies may be directed at relieving machinists of this machine monitoring role by improving the degree of information that is fed back, thus compensating for the loss of information that resulted from the change to NC technology.

Finally, the research also noted that a much higher degree of conceptual skill was required for an NC machine tool than was the case for manual machines. The probable reason for this is the increased distance between machinists and the work process which results from the NC technology. This separation requires a greater ability to imagine and understand, in the abstract, processes and events which are not directly observable.

From these considerations we can see that the role of skill and knowledge enhancing technologies should not be to just increase the level of skills and knowledge required. If we do this, we are not necessarily doing the best thing for the people involved, or the effectiveness of the system. We are concerned about making people's skills and knowledge more productive and effective. This means that we must direct our attention at using skills and knowledge to gain specific advantages.

Clearly, an NC machine requires high perceptual and conceptual skills, but these are not very productive in terms of system effectiveness. In fact, because they are potentially damaging to people through stress and boredom they are also damaging to the effectiveness of the system. In what way can perceptual, conceptual and discretionary skills be harnessed to make the overall system more productive and effective?

When we ask this question we start to see the possibilities. For example, can we develop a computer based system that will support perceptual skills, and allow machinists to identify potential problems before they occur? Likewise, can we support conceptual skills such that they are applied in a way that allows machinists to select which tools to use, and what depths of cut, feeds and speeds to use? And can we use the computer to provide machinists with the opportunity to exercise discretionary skills, by giving them the facilities to change actions in the light of operating experience or results emerging from analysis?

Control and feedback analysis

In Chapter 8 the case of NC technology was considered to demonstrate the links between organizational choice and technology. This raised the issues of user control and feedback. The systems considered were

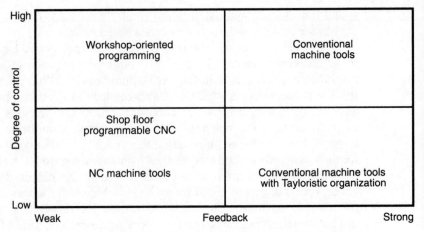

Figure 11.2 Control/feedback matrix.

categorized according to whether there was a high or low level of control, and whether there was strong or weak feedback. The cases considered are summarized in Figure 11.2.

Increasing levels of technical sophistication have tended to distance people from work processes. In the case of machine tools, the starting point was hand held tools, where machinists were directly involved in the work process. The introduction of the slide rest and handwheels, automatic and capstan lathes, NC machines and CADCAM have introduced many layers of technology between people and the work process as illustrated in Figure 11.3.

As Figure 11.2 illustrates, numerous technical and organizational developments have had an impact on the degree of control and feedback that people experience when using machines. Developments such as the WOP system described above, and the open systems method described in Chapter 10, are all aimed at increasing machinists' control of their work. However, as Figure 11.2 illustrates, the other dimension, that of feedback, has not been addressed in detail.

From this simple analysis, we can see that the idea of control and feedback analysis provides a useful framework for identifying the issues that need to be addressed during design. When we develop computer based systems, we should consider both control and feedback. If increasing technical sophistication tends to remove people from direct contact with the work process, then it is necessary to address the way computer based technology can be used to increase or maintain control and feedback.

This then represents a design requirement. How can we use the computer technology to improve both control and feedback?

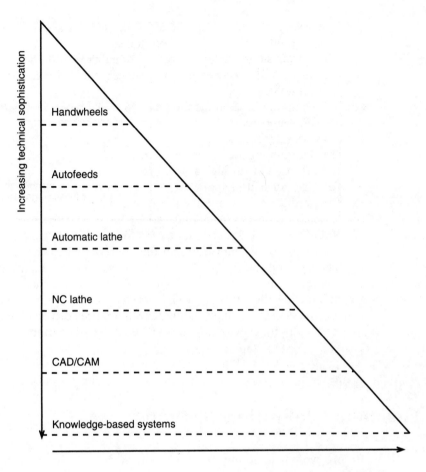

Figure 11.3 Technology/work process separation.

Summary of the design requirements

We summarize here the basic design requirements for machine tool systems:

(1) Planning and execution activities should be combined, or a satisfactory level of integration should be achieved when situations demand a degree of separation.

(2) The techniques and tools developed should, if possible, bear some resemblance to existing skills so that the technology provides some familiar starting point.

(3) The system should not introduce artificial technical barriers to cooperation, communication and team working.

(4) The system should be capable of being used in a stand alone mode, as well as integrated with CAD systems.

(5) The system should provide organizational flexibility so that organization, working practices and job designs are not over constrained by the technology.

(6) The computer based tools should be focused on providing support in the following areas:

   (a) tool selection
   (b) determining the sequence of cuts
   (c) selection of cutting parameters
   (d) changing cutting parameters
   (e) predicting the consequences of decisions
   (f) monitoring the machining process.

(7) Scientific knowledge should be used to complement the experiential knowledge of machinists, rather than to replace this knowledge.

(8) The system should provide tools which will make perceptual, conceptual and discretionary skills more productive and effective by minimizing the technologically derived need for these skills and maximizing the human–computer integration driven aspects that lead to appropriate, productive and effective use of human skills.

Geometry definition methods

Before we consider the question of providing decision support and predictive aids for machine tool systems, we must consider how the component geometry will be defined given that the system will have to work both as a stand alone CNC system and as part of an integrated CADCAM system.

Many CNC lathes work on the basis that machinists first define the component geometry, and then the type and sequence of cutting operations that are needed to make the part. This resembles the method people would use to draw a component, that is, by connecting together a series of straight lines and circular elements. This geometric method is quite different from the way machinists would make a component on a conventional manual lathe. To do this they would start with a piece of metal, and then undertake a series of machining operations (turning, facing, grooving and so on) until they ended up with the desired shape.

The method most universally used for programming CNC lathes is the first technique, which is nothing like the second. A programming method that resembles machinists' methods of working has been developed (Satine *et al.*, 1980). We will call this a workshop-oriented approach.

It is easy to learn and simple geometries can be programmed very quickly. Most of the components met in industry can be programmed using this method, but it is not used on most CNC controllers.

Another approach that was proposed in the early days of the development of NC technology is the record playback method. This involves making a part on a machine tool using handwheels. The movements of the handwheels are then recorded and stored so that they can be replayed for subsequent components. An alternative to this record playback method is the use of electronic handwheels and a graphic display to prepare a program (Gossard and von Turkovich, 1978). This emulates the process of using handwheels to generate the required cuts.

One of the reasons why the workshop-oriented method, such as the one developed by Satine *et al.* (1980), is not widely used, may be that traditional technology oriented design paradigm starts from a technical perspective, not the perspective of people's skills, knowledge and working methods. It is also difficult to program complex geometries (it can be very slow and difficult to use in these situations) using this particular workshop-oriented method. A further problem is what to do about geometries that are transferred to the CNC lathe via a communications link with a computer-aided design system. In this situation there is no need to define the geometry, and machinists have no choice but to define the sequence of cuts in a more abstract way.

Given that links with CAD systems will become more common in the future, any CNC system must be able to support this method of working. However, given that many machinists still do not have CNC experience, the solution that emerges is both to use the workshop-oriented approach and to extend this to capture the capabilities of the geometric approach.

This can be done in two ways. The first is to implement both approaches as two separate methods, in which case there are two ways of using the system. Thus the limitations of the workshop-oriented approach, from the technical perspective, and the limitations of the geometric approach, from the skill oriented perspective, can be overcome by providing machinists with both methods. The resulting system would allow machinists to easily program both simple and complex parts, and to shift to an operating strategy appropriate to the task. By providing two methods, it is also be possible to deal with situations when the geometry will be transferred down a CADCAM link.

An objection to the solution might be that it is too clumsy and inelegant and possibly over complex and expensive. An alternative solution is to integrate both approaches into one method, so that there is the possibility of using the system in an almost infinite number of ways, depending on people's preferences and the nature of the work. This would potentially overcome the objections, while still retaining the advantages of the first proposal.

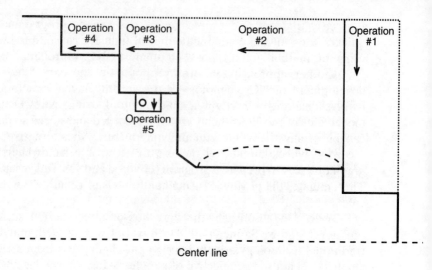

Figure 11.4   Example component.

Outline of the proposed design

There is one key difference between the workshop-oriented method and the geometric method. Definition of component geometry and cutting sequences are separate activities in the latter method, while they are combined in the former. The geometric method requires machinists to define the whole component geometry, and then define the cutting operations. Using the workshop-oriented method, the component geometry is built up by defining the cutting operations that are needed. If necessary, these cutting operations can be undertaken as they are programmed, or alternatively the cutting operations can be undertaken at the end of the programming. This choice is not normally possible with the geometric method: all the cuts usually have to be undertaken at the end of the programming exercise.

There is no need in this design situation to introduce two separate programming methods. There is no reason why the workshop-oriented method cannot be extended to work in a similar way to the geometric method, such that geometry definition and the generation of cutting sequences become separate activities.

To illustrate this, consider the example shown in Figure 11.4. The workshop-oriented method allows machinists to make this component in a number of ways. In this example, the first operation is facing, the second, third and fourth are turning, and the fifth is grooving. After each operation is defined, it is necessary to work out the cutting parameters, and then to proceed to the next operation.

To change the method of working, all that is necessary is to skip the selection of cutting parameters. A facility is then needed to enable the machinists to define the cutting parameters after all the cutting sequences have been defined. Thus, for example, once the component geometry has been defined using this method, the machinists could then decide to program the cutting operations in a quite different way, by machining sections one to four using turning operations. The machinists would then need to define the cutting parameters for the grooving operation.

The method as it stands, however, still needs to be extended to cope with more complex geometries. This is not difficult. All that is necessary is to add a menu of appropriate straight line and circular elements which can be selected as needed. The machinists could then work to define the component geometry using the geometric method.

However, the two ways of working can be integrated. For example, suppose the example in Figure 11.4 had a curved profile across Operation 2 as indicated by the dashed line. This poses no problems, because all that is needed is to use an appropriate shape from the menu to add the curved profile to the geometry of Operation 2. This can be added at any time in the programming sequence. Thus after defining Operation 1, the machinists could switch to the geometric method for the rest of the job, or just for part of the work, switching back to the workshop-oriented method as and when desired.

Having outlined the way in which the workshop-oriented method can be modified to overcome its limitations, similar comments can also be made about the geometric programming methods used on many CNC lathes. They too can be modified so that machinists can work using either method.

The proposed method that we have just outlined addresses issues of technical functionality as well as questions of usability, and those issues which relate to machinists' existing skills. The aim in adopting a workshop-oriented approach is not to fossilize techniques or working methods, but to create a flexible system which would allow skilled machinists to develop working methods appropriate to each situation, and also to provide a transition path from old working methods to newer ones. The benefits of developing a workshop-oriented approach and integrating it with other techniques is that the solutions derived from this approach are suitable as tools for skilled machinists. These techniques also provide very favorable learning curves during application.

In the example outlined above, the method of working has been deliberately shaped by the existing practices of the skilled machinists. This corresponds to the design principle stated in the previous chapter. The design principle states that technology should, where possible, be related to existing skills and working methods. This however, should be done in a way that allows room for development and experimentation, which corresponds to another design principle.

Decision support for selection of cutting parameters

Early developments in NC technology were characterized by a physical separation, achieved by technological means, of planning and execution. In the late 1970s CNC systems were developed which enabled these two aspects of machining to be combined, thus providing the potential for machinists to exercise greater control over their work.

In the preceding sections we identified selection of cutting parameters as an area where computer support could be provided in a way that would complement the existing knowledge of the machinists, by providing support based on codified knowledge. We will now describe the characteristics of a decision support system that was developed to assist skilled machinists with the selection of cutting parameters.

Design objectives

Of central importance to the design of this system was the concept that the software should allow the machinists control over the choice of cutting parameters. Also of importance was the concept of human–machine complementarity (Jordan, 1963) as opposed to the concept of human–machine comparability inherent in our technology oriented design paradigm.

The overall objective was to design a computer based decision support system that would be technically and economically satisfactory. In addition, however, the technology was to be designed so as to complement, rather than reject, machinists' skills, knowledge and experience. It was seen as important that the machinists should be actively involved in the process of selecting cutting parameters.

The technical objective of the work was to develop computer software for calculating optimum cutting parameters while satisfying a number of basic constraints on the machining process. Rather than just calling up a few stored cutting data, which are exclusively material dependent, the software would calculate cutting conditions based upon the particular machining operation, which is defined with respect to material, workpiece shape, workholding conditions and machine data. This involves taking into account constraints such as limits on workpiece and tool bending, limitations on the available gripping force at the chuck, limits on the power, torque and revolutions per minute available from the machine tool, surface finish requirements for the component and the need to produce metal cuttings (chips) of a size that could easily be disposed of.

It was also clear that owing to the limitations of the technology and the theory of metal cutting, there was a need for interaction with the software, in order that the machinists could take account of the limitations of the mathematical model and data used. However, it was also desired that the situation created should go beyond the machinists using skills and knowledge to compensate for the inadequacies of the technology. We also wished to create a situation where the skills, knowledge and experience of the users could be deployed, for example, to foresee possible difficulties and take proactive action to avoid them.

More specifically, we can identify a number of ways in which people's skills can be enhanced by the computer. First, consider perceptual skills. Many CNC systems are provided with facilities for tool path simulation. This allows machinists to identify some potential problems before machining is undertaken. Clearly this could be seen as a way of enhancing perceptual skills and reducing stress. We achieve these improvements because the machinists' confidence (that the program is satisfactory) is improved. This is now a common facility on CNC systems. We should point out that one design aim is consideration of other ways of employing the perceptual skills of the machinists within the process of determining the cutting parameters. Machinists should be allowed to identify areas where potential problems might be experienced, and eliminate them, before machining starts.

Second, we refer to conceptual skills, which in the case of determining the cutting parameters, revolve around the skill of translating the requirements specified by the geometry into cutting sequences, and the associated depths of cut, feeds and speeds. What we want to achieve here is support for these skills by making use of the scientific knowledge available, but in a way that complements rather than replaces the experiential knowledge of the machinists.

Finally, we wish to reintroduce discretionary skills to the shop floor people, by combining planning and execution and by giving control of the process back. We also wish to make good use of these discretionary skills by providing information that will allow the machinists to apply discretion over the results of the computer's calculations and not just override or edit the computer's results. The machinists should also decide when a more proactive approach is required, and should take the lead and generate cutting parameters on the basis of experience, using the computer to check the implications.

Cutting technology considerations

We must now delve into the technical details of metal cutting, because the process by which the computer generates results, that is the details of the algorithms, the way they work and so on are important. We are not just concerned with developing user friendly interfaces, but also with designing the technology behind the user interfaces, taking into account machinists' skills, needs and so forth.

There are several ways to achieve the calculation of optimum machining parameters. In this section we will discuss procedures that have been developed for the purpose of calculating optimum cutting conditions for workshop-oriented CNC lathe programming systems. These procedures have also been designed to allow for a high degree of interaction between skilled machinists and the software.

The calculation of optimum cutting conditions has exercised the minds of many engineers since Taylor (1907) first produced his slide rule in the early part of the 20th century. The modern version of the slide rule is the computer program, which is a much more versatile tool for calculating depths of cut, feeds and speeds. Unfortunately, most of the programs that have been developed are based on the assumption that they would be used in an office environment by NC programmers (Kals and Hijink, 1978; Houten, 1981), and as a result, little effort has been devoted to developing equivalent software for use by skilled machinists programming machine tools on the shop floor.

One obvious way of calculating optimal cutting parameters is to calculate the production cost for a large number of machining parameter combinations satisfying the basic physical constraints, and then select the combination of parameters that gives minimum production cost. This type of approach might be developed for an office based environment. It has two disadvantages. First, the data required for the calculations are not generally or easily available. Second, this type of search procedure is not very transparent because it is not easy to relate the method to rule of thumb knowledge and machining experience. Consequently, a more transparent calculation procedure needs to be developed which can make use of available data.

The objective was, therefore, to develop, in a way that harnesses the power of the computer, and the skill, judgment and experience of the machinists (Rosenbrock, 1977, 1981, 1982), a decision support system to assist with the selection of optimum cutting conditions for turning operations. Optimum cutting conditions means the most favorable cutting conditions for a given machining task, bearing in mind that certain simplifying assumptions have to be made in order to be able to carry out calculations, and that the machining process is subject to uncertainties and unpredictable disturbances.

The position with regard to machining economics is rather complex (Barrow, 1971). There are a number of optimization objectives that can be considered when calculating optimum cutting conditions: minimum cost, maximum production rate or maximum profit rate for each component. Furthermore, the calculations can either be based upon single pass theory or the more complex multi-pass theory. It is essential that information is available regarding such things as manufacturing costs, tool-life data and so on. However, such data are not always easy to obtain, and when they are available they are usually subject to uncertainty (Barrow, 1971; Kegg, 1971; Taylor, 1982).

In order to make more tractable the problem of developing a software based cutting technology decision support system, some simplifying assumptions are necessary. One approach is to use single pass theory, that is, to assume that all the metal will be removed in one single pass. Calculation of optimum cutting conditions, based, say, upon the minimum cost criterion, would then involve a constrained search of a feasible region in the parameter space defined by depth of cut and feed (the *a-s* space), where the boundaries of the feasible region are determined by the tool manufacturer's recommended ranges for these two parameters. This search would seek to identify the combination of depth of cut and feed that give minimum cost, given an optimum tool life and corresponding optimum speed, subject to constraints on the available machine power, the revolutions per minute (RPM) range of the machine and so on. The calculation of the optimum tool life and speed could, for example, be based on the extended Taylor equation.

The main problem with this type of search procedure is that it requires data that may be unavailable, inaccurate or difficult to obtain. A procedure that allows machinists to take account of any uncertainties, and that uses data which can be easily obtained, is therefore required.

Cutting technology algorithms: basic theory and assumptions

Since metal is most economically removed by a single cut (Barrow, 1971), and since single pass theory is much simpler to deal with than multi-pass theory, the case of single pass machining will be considered. This implies that the depth of cut should be set to the maximum possible, subject to the constraints imposed by the length of the tool's cutting edge and the actual amount of metal required to be removed. It therefore follows, for a given maximum feed, and ignoring for the moment other constraints on the machining process, that the optimum combination of depth of cut and feed lies at point A in Figure 11.5. However, owing to these other constraints, it may be that point A is inadmissible. For example, the surface finish specification may require that the feed be reduced, and in this case the optimum point would then move from point A to point B.

The exact location of the optimum point will depend on the constraints arising from a given turning problem, but it can be shown that the optimum point, as in many other optimization problems, never lies within the feasible region, but always on a boundary of this region, where the boundaries are defined by the constraints on the machining process (Rosenbrock, 1983). To show this it is necessary to consider the cost equation for metal cutting operations, which has the form

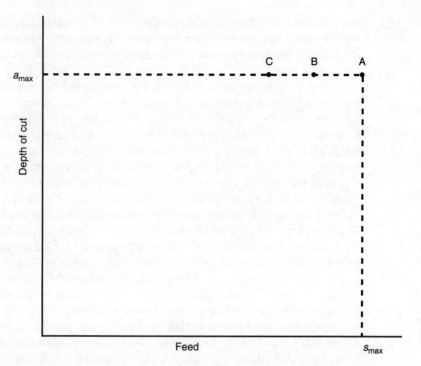

Figure 11.5 a–s space diagram with limits on depth of cut and feed defined by a_{max} and s_{max}.

$$c = p[t_1 + t_2 + t_3(t_2/T)] + q(t_2/T) \tag{11.1}$$

where c is the total cost, p is the operating cost per minute of the machine (overheads plus labor plus power and so on), t_1 is the set-up time, t_2 is the cutting time, t_3 is the time to change a tool, T is the tool life, and q is the cost per cutting edge.

A widely-used approximation for T is the extended Taylor equation

$$T = \frac{k}{v^\alpha s^\beta a^Y} \tag{11.2}$$

where v is the cutting speed, s is the feed, a is the depth of cut, and k, α, β, and Y are assumed to be constants.

The time required to cut a given volume, m, of metal, is

$$t_2 = \frac{m}{v\,s\,a} \tag{11.3}$$

so that the cost equation can be written, using Equations 11.2 and 11.3, in the form

$$c = pt_1 + \frac{m}{K^{1/\alpha}\,T^{-1/\alpha}\,S^{(\alpha-\beta)/\alpha}\,a^{(\alpha-Y)/\alpha}} \times \frac{[p + (pt_3 + q)]}{T} \tag{11.4}$$

The first term on the right in Equation 11.4 is constant for given t_1 and can therefore be ignored in the following discussion.

For the moment the only constraints that will be considered will be those relating to the maximum recommended depth of cut (a_{max}) and the maximum recommended feed (s_{max}). Other constraints will be considered shortly.

First, consider the situation when $a = a_{max}$. Then, for a given tool life T, and a given volume of metal to be removed m, Equation 11.4 shows that the cost c, decreases continually as the feed s, is increased, subject to the constraint s_{max}. It therefore follows that the optimum point is located on the boundary of the feasible region at the intersection of the constraints a_{max} and s_{max}, which is point A in Figure 11.5.

Consider now the situation when $s = s_{max}$. Then, for a given T and m, Equation 11.4 shows that the cost c, decreases continually as the depth of cut a, is increased, subject to the constraint a_{max}. It therefore again follows that the optimum point is located on the boundary of the feasible region at the intersection of the constraints a_{max} and s_{max}, which is point A in Figure 11.5.

It may happen that point A is inadmissible because some constraint such as surface finish requirement is violated, or because the tangential cutting force is excessive. Since surface finish is largely influenced by the feed, this is the parameter that should be reduced if the surface finish constraint is violated. In this situation the optimum point would move to the left of point A, say to point B. The optimum point again therefore lies on the boundary of the feasible region at the intersection of the constraint a_{max} and the constraint imposed on the feed by the surface finish requirements.

Let us now assume that point B is inadmissible because the tangential cutting force is excessive. Generally, the magnitudes of α, β, and Y in Equation 11.4 satisfy the condition

$\alpha > \beta > 1 > Y$

It thus follows that, in general, a decrease in the feed s, has a much more significant effect upon the cost c, than a decrease in the depth of cut, a. Consequently, if the tangential cutting force is excessive, it is much more economic to reduce the feed rather than reduce the depth of cut. In situations such as this, the optimum point must lie to the left of point B, for example at point C, and this point must lie on the boundary of the feasible region, at the intersection of the constraint a_{max}, and the constraint on the feed arising from the maximum permissible tangential cutting force.

It may happen that the nature of the constraints are such that the maximum depth of cut and maximum feed that can be used are less than the maxima recommended. This situation is depicted in Figure 11.6. Where then, in this situation, does the optimum point lie?

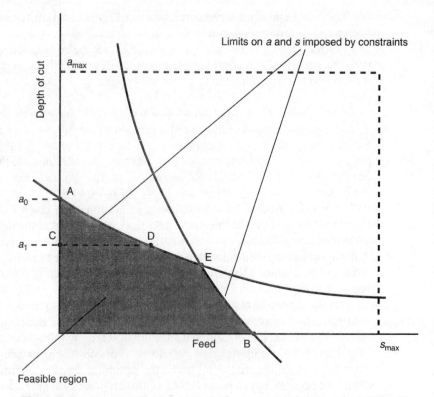

Figure 11.6 *a–s* space diagram with limits on depth of cut and feed defined by constraints other than a_{max} and s_{max}.

Equation 11.4 suggests that the optimum point is not located at point A or point B, so to find where the optimum point is located, consider point C, which corresponds to a depth of cut a_1. Equation 11.4 shows that, for this depth of cut, the cost must decrease continually as the feed is increased. It thus follows that the minimum cost for this particular depth of cut is located at point D in Figure 11.6, that is, on the boundary of the feasible region.

In the same way it can be shown that for any depth of cut in the range $0 < a < a_0$, the point of minimum cost for the chosen depth of cut is located on the boundary of the feasible region. It therefore follows that, when the constraints are of the form depicted in Figure 11.6, the optimum point for this situation lies on the boundary of the feasible region somewhere between point A and point B. Since we have observed that the optimum point lies at the intersection of two constraints, it is probable that in this case the optimum point is actually located at point E.

Now that it has been established that the optimum point always lies on the boundary of the feasible region, this knowledge can be used to

Table 11.1 Typical tool manufacturers' cutting power data assuming a tool life of 15 minutes.

Feed (s) mm/rev	Cutting speed (v) m/min	1.5	Cutting depth (a) mm 2.5	3.5	4.5
			Net power requirement (kW)		
0.1	365	1.0	2.0	2.75	3.75
0.2	300	1.25	2.5	1.25	5.0
0.3	245	1.5	3.0	4.25	5.75
0.4	215	1.5	3.0	4.4	6.25
0.5	195	1.75	3.25	5.0	6.5
0.6	170	1.5	3.0	4.75	6.25

develop simple methods for calculating optimum cutting conditions. Before outlining these procedures however, we need to consider the problem of obtaining data for use in the computer program.

Data describing the characteristics of the machine tool and hydraulic chucks can be obtained without any serious problem; the main difficulty is associated with collecting cost data and with obtaining the values of the coefficients in the extended Taylor equation.

One of the most readily available sources of data is that provided by tool manufacturers. For example, it is sometimes possible to obtain data of the form shown in Table 11.1, which are based on a tool life of 15 minutes. It would be very convenient to be able to use such data in a cutting technology procedure, rather than using the extended Taylor equation.

If the assumption is made that in most turning situations the optimum tool life is about 15 minutes, then a tool life calculation becomes unnecessary, and the use of the extended Taylor equation and associated cost data is avoided. If it is then further assumed that cutting power is given by the product of tangential cutting force and cutting speed, then it is possible to convert the data shown in Table 11.1 into the tangential cutting force data shown in Table 11.2, and to tabulate cutting speed against feed, as indicated in Table 11.3.

Table 11.2 Tangential cutting force as a function of depth of cut and feed obtained from the data in Table 11.1.

Feed (s) mm/rev	1.5	Cutting depth (a) mm 2.5	3.5	4.5
		Cutting force (N)		
0.1	164	329	452	616
0.2	250	500	250	1000
0.3	367	735	1040	1408
0.4	418	837	1255	1744
0.5	538	1000	1538	2000
0.6	529	1059	1676	2205

Table 11.3   Cutting speed as a function of feed.

Feed (s) mm/rev	Cutting speed (v) m/min
0.1	365
0.2	300
0.3	245
0.4	215
0.5	195
0.6	170

Using this data, and based upon the knowledge that the optimum point lies on the boundary of a feasible region in the a-s space, a procedure can be developed that will calculate cutting conditions which satisfy a number of constraints on the machining process. First, however, it is necessary to begin to define the boundaries of the feasible region in the a-s space. This can be done by using the maximum values of depth of cut and feed given in Table 11.2, to specify the limits a_{max} and s_{max} shown in Figure 11.7. Since the optimum point, ignoring any other constraints for the time being, lies at the intersection of a_{max} and s_{max}, this is the point from which the search will start (denoted as point A in Figure 11.7).

Now, if point A is inadmissible, then the next step will be to reduce the feed, keeping the depth of cut constant. However, it is not normal to take large depths of cut with very small feeds, as this can, among other things, result in poor chip breaking characteristics and the possibility of inducing chatter (American Society of Mechanical Engineers, 1952). At some point therefore it becomes necessary to reduce the depth of cut as well as the feed.

Little tendency towards chatter exists with a machine tool in ordinarily good condition, and with reasonably stiff work, when the ratio of chip width to chip thickness (the chip ratio) is less than 15. It may also be possible to avoid chatter under favorable conditions, when cutting steel, with a ratio of 20 to 25, but in the range 25 to 50, some chatter will be present. Beyond values of 50 the chatter will most likely be serious (American Society of Mechanical Engineers, 1952).

Brewer and Rueda (1963) report that in industry, 93% of all turning operations use depths of cut and feed in which the ratio between these two parameters lies somewhere between 2 and 20, while in 48% of turning operations, this ratio is limited to a value from 4 to 10. Based upon these observations, a constraint can therefore be imposed upon the ratio of depth of cut to feed (that is, the chip ratio). Nominal values for the upper and lower limits of this constraint can be set at 20 and 2 respectively (the need for the lower limit will become apparent in the following section). The feasible region in the a-s space is now as indicated in Figure 11.7. The search for the optimum point therefore proceeds along the line AB0, thus ensuring that the depth of cut is reduced once a given value of feed has been reached.

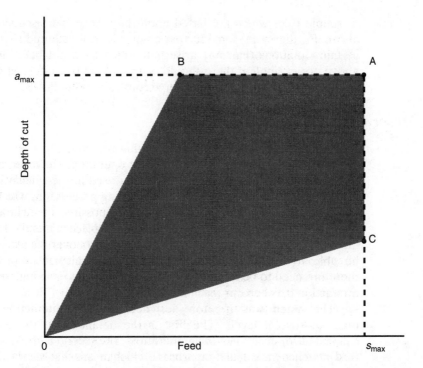

Figure 11.7   *a–s* space diagram showing the boundaries of the feasible region used in the calculation procedure.

Using the ideas outlined above, it is possible to derive a simple procedure that searches along the line AB0 in Figure 11.7 to find the optimum cutting parameters. The procedure will satisfy constraints such as surface finish requirements, force exerted on the chuck jaws, tool and workpiece bending, RPM limits, and torque and power constraints. It will also ensure, through an appropriate method, that the sum of the depths of cut all add up to the total amount of metal that needs to be removed.

It should be noted however, that as the procedure searches along the line AB0, it may be the case in some situations that the suggested cutting parameters may be well away from the optimum point. We should note that a more sophisticated procedure, derived from the first one, has also been developed that deals with this situation. This can be used if it is felt necessary to search for the optimum point with greater accuracy.

This second procedure is more complex than the first algorithm, because it seeks to establish the boundary of the feasible region in the *a-s* space in more detail. It does this by first locating the force constraint boundary, then the torque constraint boundary, and then the power constraint boundary. Once the boundary of the feasible region has been defined, the algorithm selects the optimum point based upon a number of simple rules which are based upon the theoretical discussion given above. Furthermore, some further control logic is required to deal with certain situations that may arise and which have not been described above, for example if there should be more than one intersection point between the power, torque and force constraint boundaries.

Description of the design

Procedures have been outlined above that will generate a set of recommended cutting data for a given turning operation. However, owing to the uncertainties associated with the data used in the calculations, the limited nature of the model of the machining process, and the fact that there are many disturbances which are impossible to include in the computer model (for example, a hard skin on a piece of metal), it is vitally important that the machinists should have control over the software and be able to intervene in its operation. The calculation procedures therefore need to be implemented in a way that allows a high degree of interaction between our machinists and the computer.

The system was therefore designed to enable interaction to take place at several levels. The first is the detailed cutting parameters calculated for each machining operation. The second is the parameters that influence the calculation process, which means that the way in which the computer calculates cutting parameters can be fundamentally changed by machinists.

At the first level, interaction can take place via the display shown in Figure 11.8. Each cutting parameter has two columns of data. In each of

Cutting technology							
Calculate	Edit	Display global			Bar charts		
	Fix value Un-fix value Re-calculate End edit						
		Cut number		Depth of cut		Feed	Speed
		R1	2.03		0.14		202
		R2	2.03		0.14		184
Time 4 – 23		R3	2.07		0.14		166
		R4	2.07		0.14		148
		R5	2.11		0.14		129
		R6	1.69		0.2		114
		F1	0.5		0.12		110

Figure 11.8 Display for editing calculated cutting parameters.

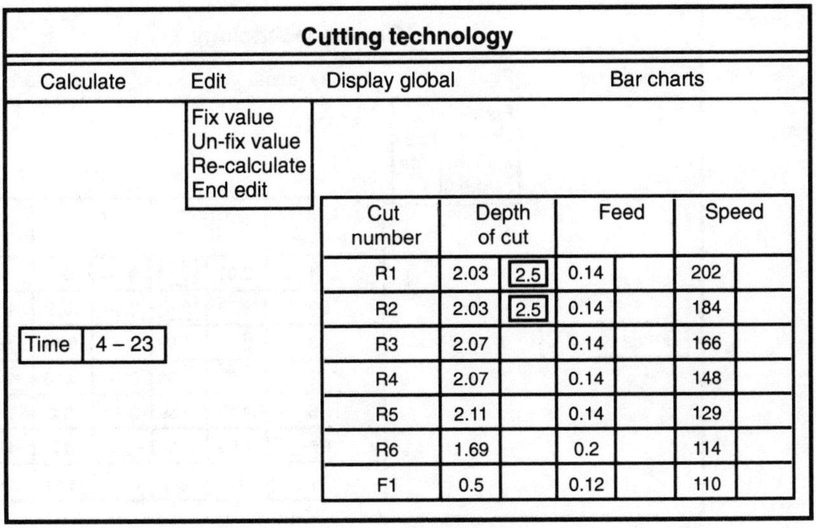

Cutting technology								
Calculate	Edit		Display global				Bar charts	

	Fix value Un-fix value Re-calculate End edit							
		Cut number	Depth of cut		Feed		Speed	
		R1	2.03	2.5	0.14		202	
		R2	2.03	2.5	0.14		184	
Time	4 – 23	R3	2.07		0.14		166	
		R4	2.07		0.14		148	
		R5	2.11		0.14		129	
		R6	1.69		0.2		114	
		F1	0.5		0.12		110	

Figure 11.9 Display for editing calculated cutting parameters showing some editing by the machinist.

the left-hand columns are displayed the values calculated by the computer for each cut. The right-hand columns are left blank, and this is where the machinists can enter cutting parameters (see Figure 11.9).

There are some simple rules for editing these displays. Any cutting parameter specified by the machinists cannot subsequently be overridden by the computer. Their input will remain fixed at the specified value, until they indicate, via a command, that the value can be unfrozen. At any stage during the interaction, the computer can be instructed to recalculate machining parameters, taking into account the input specified by the machinists. When this happens any parameters that have not been fixed or specified, are recalculated, and then displayed in the remaining empty spaces in the right-hand columns.

In Figure 11.10, an example of such an editing procedure is shown. The numbers indicated in bold are those that the machinists have input. The original computer-calculated parameters remain displayed in the left-hand columns for the purpose of comparison. Using this procedure the machinists can specify and change as many of the cutting parameters as desired, and the interaction can go on for as long as the machinists consider worthwhile.

The second level of interaction referred to above occurs using the display shown in Figure 11.11. Tool data for the selected tool is displayed as recommended maxima for depths of cut, feed and speed. The display also presents information about the number of roughing and finishing cuts that

Cutting technology						
Calculate	Edit	Display global		Bar charts		
	Fix value Un-fix value Re-calculate End edit					
		Cut number	Depth of cut		Feed		Speed	

		Cut number	Depth of cut		Feed		Speed	
		R1	2.03	[2.5]	0.14	**0.1**	202	**195**
		R2	2.03	[2.5]	0.14	**0.1**	184	**175**
Time	4 – 17	R3	2.07	**1.82**	0.14	**0.16**	166	**157**
		R4	2.07	**1.80**	0.14	**0.16**	148	**139**
		R5	2.11	**1.69**	0.14	**0.2**	129	**129**
		R6	1.69	**1.69**	0.2	**0.2**	114	**114**
		F1	0.5	**0.5**	0.12	**0.12**	110	**110**

Figure 11.10 Display for editing calculated cutting parameters following some editing by the machinist and re-calculation of those values not edited.

have been calculated, as well as default values for the surface finish speci-fication, the upper and lower chip ratio limits and the clamping factor.

The reasons for the chip ratio limits and the surface finish specifica-tion were discussed in the previous section. The clamping factor provides the machinists with the means of influencing applied cutting forces, and hence depths of cut and feeds. By reducing the value of the clamping fac-tor, the value of the gripping force, available at the chuck, can be reduced within the computer model. Thus the clamping factor allows the machin-ist to take account of unmodelled effects in the gripping of the workpiece.

The parameters displayed in Figure 11.11 can be changed by the machinists. As well as being able to change the clamping factor, it is also possible to change the default values of surface finish and the default val-ues for the upper and lower chip ratio limits, which allows the machinists to redefine the search region. It is also possible to predefine the number of roughing and finishing cuts. All these parameters can be regarded as global, and any changes made at this level will cause any previous editing at the first level display shown in Figure 11.10 to be deleted, and new data to appear in the left-hand columns of that display, reflecting the changed global parameters.

Finally, Figure 11.11 shows a cumulative estimation of the total time required to undertake all the machining operations programmed for a specific workpiece. In the display shown in Figure 11.10, there is an estimate of the machining time for the operation that is currently being programmed.

Cutting technology			
Calculate Edit		Display global	Bar charts

Fix value
Un-fix value
Re-calculate
End edit

Roughing surface finish	16.0
Finishing surface finish	0.6
Clamping factor	1.0
Chip ratio, upper limit	20
Chip ratio, lower limit	2
Number of roughing cuts	6
Number of finishing cuts	1

Maximum depth of cut (mm)	4.5
Maximum feed (mm/rev)	0.6
Maximum speed (m/rev)	365
Minimum speed (m/min)	170

Total machining time	4–23

Figure 11.11 Display for editing parameters affecting the calculation of cutting parameters.

These displays provide the machinist with the ability to edit, change and control the selection of cutting parameters. But, on their own, they are not adequate. For several reasons there is a need to provide further information.

First, it will be recalled that one of our goals was to try to make the perceptual skills of the machinists more productive and effective and to reduce stress. To some extent we have achieved this, because the machinists can see, in advance, what the cutting conditions are, and then their conceptual and discretionary skills can be deployed to change and improve these cutting conditions. However, there is no detailed information about the system states, in terms of the constraining parameters. For example, they would not know if the forces exerted on the chuck were close to the maximum values recommended. Basically, in any situation where the constraints are satisfied, there is no way of knowing or establishing how close a given constraining parameter is to its limit. Thus, there is a need to display further information on these constraining parameters, so that the machinists can perceive more about the decision situation and be better informed about the possible consequences of their decisions. However, there are also other reasons why such information is required.

The computer will generally always produce results that satisfy the specified constraints. An exception to this general rule is the speed constraint. A problem can arise with this, owing to the relationship between workpiece radius, surface speed and machine RPM. When the radius becomes small, it may happen that it is not possible to satisfy the tool manufacturer's recommended minimum cutting speed, because as the cutting radius decreases, the RPM of the workpiece has to increase in order to maintain the cutting speed above the recommended minimum. However, when the RPM reaches the maximum attainable, it follows that the cutting speed must eventually fall below the recommended minimum if the cutting radius continues to decrease. This is why, in the data shown in Figures 11.8, 11.9 and 11.10, the speed values for cuts R3 to R6 and finishing cut F1 actually fall below the minimum of 170 m/min shown in Figure 11.11. The problem can only be resolved by using a machine tool with a larger maximum RPM or a tool with a lower recommended minimum speed.

Apart from this situation, the possibility of violating constraints also increases as machinists begin to specify cutting parameters. As soon as cutting parameters become fixed, the degrees of freedom that the computer has available to satisfy constraints reduce. It is possible, in these particular circumstances, that the computer may not be able to produce results that satisfy all the constraints. Consequently, information about the constraining parameters is required.

Another problem that is not initially evident, which only emerged through discussions with the machinists, is the fact that many of the machinists' believe that often the maximum values of cutting conditions recommended by tool manufacturers are too conservative. As a result, skilled and experienced machinists sometimes exceed these maxima.

The software was therefore developed to allow the machinists to specify values beyond the range recommended by the tool manufacturers, although the computer itself was never allowed to generate any results beyond these values. Unfortunately there was no data available for cutting forces beyond these maxima, and consequently the machinists would, in effect, lose software support in these circumstances. This problem was resolved by extrapolating data, thus giving the machinists improved decision support. This further highlights the need to provide the machinists with more information about system constraints.

We can provide further information in two complementary ways. The first involves providing a display of the constraint parameters, in relation to their respective maxima and minima, in the form of bar charts, as shown in Figure 11.12. These bar charts can be displayed at any time, giving the user a qualitative feel for the system state. However, a second way of communicating further information is to use color coding of all these displays.

The color codes that are appropriate to these charts were related to the degree to which constraints were violated. Thus, green was used to indicate that all the constraints were satisfied, yellow was used to indicate that some constraints were violated by an amount up to 25%, orange was used to indicate a violation in the range 25–50% and red was used to signify a violation of more than 50%. Further colors were used to

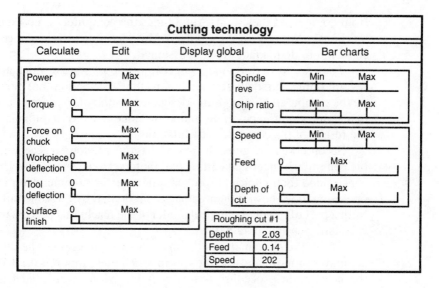

Figure 11.12   Bar chart display indicating the state of constraining parameters.

identify machinists' selected cutting parameters which activated the use of extrapolated data.

To summarize the details of the design, it can be seen that machinists have a choice in the way that they use the system. In one mode of operation they evaluate a set of recommended conditions that the computer has calculated, and then either edit or accept these suggested parameters. In this mode it is possible to ask the computer to recalculate any of the parameters which have not changed. The computer cannot override modifications. Another mode of working is also possible, which involves the machinists specifying the number of cuts required. The computer then produces detailed cutting parameters.

If desired, the system can also be used in a completely different way. In this third operating mode, the machinists select the cutting parameters, while the computer checks these values against the machining constraints (for example, power and torque limits). If any of the constraints are violated, then this information is conveyed to the machinists.

All interactions between the machinists and the computer are governed by one basic rule, which is that any parameter value determined by the machinists cannot be changed by the computer. If, as a result, constraints are violated, then warnings are displayed on the computer screen. The computer, however, does not stop the machinists from proceeding with their desired actions; it can never stop the machinists from doing what they want. At all times the computer is subordinate to machinists. We rely on their skills, knowledge, experience and common sense not to do damage. Trust is assumed.

Thus, we have developed a decision support system which achieves several things. First, all detailed and routine calculations are performed by the computer. However, the design leaves the machinists to use their machining experience, skills, and knowledge to exercise judgment over the results of the computer's calculations.

Second, we have given the machinists the freedom to accept or reject the computer's suggested cutting parameters. However, we also have not constrained their choice to tool manufacturers' recommended ranges of operation, nor allowed their choice to be limited by the constraints that form a part of the mathematical model of the machining process used for calculating cutting parameters.

Third, the system allows the machinists to determine the degree of computer support, and also the way in which that support is used. Fourth, the calculation procedure is relatively straightforward, and has been related, as far as possible, to shop floor knowledge.

Fifth, the system provides the machinists with facilities to adjust those global system parameters which have an important effect upon the computer's calculations. Sixth, results are presented in a form that can be easily assimilated.

Seventh, the machinists can examine the state of the system, that is, the mathematical model of the cutting process, to establish the situation with regard to the constraints.

Eighth, the machinists are informed of the consequences of their decisions, allowing them to compare the computer's predictions with reality. At the same time they are not restrained from carrying out their decisions.

Finally, the system provides the machinists with a choice of working methods. This allows them to develop their skills in selecting an appropriate method of working and allows them to explore and learn different techniques.

One important point that we should stress is that the system characteristics that we achieved in this design are not related to the application of ergonomics to the design of the human–computer interface. We achieved these results from considering the technology (the deep system characteristics), and not from the human–computer interface (the surface characteristics). In fact, the human–computer interface is fairly simple, and could probably be improved by considering the ergonomic issues.

This illustrates the points we were making in Chapter 8 about the need to distinguish between the surface characteristics of a system, as determined by the human–computer interface, and the deeper characteristics of a system, as determined by the technology that lies behind the interface. The surface characteristics are strongly related to ergonomics, while the deeper characteristics relate more to our view of the machinists and the importance we attach to their skills, knowledge, judgment and experience.

Design enhancements

In this section we consider ways in which the design of the system can be improved upon. We do this for the purpose of demonstrating that the design of skill and knowledge enhancing technologies is not a dead-end path that leads to fossilization of the technology and the skills and knowledge involved. Skill and knowledge enhancing technologies can be improved upon without having damaging consequences for the skills of the people, while still retaining the prime objective of making human skills more productive and effective. We first consider the cutting technology decision support system described above, and then the geometry definition method. Finally we outline how developments in the field of AI can be exploited in a way that is in harmony with the basic goals of skill and knowledge enhancing technologies, again to demonstrate the feasibility of further developing the technology.

A more sophisticated design

In this section we consider how the design of the decision support system considered above can be made more sophisticated using the concept of open systems, as described in Chapter 10.

To understand how we can use an open systems approach to design a human–computer relationship, we must use the concept of evaluative and generative decision support systems, also mentioned in Chapter 10. We have seen that an evaluative decision support system is one that takes a set of proposed decisions and evaluates and predicts the results of these decisions. A generative decision support system is one that takes a set of criteria and constraints and generates a set of decisions.

The system that we have outlined above is both generative and evaluative, which is an interesting feature of the design. Often systems are either evaluative or generative, but very rarely both. The system is generative because it will generate a set of cutting parameters for a specified problem. It is also evaluative, because it will also produce an evaluation of user specified input. And of course, in practice, the exact mix of generative and evaluative operation is highly dependent upon each individual user and the problem situation. There is no one way of operating the system, as it is flexible.

As we pointed out in Chapter 10, a common problem that we seem to face is that we cannot break out of the evaluative versus generative dichotomy. There is no logical reason for this, because systems can be designed to be both evaluative and generative.

The operating mode of the decision support system that we discussed in the previous section starts off primarily operating in a generative mode. The computer comes up with a possible set of cutting conditions and the machinists evaluate these and make any necessary changes. The system then revises its results, keeping the changes specified by the machinists. In this interactive manner, it is possible for the machinists to utilize the computer as a decision support system, but control over whether to accept the computer's recommendations is left in the hands of our machinists.

The system operates in a way that can be compared with a spread-sheet, but it is also possible to drive the system by defining global parameters and constraints. However, it is possible to argue that the design is still unsatisfactory because the machinists always have to wait for the generative results before starting to exert control by editing the calculated results. One way around this problem is to offer the machinists a blank table option, so that their own choice of cutting parameters can be entered before any calculations begin. The computer could then generate any cutting parameters which the machinists did not specify, and they could still edit the parameters if so desired. It is, however, possible to design the system to operate in a different way, which achieves this objective, but which is more integrated with the previous system description. The details of the proposed design are described below.

Across the bottom of the screen are displayed a set of cutting parameters (depth of cut, feed and speed) which the machinists have to enter via the keyboard. The computer then estimates the consequences of using these parameters in terms of the constraining variables, that is, power consumption, tool and workpiece deflection, and so on. These variables are then displayed above the cutting parameters in the form of color coded bar charts as described previously.

On the keyboard, the machinists are provided with six keys (two keys per cutting parameter). These keys allow the machinists to increase or decrease any of the three cutting parameters in user defined steps (say 5% as the default value). As soon as any cutting parameter is changed, the bar chart display of constraints (for example power) is updated, so the machinists can see the consequences of their actions. When they are satisfied with these cutting parameters, they store them, and then proceed to specify the next cut (if there is one). The computer gives support by displaying the amount of metal remaining to be removed. All the details of the specified cuts can be recalled on to the screen, at any time.

This evaluative decision support system allows the machinists to learn how changes to the cutting parameters affect the constraining variables. However, a technical and economic objection to this evaluative approach is that there is no guarantee that the cutting parameters will be optimal (in the narrow sense of minimizing cutting time). Of course, we must remember that optimal does not necessarily imply good, but nevertheless, we can overcome this objection. One way around this problem is to use the computer to advise the machinists about this situation. This can be achieved in a number of different ways.

One possibility is to offer advice after each cut has been specified, or to wait until all the cuts for a given operation have been determined and then to offer advice. This is something that each individual machinist should control. The basic principle of operation is as follows. The machinists specify the cutting parameters. The computer estimates the cutting time for these parameters. The computer also calculates the optimum cutting parameters. The difference between the machining time is indicated using a graphical display. If the machinists want to explore the reasons for the difference they can then call up further data (the optimum cutting conditions and associated bar chart displays of constraining variables, and charts showing the differences between the machinists' choices and the optimum values). They then have to decide whether to accept these optimum values.

Machinists can also do some experimentation. They could decide to keep the value of depth of cut that they originally selected, but to use the computer's recommendation for the feed and speed. They can immediately see the consequences of these changes. This interaction continues for as long as necessary. The option to generate the computer's recommendations first can also be integrated into the operation of the decision support system. In this case the computer works in a generative mode, and comes up with a recommendation, which the machinists can change.

Now consider what has been achieved. The computer is now operating in both purely evaluative and generative modes, but there is also a mixture of the two. How the system is used is controlled by the machinists. We have provided a decision support system that can be used in numerous ways. From a strictly technical and economic perspective many people would argue that this type of system is not needed. However, if we start to consider issues such as control and learning, then this sort of system is the result. Thus by using an open systems approach to the design of the human–computer relationship, we can begin to take account of these wider design issues.

Data management tools

Given the uncertain nature of the data used in the calculations, the usefulness of the proposed workshop-oriented decision support system can be extended by using the concept of hybrid knowledge-based decision support systems, the main components of which are a knowledge-base, a knowledge acquisition mechanism and an optimization-based inference engine (Singh and Cook, 1985).

The knowledge-base, rather than being a set of production rules, as are often used in knowledge-based systems, consists of a causal mathematical model (in this case of the machining process) which comprises two parts; the structural equations and the model parameters. The model parameters are obtained through the knowledge acquisition mechanism, and can be acquired from a number of sources which can be classified as hard data (for example, as given in Tables 11.1, 11.2, and 11.3), and soft data obtained in response to *what-if* questions generated by the computer. The inference engine is optimization based, and in this case can be either, or both, of the cutting technology algorithms outlined in the previous section.

As an example to illustrate the above, the equation for tangential cutting force is normally given as a linear expression

$$F_t = k_s as \tag{11.5}$$

However, the data in Table 11.2 suggests a non-linear equation of the form

$$F_t = k_s as^x \tag{11.6}$$

This equation can now be parameterized, using some standard data fitting technique, based upon the hard data in Table 11.2.

Soft data representing the experience of a number of people can be obtained from answers to what-if type questions generated by the computer. For example, a question of the form 'if the tool life is doubled, estimate what effect this will have on tangential cutting forces', can be used to form some quantification of the effects of using a tool life other than the 15 minutes assumed in the data obtained from tool manufacturers' tables. Thus hard and soft data, each given appropriate weighting according to the machinists' level of confidence in any particular part of it, can be used to parameterize the structural equations, which could include, given some appropriate assumptions, the Taylor tool-life equation given by Equation 11.2.

Graphical tool path editing

The cutting technology decision support systems that we have described thus far relate to situations where the machining involves making cuts parallel with the component center line. In some situations cuts follow the profile of the desired workpiece geometry, and for these situations a more powerful form of editing facility is helpful.

When we edit a depth of cut in the display shown in Figure 11.8, the depths of cut are changed along the whole length of the cuts. When undertaking profiling, however, a situation might arise which involves changing the depth of cut along a limited section of the profile. Graphical editing facilities can be used to deal with this type of situation, which will allow the machinists to redefine the tool path. Basically this can be achieved by providing facilities that allow the machinists to use a computer mouse to specify a number of points on the screen display of the tool paths. These new points correspond to the required path. The computer will then draw a smooth curve through these points. The feeds and speeds can be edited as previously described using the type of display shown in Figure 11.8. While the operation of the cutting technology software remains unchanged, the model of the machining process embedded in the software is more complex because the profiling situation is a much more complex activity.

Concluding comments

In this chapter we have described an example of skill and knowledge enhancing technologies. So far, however, we have only considered skills and knowledge that to a large extent already exist, and the application to process-oriented functions. We should also consider the development of skill and knowledge enhancing technologies for skills and knowledge that at the moment are not perceived as part of our people's work. For example we could think about several other areas where these technologies might be applied, such as:

- *Innovation skills* Skills related to using creativity to find better ways of doing things.
- *Team skills* The skills required for effective cooperation and collaboration, both within the machine tool system and with other sub-systems.
- *Communication skills* Skills required to effectively transfer insights to other people.

We will consider this in the next chapter under issues of future developments.

Key points

- A key step in the design of skill and knowledge enhancing technologies is to undertake a skills, knowledge and task analysis.

- The focus of the design should be on making use of people's skills, but in a way that is satisfying to the users, and without over stressing them.

- User control over the technologies is an important issue, as is the capability to accommodate individual working styles and so on.

References

American Society of Mechanical Engineers (1952). *Manual on Cutting of Metals*. New York: ASME

Bainbridge L. (1983). Ironies of automation. *Automatica*, **19**, 775–9

Barrow G. (1971). Tool-life equations and machining economics. In *Proc. 12th Int. Machine Tool Design and Research Conf*. Manchester, UK, September 1971

Brewer R.C. and Rueda R. (1963). A simplified approach to the optimum selection of machining parameters. *Engineers Digest*, **24**(9), 133–51

Gossard D. and von Turkovich B. (1978). Analogic part programming with interactive graphics. *Annals of CIRP*, **27**, 475–8

Hazelhurst R.J., Bradbury R.J. and Corlett E.N. (1969). A comparison of the skills of machinists on numerically controlled and conventional machines. *Occupational Psychology*, **43**, 169–82

Hekeler M. (1989a). Traub-IPS: The Workshop-oriented Programming System. *Technical Literature*, Traub AG, Reichenbach/Fils, Germany

Hekeler M. (1989b). Ergebnisse des Pilotanwenders (MTU Motoren- und Turinen-Union Friedrichshafen GmbH). *Technical Literature*, Traub AG, Reichenbach/Fils, Germany

Hekeler M. (1990). Workshop-oriented Programming (WOP) – A Standardised Programming Technology for Programmers and Operators. *Technical Literature*, Traub AG, Reichenbach/Fils, Germany

Houten van F.J.A.M. (1981). The development of a technological processor as a part of a workpiece programming system. *Annals of CIRP* **30**(1), 363–8

Jordan N. (1963). Allocation of functions between man and machines in automated systems. *J. Applied Psychology*, **47**, 161–5

Kals H.J.J. and Hijink J.A.W. (1978). A computer aid in the optimisation of turning conditions in multi-cut operations. *Annals of CIRP*, **27**(1), 465–9

Kegg R.L. (1971). Selection of cutting speeds based on uncertain data. In *Proc. 12th Int. Machine Tool Design and Research Conf*. Manchester, UK, September 1971

Kidd P.T. (1992). Interdisciplinary design of skill-based computer-aided technologies: interfacing in depth. *Int. J. Human Factors in Manufacturing*, **2**(3), 209–28

Kelly M.R. and Lan X. (1990). Does decentralisation of programming responsibilities increase efficiency? An empirical test. In *Ergonomics of Hybrid Automated Systems II* (Karwowski W. and Rahimi M., eds.), pp. 379–86. Amsterdam: Elsevier

Rosenbrock H.H. (1977). The future of control. *Automatica,* **13**, 389–92

Rosenbrock H.H. (1981). Automation and society. *Systems and Control Letters,* **1**, 2–6

Rosenbrock H.H. (1982). Robots and people. *Measurement and Control,* **15**, 105–12

Rosenbrock H.H. (1983). *The Calculation of Cutting Conditions.* Unpublished UMIST Project Steering Committee Paper No. 106, UMIST, Manchester, UK

Satine L., Hinduja S., Vale G. and Boon J. (1980). A process oriented system for NC lathes. *Int. J. Machine Tool Design and Research,* **20**, 111–21

Singh M.G. and Cook R. (1985). A new class of intelligent knowledge-based systems with an optimisation-based inference engine. *Decision Support Systems,* **1**, 299–312

Taylor F.W. (1907). On the art of cutting metals. *Trans. American Soc. Mech. Eng.,* **28**, 31–350

Taylor J. (1982). A combined approach to obtaining and using tool life data. In *Proc. 23rd Int. Machine Tool Design and Research Conf.* (Davies B.J., ed.). London: Macmillan

PART FIVE

Agile manufacturing: the future

12

Issues, problems and future developments

Introduction

To conclude this book we consider some issues that need to be addressed by the research community and research policy makers. Where necessary, we highlight the problems that stand in the way of the development and adoption of agile manufacturing. We will also look at some future developments that are likely to occur, focusing specifically on skill and knowledge enhancing technologies.

Issues and problems

The legacy of the Taylor Model

The big issue is not whether we should become involved in the development of agile manufacturing, but to what extent our own existing beliefs, goals, objectives and methods will continue to be shaped by the old manufacturing paradigms. We can easily adopt the label of agile manufacturing, but can we easily discard the thinking behind the Taylor Model which represents an engineering and management culture that has developed over the past 200 years? Do we really understand the differences between agile manufacturing and traditional manufacturing, and the profound implication of these differences for the things we do and how we do them? Will our research into agile manufacturing be just the same as research into other aspects of manufacturing such as CIM, and be largely influenced by our Taylor Model thinking? Will our work be technology driven and monodisciplinary, or will it be more balanced and truly interdisciplinary?

In this section we focus primarily on some recommendations for future research in the area of agile manufacturing, based on an interdisciplinary approach and on a balance between organization, people and technology. The emphasis of the recommendations is therefore on organization and people issues as well as technological research. We also highlight some of the problems that stand in the way of implementing the proposed actions.

The need for an integrated approach

We are learning that the old approaches to manufacturing, which are largely based on separate and isolated functional departments, have outgrown their usefulness, and have become a competitive liability. The fragmented approach to manufacturing is slowly being replaced by an integrated approach, the key words being empowerment, simultaneous activities, coordination, cooperation, sharing and team working. However, this message has still to penetrate into the operating philosophy of government departments and other governmental types of organizations that fund research activities.

No organization can expect to deal adequately with the development and implementation of measures to support the development of agile manufacturing, without first adopting a new approach itself. Agile manufacturing cannot be addressed in a simple, monodisciplinary way. Many of the issues in agile manufacturing need to be approached in an interdisciplinary manner. For example, it is necessary to broaden the coverage of manufacturing research to include organization and people issues. However, a human factors research programme on its own, or within a technical research programme, is not adequate. What is also required is to integrate these aspects into the technology development research.

This objective of integrated research, however, is not easy to achieve. Many of us still believe that the human factors problem can be traced to a lack of research funding for human factors aspects of manufacturing. But this is only one issue. Once this funding problem has been resolved, the next step is to realize that all the areas of research are interrelated. To fund separate projects, some dealing with human factors and some dealing with technology, is largely a waste of resources because this type of research is only suitable for traditional manufacturing. Agile manufacturing research should be based on integrated projects.

It is important that research should be interdisciplinary and not monodisciplinary. Thus, for example, questions of skill and knowledge enhancement, technology deployment, organization, psychology, user training, technology transfer and motivation must be considered in the R&D phase and should be part of the technology development process. These issues should be integrated into technological research, not just left as separate research issues to be dealt with after the technology development is complete.

The research issues in agile manufacturing are much broader and much more interdisciplinary than in the past, and cannot therefore be addressed by any one professional group on its own. The barriers that exist between monoprofessionals need to be broken down and eliminated. This will be hard to achieve, and is not likely to happen overnight.

We have become used to working within our own disciplines. We have traditionally taken little or no regard for the issues and insights generated elsewhere. We will, therefore, not suddenly start to cooperate just because project funding is available for such projects.

What is most likely to happen in these situations is that we will continue with our old ways, but will try to pretend that we are working in an integrated way. This is certainly what has happened in Europe and Scandinavia on such projects, but the organizational politics of such projects prevent the full truth from being told. No one involved in any research project has any interest in telling the world about their failures. Failure is not valued, and until we start to recognize the importance of analyzing failures, and disseminating the lessons learnt, we will not make any progress towards interdisciplinary integrated working. The problem is that research funding bodies, journals, research institutions and so on do not want to know about failures, and only reward success.

Awareness of agile manufacturing

We still do not fully appreciate the scope and importance of organization and people issues in agile manufacturing. We have a tendency to think of human factors, which we perceive to be primarily an organizational question, or a quality of working life issue, or we associate it with training or the ergonomics of human–computer interfaces. Moreover, while we have an increased awareness of the need to improve the management of change, we tend to view this solely as a question of how best to deploy more technology.

We are still not fully aware of the potential for improvements in profitability and competitiveness that can be derived from tapping into and mobilizing people's competencies, that is, their skills, knowledge, judgment, creativity and experience. The need to remove organizational layers is widely talked about, but it is not clear whether the motivation for doing this is related to cost savings, or to achieving broader objectives.

For example, there is a belief that Information Technology has made a large number of our middle managers redundant, because the monitoring and controlling actions that they performed can now, to a large extent, be done with the aid of computers. However, this misses the point completely. The reasons why we have so many middle managers in the first place is because of our command and control mentality that prevails in our approach to management. When we start to empower people, many of our middle managers are no longer required to fulfill control and monitoring duties. Also, the role of computers has to change from one of monitoring and control, to one of information and communications support. Thus, the purpose in removing organizational layers is not just to flatten the organizational hierarchy. We should see such moves as a first step in the complete dismantling of the command and control organizational hierarchy. This is not yet widely appreciated or understood.

Education and training

The education and training of managers and manufacturing systems engineers is an area that needs some attention. We need to consider the skills and knowledge that our managers and engineers should be acquiring from undergraduate courses. At the moment it seems that the education of most managers and engineers is firmly rooted in the production engineering culture of the 19th century.

Education and training will be a key area for the success of agile manufacturing and our exploitation of research results. There are two primary reasons for the importance of education and training.

First, as we have already pointed out, agile manufacturing is not just a question of addressing issues such as organizational aspects and psychological topics in isolation. These have an impact on technology development, which should now be addressed in an interdisciplinary way. Second, the success of agile manufacturing depends to a large extent on the availability of well educated and trained, highly skilled people throughout the enterprise.

New knowledge and new methods of working are needed. Most of our managers and engineers do not, at the moment, have enough knowledge or sufficient skills to work effectively on interdisciplinary projects.

Demographic changes also imply that greater emphasis needs to be placed on the retraining of older people. The increasing emphasis that younger people place on quality of working life will mean that continuing training will have to become the accepted norm if we are to attract and retain younger people.

Universities and colleges need to develop appropriate education and training for managers, engineers, and technicians. Emphasis should be placed on:

- Education and training for a lifetime of learning.
- Developing social, teaming and communications skills for group working.
- Learning by doing.
- Increasing links between industry and educational establishments.
- Open learning approaches.
- A psychology of learning driven approach to the development of multi-media learning technologies.
- The training needs of small to medium size companies.
- Broadening of skills and knowledge.

There is a requirement to develop interdisciplinary manufacturing systems engineers. There is a need to develop design team structures to support interdisciplinary design. University undergraduate courses need to be revised and training provided for professors as well as engineers working in industries.

Management competence also needs to be improved. Managers need to be helped to develop a stronger people orientation, and they need to become more familiar with modern management science theory and practice. Training is also needed to help managers deal with change management and to develop styles of management in keeping with the new emphasis on trust, empowerment and team working.

The training of people for the computer age also needs to be given more serious attention. Empowerment implies increasing competence. We do not need hierarchical managers, narrowly oriented engineers, semi-skilled machine operators and single skilled people. We need multi-skilled, computer competent people. Everybody must acquire team working skills and become more cooperative. While the technical specialist will still be needed, many manufacturing systems engineers will need to become manufacturing strategists and systems integrators, with a broad understanding and knowledge base.

All these changes are problematic. The whole of our educational system is rigidly divided into disciplines. We do not have many inter-disciplinary departments in universities. When we visit an industrial engineering department, we tend to only find industrial engineers, or other related engineering disciplines. There are few, if any, non-technical members of staff. When non-technical issues are taught, this is usually by people from other departments. The issues that lie between the various disciplines are almost never explored. This, unfortunately, reinforces our culture of monodisciplinary methods and thinking. If we want to change the way that managers and engineers think and act, then we have to change their education. But before we can do that, we have to change the educational system that reflects the very structures and divisions of knowledge that agile manufacturing has made redundant. And we must also re-educate our educators.

Agile manufacturing research

Strategic issues

It is clear that agile manufacturing requires our research community to make a strategic shift away from the development of automation technology, especially in the area of decision-making, towards using technology to support people. The emphasis needs to be on developing skill and knowledge enhancing technologies, rather than skill substituting technologies. We should develop technology which leaves room for the exercise of people's skills, knowledge and judgment. Technology should be used to make these distinctive attributes of people more productive and effective. Our efforts to reproduce these unique characteristics in computers is likely to become more and more difficult as the complexity of the decision-making environment continues to increase. Most of the easy problems in decision-making have now been dealt with. The ones that are left are the difficult ones, which, if they are to be tackled successfully, will require a completely different approach.

It is also clear that we are unlikely to be able to develop skill and knowledge enhancing technologies on our own. Part of the expertise needed lies outside our area of knowledge. We should therefore collaborate with organizational scientists and psychologists and address the development of technology as an interdisciplinary subject.

There is also a growing need to adopt a broader approach to technology development and deployment. This should not be a purely technical one. Development projects should be expected to employ a holistic approach, taking into account all the factors necessary to bring about change. These include skill and knowledge enhancement issues, technological requirements, management and organization, training and motivation of staff and technology deployment. Projects should be balanced, addressing several elements including organization, people and technology.

It is important that we change our assumptions about organization and people issues. These are not secondary matters, nor are they issues that should only be dealt with at the implementation stage. In agile manufacturing they permeate all aspects of manufacturing enterprise design, including research and development. We should assume, therefore, that all our projects have an organization and people dimension. We should make it an acceptance condition that all research proposals identify the organization and people issues and specify how these will be dealt with, or alternatively, demonstrate that organization and people issues are not relevant. Our project evaluation teams should include experts with knowledge and experience of this area. We need to develop criteria and guidelines to help our research and development people to deal with these aspects of their proposals. These criteria and guidelines should address issues such as organizational structure, the role of people, skill and knowledge enhancement, human–computer interaction, ergonomics, motivation, job satisfaction, training and health and safety.

Those in manufacturing who become involved in research and development proposals seeking government support should be expected to give details of their organizational structures and practices. Organizational structures and procedures should be justified and organizational redesign objectives should be stated. This information should be taken into account during the evaluation of any project proposal.

Once a government funded project is approved and running, project monitoring and formal reviews should pay particular attention to the way that organization and people issues are being addressed by projects. Probing questions should be asked. The importance that is attached to interdisciplinary working should be made clear through the performance criteria used to evaluate projects.

Specific research issues

Research needs to be undertaken on a wide range of topics. Consideration should be given to the following:

- The concept of agile manufacturing enterprise design. There is a need for methods and tools to support an interdisciplinary approach, with special emphasis on combining top-down and bottom-up methods, holistic approaches, organizational simulation, appropriate and selective use of technology, increased user involvement and rapid prototyping. These are all relevant tools which will be required to support a spiral approach to the design of agile manufacturing enterprises.
- More emphasis on developing decision support systems that expand the range of possible decision alternatives. Avoidance of a single minded emphasis on the speed with which a decision is made with more emphasis on the quality of the decisions.
- The need to address research in manufacturing as a whole, not just research into new manufacturing technologies. The need to develop new management practices, technology deployment techniques, new reward systems, more sophisticated financial justification techniques, new management accounting methods and so on to support agile manufacturing.
- The development of skill and knowledge enhancing technologies focusing on applying insights from the organizational and psychological sciences. Condition monitoring, database management and networking, applications of genetic algorithms, neural networks and so on to support decision-making, vision systems, workshop-oriented programming of robots and machine tools and computer supported cooperative working.

- Technologies that will support a shift in market conditions towards one-of-a-kind production (OKP). Agility in manufacturing as a key aspect.
- Technologies to support group working. Increasing emphasis on team or group working. Computer supported cooperative work.
- Technologies to support the learning company or organization.

Future developments

In the preceding chapter we outlined several developments which constitute skill and knowledge enhancing technologies. There are two particular areas where further development can be expected. One is the use of artificial intelligence (AI) technologies and the other is in the area of cooperative working. We will consider AI first.

AI is a rather unfortunate term for it conjures up emotive issues of *intelligent machines* taking over intellectual work that has hitherto been immune from automation. It also generates philosophical discussions which center around the possibility of developing computers that think, which leads to endless speculations largely based on opinions. These roughly divide into those who believe that computers can be made to think, and those who do not. Both sides in the argument have a particular, special interest, or a particular or perhaps peculiar narrow focus on the world. It is not our aim to promote these new technologies as panaceas, but neither do we wish to adopt an anti-technology or anti-AI position.

We will content ourselves with noting that in practice we are dealing with programming paradigms. We will concern ourselves with the practical issues, not with the philosophical arguments which can never be more than, at best, well formed and argued opinions, and at worst, narrow, special interest dogmas.

We prefer to adopt a view of AI based on the concept of programming paradigms. We do this because it takes account of established programming practices known as the procedural paradigm. This is the programming paradigm that many people will be most familiar with. It is based on defined routines which are executed in some predefined way depending on the inputs. We have seen over recent years the emergence of more advanced programming paradigms. Some of the more popular of these include the:

- *Rule-based paradigm* This involves representing knowledge by the means of *if-then* rules, with logical premises and conclusions. This allows forward chaining in which one starts with premises and arrives at conclusions, and backward chaining in which one starts with a set of conclusions and derives the premises which are valid given these conclusions.

- *Frame-based paradigm*   This relies on using structured knowledge for capturing regularly occurring circumstances. Each frame includes a number of slots with inheritance, predicate attachments and active values.

- *Logic-based paradigm*   This involves dealing with logical predicates and assertions.

While these programming paradigms are part of the AI toolkit, some of the procedures that are executed in conventional programs are also knowledge-based, in that specific knowledge relevant to the control of the program flow, or necessary for program execution, is included in the program.

In modern programming environments we should not be concerned with the exclusive use of any particular paradigm because there is no single best programming paradigm for all purposes. In complex problems it is, in fact, necessary to combine several paradigms to fit the various tasks. Using these various paradigms makes it easier to achieve these different tasks. For example, what can be difficult to achieve using a rule-based paradigm, might well be quite easily achieved using the procedural paradigm, and vice versa. We should view these paradigms, not as a threat to the skill oriented design paradigm, but as tools to support the achievement of the sought after goals and functionality. For example, we could embed a rule-based component in some software in such a way that the users, or an outside observer, might never know this, unless told.

In what way might we use these programming paradigms to support skilled people? There are several possibilities, which have not yet been widely perceived.

As we noted in Chapter 10, Coombs and Alty (1984) argued that experts are rarely required to solve well defined problems, which is what traditional expert systems operating in the transactional mode are designed to do. Instead, experts work on problems which involve two or more domains of knowledge. What we require is for an expert in one knowledge domain to receive advice from experts in the other knowledge domains, and this involves using expert systems which contain expertise from these other domains.

Within the framework of open systems, as discussed in Chapter 10, these advanced programming paradigms can be used to support people rather than replace them, and this requires that we establish the extra skills and knowledge people require in order to work more effectively. We must also select an operational mode that leaves people with the freedom to act in the way that they want.

We have, of course, so far focused mostly on the individual human–computer relationship and the skills and knowledge of individuals. The other dimension of skill and knowledge enhancing technologies is the support of integration between people, and the support and enhancement of the skills of interpersonal working.

This latter area is one where a lot of future developments can be expected. We are talking about what has become known as **computer supported cooperative work** (CSCW). This has particular relevance to several areas. One obvious area is concurrent engineering, where it will become more and more important to support dialogue and cooperation between designers, and those involved at the sharp end of manufacturing on the shop floor. We should tap into every ounce of intelligence available and use it to bridge the gaps between thinking and doing, and designing and making.

The other obvious area where CSCW can be applied is in supporting cooperation between office based programmers and skilled machinists working on the shop floor. In situations where we may have to do the programming away from the shop floor, we should make the programming a collaborative effort between programmers and machinists.

How we use computer technology to make the skills involved in cooperative working more productive and effective, is something yet to be addressed in detail. We describe below some of the results of efforts that have been made in this direction.

Future generation skill and knowledge enhancing technologies

Traditionally, design of technology has focused on process-oriented tasks, usually attempting to automate people out of the decision-making process. People's roles have normally been restricted to handling tasks that cannot be automated, and dealing with unpredictable and unexpected events. Integration has usually been restricted to interfacing between computer based technologies and sharing data within computer applications.

The design of skill and knowledge enhancing technologies is based on a wider understanding of integration. In Chapter 2 we defined three complementary forms of integration:

- People integration (people communicating and cooperating with people).
- Human–computer integration (people interacting with computers).
- Technological integration (machine interfaced with machine).

We have become all too familiar with the **technological integration** perspective, which might more appropriately be described as the **technical interfacing** perspective. In Chapter 2, however, we tried to define some of the characteristics of the agile manufacturing enterprise of the future. One aspect is the human networking organization, which involves many linkages between people, groups of people, functions and so on. In each enterprise there will be a unique set of critical linkages, which will change with time as the nature of the business and the market changes.

In what way could the **people integration** aspects of these critical linkages be developed, and in what way could **human–computer integration** and technological integration be developed to support the people integration aspects of the critical linkages? To answer these questions we have to start defining the attributes (skills, knowledge and so on) that would be needed, and then decide how these could be made more productive and effective through the use of skill and knowledge enhancing technologies. Immediately, the nature of future generation skill and knowledge enhancing technologies becomes clear.

Presently, most computer based technologies are process task oriented, that is, they are primarily concerned with the tasks associated with material transformations such as programming and operating a machine tool and this is where the focus of attention has been placed with the development of skill and knowledge enhancing technologies. Future generations of computer based technologies will also be process task oriented, but there will be additional technologies, some of which go beyond the traditional process task oriented technologies. These will include technologies to support experimentation and learning activities, and technologies to support the linkages within the human networking organization.

Experimentation and learning technologies

These technologies will be concerned with:

- Supporting the process of continuing improvement.
- Helping users to extend their understanding of problems.
- Providing advice in adjacent areas of expertise.
- Supporting experimentation and learning activities.
- Informing users about consequences of proposals and decisions.
- Helping to identify potential problems and failures.

These technologies should not be confused with computer-aided learning and training technologies. Here we are talking about technologies that will help people to extend their understanding of a problem domain through the use of conceptual and procedural guidance, or support experimentation and learning exercises that are particularly focused on finding better ways of doing things.

Linkage technologies

These technologies will be concerned with supporting the process of forming and developing critical linkages within the enterprise. They will:

- Support the identification and formation of critical linkages.
- Help empowered people to contribute to team activities.
- Support inter-group and intra-group activities.
- Identify core competencies.
- Support inter-enterprise and intra-enterprise innovation networks.

The emphasis is on using technologies to support empowered individuals in their efforts to join, form or participate in teams, and to make people's contributions to the work of these teams more productive and effective.

For example, if we consider the HCIM reference model introduced in Chapter 10, then we can tailor this to a specific enterprise, as shown in Figure 12.1. The external group could in this case be a group of people who use our products. One of the internal groups is the product development group. This latter group could be in direct contact, through information and communication technologies, with our customers. New design proposals could be put to our customers for comments, or information could be gathered directly from our customers on the performance of our products.

It could be that one of our customers has a problem, and we could then ask members of our external group whether they have encountered similar problems. Or it could be that a problem has been identified by our external group. This has been communicated to us for action. We then take action to inform all our customers of the potential problem and we undertake remedial action before it becomes a problem for our customers.

Of course, members of the external group are not necessarily managers or engineers in the customer company, but the people who actually use the products. For example, our customers might be shop floor people or design engineers. Direct communications with these people are now possible using e-mail. But a more sophisticated set of tools needs to be designed to support a rich dialogue between groups, whether they be internal or external. And of course, we are not simply talking here about a technical communications problem, but about a many faceted problem of inter-group behavior and communication, in areas that might potentially be technically very complex.

Final comments

Research in the area of agile manufacturing needs to be addressed in a more interdisciplinary way. Unfortunately, this is not yet widely appreciated or understood. Research programmes are still structured as if there

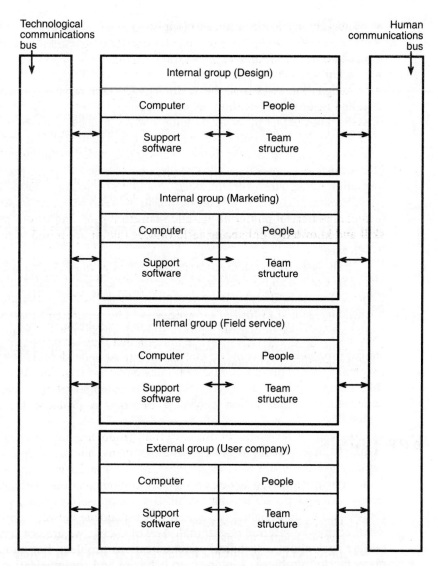

Figure 12.1   Human and computer integrated manufacturing reference model tailored to a specific enterprise. *Source:* Cheshire Henbury. © 1989. Published with permission.

were no interdisciplinary issues: everything fits into well defined boxes, with no overlap. The general lack of understanding, coupled with bias towards monodisciplinary research projects, makes it difficult to undertake interdisciplinary projects.

There are barriers imposed by tradition that will frustrate attempts to develop agile manufacturing. It seems inevitable that research will ultimately become more interdisciplinary. The question is when? The need is already there, but the environment does not foster such approaches.

Throughout this book we have maintained that we are facing a paradigm shift away from the Taylor Model to a new paradigm which we called agile manufacturing, in which people's attributes, such as their skills, knowledge, innovative ability and so on will play a central and leading role. This change of paradigm demands a new way of operating, new values, and a new type of computer based technology which is designed to make people's skills and knowledge more productive and effective. However, the deep rooted nature of the old paradigms will make it extremely difficult for us to recognize the importance and commercial potential of agile manufacturing, and to develop the skill and knowledge enhancing technologies that are required to make it a success.

There is tremendous commercial potential here. There is also an urgent need to address research and development in this interdisciplinary area, for it is likely that important new discoveries and interesting insights, leading to further innovation, will be generated by working in the areas between disciplines. It is an open question whether it will be Americans, Europeans or Japanese who will pioneer the development and commercial exploitation of agile manufacturing.

Key points

- Overcoming the legacy of the Taylor Model is a major barrier to progress.

- There is a danger that agile manufacturing will be interpreted as a technological concept and will lead to the generation of more and more technology, but not to the development of the capabilities to deploy the technologies.

- We need to better define agility and to identify those factors which enable agility and those which detract from agility.

- The development of agile manufacturing requires an integrated approach. Piecemeal and fragmented research by different disciplines will only hinder the development of the concept.

- Education and training are crucial to the success of the concept.

- There is a need to make a strategic shift in the area of decision support technologies towards the development of skill and knowledge enhancing technolgies.

- There is a need to develop a broader approach to technology development and deployment, and to make deployment a technology development criterion.

- We need to develop tools to support a spiral approach to agile manufacturing enterprise design.

- Research into manufacturing needs to focus on manufacturing as a whole, not individual parts.

- There is a need to develop and deploy technologies to support development of linkages within agile manufacturing and to support experimentation and learning.

References

Coombs M. and Alty J. (1984). Expert systems: an alternative paradigm. In *Developments in Expert Systems* (Coombs M., ed.), pp 135–57. London: Academic Press

Index